D0392280

The Craft of Play Directing

THE CRAFT OF PLAY DIRECTING

Curtis Canfield

YALE UNIVERSITY

DRAWINGS BY W. OREN PARKER

Holt, Rinehart and Winston, Inc.

NEW YORK · CHICAGO · SAN FRANCISCO · TORONTO · LONDON

LIBRARY
LEWIS-CLARK
STATE COLLEGE

63865

03-041610-8

Copyright © 1963 by Holt, Rinehart and Winston, Inc.

All rights reserved

Library of Congress Catalog Card Number 63-19110

Printed in the United States of America

90123 18 987654

▲▲▲

ACKNOWLEDGMENT is gratefully made to the following for permission to quote copyrighted material:

To Archibald MacLeish and Houghton Mifflin Company, Boston, for a segment from *J. B.*

To Oxford University Press, Inc., London and New York, for lines from Christopher Fry's *The Lady's Not For Burning.*

To Grove Press, New York, and Methuen & Co., Ltd., London, for lines from *The Hostage* by Brendan Behan.

To Random House, Inc., New York, for lines from *Arsenic and Old Lace* by Joseph Kesselring. Copyright 1941 by Random House, Inc.

To William Heinemann, Ltd., London, and to Charles Scribner's Sons, New York, for excerpts from Henrik Ibsen's *A Doll's House* and *John Gabriel Borkman,* translated by William Archer.

To Anderson House, Hinsdale, New York, for passages from *Winterset* by Maxwell Anderson. Copyright 1935 by Anderson House. Copyright renewed 1963 by Gilda Anderson, Alan Anderson, Terence Anderson, Quentin Anderson, and Hesper A. Levenstein.

To Curtis Brown Ltd., London, and Constable & Co., Ltd., London, for a scene from *Tobias and the Angel* by James Bridie.

For quotations from *The Cocktail Party* by T. S. Eliot. Copyright 1950, by T. S. Eliot. Reprinted by permission of Harcourt, Brace & World, Inc., New York, and to Faber and Faber Ltd., London, the publishers of T. S. Eliot's *Collected Plays.*

For a passage from *Murder in the Cathedral* by T. S. Eliot. Copyright 1935, by Harcourt, Brace & World, Inc., New York, and Faber and Faber Ltd., London, and reprinted with their permission.

For excerpts from *Death of a Salesman* by Arthur Miller. Copyright, 1949, by Arthur Miller. Reprinted by permission of Elaine Greene, Ltd., London, and The Viking Press, Inc., New York, who ask that the following statement be included: This play in its printed form is designed for the reading public only. All dramatic rights in it are fully protected by copyrights, both in the United States and Great Britain, and no public or private performance—professional or amateur—may be given without the written permission of the producers and the payment of royalty, except that they may be used as classroom exercises. As the courts have also ruled that the public reading of a play for pay or where tickets have been sold, constitutes a public performance, no such reading may be given except under the conditions above stated. Anyone disregarding the author's rights renders himself liable to prosecution. Communications should be addressed to the author's representative, Ashley-Steiner, Inc., 555 Madison Avenue, New York 22, New York.

To Sean O'Casey, Macmillan & Company, Ltd., London; St. Martin's Press, Inc., New York; and The Macmillan Company of Canada for quotations from *Juno and the Paycock* as published in *Two Plays* (*Collected Plays,* Vol. I), by Sean O'Casey.

To the Public Trustees and The Society of Authors, London, for excerpts from *The Doctor's Dilemma* by George Bernard Shaw.

For quotations from *A Streetcar Named Desire* by Tennessee Williams. Copyright 1947 by Tenneesee Williams. All rights reserved. Reprinted by permission of New Directions, Publishers.

LEWIS-CLARK
STATE COLLEGE

Preface

This is a book about the stage director's craft. It discusses the director himself primarily as artisan rather than artist, and is concerned with the techniques and methods he uses to obtain given effects as well as with some of the qualifications and insights he must have if he hopes to become an expert in his profession.

Little attempt has been made to deal with the mystiques of the art of creation, with esthetic theory, or with a philosophy of the theatre. The assumption is that before he can take those all-important steps that will lift his productions to the plane of art, the director must possess craftsmanship, the knack of knowing how to use the tools of his trade. Before anyone can paint a masterpiece he must learn how to handle a brush and arrange his palette. If he doesn't know how to control his chosen medium of expression, all the artistic imagination in the world will be of little use to him, as little as it would be to a sculptor who could not put mallet to chisel without splitting the block.

The man or woman who embarks on a career in the directing field must possess a personality capable of coalescing the talents of many people in an act of mutual creation, to an end result, hopefully, that will be a work of art, not merely a piece of efficient workmanship.

Yet it can be argued that the artisan precedes the artist, whether in the fields of painting, sculpture, or play production, and a stage production has to be workmanlike and efficient before it can truly be termed artistic. Actually, a good deal about the craft and technique of making a production effective with an audience can be both taught and learned. Even for those who already possess the power to raise a production to the level of high art, there may still be something to learn about smoothing and streamlining basic techniques, and this is, of course, why books continue to be written on the subject. There are already many useful ones in print. Knowing this, I have tried to avoid repeating unduly what has already been said many times before about the rudiments, strong and weak moves, body positions, the divisions of the stage and so on. It is assumed that the reader is acquainted with these fundamentals and is eager to discuss aspects of the field not fully covered by them, but necessary none the less.

The procedures recommended and demonstrations used throughout the book are founded on an analytical or logical rather than on an intuitive or emotional base. The director's functions, qualifications, and areas of responsibility are described or defined; some tested methods of play analysis and staging are illustrated; and various ways have been suggested for approaching individual as well as ensemble problems in acting.

A step-by-step progression is followed from the director's first reading of the manuscript, through the several stages of preparation to final performance.

Part One considers the play itself and is concerned with matters of interpretation and analysis. Part Two is confined to the actual problems of putting a play on the stage. Major discrepancies and differences between some directorial approaches or methods have been discussed as objectively as possible.

Books on directing are almost invariably written by directors; this one is no exception. There is a natural tendency in them to place the director, implicitly or explicitly, very high in the theatrical hierarchy. Some have enlarged the director's stature out of all proportion to his actual contribution to performance.

To keep things in perspective, let it be said at the outset that I am as conscious as anyone of the historical fact that many plays have found success with the public without the benefit of much direction at all. And I have with me always the sobering thought, encouraging humility, that few directors anywhere have reached the pinnacle of triumph in a production without the help of good actors or good scripts.

Professors John Gassner, Alois Nagler, Nikos Psacharopoulos and Mr. Robert Leland Starnes, colleagues at the Yale Drama School, read the manuscript and offered valuable suggestions from their several points of view. I am most grateful to them, and also at the same time mindful that they did not always agree with my viewpoint.

Two of my former long-time associates at Amherst College, Ralph C. McGoun and Charles Ensign Rogers, supplied me with needed productional and other material. Mr. Rogers generously let me use his designs for the first act of *The Doctor's Dilemma* and the tenement scene in *Winterset*. To Philip Eck I owe thanks for permission to use his ground plan for the *Winterset* exterior, which was based on an earlier plan by Mr. Rogers. W. Oren Parker, Assistant Professor of Scene Design at the Yale Drama School, graciously executed the line drawings.

The Rockefeller Foundation made it possible for me to study directing techniques in the British theatre and to obtain some perspective from a vantage point in London on what I was trying to do.

I am deeply indebted to Margaret Pinckney King for providing me with a perfect place to work in Chilmark, Massachusetts; and to my wife, Katharine Newbold Canfield, for her never-failing interest and encouragement.

CURTIS CANFIELD

New Haven, Connecticut
July, 1963

Contents

PART ONE: *THE DIRECTOR'S MATERIAL*

CHAPTER ONE · THE DIRECTOR'S CRAFT 3

His Relation to His Material 5
His Contributions to the Production 8
The Nature of His Qualifications 11
The Diversity of Directorial Types 22

CHAPTER TWO · MAKING THE APPROACH 25

The Directorial Attitude 25
Locating the Play 27
Dramatic Types 28
Dramatic Styles 29
Dramatic Modes 35

CHAPTER THREE · WHAT THE PLAY CONTAINS 37

The Story 37
The Subject 39
Characterization 46
Atmosphere 49

CHAPTER FOUR · STRUCTURE AND MEANING 52

Act Divisions and Their Functions 52
The Elements of Drama 56
The Director Analyzes the Play 59
The Director Analyzes a Single Scene 64

CHAPTER FIVE · LITERARY STYLE 83

The Uses of Dialogue 83
Verse Drama 88
Poetic Prose 91
Using the Language 94
Imagery and Metaphor 99
Dramatic Devices 107

PART TWO: *THE DIRECTOR'S MEDIUM*

CHAPTER SIX · BLOCKING 115

When to Block 115
The Purpose of Blocking 120
When the Actor Blocks Himself 122
The Actor's Real Responsibilities 125
Prerehearsal Blocking 126
How Detailed Should Early Blocking Be? 128

CHAPTER SEVEN · DEVELOPING THE GROUND PLAN 130

The Director's Contribution 130
Locating the Acting Areas 134
The Breakdown into French Scenes 136
Exterior Ground Plans 150

CHAPTER EIGHT · THE DIRECTOR BLOCKS THE PLAY 161

General Principles 161
Two Characters in a Single Scene 169
Two Characters in Successive Scenes in a Single Set 194
Traffic Problems—Several Characters in a Small Set 231

CHAPTER NINE · CUTTING, CASTING, FIRST READING 245

Cutting 245
Casting 254
The First Reading 261

CHAPTER TEN · THROUGH REHEARSALS TO PERFORMANCE 266

Various Procedures Examined 266
Directing the Individual Actor 270
Directing the Ensemble 291
Technical Rehearsals 300
Dress Rehearsals 302

APPENDIX: · THE COLLEGIATE THEATER 307

Objectives 307
The College Director—Scholar or Showman? 310
Play Selection 313
Purposeful Programming 318
Using the Talent 321
Student Productions 322
Schedules 323
Finances and Publicity 325
The Dramatic Society 328

GLOSSARY 331

INDEX 339

PART ONE

The Director's Material

CHAPTER ONE

The Director's Craft

To each is given a certain inward talent, a certain outward environment of Fortune; to each by wisest combination of these two, a certain maximum of capability.

CARLYLE: *Sartor Resartus*

It is the function of the theatre to express the fictive creatures of the playwright's imagination in terms of lively human beings; to let them, the actors, give voice to his words and perform the actions he has set down for them in the text; and to translate his often sketchy notes about the physical environment in which his characters operate into palpable realities of form, color, and light.

Thomas De Quincey thought that the theatre came into being because it was the only practical way of exposing a large number of people to an author's writings in the days before the custom of printing and reading books became universal. The stage was a manner of publication, an oral one, as it were. Be that as it may, the theatre is a medium of communication, a vivid way of telling a story. As such, it has persisted in spite of the now widespread habit of reading. There are many reasons for this, but chief among them is that under ideal conditions a performance can enliven and illuminate a text with far more skill, insight, and power than the ordinary reader can bring to it himself. If it cannot do this there is no justification for any theatre's existence.

The theatre's continuing life depends on its handling the playwright's material so as to make the most telling impression on the sensibilities of a public audience. The superintendence of this effort in the modern theatre is in the hands of the director. It is he who is charged with the responsibility of transferring the material from text to stage, from the medium of literature to the medium of the theatre.

One of his major objectives is to maintain consistency in the behavior of the characters, to supply material not provided specifically in the text to help the actors envision their immediate objectives in the play, and to give them a complete and rounded background context which explains why they are doing what the playwright requires them to do.

It is under the director's guidance that the play's ideas are projected into a three-dimensional space peopled with actors. These in turn, by controlled speech, feigned emotions, and prearranged deportment, working at predetermined levels of emotional intensity and with calculated variations in the rhythm and tempo of their moving and speaking, give the play animation and tongue.

Sometimes it is the actors' object to convey an illusion of reality, to pretend with the audience that the life they are enacting is really taking place. At other times they pursue a different course, as for example in symbolic drama, where they may seek to represent abstract personifications of human qualities or attributes, rather than actual people; or in other styles in which normal human behavior is exaggerated, conventionalized, or stylized to make a dramatic point.

But whether the intended effect is to be lifelike or otherwise, stage life is seldom haphazard, although at times it must seem to be. It follows a pattern and a design. Even when conditions of chaos are supposed to prevail onstage the chaos must somehow be carefully organized and ordered—in short, directed; otherwise what is created will not partake of the essence of art. Art always connotes artifice, the deliberate imposition of form and meaning on some segment of experience plucked from life's disorder. The director is the prime functionary who has to see to it that all the disparate parts of the production are ordered and meshed in accordance with the play's objectives.

Because of the way the theatre operates in this country and in many others for that matter, it is necessary for actors to repeat their performances, if the play is popular, for several months or even years. What the director is called upon to achieve is a standard of performance from which there shall be no significant deviations during the run. And the only way that this can be attained with any degree of certainty is by hardening every aspect of the production, the moves, business, gestures, inflections, cueing, tempo, and all the rest into a fixed and immutable pattern. There may be a few but unimportant exceptions to this—in a theatre of improvisation, for example, which exists without the benefit of a playwright—but in general the success of a production depends on how well preplanned effects can be made to create cumulative emotional and other responses in an audience night after night for an extended period of time. For better or worse, in modern times it has fallen to the lot of the director to be the architect of the master plan of a production as well as the executive who puts that plan into operation. He is concerned with conscious calculations, and must so conceive and arrange his plans that the production stays within its fixed bounds without seeming to be planned at all, particularly in realistic plays. So that while everything about the performance is foreordained, systematized, and made as smooth in operation as any mechanism, it must appear to the eyes of the beholders as something spontaneous, warm, lively, and not at all mechanical. The actors must speak their lines as though they had just thought of them, the "illusion of the first time," and the whole effect must be as fresh on the hundredth night as it was on the first.

His Relation to His Material

The director has much less control over his medium than do his fellow artists and artisans in other fields. The painter working with color, brushes, and canvas; the sculptor with marble, wood, metal—or any element that will hold its shape—may meet some difficulties in trying to impose form and meaning on these inert materials, but the fact remains that these materials can eventually be brought to respond absolutely and without challenge to the artist's will. The director works with human beings: playwrights, actors, and designers who are craftsmen or artists in their own right, with wills and temperaments of their own. He cannot treat these sensitive people as though they were docile clay. For one thing the law and unions give them certain inalienable rights. For another, since so much depends in the collective process of mounting a play on the frictionless coordination between many minds and skills, and also because in many cases his fellow workers may be as eminent in their professions as he is in his, he would endanger the whole enterprise if he were so foolish as to try it. In any case it will be pleasanter all around, and more profitable too, if in the long run the director assumes from the beginning that in the hectic preparation period sweet reason can prevail, that the naked display of his power is quite unnecessary, and that he can get the best from his actors and associates by enlisting their cooperation instead of having to demand it, by using persuasion instead of command, and by always having better reasons than theirs for wanting them to interpret a character, speak a line, or execute a move in one way rather than another.

There is another significant difference. The director's master plan of a production must be based on the play's text. He is not free to express himself as unrestrainedly as artists in other media who draw their inspiration and select their subject matter directly from their untrammeled imaginations or from the boundless world of nature.

The painter and sculptor are free to choose what they want to say without stint, provided only that they stay within the bounds of their media. The director is not in a position to do this. It is the dramatist and not he who chooses the subject and decides how it shall be treated. The medium of the playwright thus becomes the director's material, and whatever creative energies he expends must be expended upon that material. He cannot change it or add to it without permission.

This limitation does not diminish the director's importance in any artistic sense. Even if his job is largely restricted to the interpretation of someone else's original ideas this does not mean that he cannot work creatively within his own medium, that is, with the actors and the stage space, any more than our leading musical conductors should be held in any less esteem as artists because their subject matter is confined to the scores provided for them by composers.

There is further analogy between directing and conducting. Each involves two processes, separate but on related planes. In the first, decisions must be reached about what the text is saying. This is the area of interpretation. The second is the area of execution. Here solutions must be found to problems about how best to express dramatic meaning in terms of the presentation. For the director this means finding a way to express the material in the text by means of stagecraft.

Interpretation and presentation encompass the entire function-field of stage directing. Both are equally important. Consummate acting, beautiful stage pictures, audible speech, expressive movement, along with relevant niceties in the costumes and lighting effects are of no use at all if the point of the work is misapprehended or fails to emerge. And, conversely, a director may have the most exciting and imaginative concept of what a play means and still through lack of aptitude in presentation be unable to get the actors to express that meaning in performance.

Any act of interpretation by its very nature is inescapably subjective, whether it be in music, literature or the drama. Just as beauty is said to reside in the eye of the beholder so the truth of a play, a painting, or a musical score resides in the perceptions of the interpreter. In a very real sense a symphony orchestra does not play the notes of the score so much as the image of the score as this has been registered on the mind of the conductor. In the theatre, likewise, it is not the text alone, and by itself, that furnishes the material for actor, designer, and technician—it is the text as understood by the director. The director's vision or hunch of what the settings should be serves as starting point and guide for the designer. And, depending on the amount of control the director exerts over them, the actors project not their own independently contrived images of the characters, but images which have been shaped and modified to conform to the director's ideas about what they should be.

He must justify the right to exert this sort of authority. And the only way he can do that is to prove he has the ability to see things in a manuscript which are neither apparent to the common gaze nor immediately discernible in total synthesis to his professional colleagues in the production.

What he is able to see depends on the sum of the factors that make up his personality: his knowledge, experience, sensitivity, instincts, and the power of his imagination.

How does the director as interpreter proceed?

In any number of ways, of course. But one would expect that in general he would draw from a complex play whatever ideas and meanings his personal sensibilities, prejudices, and immediate goals have conditioned him to select from the multiple choices the text offers him. Each single idea or particle of meaning which he has thus caught and held would eventually be synthesized, by intuition or ratiocination, into what might be recognized as a total concept. And this, furnishing him with the play's subject and the conclusions his understanding draws from the playwright's treatment of that subject, form the essential spine or core of meaning upon which his production will be built.

When he deals with a modern play by a living author even the most willful and creative director has to curb any impulse he might have to read meanings into it that are obviously contrary to or different from those intended by the playwright. The playwright owns the text and no one can tamper with it in any way without his consent. The director, then, must be content to confine himself to discovering what the playwright's intention is, and having discovered it can then proceed to handle the production in such a way as to realize that intention.

In the case of a revival, however, when the author is not around to defend his rights, and when the play in question happens to be well known and frequently produced, there is little to prevent the director from shifting his approach from an attempt to find out what the author meant to one in which the main purpose is to adapt and if necessary transform the text so that in the end it reflects and coincides with what the director alone wants it to mean. The main effort then is aimed toward finding new meanings, new angles, new emphases; and all for the purpose of creating a fresh, original, or unhabitual view of the old work.

There is no doubt that the pressure of the personality of the director, when he elects to bring it to bear on the textual material and later on the actors, can and often does bring about variations in meaning even in copyrighted plays. The variations may be slight or they may be extensive according to the strength of the director's will. What emerges in the production may be different, or better, or worse than what the original creator intended. The point to be observed is that, except in the unlikely case of a director who has no will or ideas of his own, something of the director is bound to be rubbed into the final product as seen by the audience.

His Contributions to the Production

Exactly what a director adds to a play, how much of himself is in it, is hard to measure. Take the matter of script revisions. In order to establish the extent of the director's influence in this crucial area, one would have to compare the original draft as the director received it with the final playing script, and have evidence to show what alterations had been made in it specifically at the director's behest or on his initiative. The same difficulty of assessment applies to performances. It would be necessary for someone to attend every reading, every coaching session, and every rehearsal before he could discover how much in an actor's playing, from the whole concept of the part to each single vocal inflection or tiny gesture, was primarily the result of the director's inspiration and guidance and how much had been evolved by the actor alone without the director's help.

It is equally hard, particularly for the layman, to appraise the amount and quality of the director's contribution to the play's total effect. One often hears the cliché that the best direction is the kind that conceals itself. This is to say that the director fulfills his function most adequately and successfully when his hand, the significant trademark of his inventiveness and originality, is not detectable in the performance as such.

To say that a play does not seem to have been directed may be a compliment indeed if the play is realistic in style, colloquial in speech, and contemporary in dress and setting. Here the spectator's appreciation of the director's work centers in admiration for the play's lifelike quality, the polish, assurance, and adroitness in the playing that makes it appear as if the actors are not acting at all but behaving naturally and living the parts. In plays of this type I think everyone would agree that the direction could be considered good if it provides the results described. But in a revival of a classic, a poetic or ritual drama, or in any play in which verisimilitude is not the end and aim, the kind of unobtrusive direction so praised in dramas of realism, if applied, would lead to nothing save an unexciting production.

Such plays demand authoritative and discernible directorial treatment; their success depends on it. What is wanted in revivals, and particularly in Shakespearean revivals, is not novelty exactly but a distinctive approach of some sort, a new look, new faces in the cast, different designs, and a justifiable stress on variations in the statement of the theme and in the presentation of the characters. The special interpretation brought to the main roles is of major interest. And all such innovations are amply justified when they lead to new insights into the greatness of the plays and extend their range of impact. The influence of the director may be detected in them in the whole style, drive, intensity, and pace of the performance. Franco Zeffirelli's artistry as director–designer of the Old Vic's recent revival of *Romeo and Juliet* informed every part of that gymnastic production. It had a new beauty and a new reality. The director's obvious and insistent influence on it, far from detracting from the familiar values of the play, made them stand out more clearly as the result of the vitality and energy with which they were approached.

If Zeffirelli had been wrongly persuaded to efface his personality from that production, the most noteworthy and pleasing thing about it would have been lost.

But the important point is that Zeffirelli began his search for his new approach in the text itself rather than in his own soul. There is no better place to start from, particularly if the director is a beginner. If he is dealing with a standard work of literature, he should follow up his study of the text with an examination of the critical commentaries on it. Some directors are conscientious enough to examine the whole corpus of the dramatist's work with particular attention to the major offerings, in order to get perspective on his general style and point of view.

By steeping oneself in the commentaries and in the play's historical context, one can avoid the distortions and aberrations of meaning that follow from an overpersonalized approach.

A director's virtuosity may persuade large segments of the audience to accept themes never before perceived and conceptions of character never before thought of in orthodox or conventional productions. These may be themes or meanings of which the author himself is unaware, as will be illustrated in a moment. Yet knowing this, the tyro in direction, tempted to do something drastically new with an old script, might well heed Stark Young's advice that, "Virtuosity sinks or swims by the significance of its idea." The compulsion to transform *Troilus and Cressida* into a romantic tale of the American Civil War, or *Julius Caesar* into an anti-Fascist tract should be balanced against the advantages to be found in staging these plays as the author, who presumably knew his business, intended them to be staged, and in adhering as closely as possible to his purposes and conclusions.

No one can say that one method is wrong and the other right. The verdict lies always with the theatre's only jury, the audience. If the play fails the director is wrong; if it succeeds, he is right.

But whether he searches for meaning in the play or within himself, the search is the director's fundamental preoccupation.

One would think, when the meaning of a play is unequivocally stated in the text, as it is in *Winterset* when Mio says he would rather live by love than hate, that any question of the author's intention would cease to be a matter of subjective opinion. But the theatre being what it is and directors being what they are, such is not always the case. The phrase, "for me" in any sentence beginning, "Well, for me, the play means . . ." invalidates all objective evidence, including the playwright's own, and admits no argument based on it.

No less august an authority than Constantin Stanislavsky maintained the principle that the actor and the theatre manager, meaning the director, "must first probe for the fundamental motive in the finished play—the creative idea that is characteristic of the author."[1] He admonished the director to "go straight for the most exact and profound conception of the mind and ideal *of the dramatist*," and "not change that ideal for [his] own."[2] Yet Stanislavsky demonstrated in practice an entirely contradictory attitude, at least in one instance. He staged *The Cherry Orchard* as a tragedy against the explicit objections of Chekhov, who insisted that what he had written was a comedy.[3]

Strangely enough, in this most mercurial and wayward medium, the play has validity both ways, whether its comic or its tragic values are stressed.

The lesson for the would-be director here is this: whenever the absolute truth lies concealed in the text, and it is hardly ever overt in the good ones, and whenever there is a clash of opinion, as there usually is, between creative persons about what and where that truth is, the views of the one with the most patience, the stronger will and the larger reputation will prevail—unless one of the contenders happens to be the playwright and invokes his legal right to protect his property. He who would avoid the clash of such battles, and they are an inevitable and accepted condition of theatrical life, should not aspire to become a director.

The Nature of His Qualifications

Who should attempt to enter this highly-selective profession? What sort of background is needed, what qualities of mind and heart? What types of training and experience should be sought?

[1] Stanislavsky, Constantin, "Directing and Acting," in *Acting, a Handbook of the Stanislavsky Method,* compiled by Toby Cole. New York: Lear, 1947. p. 22.

[2] Ibid.

[3] See Latham, Jacqueline A. M., "The Cherry Orchard as Comedy," *Educational Theatre Journal,* March, 1958.

The roads to success in the field are numerous and have been traveled by many diverse personalities, using a wide assortment of technical methods. It is impossible to recommend one simple course of action or one method as superior to all others; and it is difficult to arrive at a meaningful generalization about an ideal system of preparation. Perhaps the most sensible approach is to look first at some of the things a director is called upon to do, to examine the areas in which he is expected to show power and proficiency. Thus by stating the nature and the dimensions of the job, the nature of the qualifications required to do it may be suggested by implication.

The director's sphere of activity, like Gaul, is divided into three parts.

The first is in the field of dramatic literature, an extensive knowledge of which is a necessity. This does not mean that the candidate must have an encyclopedic memory for plots, names, and dates—the lumber of pedantry—but rather that he should have a wide-ranging appreciation of what the drama has been and can be in the hands of the masters of playwriting. Without such knowledge or sensibility it is unlikely that he will be able to establish high standards of judgment for measuring what is good or bad in a text. To evaluate a play's potential as literature one must know how to assess it in comparison with models of known excellence.

Here the director performs a function not unlike that of the literary critic. He must know how to deal with language, the styles of composition, imagery, themes, structure. In other words he must have the ability to analyze a play as a work of literature and bring to bear on it the same batteries of comprehension, comparison, and evaluation that the professional critic aims at a novel, a poem, a biography, or a book of essays.

Next, he must have some knack for playwriting, or at least for play-doctoring. An important part of his work is collaborating with the dramatist in what has come to be an indispensable feature in the preparation for production: namely, revising and polishing the script. He is expected to bring to this collaboration a sharpened and if possible an infallible sense of what *goes* in the theatre, what keeps the audience warmly attentive, and what does not. I don't know exactly how a director can acquire this instinctive "feel," this sixth sense of knowing what will be effective on the stage. I only know that every good director has it.

In the main, he is called upon to help the playwright in such things as bringing scenes into sharper theatrical focus, or fixing the placement of key words in a speech so that they will get proper emphasis, or adjusting the rhythm of a line so that it comes easily off the actor's tongue. He can help to clarify motives, to expedite exits, prepare entrances, heighten climaxes, and even to rearrange the order of scenes in a plot-sequence for maximum theatrical effect. He must know why lines should be cut, and how to cut them without damaging important dramatic values.

Some directors, Joshua Logan and George Abbott among them, overhaul scripts so drastically that they become entitled to list themself as coauthors. Others are content to make suggestions to the playwright about making the product stageworthy without infringing on his prerogative to accept or reject the suggestions as he sees fit. In either case, the ability and willingness to supply positive ideas for tightening and clarifying the manuscript go hand in hand with one's grasp of the play's literary values.

Finally, it is obvious that the director's mastery of the core subjects of his medium—acting, design, and lighting, should be absolute. And it helps further if he knows at least the basic elements of the several peripheral arts that often contribute so heavily to a production's total effectiveness: music, dance, painting, and sculpture. Nor does it harm if he has a nodding acquaintance with the principles of fencing, tumbling, pantomime, and choral singing. To these accomplishments may be added a solid academic background in the history of the theatre, valuable primarily as a means of keeping in mind styles of acting and staging in the various historical periods.

The director must also be inventive. Douglas Seale said recently at Yale that the problems the director is most frequently called upon to solve, particularly in classic drama, are of a type that do not call for psychological or philosophical solutions, but demand a kind of technical or practical improvisatory approach involving the application of shrewd common sense. He cited the scene in *King Henry VI, Part Three,* in which Queen Margaret places a paper crown upon the head of York, as a typical example of the kind of problem with which the director is so often confronted. The directorial problem here is to decide where and how Margaret is to get such a crown on the open plains of Sandal Castle and to supply some plausible reason for its being there.

Much of the director's inventiveness is given over, as in the above, to stage business. He must create it for actors who can't do it themselves, and pass judgment on the effectiveness and appropriateness of the inventions of those who can.

Inventiveness may take the form of a series of subtle touches in the handling of minor details, which by accumulation deepen theatrical effect. When applied successfully as in the case of the aforementioned Old Vic production of *Romeo and Juliet,* spectacular results can be achieved. For instance, Zeffirelli so arranged the action in Act III when Mercutio is stabbed by Tybalt that as Romeo throws himself between the contestants the blow goes unperceived by all the company. Romeo, relieved and pleased that he has broken up the fight before any damage has been done, joins other members of his party at one side of the stage, joking and laughing. Mercutio, entirely alone, and alone also in the knowledge that he has received a fatal wound, speaks his "I am hurt. A plague o' both your houses" out of earshot. The actor continued to stand apart through most of the "not so deep as a well" speech, handling it as a soliloquy, until just toward the end when at last Romeo draws near and perceives that his friend has been seriously injured. In contrast to the conventional method of staging this scene, which has Romeo stay by Mercutio's side throughout, fully aware of what has happened to him, Zeffirelli made possible a new moment of touching discovery which was all the more poignant because of the contrast between Romeo's first feelings of careless relief and his anguish when he perceives the truth.

The director's inventiveness is seen also in the way he capitalizes on opportunities given him by the properties and his effective use of them, in conjunction with the sets, costumes, and lights, to extend dramatic ideas. The following demonstration is offered to illustrate how the comic impact of a scene may be heightened and elaborated upon by business involving props. It may be useful more as a sample of directorial attitude than anything else, although the excerpt, taken from *Tobias and the Angel* by James Bridie, was tested in performance and drew a satisfactory public response.

The play is based on the story of Tobias in the Apocrypha. Tobias, in the company of the Archangel Raphael disguised as a Porter, goes through several marvelous adventures. Among them is his love affair with Sara, daughter of Raguel, the rich Jew of Ecbatana. In the scene Tobias tells Raguel that he wants to marry Sara and this elicits from Raguel some disquieting news about certain obstacles in the way of Tobias's success in the courtship.

As will be seen, the major dramatic movement in the segment is Tobias's progressive decline from a state of confidence through growing apprehension to cowardice, all caused by Raguel's reluctant recital of the reason why his daughter has never married. The treatment is playful and mischievous throughout.

The scene is a walled garden attached to Raguel's sumptuous house in Ecbatana.

(*Enter* RAGUEL *with girls carrying a basin, a ewer, a bottle of wine and some fruit in a great dish. Azorah and Sherah prepare Tobias for his meal. While they are washing his hands and feet he talks to Raguel.*)

TOBIAS: Raguel, this is very handsome of you.

RAGUEL: It is the least I could do for your father's son. Ah! Is this your friend?

RAPHAEL: Your servant, sir.

TOBIAS: Yes, this is Azarias.

RAPHAEL: The son of Ananias.

RAGUEL: Indeed? Ah, yes. I didn't know he had a son. However, I am glad to see you. Any friend of Tobias is welcome here. Do you serve your master, or would you prefer to go to the servants' hall. You must be hungry.

RAPHAEL: I shall go to the servants' hall. I am a servant.

TOBIAS: Oh, I say, Azarias . . .

RAPHAEL: I shall go. Remember what I told you. (*He goes.*)

RAGUEL: An extraordinary fellow. I suppose he's faithful enough. But

I do feel these people who have come down in the world are a little apt to be familiar, don't you think? Good looking fellow, though.

TOBIAS: Raguel, it's about Sara . . . (*Raguel puts a piece of Turkish Delight into the mouth of Tobias.*)

Raguel is a generous host but this time his hospitality is enlarged by an urge to prepare his guileless guest for the disturbing truth of his daughter Sara's previous marital experiences. He knows Tobias is interested in his daughter. It is natural for him to ply Tobias with delicacies because Raguel's whole nature, as seen earlier, revolves around the idea of food. He is possessed by it. He thinks everyone is always hungry, and he harps continually on feasts, breakfasts, and collations. Food colors his speech and even dominates his subconscious, as when he refers to Sara as "the apple of his eye." It is, in fact, his humor.

The comical implications of this aspect of Raguel's character must be projected in the form of stage business, and the direction about his putting the piece of Turkish Delight into Tobias's mouth offers the first opportunity.

It will be noted that Raguel interrupts Tobias at exactly the right moment, and on the right word, "Raguel, it's about SARA.*" Raguel wishes to avoid discussing the issue prematurely. The sweet is meant to bolster the suitor's courage, encourage his confidence, and disarm his shyness.*

A minor problem: the audience does not know exactly what is being conveyed into Tobias's mouth. To remedy this an explanatory line may be improvised. No harm will be done; even Shakespeare recovered from Cibber's improvements. So . . .

RAGUEL: Taste that bit of Turkish Delight!

His fingers should deliver the confection with an arching motion, like a harpist plucking a chord. The actor should not anticipate the gesture. If he begins the motion before the word "Sara," we lose his motive for cutting Tobias off.

Some reaction from Tobias is needed to complete the sequence. He gulps, swallows the gummy stuff whole and then proceeds, somewhat disconcerted by his host's sudden move.

TOBIAS: Thank you. I was saying, it's about Sara.

RAGUEL: Ah, yes, yes. A nice girl. Domesticated and so on. She is the apple of my eye.

TOBIAS: She must be. Raguel, I want to marry Sara.

RAGUEL: Well, that's plump and plain, anyhow.

"Plump and plain" may be a pun directed at Tobias himself, since he has been referred to elsewhere as a little fat man. But Raguel's mood of the moment is too serious for him to be conscious of having made it.

TOBIAS: Yes. I have always studied to be both plain and plump. What have you to say about it, eh?

RAGUEL: It is a little unexpected. I mean, you hardly know each other. It is a great honor that she has found favor in your sight. I need not say how delighted I should be to see her comfortably married to a respectable young man. And I don't think there is any possibility that you will quarrel about the settlement. Only, as I say, it is rather sudden. And Old Tobit did me many a good turn in the old days. . . .

Something hidden is worrying Raguel and the speech should convey this uneasiness. A wistful sigh should escape him on "I need not say how delighted . . . etc." But he pulls himself together immediately when he speaks about the marriage settlement, in spite of his misgivings about the outcome.

It might be effective to try the Turkish Delight business again here. The audience has been prepared for it, and will know it is coming the minute Raguel reaches for the dish. The repetition can be justified because it performs the double duty of commenting on Raguel's personality while explaining his solicitous feeling toward his possible son-in-law.

Since "settlement" is a new and important subject, the business can be completed on the word. With delicate timing and the added help of Tobias's expression of alarmed anticipation, the audience response should be larger than on the first try.

TOBIAS: All the more reason why you should make his son happy.

RAGUEL: I know, I know. But it's only fair to tell you. . . . Well, there are stories going about. Not too pleasant ones either. It's all superstition and old wives' tales, of course, and I should never mention them to you if you were not an old friend, in a way of speaking, and an enlightened, educated man like myself. You know these Persians. A pack of heathens. Believe anything.

Raguel procrastinates brilliantly. His dire hints are balanced against words of reassurance and flattery for the puzzled lover.

The reference to the Persians is made concrete by addressing it to the waiting handmaidens, who react surlily, conscious of their Iranian supremacy.

TOBIAS: Go on.

RAGUEL: (*To the girls.*) You clear out now. I'll look after the guest. Look sharp. No loitering. (*The girls go.*)

Raguel's irritation is caused as much by Tobias's crude insistence on being told the whole story as it is by the handmaidens' insolence.

Have some grapes. Or a citron? These pomegranates are very good. These nectarines are not bad. Home grown. Yes. About Sara. Try a mango.

Again the comic delay about coming to the point is achieved with the offerings of fruit. Tobias, of course, refuses.

Would it be possible to try the candy business again? No. Twice is permissible, but a third time would be in dubious taste and interfere with the progression of the scene. Nevertheless, a mere suggestion should offend no one's sense of propriety.

Raguel can beam at Tobias, and draw back his hand as if in preparation for the familiar hand-to-mouth routine. But this time Tobias can be on his guard and decline. The business can precede the speech, in which case, "Have some grapes" would follow as a logical alternative to Tobias's refusal of the candy.

Thus the business serves to close the gap between two otherwise disassociated ideas.

RAGUEL: (*Cont'd*) You know, my lad, the poor girl has been the victim of an extraordinary series of coincidences. They *are* coincidences, of course, but they are nonetheless heartbreaking.

The speech must not be said too seriously; the pathos should have an edge of the ridiculous inasmuch as Raguel's solicitude for Tobias's safety is somewhat neutralized by his parental obligation to give his daughter what happiness he can. He is worried and solicitous, fearful and hopeful, at the same time. In order to convey his comically abstracted mood, let him do what comes naturally. Since his hand is on the mangos, let him eat one. If he bites into it on the word, "heartbreaking," a proper balance between emotion and appetite is obtained.

TOBIAS: Go on. I need not tell you this is very interesting to me.

RAGUEL: Well, to tell you the truth, she has been betrothed and even married before. To be absolutely frank, more than once.

The beginning of the revelation.

TOBIAS: Seven times.

RAGUEL: So many as that? Let me see. Five times, at any rate. No. You are right. Seven times. Tragic. Awful. Most reputable decent, young fellows.

Disconcerted by Tobias's knowledge of these details, his inflection rises in some alarm. Admitting the truth he bows, with a sigh, to the inevitable.

TOBIAS: What happened to them?

Trilby under the spell of Svengali.

RAGUEL: Well, we don't exactly know.

His hysteria mounting. The coming revelation is so simply designed that it can be parsed like a sentence. The nominative is "Asmoday," the verb, "murdered," and "seven husbands" the collective object. The playwright with much comic art delays the completion of the sentence until all the humorous changes can be rung.

It's a frightful trial to poor Sara. It's not her fault. I don't know how she has survived it.

Sadly.

But they say . . .

The advance on the subject. To prepare for this Raguel should whip around, his hands extended as if he were hypnotizing Tobias, and intone what follows, not varying the pitch.

. . . she has been so unfortunate as to be the object of admiration of one of their horrible heathen gods —the foul fiend . . . (*He whispers.*) Asmoday.

He hisses the chilling syllables directly into Tobias's ear.

TOBIAS: Who?

Before Tobias speaks, his curiosity must be shown overcoming dread. Spoken with a wide-eyed expression, half stupid, half innocent.

RAGUEL: Asmoday!

Straightens up, impatient at this display of abject ignorance. Accompanied by a wide gesture for emphasis, the exclamation's staccato unnerves Tobias and this causes Raguel to resume hastily his old reassuring manner. He laughs emptily, shaking his head in a deprecating way.

You and I don't believe in such things.

Tobias answers this with a wan smile. Then gradually both smiles dissolve. Raguel's expression becomes something fearful to behold. What follows reflects his true feelings and requires an alteration of mood. He speaks with great rapidity.

They say he has a tail like a dragon and a foul breath. Nasty ideas.

Gesticulating.

It is getting chilly. Shall we go in?

Following directly as part of his fright.

TOBIAS: No. Tell me more.

Now willing to hear the worst.

RAGUEL: It is a strange country, this, with its great pink, snow-topped hills, and its thick, dark groves. Terrible things happen here. I wish we lived in a homely and quiet land, where there are no devils walking in great winds at night. What did you notice first when you came to Persia?

Raguel's description of the forbidding landscape sets the atmosphere for the coming of the verb. Notice how the playwright holds back its utterance until just the right moment when it will topple Tobias from the heights of bravado.

TOBIAS: That no birds sing here. There is hardly a sparrow.

RAGUEL: And in the dusty desert there are birds all the way. I have only heard one nightingale and one lark since I came here, forty years ago.

TOBIAS: That is very strange.

RAGUEL: It is very strange in a country all trees and fountains and running streams.

TOBIAS: I will take Sara away from here.

With an effort at boldness.

RAGUEL: Go away from here yourself, my son.

Sweeping to the attack.

Sara is still a maid, and will be so, alas! till she dies.

Swiftly.

The "alas!" is a wail.

There is a pause. The long-awaited verb is here.

Her seven husbands were murdered--------strangled.

Pause

TOBIAS: How?

More than a mere question. Tobias's hand should go to his own throat as if in dreadful anticipation of what might happen to him.

RAGUEL: I cannot tell.

Hopelessly.

The verb is now repeated for the sake of emphasis.

But every one of them was strangled on his wedding night . . . She remembered nothing.

TOBIAS: Ough!
It is growing dark and cold.
(*Raphael, without: "Tobias!"*)

Fear and a faint heart make him sensitive to the night. His self-confidence has vanished, and Raguel's nourishing viands have been given him to no avail. His teeth chatter . . . and the scene reaches a turning point.

The enhancement of a scene by the telling use of properties, as attempted in the foregoing, is the objective toward which much of the director's power of invention is aimed.

Now, and in brief, let these further qualifications be listed: The director's ear must be sensitive to all modulations of the voice and to the subtle relationships between those modulations and meaning. His eye for line, mass and form must be acute enough to allow him to perceive the correspondence between an actor's physical attitudes and the emotions he is expressing, and his sense of the pictorial must be fertile enough to lead him to arrange figures on the stage swiftly and precisely so that the compositions convey dramatic ideas with force and beauty.

There are other miscellaneous areas where proficiency is required, in making or revising the ground plan for instance, or in knowing how to select a good cast.

The Diversity of Directorial Types

Few professions demand such a variety of talents in so many discrete fields. And I imagine few directors are equally capable as scholars, technicians, critics, writers, psychologists, and showmen. Yet there have been and no doubt will continue to be those who possess in some measure the necessary flexibility to excel in all departments, who have the intellect to understand and evaluate a manuscript and the knack for putting it on the stage in such a way that it touches the minds and hearts of many people.

Rarely, however, do the qualities needed to make a perfect director reside in one person in ideal proportions. One or two qualities usually dominate and tend to eclipse the rest or, at least, tend to make the director gravitate toward plays which call for his special skills and offer material in which his particular propensity can be displayed to advantage—plays, in short, which lead to his strength.

For example, it is unusual to find a director with equally sensitive sensory perceptions. In one, the eye will be the most fully developed sense, in another, the ear. Those whose visual acuity overbalances other senses find their best outlets in plays requiring pictorial niceties, the vivid use of color, striking composition, and pleasing movement. These are the choreographers, who delight in opportunities to put their optical talent to use and whose most successful productions are those which appeal primarily to the eyes of the audience. Those whose sense of hearing dominates, the masters of sound, will be drawn naturally to plays in which the dialogue may be treated as song. They will assault the ears of the audience with lyrical vocal effects, musical inflections, and carefully-cadenced speech, and make theatrical capital out of stage sounds and musical accompaniment.

In others such sensory perceptions as these may be weak. Instead they may have a bent for probing and analyzing the springs of character. These are the psychologists, experts at digging into motives, hidden complexes, inner drives and such. Their system of directing will include large measures of complex analysis in which they will explore with the actors every facet and dimension of the characters to be portrayed, relentlessly pursuing every innuendo and nuance in the psychological relationships between the characters as well as their antecedent case histories. Their main exertions will be directed toward establishing the truth of each characterization and the interconnections between the truth of the character and the truth of the performer as he reaches for it. This will be followed by efforts to find the technical means to project these mutual discoveries over the footlights in truthful form, but also in such a way that they are readily identifiable by the spectators. The one danger in all this is that such directors can become so involved in behavior that they do not have time or energy to solve the mechanical problems of translating their findings by means of acting technique into actions and speeches that register specific as well as theatrically effective points with the audience. Examples of this sort of imbalance, and there have been many in recent years, supply most of the material to critics of the Stanislavsky method.

Directors differ from each other in another way. Some are temperamentally unfitted to deal successfully with comedy, having little sense of humor. Others with a keen sense of fun and an eye for the absurd may be made uncomfortable when confronted with the prospect of staging a script that has little in it except gloom and a tragic conclusion.

Yet, while granting that the directorial temperament may take many forms and is a thing of infinite diversity, and further that a director's personality traits as well as his physical attributes—his hearing, eyesight, sense of balance, and so on—may all be limiting factors which make him good for some plays but poor for others, the point should be made that the best way for a director to develop, if he aspires to perfection, is to find out what his weak points are, to acknowledge them as such, and then go ahead to shore up those weaknesses while developing his naturally strong talents to their greatest strength.

Unless a director suffers from some physical defect, there is no reason why he cannot train his eye to be as sensitive as his ear. Anyone who has a flair for staging exciting pictorial arrangements or for inventing interesting stage business can learn, by applying himself, the fundamentals of psychology and psychoanalysis and go ahead and apply them in a theatre context.

Every director worth his salt will eventually discover his own directing method and his own technical procedures. These will be based on his personal habits and his inclinations as an artisan or artist. If he is sensible they will be designed to feature his strong points and cover his faults or deficiencies. On the way he should pursue whatever course of training or study best conditions him to learn how to adapt himself and his method to the special demands of the individual script, regardless of its type, style, or mode. The goal to be achieved is excellence and flexibility. He can only attain these when he has mastered all the instruments of understanding, perception, and imagination that he has in his possession and continues to enrich them by experience.

The genius of the stage and master of his art needs neither books nor advice. This volume was certainly not written for him. But those who still have something to learn about the craft and whose techniques can stand improvement may find it of use.

CHAPTER TWO

Making the Approach

Nature and Art are two things.

VICTOR HUGO: *Preface to Cromwell*

Reading a new play is an adventure, happy or unhappy as the case may be. In time the director or producer learns to approach the experience with wary optimism and a determination not to allow a surfeit of poor scripts to dull the edge of belief that the one he is about to read may be a masterpiece.

The Directorial Attitude

If a script is hopeless, dull, and impossible to stage, these impressions will register on the mind of an experienced theatre man before he has read twenty pages, and there will be little reason for him to proceed further except to verify his opinion with a look at act endings. The bounds of courtesy need not be extended to include the close reading of every page of a stupid or inept work.

But, if the script arrests attention and has recognizable quality of any sort, every word of it should be read through at one sitting without interruption or distraction. After all, a text represents weeks or months of effort by the writer, and if it does show merit the director should give it his whole attention for two or three hours.

It takes more courage to pick a new untried script on the basis of one's lonely personal conviction than an established play whose worth was proclaimed by impressive critical raves. The college or community theatre director, however, should weigh the shortcomings of a new play against the challenge and opportunity it gives him to till new ground. Who knows when one may discover fresh talent that will eventually enrich the whole theatre? An audience's response to original work can be extraordinarily warm. Interest in new writing is often keener than in old and perhaps overfamiliar work. This may be due to the fact that the audience has been trained over a long period to look upon such work as plays-in-being rather than finished products, although these are offered without apology. The director who has the confidence of his audience can usually go ahead on the assumption that any new effort will get a sympathetic hearing, and he will be performing a real and creative service for the community as well as for the playwright.

Approaching any script, new or old, the director should be positive and receptive, not critical in the negative sense of that term, or at least not hypercritical. This is a time to try and perceive attributes, not to dwell on shortcomings. The number of great plays in the world is small. The practical realities of putting a season of plays together demand that the director balance his highest artistic principles against the sobering thought that in drama as in poetry, "it is only a moment here and a moment there that the greatest writer has." [1] To ask that every new play under consideration compare favorably in every respect to *Hamlet*, *The Cherry Orchard*, *Death of a Salesman*, or *Tartuffe* is the surest way of keeping a theatre dark. It is certainly more practical and probably better to try and strike a mean between the ideal and the possible, the perfect and the attainable.

As he reads, the director will obviously be looking for meaning, the author's intention, the gist, all of which calls for intellectual awareness, but he should try also to let the work touch him emotionally if it can. For the theatre appeals to feelings first and to intellect second. A play's ideas may interest the thoughtful segment of the audience enormously, yet it is the passions it arouses which give it impact on a mass scale. Ideas, if they are popular and stimulating, add dimension and depth. Yet it should not be forgotten that the theatre is a form of art that addresses itself to the many, and all at once. The test of a play's success in evoking collective response lies in its power to make us laugh or cry, to arouse our pity and sympathy for some characters or resentment and hatred for others. And the more we insist that the public stand apart from a play in order to make a conscious judgment of its esthetic or philosophical worth, the less chance there is for its universal appeal to make itself felt. And this universal appeal is what draws us into the play life we are witnessing in a magical and a persuasive way that momentarily

[1] Robert Frost's letter to Sidney Cox, January 2, 1915, in Sergeant, Elizabeth Shepley, *Robert Frost, The Trial by Existence*: New York: Holt, Rinehart and Winston, Inc., 1960.

lets us forget our own. The director who lets the play speak to his heart as well as his head will probably do a better job of selection than one who is blind to this ambivalence in the theatre's appeal.

If the play he is reading is realistic, he should approach it as reality itself. By bringing himself to view the characters as human beings living and speaking in a world which for the moment is not a thing of artifice to be made up of wood and canvas but the world of nature, he will be less likely to fall into the error of leaping too quickly to considerations about how it should be staged.

He can find almost as many legitimate reasons for selecting a play as there are plays. It may offer an opportunity for his best actor, it may require but one set, it may have one splendid scene, a powerful idea, a good story, a thunderous climax, or a moving close. Any of these may justify the choice, but the chances of success are better if the script offers several such qualities rather than just one.

Sound characterization, a timely theme, an interesting plot, and anything that adds cumulative interest to the flow of events and builds anticipation about the outcome are operative factors pulling toward acceptance.

Because the director's primary objective in this initial contact with the text is to obtain a grasp of it as a whole and in large perspective, there is little to be gained by stopping to make extensive notes about needed revisions, cuts or emendations; to question isolated items of construction or characterization; or to set down suggestions for improving the style or tightening the dialogue. Nor need he indulge in long analyses of what sort of lives the characters led at a time antecedent to the beginning of the play, nor in elaborate penetrations of their respective psyches. All these, if need be, can come later.

He may decide to go ahead with the script after a single reading, or after ten. It all depends on the quality of the text and his own temperament. Elia Kazan is said to have read *J.B.* at least half a dozen times before agreeing to direct it.

Locating the Play

Plays differ so widely in form, tone, and intention, that one of the first things a director may wish to do is to label the work he has chosen in accordance with accepted and universally applied methods of literary classification. In order to put it in its proper genre, and be able to compare it with other work in that same genre, the director must establish its type, style, and mode. For the knowing theatre man this will be easy—an almost automatic reflex. But it will do no harm to review briefly the categories that help to set off one play from another.

Dramatic Types

Drama is divided into two major types: tragedy and comedy; the chief differences between the two being based on a divergence in tone, aim, effect, and nature of conclusion.

Strictly speaking, the term *tragedy* in academic circles is reserved for works of high literary quality written either in verse or poetic prose whose personages are of some stature and importance. The prevailing tone is serious and the events normally calamitous though not necessarily fatal for the hero. The heroes and heroines of tragedy, while not absolutely required to embody one or more human virtues, are more likely to be admired as true representatives of the type if they display some strength, be it of will, mind, or heart—and that strength, whether it be used for good or evil purposes, should be of heroic proportions. It is the lot of tragedy to depict the pitiful or awesome aspects of life, and this it does by showing its characters struggling in the grip of some unhappy fate. But admixed with the suffering may be exaltation. This may be observed in the very perfection of the writing, as in Sophoclean tragedy, where the exquisite chiseling of the verse diverts us from the painfulness of the subject it describes, just as Shakespeare does in *Romeo and Juliet* with the extravagant splendors of his metaphors. Or it may bc found in the presentation of people who meet their fates well and bravely as do Oedipus or Antigone. Purists refuse to bestow the title Tragedy on many works not written in Greece during the fifth century, B.C., or in Renaissance England, although they admit a few from other periods if they are closely imitative of the accepted models or based on Aristotle's theories of tragedy. But there is no absolute definition for the term, and it seems overcautious to deny its application to some modern plays that conform generally to the requirements stated above except that they are not written in verse and are peopled by characters from everyday life.

Comedy is a word which has come to be applied in its strictest sense to plays with some larger purpose than that of mere amusement. It describes a literary style, not devoid of some thought or trenchant commentary, whose prevailing tone—if not exactly hilarious—is at least benign or wry, satirical, or humorous. Some plays labeled *comedies* by their authors have proved to be very grim indeed, so that the term has become somewhat like a coin whose features have been worn off with use. Such *comédies humaines* and others like them with serious themes are also termed *drames,* signifying a hybrid type once called *tragi-comedy.*

Subtended from tragedy and comedy are their somewhat disreputable but nevertheless sturdy satellites, the so-called *minor types:* melodrama and farce.

To be added to these are certain special types whose descriptive titles denote their special subject matter: the problem play, the comedy of manners, the tragedy of blood, the Agitprop play and so on.

Aside from the convenience of the labels it is often helpful for a cast that has begun to waver in its grasp of the fundamentals of a work to be reminded of the meaning of the term by which the play is classified, and to be shown specifically how it conforms to the essentials of that type; although this should be handled cautiously. If too much stress is placed on the fact that the material is a tragedy, for instance, the playing may become solemn where it should be something else. Zeffirelli's production was memorable because Romeo and Juliet were, to the life, two young people in love. At no time did they give any indication that they knew they were playing tragedy.

Dramatic Styles

Two broad terms are used to mark the difference between plays that are intended to create an illusion of reality and others which are not. If a play is obviously aimed at representing normal and everyday human experience in recognizable natural settings, and if the characters speak ordinary sounding conversation, the style is termed *realistic* or *naturalistic.* If, on the other hand it is an abstract or conventionalized reflection of human activity, frankly artificial or playlike with little conformity to the way people actually behave or talk, and if the settings merely suggest real places instead of representing them, the play is said to be in the *nonrealistic* or *theatricalist* style.

REALISM

It should be noted that realism in theatre parlance is a highly qualified term. A play may be lifelike, but it is never life. No matter how closely it tries to imitate it, it remains art, a thing of artifice. Hamlet, dead from the thrust of Laertes' poisoned rapier, will always rise to take the curtain call.

Henrik Ibsen's social plays provide the norm for realistic drama, and it is hard to find many "nature-imitating" plays which make up the bulk of today's playwriting that are not based on the Ibsen model. In *A Doll's House, Ghosts, An Enemy of the People,* and *The Wild Duck,* contemporary characters drawn from carefully observed life are placed in possible situations and held together by the unifying effect of a meticulously articulated main plot. They speak, act, and move just as one would expect characters in real life to do. But just the same, what they do and what they say, the things that happen to them, and the order in which those things happen are all part of a tightly organized compositional scheme designed both to keep the whole within the frame of the real and the probable and to achieve at the same time certain preordained, plotted, theatrical effects. Ibsen certainly strove to create illusion, but he never did so if it interfered with or obstructed the scoring of dramatic points, and he made sure such points would register with the audience.

From the Ibsen norm a play may move, stylistically speaking, toward one of two opposed extremes: toward naturalism or toward the more obvious conventionality of the "well-made" play.

NATURALISM

The aim of this style is to suggest that the spectator has inadvertently stumbled into an actual place outside the theatre and is eavesdropping on a segment of actual life.

Gorki's *The Lower Depths* is cited most frequently as a leading example of this style. It differs from the Ibsen norm in that it has no main plot, no connected narrative, and no particular dramatic focus. Without a central plot, it contains no characters upon which interest can center for any length of time, and the author deliberately avoids using a firm structural outline. This of course is all in keeping with his purpose, which is to show the nightmare world of a Russian slum in its chaos, purposelessness, untidiness, and brutality. To reproduce this chaos and purposelessness accurately and honestly, the medium itself had to display these same characteristics, or so the naturalists thought, even at the risk of having the plays themselves seem haphazard and formless.

The Lower Depths is unsullied by the artifices and devices that form the backbone of conventional showmanship and theatricality. There is little attempt to reach an explosive climax after tidy exposition and well-calculated rising action. There are no punch curtains, no prepared entrances. Thrown out with these are all the familiar paraphernalia of suspense, misunderstanding, and complication that brought popular acceptance to the familiar stencils of the "well-made" play, including its easily identifiable stage types, the hero, the heroine, the villain, and so on.

Nor are there any leading roles. Each person in the play is not a theatrical character but an individual, and neither more nor less important as such than any other. Each personage, in fact, may be thought of as a separate thread in the action, just as in the case of plays written in the theatrical tradition. But in naturalism what happens to each thread in the course of the dramatic action is different. Instead of the threads being twined or knotted together to provide a tight weave whereby each personality is bound closely to the central matrix that is the main plot, naturalism concentrates on the truth and vividness of each individual, on the particular coloration of each separate thread. It is not concerned particularly with the way each thread is interworked with the rest.

Thus each man or woman in a naturalistic play may be said to have his own plot just as each has his own individual life. It is not regarded as necessary to relate these individual plots in any arbitrary way to the plots of the others, although some interconnections are, of course, inevitable.

The matrix that holds the characters together in *The Lower Depths* is not the central story but the milieu. This is not to say, however, that there is more characterization than action in naturalism. In Gorki's play there is action galore and plots in profusion. There is a murder plot, there are assignations, a death on stage, a murder off, a hanging, a maiming, a scalding, and other evidence of the savagery of the destitute's life. But all these events are off on the periphery and unrelated to a central core. Instead of a single tight plot there are a dozen loose ones, and most are advanced not by dramatic means but by narration and recapitulation as in the novel form. The inevitable diffused effect which this treatment creates and which is so apparent also in the plays of Anton Chekhov, may well result from the playwright's inability or reluctance to disentangle the essentials of the theatrical form from the novel form.

IMPRESSIONISM

The term *naturalism* has most frequently been applied to dramas dealing with submerged members of society living in squalor as they do in *The Lower Depths* or in Tolstoi's *The Power of Darkness*. Yet, when much the same dramaturgic method is used in plays dealing with the upper class, as in Chekhov, the result is called *impressionism*. Actually the same devices are used in both. Each character seems wrapped in his own monodrama. We are permitted to catch only a brief glimpse of each one at a time, picking them up, as it were, in disassociated fragments like the pieces in a jigsaw puzzle. Only at the end can the fragments be put together and added up in the mind of the spectator to make a cohesive whole.

This same fragmented style, coupled with murkier intentions and much further removed from reality, descends almost in a straight line from naturalism to the present-day Theatre of the Absurd, lower-class life and all.

Impressionism, like naturalism, is a variant of the realistic style. The term is derived from a style of painting which sought to reproduce scenes in nature as these were softened and blurred by the surrounding atmosphere of light and air. Impressionist painters produced such effects by eliminating black from the palette, by eschewing hard outlines, and by building up their pictures with short strokes of primary colors, often set in such close juxtaposition that the blending had to be done by the eye of the spectator at a proper distance away. The broken line and the shimmering vagueness of Monet's studies of haystacks under different light conditions, and Seurat's *La Grande Jatte* are popular examples of this technique.

As applied to the theatre, the term describes a style of writing based loosely on the same principles as found in pictorial art. Its best examples are the full-length plays of Anton Chekhov although some contemporary playwrights, Saroyan and Odets among them, have adopted the style successfully.

Chekhov, in agreement with his fellow-dramatist, Gorki, thought that the best way to put truthfully observed life upon the stage was to avoid the commonplace conventions and clichés of popular playwriting. He, too, applied the broken technique for building up the features of his characters in a series of spaced touches, giving us fleeting impressions of a character's life and traits in such a way that the whole person was not revealed until the observer had a chance to put together, sometimes in retrospect, the fractured parts strewn through the text.

Not that this technique is wholly new in dramaturgy. Delayed revelation has always been a stock-in-trade with writers in any theatrical genre. The difference lies in the fact that these compartmented bits of autobiographical revelation, at least as Chekhov handled them, seem in most cases to be drawn out or uttered spontaneously, frequently without clear relevance to the subject of the conversation in the scene. The result, in spite of some vagueness and diffusion particularly in presenting the logical association of ideas, is the creation of scenes which have the vividness of reality, all the more so because they convey some of the casualness and artlessness of actual life. The hard outlines of the plot and the hard outlines of the characters are concealed or muted and, in the hands of a masterful artist like Chekhov, the results are as brilliant and lifelike as they are in Monet's paintings. Both impressionism and naturalism came into being as part of an effort to convey a deeper sense of life and meaning than could be found in conventionally molded entertainments. Only a stage where truth prevailed could contain the revolutionary idea that the medium could become an effective instrument of social conscience. And plays which presented the unvarnished truth about life in the lower strata of society, as Gorki's and Tolstoi's did, were manifestations of the new belief that the theatre might function as a force in the drive to curb social ills. *Awake and Sing* and *The Time of Your Life* follow the pattern but with a large addition of comedy to make the message palatable. Just as Monet, Degas, Cézanne and Seurat may be said to have broken away from academic methods of painting and the French Academy's ideas about what subjects were acceptable and what were not, so these playwrights reacted against the mechanical sterilities of the Sardou school both in form and ideas.

NONREALISM OR THEATRICALISM

Here the aim is to represent experience in abstract or imaginative form. The stage is to be used and accepted frankly as a stage, a place where

LIBRARY
LEWIS-CLARK
STATE COLLEGE

63865

certain conventional ways of expressing ideas are accepted by common agreement. The playwright along with the actor is freed from any obligation to indulge in the kind of trickery needed to make what is happening seem actual. What is presented is the world of the imagination. Nothing in that world is governed by natural laws, and the product is responsible only to its own integrity as a form of art.

Included in this style as its chief subdivisions are fantasy, symbolism, expressionism, surrealism and constructivism.

A fantasy shows a world that never was and never could be. Examples of the style range from fairy tales like Barrie's *Peter Pan* to bizarre samples of science fiction like *A Visit to a Small Planet*.

Symbolism, present in many styles, pervades the one to which its name is given.

The mystical plays of Maeterlinck as well as Yeats's later imitations of Nō Drama employ symbolic association to conjure up images of death, night, and silence. Yeats uses masks, music, and ritual further to remove this style from the commonplaces and indeed from some of the clarities of nature.

The characters in expressionist drama represent large, general, symbolic types rather than individuals, and plays written in this style state whatever messages they contain about man in terms of generalization rather than by specific and personal illustration. The features of the actors are depersonalized by masks or make-up, the movement is mechanistic, the scenery distorted, often for the purpose of suggesting how things look to the eyes of the leading character. All these combine to express modern life under the impact of the machine.

Neither this style nor its offshoot, constructivism, so named because the structural skeleton of the sets is exposed to the view of the audience (and usually with the same esthetically unpleasing results as would be found in looking at mere bones), has survived to any appreciable degree in the American theatre of the present day.

Surrealism, like its stylistic counterpart in painting, presents to view a combination of lifelike, or at least empirically recognizable elements and subjective and often distorted symbols, like the melted watches of Dali, in strange contexts and unfamiliar juxtapositions. The sand box in *The Sand Box* by Albee, the plane "Fugitivo" in *Camino Real*, the creature at the end of the rope in Beckett's *Waiting for Godot*, are meant to have significance and to convey overtones of meaning the way most symbols are meant to do. Some surrealist playwrights, however, use them in such a way as to shroud the proceedings in an aura of obscurity, sometimes for intentionally comic effect. The fun comes in trying to decide whether what one is seeing is profound or nonsensical.

Once he has identified the style of a play, the director can establish a base of comparison with others of similar style, and armed with this knowledge may be in a better position than he would be otherwise to determine the proper scheme of production for it.

Theatricalism for the most part calls for an artificial style of playing which includes exaggerated departures from what are considered normal in the players' postures, motions, speech, and facial expressions. These abnormalities of behavior and aspect are intended to match and even heighten the departures from actuality contained in the text and called for in the sets. Costumes and make-up are similarly carried to a point of extravagance. Such productions are said to be *stylized*, another unfortunate term because any production, naturalistic or otherwise, has a style. But the word is perhaps adequate to describe the theatrical hyperbole imposed on the productions of those plays which break the mold of illusion and enter the realm of the suggestive and the unreal.

Dramatic Modes

Another and familiar way to differentiate between plays is to divide them into two classes based roughly on the typical form and style of plays in the historical epoch from which they are derived. Plays which follow ancient Greek and Roman models are set in the Classical mode; those which imitate the Shakespearean model in form and feeling are placed in the Romantic mode. The first is tightly written, centripetal in effect, its action strictly confined in time and space, its attention concentrated on a single event or action of some magnitude, and using a small number of characters. In Classicism the fundamental aim is to distill essences, to cut away altogether whatever tangential material is extraneous to the main plot or may interfere with the play's singleness of impact.

In Romanticism, however, a different end is pursued. Austerities and limitations in style and form are discarded in favor of flexibility and freedom from restrictions in form and subject matter, the object being to convey a livelier sense of life than that which is found in the classic mode. For the sake of color, atmosphere, picturesqueness, and a newer realistic look, the basic unities of time, place, and action which lie at the heart of the Classical mode are abandoned. Hence, the Romantic mode is loose, centrifugal, extravagant, free. The playwright's imagination is to be allowed to soar unhampered by rules and laws, whether these apply to spatial, temporal, or metaphorical matters. Comedy and seriousness are intermingled. Scenes are changed at will and the action of the play may cover many years. There are no restrictions on the number of characters or on the number of subplots.

To see the basic contrasts between these two modes set off in sharp relief, one should compare Dryden's *All for Love* with Shakespeare's *Antony and Cleopatra.* Dryden tried to bring the history of these heroic figures into line with the Aristotelian unities, to tame the "pestered extravagance" of Shakespeare's metaphorical usage, and to narrow down to reasonable limits its wide-ranging global scope. The results were disastrous, but the play gives a striking illustration of the divergencies between the two approaches.

While a grasp of these academic classifications is useful in that it gives the director a context and a frame of reference from which to approach the work in hand, just as a large-scale map gives him a specific geographical location, his real task begins with the detailed close analysis of the script, and this means a concentration on its subject, structure and style. It does not matter about the order in which he studies these three key elements. He may even take them all together at one and the same time. But he must know all there is to know about all three; otherwise he is no true director but merely a prompter or stage manager.

CHAPTER THREE

What the Play Contains

> One might almost say that a play ought to be the work of two men of genius, one of whom should make the plot, and the other write the dialogue.
>
> DIDEROT.

At the outset of his study of the play the director has his eyes open for the three basic elements which are present in every theatre work: content or subject, structure, and style. He must finally recognize and understand them as literary and dramatic values. Furthermore he must perceive how they interlock, how the structure supports the theme, and whether or not the language chosen and the way it is used are appropriate to the framework and befit the nature of the subject.

Because every play is unique these values vary widely. In one, what is said may be far more important than the way it is said; in another, the style may overcap the theme; and in still another, the playwright's skill in building the plot sequences may far outreach his ability to convey a message. The director must decide where the main strength of a script lies and make creative capital of it. If there are deficiencies he must take steps to conceal them and divert the audience's attention to stronger values.

The Story

The content includes story, theme or meaning, and characterizations.

The story (the narration of happenings) is contained within the framework of the plot. To tell the plot is to describe the play's physical action. The details of the physical events when regarded in the sequence the playwright has provided comprise the structure of the plot. A play's structure depends, then, both on the nature of the episodes or incidents which are selected to tell the story and also on the sequence or order in which these incidents are set down in the flow of the play's time. The story of a play is always about its people, its characters. The events of the plot exert an influence on them, and they on the events; and in many plays the plot situation is merely the means of putting the characters to some sort of test, to see whether they triumph or crumble in the process. The progression of personality development is as much a part of the forward action of the plot as are the basic changes in situation that supply the motion of the play's external events.

In the minor dramatic types, these external events are about all the director has to work with. This is because the dramatist has placed his stress on what the characters do, with their fists, arms, legs, and faces, and not on why they do it. The aim of melodrama is to create suspense and send chills up and down the spine by setting the characters in dangerous situations where life rather than principle is at stake. Excitement takes precedence over psychological truth; and the characters tend to serve as pawns or familiar types, placed in difficult situations not so much of their own making but as arbitrary environments designed to produce maximum though commonplace emotional effects.

In the farce, also, the plot predominates over theme and characterization. The characters are displayed in improbable situations, often bordering on the outrageous, for the sake of getting laughs. The absurdity springs from the physical action which is often in the form of slapstick.

In both these types, the director must "play the plot," that is, punch the plot lines, crisply time the business, and maintain a swift tempo. To conceal the machinery and make the incredible appear likely, he will probably increase playing pace and raise volume to sharpen the climaxes. The creative demands made upon him are technical rather than esthetic or philosophical, although a good deal of imagination may be needed to invent comic business in farce and sustain suspense in melodrama. It is far better to use rehearsal time for precision drilling than for probing psyches and unearthing occult or subsconscious motivation.

It would be foolish to minimize the importance of a good story in the list of dramatic values. Drama began as a way of telling a story and remains so in spite of some modern aberrations which dispense with narrative altogether. But it may, and perhaps should be only one of many values present in a text, serving as a sort of avenue down which one may travel to more significant matters of meaning. The events in Carson McCullers's *The Member of the Wedding* are few in number. Nothing much *happens*. A young girl, Frankie Addams, longs to go to live with her brother and his bride after their wedding. In this she is frustrated and runs away from home, only to return after a few hours. Thus the central external action of the plot is based on the slightest sort of incident. Other events occur offstage and have to be recapitulated. Among these are the deaths of Frankie's little cousin, John Henry, and of her servant Bernice's foster-brother, Honey Brown, who, we learn, has hanged himself in jail. Here the plot may be said to be merely a tentative, almost impalpable, fabric whose principal use is to hold the personalities of the play together in their environment.

It should be noted also that some plays of the highest quality, O'Casey's *Juno and the Paycock*, to name one, succeed in spite of the fact that their plots are made up of hackneyed materials. They possess other values in theme, subject, style, and human insight in such significant proportions that any weakness in the plot becomes a minor flaw.

The Subject

The universal subject of all drama is man. But the essential subject of a play describes some particular aspect or condition in the behavior of men and women as revealed in a specific environment and at a specific time and place. To state a play's subject is to describe the general, pervasive, informative idea it illustrates, dissects, or proclaims. It is the topic which the actions of the plot advance. The subject of *The Member of the Wedding* is adolescence, and it is through the personality of Frankie Addams that we are given glimpses of much of the poignancy, the rages, hopes and uncertainties of life in that in between age. The subject of *A Doll's House* is marriage, of *A Streetcar Named Desire* the decay of gentility, of *Cat on a Hot Tin Roof* disease. The subject of *The Doctor's Dilemma* is medical ethics, of *Winterset* the redeeming power of love.

A playwright is seldom content merely to state or illustrate the subject. He usually wants to make a comment on it or to draw a conclusion about it which may help to illuminate some truth about the human condition. A play may ask a question about the subject and attempt to answer it, as in Augier's *Marriage of Olympe*, whose subject is the same as *A Doll's House*. The question Augier asked is whether or not a marriage between an honorable man and a prostitute can succeed. The action supplies the answer with true Gallic logic: it is "no," provided the wife remains at heart a prostitute. A play may ask a question and find at the end no answer at all, only a still larger question.

More often than not a play may state a certain proposition about the subject, and the plot will then be used to test that proposition or demonstrate it in such a way that a conclusion may be drawn which supports or refutes it. Such a conclusion is the theme or lesson. *Macbeth* illustrates the theory that ambition left to run unchecked leads man to savage acts contrary to moral law. Macbeth's bloody end and his wife's insanity and death suggest that the additional point Shakespeare makes is that naked ambition leading to crime brings retribution.

From *The Member of the Wedding* it is possible to conclude that youth possesses a resiliency that overcomes disappointment and permits the adolescent to turn to new interests and a new life; and this in contrast to age, represented by Frankie's mother-surrogate, Berenice Sadie Brown, who cannot shake off the past.

A Doll's House puts a conventional, one-sided marriage to the test of a woman's awakening experience. Its inescapable lesson is that in marriage there cannot be true union until man accepts his wife as his social and intellectual equal, and respects her rights as an individual. Applying this specific case to marriage in general, it would appear that Ibsen was advocating a reform in the prevalent social attitude toward marriage which seemed to be based on the idea that as long as the outward amenities were observed it was the natural and accepted thing for a man to look upon his wife as his plaything and chattel.

In *A Streetcar Named Desire*, Tennessee Williams suggests the inevitability of the conflict between a representative of a faded and corrupt but gentle social class and another who stands for everything that is brutish, vulgar, but withal honest in American society. In the clash the symbol of degraded gentility is destroyed.

Cat on a Hot Tin Roof demonstrates the proposition that whole sections of our affluent society are degenerate, its people crippled or diseased in a moral as well as a physical sense. The bleak conclusion seems to be that there is no way out.

One important question which *The Doctor's Dilemma* raises is the relative worth of human life. To illustrate it the playwright confronts us with a specific situation. He poses the question: should an immoral artist of undoubted genius be saved from death at the expense of another man who is a respectable nonentity. In this case the doctors representing society punish the artist who flouts conventional morality by letting him die. But the play is a comedy and its conclusion shows society rebuked and the genius apotheosized.

Winterset places a youth in a dilemma where he must choose between a life motivated by hatred and revenge or one marked by goodness and love. Anderson's faith in man's nobility is demonstrated by the hero's choice of the latter way, even though it results in his death.

It should be understood that these generalizations representing an effort to enlarge the specific case and express the thought behind it in universal terms are not to be taken as dogma. They represent the opinions of one individual who, having weighed for himself the evidence of the facts has arrived at his own personal interpretation of what they mean. Someone else might think his conclusions hopelessly wrong and choose meanings completely at variance with his.

Be that as it may, it is clear that no director can afford to embark on a production without coming to a definite decision in his own mind first about whether or not his play has a subject, a theme, a proposition, and a conclusion, and if it has, to describe or define as precisely as he can what they are. He may make mistakes, but it is central to his place and function as a director to make up his mind what the playwright's intention is and identify the side the playwright is on. If he fails to do this he has no guiding intellectual principle nor fundamental logical base from which to start to make the production his own. And without such a base the point of the work can convey itself to the audience only by accident. The aimlessness and confusion of many performances can be blamed on the director's failure to hold before his cast the image of the play's true subject and what the playwright meant to say about it.

A play may have several subjects and multiple layers of meaning, just as there are multiple themes and motifs in a symphony. If so, the director must understand them all; but there is no law compelling him to treat them all with equal emphasis. It is his province to select from these many themes the few he considers most important. His choices will determine the slant of his production. Part of our enjoyment in witnessing revivals of old plays is to see which themes are stressed and which suppressed. Look at the number of valid conclusions that may be drawn from a complex work like *Death of a Salesman* wherein several themes, all of them important, hold the play together almost independently of the plot.

On the sociological level the play deals with the thought that personality, the ability to make oneself liked, is an outmoded formula for success in modern business. There is, besides, the contrast between the present impersonality and heartlessness of business methods and the friendly way of salesmanship in the past when selling was a dignified and respected profession. Another sociological commentary is to be found in its illustration of the incompatibility between rural, outdoor men and the complexity and competition of metropolitan life, and in its disclosure of some of the problems imposed on the small householder by the pressure of increased population and the mushrooming of tenements in our cities.

On the emotional level the play, in the words of its director, Elia Kazan, is a "love story between a father and a son." But it also contains essential material on the effects that relationship and that love struggle have on the patient wife, Linda Loman.

Of no less importance in the play's conclusion are two personal discoveries by Biff which have a profound effect on his character and his life, the painful one that his father is not a demi-god, and the second that contains some seeds of hope, his discovery that his chance for happiness lies quite outside the sort of success his father envisioned for him. The younger son, Happy, fails to learn anything from his father's death and this failure is just as telling in a negative way. There is also the dramatic contrast between Willy's softer, tamer, more domesticated instincts and his brother Ben's ruthless pioneering spirit, a contrast which supplies its own comment on the declining vigor of the American male.

Above and beyond these considerations, Willy's psychological relationships are explored in depth, and from several perspectives. We see him as husband, father, and brother. We see the kind of man he is when he is with his friends, his employer, and his mistress. Of thematic importance, too, is Willy's concluding sacrificial act, an act in expiation of his guilt at having disillusioned his son in the crucial scene at the Boston hotel. This serves to give him a tragic dimension at variance with the concept of him as a "low man."

Awareness, understanding, clarity of mind—these should be stressed first, before instinct, intuition, or subjective feeling as the necessary materials of the director's craft. They are certainly needed in that phase of preparation that includes analysis of meaning of the subject.

But let us go back once more to the question of choice in selecting certain themes to stress.

While the director of a Shakespearean play may feature one theme at the expense of others by the simple process of cropping the text, he cannot do this in a modern work without running foul of the copyright laws. Besides, in a play like *Death of a Salesman* the themes are knitted too closely together to admit of much separation. They must all be developed together and accented equally.

The first step is to recognize a theme when it appears.

The following illustration from Arthur Miller's play may serve to show how one subject, like a single thread, has been woven into the play's fabric, and how different aspects of it are brought into view. Each time the motif emerges some slight accretion of meaning is added to what came before, and the accumulating shreds of evidence all bearing on the same subject serve to amplify and elaborate it until at the end, with maximum suspense obtained by delayed revelation, the whole configuration of the theme as well as its import is displayed.

The single motif in this case is Biff's hostility toward his father, Willy. The reason for this hatred between father and son is the play's central mystery and its ultimate revelation furnishes the play's climax.

Biff's attitude toward his father is first hinted at in an early scene:

> BIFF: There's one or two things depressing him, Happy.
> HAPPY: What do you mean?
> BIFF: Never mind. Just don't lay it all to me.

Twenty-five pages later the subject recurs, and we get from the mother the first overt statement that there is a gulf of bitterness between father and son:

> LINDA: (*To Biff*) When you write you're coming,
> he's all smiles, and talks about the future,
> and . . . he's just wonderful. And then the
> closer you seem to come the more shaky he
> gets, and then . . . by the time you get here . . .
> he's arguing, and he seems angry at you. I
> think it's just that maybe he can't bring himself

to . . . to open up to you. Why are you so
hateful to each other? Why is that?

Biff's resentment against his father's alleged lack of respect for his mother is now expressed with such violence as to suggest that his feelings against his father rise from some hurt he has inflicted on Linda, although we still remain in the dark about the reasons for it:

BIFF: (*To Linda*) Stop making excuses for him!
He always, always wiped the floor with you.
Never had an ounce of respect for you.
HAPPY: He's always had respect for . . .
BIFF: What the hell do you know about it? . . .

And seven pages later—

WILLY: Will you let me talk?
BIFF: Don't yell at her, Pop, will ya?
WILLY: (*Angering*) I was talking, wasn't I?
BIFF: I don't like you yelling at her all the
time and I'm telling you, that's all.
WILLY: What're you takin' over, this house?
LINDA: Willy . . .
WILLY: Don't take his side all the time, goddammit!
BIFF: (*Furiously*) Stop yelling at her!
WILLY: (*Suddenly . . . beaten down, guilt-ridden.*) Give
my best to Bill Oliver . . . he may remember me.

Earlier, Linda has been questioning Biff about the cause of friction between them, but Biff has evaded the answer:

LINDA: . . . And you! What happened to the love you
had for him? You were such pals . . .
BIFF: He threw me out of this house, remember that.
LINDA: Why did he do that? I never knew *why?*
BIFF: Because I know he's a fake and he doesn't like
anybody around who knows!
LINDA: Why a fake? In what way? What do you mean?
BIFF: Just don't lay it all at my feet. It's between
me and him; that's all I have to say . . .

On the next page, Biff reacts sharply to Linda's mention of "a woman"; and although she explains that she was referring to an anonymous witness to Willy's smash-up, Biff's suspicious tone is obvious enough to make us guess he must know something about the woman in

Boston who has been introduced earlier. Then at a crucial point before the close of the first act Linda returns once more to the question:

LINDA: (*Timidly*) Willy dear, what has he got against you?

But it is too early in the play for us to expect an answer:

WILLY: I'm so tired. Don't talk any more.

It is not until we are well into the second and final act, in a scene between Willy and Bernard, that the crucial subject is brought up again, and we are carried another step toward solution of the mystery.

WILLY: (*Confidentially, desperately.*) You were
his friend, his boyhood friend. There's something
I don't understand about it. His life ended
after that Ebbetts' Field game. From the age
of seventeen nothing good ever happened to him.

The perceptive Bernard connects Biff's spiritual collapse with his visit to Boston, but Willy again delays the revelation by resorting to an angry evasion and the scene is interrupted by Charley's entrance. Willy then undergoes three deeply humiliating experiences, each providing an emotional crescendo, before the shattering flashback of the scene in the Boston hotel. With Biff's discovery of his father and his "woman," the scene which lay so deeply buried in Willy's memory finally is reached, with much climactic force.

The progression of such an idea as this, so closely related to the physical action, illustrates the play's psychological structure. The climactic *act* of Biff's discovery, as moving and highly emotional as it is, serves the deeper purpose of filling in the missing piece which explains Biff's whole attitude toward his father from the play's beginning. That discovery changed his whole psychological attitude toward the world and was the decisive factor in all his subsequent behavior. It is, hence, a climactic point in the psychological structure and tightly connected with one of the major themes. In the progressive unfolding of ideas, attitudes, and emotions, the dramatist uses the same devices as he would employ in arranging the play's events, including suspense, surprise, and intensification leading to a climax. It is up to the director to identify and understand how these ideas are developed, and then to explain them to his cast.

In a complex play a dozen or more subject threads may be drawn into the flow of the play's time. The way the dramatist intertwines them, the relative speed in which they grow in relation to each other, the amount of stress given to each one, and the way references to them are spaced in the text all determine the psychological structure. The development of subject ideas or themes constitutes a kind of dramatic action that is just as legitimate as the progression of events and, from the point of view of the thoughtful playgoer, even more valuable.

An integral part of the playwright's technique is bound up in the manner in which he keeps these different subject ideas going forward.

In the normal course of composition, since he cannot develop them simultaneously, he strings them out like beads, with appropriate bridging in between. One idea is introduced, developed to a certain point then put aside in favor of the second, and then a third, and so on. Keeping the stages of development of these subjects roughly parallel to each other is the mark of a playwright who knows his craft. The director who knows his function will take steps to isolate these ideas and put each one in a certain stage space. To keep the subjects straight and to insure that they register with the audience, he may elect to have each scene which contains reference to one specific idea played in the same acting area, or in some other way connect the physical action to the psychological.

Characterization

In a play's content are included any observations or revelations the author may have about human personality. In fact, the chief value of many works designed for the stage springs largely from the inspired view they give of the nature of man. It is thus essential for a director working in a medium that features men and women in all sorts of situations and under all kinds of conditions to be knowledgeable in the ways of humankind. Conscious insight, again, is the one indispensable weapon in his armory, and takes precedence over every other asset, including technical skills. Every director should be a working psychologist.

He gathers evidence on which to base his concept of the play's personalities from his observation of what they say and do, and from his deductions about the motives behind their words and actions. There is nothing occult about the process. Once the underlying motives of the characters are understood, the way or manner in which they speak the lines and perform the action can be decided upon, but not before. More often than not it is the motive that reveals the man more clearly than the words he uses. Most playwrights include a word or two in the text to describe the emotion behind a speech whenever there may be some doubt about the way the actor should speak it; if the motive is neither apparent in the text nor explained by the playwright the director and the actor must supply it. That the invented motive should be consistent with the image of the whole character, supported by evidence in the text, goes without saying.

The nature of a character emerges also from the sum of opinion expressed about him by other characters in the play. The director will not, of course, take all these at face value but weigh them in terms of the motives of the people expressing them, their reliability as character witnesses and the worth of their individual judgments.

Character sketches supplied by the author as well as physical descriptions, which have become standard in theatre practice, provide the starting point. Associating the character with a real or fictional counterpart can be helpful to a director who wants to give the actor a simplified frame of reference, a handle, to help him establish the general outlines of the person he is to play.

Dramatic characters range from one-dimensional figures like Morose in Jonsonian comedy to creatures of infinite complexity, like Hamlet. The extremes pose two somewhat different problems for the director.

To make Morose interesting, the director and the actor must concentrate on finding shades and nuances within the narrow compass of Morose's single humor, and paint him, as it were, in different tints of gloom.

Where there are many aspects of character to choose from, as there are in Hamlet, the director is free to focus on whichever best serves to implement his predetermined view of what this Hamlet will be like, and to undercut or modify those which do not. The individual actor's style and quality, as well as his physical appearance, provide the principal variables that make one interpretation of a familiar role different from another. Hence, it is sensible for the director to stress those temperamental aspects of the character that fit the performer's capabilities and personality.

To analyze a character, first establish his relationship to the original situation and his emotional involvement in it. Is he the protagonist or the antagonist? Active or passive? Subdued or dominant? If he is neither, whose side is he on? What has he to gain or lose by a change in the basic situation? Once he is located in the action, it is a matter of routine to establish further facts about him, his occupation, his beliefs, his station in life. It is important also to know what he has been doing just before the rise of the curtain and the nature of his emotional state, his objectives in the play, and the latent power within him to reach them.

Take a familiar example, Macbeth.

The known facts about him are disclosed early. He is a fighting general fresh from a bloody victory on the battlefield, a man inured to violence and the taking of human life. It would take someone with inordinate physical strength to have unseamed Macdonwald "from the nave to the chaps," and Macbeth has done just that. From the description of the havoc he has wreaked against the Norwegians we must infer he has been a veritable madman on the field, showing an appetite for slaughter far exceeding the demands of conflict.

From this it is not difficult to conclude that he must be represented as a powerful specimen as well as a dangerous one, uncontrollable and frenzied in excitement, perhaps already at the mercy of fits or seizures that will make themselves manifest in the banquet scene. Nevertheless, what is pictured on the basis of textual evidence is a man of great vitality.

Yet notice that his first reaction to the Witches' prophecy is certainly not that of an unthinking man of action, of mere brawn. What the Witches say when they hail him as future king sends him into thoughtful silence; he is "rapt," as Banquo tells us. His first asides reveal a mind running to the contemplation of large issues, "the imperial theme." He speculates clearly and incisively on the two ways to the throne open to him. The intensity of his revulsion toward the thought of murdering Duncan, a horrible prospect that unfixes his hair and makes his heart thump against his ribs, could be found only in a man of sensitivity who has a profound sense of right and wrong, and one whose emotions are not only violent but close to the surface. Yet he has full control over himself. A moment after his emotional disturbance at the thought of slaying Duncan, he becomes gracious and polite to Angus and Ross, and shows friendliness and consideration for his fellow general, Banquo.

Lady Macbeth tells us more about this side of him in I, 5. We learn from her that he is "too full o' the milk of human kindness to catch the nearest way" to the crown, having in her view the ambition but not the illness (evil) to attain it.

The picture that begins to emerge is that of a man with violent inclinations who keeps them steadily in check, for a time at least, by moral sensibility. These two opposed characteristics will form the basis of his inner struggle up to the moment of decision when he resolves to murder the king: an ambition to have the throne inflamed into savage desire by his demonic wife set against the force of conscience which momentarily restrains him from the horror of regicide. In a larger sense, these two sides of his nature, some think, may be taken as expressive of the universal struggle between barbarism and the oncoming forces of Christian civilization. The whole forward action up to MacDuff's discovery of Duncan's murder is marked by alternating scenes in which Macbeth is gripped first by one force and then by the other.

Once the director has settled on some such idea or theory about a character, however self-evident or simple it may be, and the simpler it is the better it may read to the audience, he has a working concept, an informing image of the personality in question from which to start the actor on his task of building the characterization. The rest is largely a matter of enriching and filling in the details, relating them wherever possible to the main concept. When this is done correctly what should result is the familiar but nonetheless desirable ideal of unity with variety. The simplified outline of the chief features of the character is there like a monolith, but subtilized, shaded, deepened by variations in detail.

Atmosphere

Atmosphere evolves from the sum of all that goes to make up the scene's environment, the viewable elements, when combined with everything that can be heard, the auditory elements. The setting, the lights, the sound as well as the pace and rhythm of the actors' voices, with music or sound effects fitting the time, place, and idea of the scene, all these together, orchestrated, evoke theatrical mood.

The design of the setting discloses the physical envelope in which the action will pass. It places the play in its historical period, suggests the sort of action that will ensue and establishes the status of the characters. The power of a setting to create atmosphere is enormously enhanced by the lighting, which unlike the fixed substantive set, is dynamic and alive, capable of changing in color and intensity as often as need be to match any emotional or other change in the text. Light can be used to suggest differing depths or nuances in a single mood or it can accompany and underline shifts from one mood to another. It alone can tell us at once something about the season of the year, the time of day or night, and just as importantly in some plays, the state of the weather.

Indeed, light is so potent an instrument of evocation and lighting designers usually so enthusiastic about exploiting its potential that the director may be called upon to exert a restraining influence to keep its use within bounds. Nothing can be more distracting or more destructive to the meaning of a scene than the kind of overactivity at the control board that produces constant nervous fluctuations in the illumination. Fast changes of cue are a particular source of annoyance because they make the audience conscious of the lights when they should be paying attention to the lines. The director must insist that whatever changes have been agreed upon should be made unobtrusively, and that no changing should be done at all unless it serves to explain the idea of a scene or the emotional conditions of the characters.

A good dramatist suggests how atmosphere can be used as a source of revelation. It is up to the director to so order the synchrony of sight and sound that the revelation counts. The gloom pervading Ibsen's *Ghosts* is the product of theme and situation, but it is deepened and echoed by the darkness outside and the cold rain falling. When Oswald cries out pathetically for "the sun, the sun" toward the close, the weather becomes inseparably linked to the point of the work and indeed the chief instrument of its expression. The sunlight, just as in the final scene of *Peer Gynt*, becomes the symbol of truth and reason, but here coming too late to dispel the dark ignorance and muddled thinking that caused Mrs. Alving to continue the mockery of her marriage with the dissolute Captain in deference to outward convention. For Peer Gynt it means the dawning of the idea that the true meaning of his life and his real destiny lay where he least expected to find them, with Solveig in his native place.

Endlessly dramatists have capitalized on atmospheric effects to heighten meaning. This is as it should be because much of the strength of the theatre as a medium of communication is drawn from its ability to utilize such nonverbal instrumentation. It is fatal for a director to overlook its possibilities, or to miss opportunities to use it to underscore the idea of a scene. In *The Lady's Not For Burning,* for instance, he must be aware of the intimate connection between the weather and the shifting emotional tones of the first act. April sunshine and April showers alternate in quick succession as if fighting for dominance, and alternately the birds outside sing and are silent, exactly matching the flow of action that itself alternates between comedy and serious drama. Offstage storms, from *King Lear* through Ostrovski's *The Storm,* Chekhov's *Uncle Vanya,* and Anderson's *Winterset* to *Cat on a Hot Tin Roof* not only provide excitement from the wings but reflect and by reflecting intensify the matching emotional upheavals in the characters themselves. The soothing chirp of the familiar cricket in *Uncle Vanya* stresses and extends the idea that peace has at last descended on Vanya's troubled household with the departure of the disturbing elements, the Professor and his wife. And in that same play Telyegin interposes the soothing music of his guitar when tempers rise as if in hope that the strains will bring calm to ruffled feelings. Amanda's phonograph spreads nostalgia over *The Glass Menagerie,* and the sound of the flute in *Death of a Salesman* carries Willy Loman back into the past and to the memory of his pioneer father. The moaning foghorn in O'Neill's *Bound East for Cardiff* serves as a constant reminder of the fog that envelops the ship and finally causes the death of the leading character. The gradual acceleration of the tom-tom beat in *The Emperor Jones,* synchronized at the start with the normal human heart beat, increases the excitement of Jones' flight through the forest.

Vivification of the dialogue by these means, although they are sometimes decried as specious by the literary minded, is a legitimate and highly important theatre device. It remains the director's responsibility to use such effects in the right amount and at the right time. This calls for judgment, taste, and often considerable self-restraint.

One thing to remember is that while atmospheric effects may surround and infuse a scene, the mood as conveyed by the players is central to it. A director who overplays the peripheral elements at the expense of the actors and what they are doing runs the risk of losing the audience's attention through inaction.

CHAPTER FOUR

Structure and Meaning

> LYSIDAS: What, Sir! When the protasis, the epitasis, the peripetia—
>
> DORANTE: Nay, Monsieur Lysidas, you overwhelm us with your fine words . . . Humanize your discourse a little, and speak intelligibly.
>
> MOLIÈRE: *La Critique de l'Ecole des femmes.*

An understanding of a play's basic structure and the reasons why the playwright put it together as he did can help lead the director to an understanding of what it means. In well-composed works there is a reciprocal blending and interaction between form and content, particularly in shading of meaning and subtleties of emphasis. It is sometimes possible to reach a conclusion, for instance, about the relative importance of one of a play's dramatic ideas from its physical position in the framework of the story or by noting the amount of preparation or delay that precedes its disclosure, which in turn affects its placement in the plot.

Constructed one way it will be a play in which action and movement predominate. In such case the director's problems will be confined largely to controlling movement and refining business. Constructed another way there will be very little action and few events. Nothing much will *happen,* and the director then will find himself dealing mainly with psychological matters, interpretation, and vocalization.

Act Divisions and Their Functions

The director should share his knowledge about the play's structure with the actors on the assumption that the better their grasp of it the more intelligent may be their approach to studying their roles. For it is essential that the actor should see the person he will be trying to portray against the background of three different perspectives: at first the character in totality, in terms of his place in the play as a whole; then in terms of his place in the large compositional blocks—the acts or scenes into which the play is divided; and, finally, against the diminished but highly detailed perspective of the French scenes in which the character appears.

Separating a play into acts is the customary way of marking off the logical stopping points in the story. What they usually contain are unified and homogeneous phases in the development of the action that carry the personages to a moment of impasse, turning-point, or climax. Dramatic action is measured in terms of the changes introduced in the original situation or by alterations in the intensity of the emotions as new situations unfold. An act usually continues until some striking innovation in that situation has had time to manifest itself or until the emotional intensity of the characters gathers into a climax.

Each act may have its own separate subject as well as its own separate function. Henrik Ibsen, along with many other dramatists of his time, tried to make sure that the essential point of an act would not be missed by giving it a subject title. He labeled *A Doll's House* in this manner:

Act I. The Troubles of Nora
Act II. A Painful Position
Act III. The Most Wonderful Thing

Though this practice is no longer fashionable, it at least has the virtue of reminding us that each act has its own special identity and represents a self-contained and specific segment of dramatic progression in the development of the story.

If the playwright does not supply a title explaining the subject of each act, it is not unwise for the director to do so himself. It is a way of helping him and the cast to stay on the main track of the plot. Actors tend to become absorbed in details early in the rehearsal period. To prevent them from failing to see the forest for the trees, the director by using titles can force their attention to the massive organic structure of the piece, not only at the start of rehearsals but continuing throughout. It is a sensible way of keeping them continuously aware of the relationships between the minutae and the basic subject blocks of which these are a part. For a perfect technical execution in the acting of a scene is of little or no value if it is imperfectly or ambiguously connected to the main point and leading subject of the whole act and not clearly related to them.

An example of this occurred in a recent Yale production. The middle act of a three-act original play was given over to a long static scene between a father and his son. The two had been separated for some years and there was much quietly emotional catching up for them to do, mainly about troubled family matters. The conversation was in a subdued key and there was little forward plot motion. Into the center of this scene and dividing it in half was another between the father and a newspaper reporter who had come to interview him. In rehearsal, the reporter was played thoughtfully and honestly on a low vocal level, and the actor's characterization was convincing enough if one considered the scene by itself. The trouble was that it was too much in the key of the scenes which preceded and followed it. In perspective what the interpolated scene had to supply in the act was something in contrast to the rest, an exclamation point, a lift, something to give the center a momentum which the two ends of the act did not have. Once the actor was made to see this need to supply a different value and pitch from the father-son scenes, his ensuing vigorous attack on the words brought everything into its proper focus. Perhaps this is a somewhat negative illustration of the need to give titles to acts, but in this case, all that was necessary was to indicate that the reporter's scene had nothing to do with the title–subject, being merely an interpolation or interruption of the development of the leading idea and therefore susceptible to and demanding an entirely different approach.

What Ibsen was setting down with his titles were the three essential parts of almost any conventional plot. "The Troubles of Nora" is exactly what the act is about and supplies a description of the whole play's basic situation. It shows how and why the heroine is in trouble and explains the nature of the forces opposing her. In Act Two her difficulties are intensified to a point where they become intolerable. Her position, indeed, becomes so painful that it threatens not only her family's happiness but her own existence. Finally, although "The Most Wonderful Thing" may excite our pleasurable anticipation of a happy solution and a way out of the entanglements, a reading of the act shows the title to be ironic.

Thus it is seen that the acts, together with their subjects, are essential divisions in the spacing of the play's mechanical structure. The acts *are* the mechanical structure. When we speak of plot structure, we mean the episodes or events used to tell the story as considered in relationship to the order in which the sequence of episodes is arranged.

As the time sequence of the action in *A Doll's House* is continuous, the plot may be described as linear, that is, the beginning, the middle, and the end of the main action are shown in order with the events following each other in a logical progression through operation of the law of cause and effect. Ibsen, using the simplest of dramaturgic formulas, has put each part of his story—the beginning, the middle, and the end—into separate acts of their own.

The same operative principle is followed in the five-act form when the linear plot construction is used except that the two additional acts make possible a more leisurely progression through the action:

Act I. The beginning
Act II. The end of the beginning
Act III. The middle
Act IV. The beginning of the end
Act V. The end.

It is possible to chart this sort of orthodox play structure with an almost mechanical certitude. The beginning contains the complication. The characters are introduced, the situation is described, and a start is made into the forward action, and that is at the moment when the original situation begins to change, or when someone sets out to change it.

Next, the consummation, a continuation of change in the original situation, through the rising action with a tightening of tension to a major climax, that explosive instant when something happens to prevent a return to the original situation, in other words, at the moment of climax the action reaches an irrevocable turning point.

And last, the consequences, when the situation, having been brought to the point of issue by the climax, is now carried beyond that point and displays, in the falling action or denouement, the characters' attempts to adjust to the postclimactic conditions. The close or catastrophe, the concluding event, is the final result of the climax and shows the characters now in new and unchangeable relationships to each other; and these are either entirely different from those which existed in the original situation or are the same relationships heightened to a new point of intensity.

It will be readily seen that these terms apply primarily to the outward events of the plot and describe merely the mechanical arrangement of the story. Except for supplying the framework, they have little reference to the essential dramatic subject, the theme, the characterizations, and the ultimate point of the work, although they do bear on dramatic values dependent on time and timing such as suspense, reversal, and discovery.

Because playwriting is an art and therefore not subject to laws of any kind as science presumably is, the events of a plot do not have to follow a time continuum, nor even the logical sequence of cause and effect. The playwright does not have to start at the beginning of an action. He may, if he wishes, start at the end of a long series of actions and go backwards, as Sophocles does in *Oedipus Rex,* or he may start in the middle or toward the end and go backwards and forwards at the same time, as Arthur Miller does in *Death of a Salesman.* Such plays use what is known as algebraic as opposed to linear plot structure.

One of the chief differences between Classical and Romantic structure is in the point of attack, that moment in the life history of the characters at which the playwright elects to begin his story. In the Romantic mode, the point of attack is early and the chief events are shown in the action. In the Classical mode, the start is made near the end of a long series of prior actions, usually just before the catastrophe, and the background events are not shown but recapitulated by narration.

The Elements of Drama

Every play has its own unique structure, its own point of attack, and its own time scheme. Most plays, though not all, contain elements of conflict and climax. What is essential is that the director must recognize the first and be able to explain it to his cast, and to know exactly where in the text the second occurs. Vital elements, which few plays can afford to be without, are, once more, the introductory materials which explain who the characters are and what they are up to; a time of change in which the original situation develops or disintegrates with some telling reciprocal effect on the characters; a moment of crux which unalterably changes the situation that prevailed at the beginning and prevents a return to it; and a conclusion which may or may not solve the problem of the play if it has one, resolve the characters' difficulties if they have any, or point a moral if the author has one in mind.

The theatre has been for so long an arena where rebels fly in the face of any kind of formalism that it is not surprising to find some playwrights, among them Samuel Beckett in his *Waiting for Godot*, denying us even the slightest opportunity to know the cause of the basic situation or the relationship between the characters. They prefer to keep these veiled in mystery along with the aim and end of the plays, which are intentionally obscured.

In spite of the fact that there are some exceptions to the rule, conflict and clash are basic essentials of the dramatic form, although the kind of conflict shown may vary from violent physical combat to a difference of opinion or outlook. Where conflict provides the dramatic base and is the source of the play's momentum, the contending forces must first be arrayed against one another and then set in motion. The issues at stake between them are decided at the point when they collide, the moment of decision, and this is often the moment of highest emotional intensity. It is out of this clash at its bursting point in the climax that the new situation is prepared and, after it, begins to emerge. In the denouement, time is allowed for the spent forces to recede and the tension to ebb, if only for the purpose of letting the audience collect itself for a moment, and for the author to have a chance to sum up the effect of all this activity on the fortunes of the *dramatis personae,* before preparing for the final crescendo that brings down the curtain.

Most plays go forward with a pulsating motion, with moments of tension alternating with moments of relaxation, in a series of climaxes separated by anticlimaxes. The energy pushing the action to these climactic peaks may be derived from an emotional, psychological, or physical source. Whatever its nature it must represent an upward gathering of increased pressures leading to an inevitable explosion, to be followed by a dissipation or declension of that energy in the anticlimax. In the dynamic onrush of the action, punctuated thus by pauses and rests, each successive climax may reach a point of tension higher than those which preceded it. The highest point reached represents the main climax or the crisis. Thus if one were to try and picture the changing intensity of a play on a graph, the result would look like the serrations on a fever chart, although the highest point might be located anywhere on the chart, even at the very beginning. More often than not each pulsation will be isolated in its own French scene, and each of these smaller subdivisions when examined carefully may be seen to contain in smaller form the same upward sweep to climax and down to anticlimax as are contained in the play as a whole.

Of course, there is nothing to prevent the inclusion of more than one climax in a French scene; indeed in the demonstration which follows there is a whole series of them.

The peaks and valleys of the structural contours of a play are the director's guide and he must follow them faithfully if the whole emotional build of a performance is not to go awry. He must adjust the pace, the rhythm, the vocal pitch, the number of movements, and the speed of these movements in as close a relation as possible to the climactic and anticlimactic points. If he follows the play's external form, he will know when to let the actors coast and when to speed them up, when to increase emotional tension and when to slacken off. Fine shading, nuance, variety, all are obtained when the pitch of performance corresponds exactly with the structural variations described.

If a play contains one main climax, the director must measure and arrange his builds in the subclimaxes so that they do not overshadow or exceed in tension the principal one. It is the main climax which furnishes him with an end point or pinnacle to which the pitch of emotions before and after it must be subordinated.

Respice finem. The director must first decide upon the maximum height of tension required in the main climax and then use that as the standard by which to measure the subclimaxes in the rising action and the denouement.

The director's study of a play's plot structure proceeds concurrently with his efforts to discover its central idea or dramatic subject inasmuch as the true function of plot, except in minor types, is to set forth, support and illuminate the dramatic idea, as seen in the previous chapter. But his study must include not only the general conclusions and the central idea of the whole work, but must extend to each episode in the plot in order to find the meaning in the segment that can be related to the total meaning. Thus it might be said that the killing of Blick by Kit Carson in Saroyan's *The Time of Your Life,* an isolated and indeed somewhat remote episode since it occurs offstage, has a real connection with the play's theme. If this theme is to show that beauty, gentleness, generosity, and great natural gifts are to be found in unexpected places in American society, particularly in its submerged sections as represented in Nick's Bar, then the Blick-Carson episode suggests that this "debased" society is able to protect itself, violently if necessary, against the evil forces of oppression.

The climactic scene of the rape of Blanche Dubois by Stanley Kowalski in *A Streetcar Named Desire* is a forceful episode in the plot and productive of almost melodramatic excitement. But its real significance is in its illustration of the play's basic ideas that people in different stages of development in the same society are at war, and that in the specific society Tennessee Williams is talking about, the savage and ignorant elements in it, strong and healthy as they may be, will take violent revenge upon and destroy the decadent elements of that culture, however delicate and gentle they may be. The faded remnants of the antebellum South stand no chance against the loudmouthed and uncouth aggressiveness of Stanley's new Americanism.

The Director Analyzes the Play

What follows is a suggested way of proceeding to analyze a plot, identify act functions, establish relationship between acts and the whole design, isolate special dramatic values, and draw certain conclusions about the meaning of the play taken as an entity. Serving as our example will be George Bernard Shaw's *The Doctor's Dilemma,* a hardy perennial constructed by a master of craftsmanship. We will turn to it again later when the close analysis of a single scene is demonstrated.

Included are a synopsis of the plot, a statement of the function of each act and its working title, a description of the plot structure, a statement of the theme, remarks about the characters, and some notes about atmosphere. Stylistic considerations have been omitted because these are treated as a separate subject in the next chapter.

THE SYNOPSIS

Act I. The original situation.

Sir Colenso Ridgeon has discovered an element, opsonin, that encourages the white blood corpuscles to devour tuberculosis germs. It is a difficult and dangerous cure and the number of patients he can accept is severely limited. In a scene of persuasion the protagonist, Jennifer

Dubedat, forces Ridgeon, the antagonist, to adopt a course of action he did not wish initially to take. She pleads with him to try and cure her tubercular husband, Louis. Ridgeon is so impressed with Louis's paintings as well as with Jennifer's attractiveness and beauty, that he practically promises to cure the artist, but postpones his final decision until after his doctor friends have had a look at the patient.

Suggested title: "A Woman's Plea."

Act II. The complication.

Louis Dubedat is revealed as dishonest and immoral but enormously gifted. It is learned that Ridgeon's fellow doctor, the poor but honest Blenkinsop, has also contracted the disease.

Because he can accept only one more patient, Ridgeon must choose between the mediocre Blenkinsop and Dubedat, the scoundrel whose art may delight mankind. He weighs the factors affecting his decision, among them his growing love for Jennifer.

Title: "Ridgeon's Dilemma."

Act III. The consummation.

Dubedat's brash iconoclasm and his mockingly amoral attitudes set the doctors against him. When Jennifer makes it clear that she would kill herself if she ever discovered that her husband had been unfaithful to her, a discovery that the doctors know is inevitable, Ridgeon withdraws from the case. Louis is turned over to the ministrations of Sir Ralph Bloomfield Bonington, a brilliant quack. Ridgeon and Sir Patrick Cullen know that this action is tantamount to condemning the artist to death.

Title: "The Turning-point."

Act IV. The consequences.

Sir Ralph's application of Ridgeon's therapy proves lethal as expected and Dubedat succumbs, unregenerate to the last. Jennifer's love for him remains unshaken. She dismisses Ridgeon coldly.

Title: "The Death of the Hero."

Act V. The epilogue.

Jennifer has remarried and Ridgeon discovers that he has committed a "wholly disinterested" murder. Louis is apotheosized in Jennifer's

idealistic biography of him entitled "The Story of a King of Men."
Title: "Dubedat's Revenge."

The structure of the plot is linear and conventional, with the first act representing the beginning, the second the end of the beginning, the third the middle, the fourth the end, and the fifth a postscript. Each act contains its own rise to climax, the climax itself, and its own anticlimax. The climax of the first act comes at the point of reversal when Ridgeon, changing his mind, decides to take Dubedat as a patient. The second act contains a series of small crises each contributing something to the gradual change in the doctors' views of Dubedat. As evidence of his rascality piles up their feelings shift from friendly indulgence and polite acceptance to rejection. One single incident serves to sway the balance of judgment against him. It is Blenkinsop's revelation that he, too, has consumption. For Ridgeon this is the last straw. The climax of the third act is Sir Ralph's decision to enter the case. In the fourth act it is Louis' death.

Identified by type, the play is a satirical comedy; its style is realistic; its mode follows the Romantic rather than the Classical pattern.

So much for the framework.

The director's analysis at this point has scarcely begun. His outline of the plot's main features serves only as a kind of map which, although it shows the road the play takes, makes no reference to the nature of the topography nor to the quality of the landscape.

FROM STRUCTURE TO IDEA

What now must be ascertained are the values that give the play its quality as a work of literature and as a commentary on life. These are: the choice of subject, the witty, crackling style with which the subject is discussed, the free-wheeling personalities and the trenchant revelation of their motives, the contrast between the artist's view of acceptable behavior and society's, and finally the play's seriocomic atmosphere.

One of Shaw's chief targets in the play is the pretentiousness and stupidity of men of medicine, engaged, as Paddy says all professionals are, in a "conspiracy against the laity." Shaw attacks them wittily and makes satirical capital out of the foibles and monomanias of those who are supposed to represent England's greatest in the field of medical science.

But there is a serious problem behind the fun: What should society do with its geniuses who make a mockery of morality and religion? The intellectual fireworks that accompany Dubedat's doughty and clever defense of his Bohemian position lie at the heart of the comedy. There is also the intriguing question: What happens when medical ethics are complicated by personal feeling? Should Ridgeon cure Dubedat and thus preserve the beauty that may come from his brush, or kill him and marry his wife?

Shaw poses his questions clearly. The answers are not always decisive, nor is it Shaw's purpose to make them so. He is content most of the time to allow the answer to rest in irony. Ridgeon, by his refusal to cure Dubedat, succeeds in preventing Jennifer from discovering that her husband was a bounder and worse; but he also prepares the way for Dubedat to be enshrined in her heart as a deathless idol, which was far from his intention.

To what extent are the characters important as instruments of revelation about the nature of man? What does the playwright tell us, through them, about man's goodness or basenesss, his absurdity or sublimity?

The men are familiar but well-differentiated types, some of them like B.B. verging on caricature. Walpole is an energetic monomaniac; Blenkinsop good and kindly but a failure in his profession; Ridgeon conceited, pompous, and emotionally unsettled at a critical age. With the exception of Blenkinsop and to a lesser extent Sir Patrick Cullen, the Nestor of the group, these men air opinions, strike attitudes, and rationalize endlessly about their calling. They react intellectually to every stimulus, but they do not *feel*. They do not respond emotionally to situations, and this is what makes them figures of high comedy.

In contrast to them, Jennifer Dubedat emerges as a warm human being who has a capacity for love and grief. Unsophisticated, forgiving, wholly womanly in this man's world, she redeems the play's claim for attention as a human document. Without her to preserve the balance between thought and feeling, the play would be no more than an amusing intellectual tour-de-force. She leavens the brittleness of the satire, and her compassionate spirit spreads a touch of something vital and true over its dry surface.

The two sides of Dubedat's nature are pointed up by the difference between Jennifer's and the doctors' views of him. To Ridgeon and the others he is an unprincipled bounder. But they do not see him through the eyes of love. To Jennifer he is a defenseless genius, still a child whom her devotion must protect from poverty and the world's indifference. Instead of blaming him for his affairs with women, which are in her estimation insignificant and meaningless, she blames the women who tempted him. To her, his vagaries are mere symptoms of thoughtless aberration in a genius and not to be taken seriously. Because she is an intelligent woman and her judgment of him not wholly naive, Shaw is obliged to show in Louis some of the charm and depth that would attract a woman like Jennifer to him. What can be said in his favor? For one thing, he is a master painter. He is intellectually fearless (he dies well). He is poetic by nature, supremely sensitive to beauty, and selfless in his dedication to art. He has a remarkable sense of humor which does not forsake him even in his last moments; he has the forthrightness to acknowledge his "troublesome self," and is happy to escape from life into the only immortality he believes in—"in the heart of my beautiful Jennifer." His final defense of his position presents as eloquent a case as can be made for all the gifted rebels in the world who may have been nuisances to society but whose contributions to it have been a source of perpetual enrichment. And lastly, he has the gift of eloquence, the poet's tongue as well as the artist's hand:

> But in my own real world I have never done anything wrong, never denied my faith, never been untrue to myself. I've been threatened and blackmailed and insulted and starved. But I've played the game. I've fought the good fight. And now it's all over, there's an indescribable peace. I believe in Michelangelo, Velasquez, and Rembrandt; in the might of design, the mystery of color, the redemption of all things by Beauty everlasting, and the message of Art that has made these hands blessed. Amen. Amen.

What of the atmosphere of the comedy?

The moods are determined by whatever character happens to dominate the scene and follow from what the characters are. Thus, when B.B. holds the floor the mood is comic and satirical; when Ridgeon prevails it tends to be sententious and heavy; when Jennifer is present it is serious and touching. The death scene, surely one of the longest in dramatic history as well as one of the best, is a nice blending of tragic and comic elements.

The tone of each act varies roughly in accordance with its structural function. The start of Act One is lively and vigorous. The energy of the discussion more than compensates for the delay in starting the forward action. Jennifer's scene with Ridgeon changes the mood from high comedy to something more urgent and serious. In Act Two the beauty and peace of the summer night prevail for a time, but its serenity is marred by surprising revelations—Blenkinsop's illness, Minnie Tinwell's marriage to Louis, Dubedat's carelessness in money matters. The mood of Act Three is split in two. Comedy prevails at the start but gives way to seriousness when Jennifer again pleads with Ridgeon to save Louis' life. In Act Four the tone is more sombre but even the death scene has its comic punctuations. The mood deepens again before the close when Jennifer takes charge. Act Five is comically wry and ironic.

There are no theatrical aids to enhance moods, no music or sound effects, and none is called for. The sets are realistic, the lighting natural, and, except for some exaggerations of expression by comic characters, the general approach to the style of playing should be realistic or representational.

The Director Analyzes a Single Scene

With some such understanding of the play's meaning as shown above firmly in his grasp, the director is now ready to proceed to the next phase of analysis: close scrutiny of the separate French scenes of which the acts themselves are composed.

These are textual segments based on a stabilized number of characters present on the stage at the same time. A French scene begins with the entrance or exit of a character and ends in the same way with the entrance or exit of a character. It is not confined to the presentation of a single subject but may contain several, and these do not necessarily have to be related to each other. Likewise it may contain several moods or a single mood that may vary considerably in intensity during the course of the scene. It has already been pointed out that in many cases a French scene may possess on a small scale its own self-contained structure: an introduction, a rise to climax or turning point followed by a relaxation of tension in its own denouement or anticlimax.

The French scene is the director's normal work unit. In his prerehearsal preparations he will separate these units, block them one at a time, and later attend to bridging the segments into a unity. As he works on details in the later stages of rehearsals, each French scene will be approached separately and form the single object of concentration. He will then narrow attention to the even smaller fragments of which the French scene itself is composed. For just as molecules are divided into atoms so the French scene is made up of subscenes which are finally the more or less indivisible building-blocks upon which the whole structure of the play rests.

These subscenes have been described in a variety of ways. John Dietrich calls them "motivational units," [1]—a handy term. Each is a consistent and homogeneous entity, with its own single subject, the thought being expressed in continuity, with characters in a single stabilized relationship to one another, and the whole imbued with one dominant emotion which may vary in intensity but not in nature. Furthermore, the characters are motivated by and respond to only one given set of stimuli, and these are not replaced or transposed in the course of things by new factors bearing on that motivation. And of course it should be clear from this that the dialogue is confined to considerations of one single topic.

Only by squeezing out the essential meaning and mood from these lesser units can the director differentiate sufficiently between them to achieve variety. A performance, like a mosaic, exerts its total effect by the subtlety with which each one of these tiny pieces is set forth and handled in relation to every other piece. The onlooker may be aware only of the broad effect of the whole, but whatever richness of texture and plasticity the whole contains is the result of the director's efforts to give each motivational unit its own special coloration, tempo, rhythm, intensity, and shape, so that when viewed it has its own individual quality and integrity that makes it different from every other unit. These basic building blocks give the director his procedural base for ringing all the possible changes of emotion, motivation, idea, and attitude in the French scene. And it is in the progressive motion of the changes from one subscene to another, and in the accumulation and intensification of dramatic values as one subscene follows another, that the dramatic action of the whole lies.

There being no set rules to guide the director as he undertakes the

[1] Dietrich, John E., *Play Direction*. New York: Prentice-Hall, Inc., 1953.

necessary close analysis of each scene in his play, it might be profitable for the student to study a specific demonstration of one way to set about it. The example chosen, a scene from the second act of Ibsen's *A Doll's House*,[2] between Nora Helmer and her friend, Doctor Rank, should have the advantage of being familiar to almost everyone. It offers also an excellent sample of what a master of stage conversation can do with flat prose, the simple basic vocabulary of everyday speech. Here it is used with much subtlety to convey every facet in the changing interplay between these two characters.

So many uses are made of the dialogue here, that the commentary has been kept abreast of the lines to make it easier to follow.

The commentary itself seeks to penetrate deeply into the lines in order to discover what they mean, and to disclose the motives which prompt the characters to speak them, with an eye to establishing points which the director will eventually try to lead the actors to make. The analysis makes no claim to completeness, and others may find much more in the scene than I have. Set down are working notes subject to alteration and adjustment as both director and actors learn more about the material as they work with it.

Some directors would not dream of writing down their ideas this way, nor is it always necessary or desirable that they should. Jotting down ideas does not and should not mean that they are irrevocable. But having notes in such form as shown in the following demonstration provides a ready reference for use when circumstances in rehearsals demand them, and they save the director from the inconvenience of having to carry them all in his head.

Little attempt has been made to suggest how to block the scene or to play it. At this juncture the focus is deliberately confined to textual meanings, psychological attitudes, motives, and the characters' reactions to each other.

A Doll's House

In the antecedent action, Nora Helmer has been driven by circumstances almost to the point of suicide. Years before she had forged her

[2] See also the analysis of the scene between Ridgeon and Jennifer in Act One of *The Doctor's Dilemma*, p. 174.

father's name on a promissory note in order to save the life of her husband, Torvald, at a time when he was desperately ill and needed rest and a change of climate. Nora's love for him and the critical need to get the money to save him overrode her scruples. Nils Krogstad, employed at Helmer's bank, holds the note and is aware of the fact that Nora has forged her father's signature on it. Fearing that he will be discharged from the bank, he threatens to expose Nora's criminal act in order to blackmail Helmer into retaining him and even rewarding him with a promotion. Nora firmly believes that in any showdown, Helmer will respond to Krogstad's revelations by shouldering the blame himself to protect her. But in order to forestall the necessity of this, she contemplates doing away with herself. At a crucial moment, with Krogstad about to deliver the fatal evidence to her husband, Nora greets her visitor, Rank. He is wealthy, with no immediate family ties, close to the Helmers in friendship. Just prior to the scene, Mrs. Linden, Nora's confidante, has made the suggestion that if Rank were made aware of Nora's predicament, he might lend or give her the money to redeem the note and extricate herself.

NORA: Good afternoon, Dr. Rank. I knew you by your ring. But you mustn't go to Torvald now. I believe he's busy.

Notice that everything counts. The familiar ring marks Rank as a constant visitor. Torvald has just told Nora to tell Dr. Rank where he might be found. Her white lie shows how anxious she is to avail herself of the opportunity to prevail on Rank to come to her rescue.

RANK: And you? (*Enters and closes the door.*)

NORA: Oh, you know very well, I have always time for *you.*

A friendly compliment, but the flattery is intentional. She wants him to know he is high in her favors.

RANK: Thank you. I shall avail myself of your kindness as long as I can.

Rank accepts Nora's compliment as normal politeness. His mind is occupied with his own sickness. The phrase "as long as I can" has an ominous overtone, which Nora detects.

NORA: What do you mean? As long as you can?

Note how much of this is built on questions and answers. The characters here begin to speak at cross-purposes. From what follows it is clear that Nora thinks Rank means he will continue to seek her company until the news of the forgery comes out and brings their friendship to an end. Ibsen lets this misapprehension continue, and this adds a little suspense. It also points up Rank's delicacy and reticence. He does not wish to confront Nora too abruptly with the ugly fact of his approaching physical collapse. Once he has established it, however, he does not flinch from painting the enormity of his tragic condition in strong colors. Nora shows a touch of alarm in her question, otherwise there is no motive for Rank's response.

RANK: Yes. Does that frighten you?

Again from what follows, Rank feels that her fear and concern are for him, when of course they are for her own fate and future. Each exists for the moment in the vacuum of his own troubles, an ironical oblique view at a general human tendency.

NORA: I think it's an odd expression. Do you expect anything to happen?

Nora is on her guard. What she suspects is that Rank knows something about her crisis with Krogstad.

RANK: Something I have long been prepared for; but I didn't think it would come so soon.

The ambiguity of subject in the subscene continues.

NORA: (*Catching at his arm.*) What have you discovered? Doctor Rank, you must tell me!

The gesture reinforces the urgency of her question, and the exclamation point shows she can no longer stand the uncertainty of not knowing what it is that Rank is driving at.

RANK: (*Sitting down by the stove.*) I am running down hill. There's no help for it.

This is the miniature climax of the first subscene. The ambiguity is dispelled as Rank's illness becomes the subject of the second sub-scene. Note the stage direction. Ibsen rightly visualizes the foregoing as being played with both characters standing. Rank gives visual expression to his bodily weakness by sinking into a chair. The change of position also terminates Nora's misunderstanding of the conversation and halts the delay in Rank's revelation of his condition.

NORA: (*Draws a long breath of relief.*) It's you . . .?

Anticlimax. Nora's fears that Rank may have discovered her guilty secret are dispelled. Preoccupation with her own troubles has been so great that she does not react to this disclosure of Rank's misfortune as one might expect a devoted friend to do. But her reaction is normal and instinctive, not exactly unselfish, perhaps. However the weight of evidence in the play shows her to be concerned more about the welfare of others than she is about herself, at least up to the turning point in the last act. Now as well as later in this French scene, the gravity of her own situation dulls her responses to the gravity of his, and perhaps explains her evasion about facing up to it.

RANK: Who else should it be?—Why lie to oneself? I am the most wretched of all my patients, Mrs. Helmer. In these last days I have been auditing my life account—bankrupt! Perhaps before a month is over, I shall lie rotting in the church yard.

His own self-absorption, as complete as Nora's, has left him unaware of the fact that she has been misconstruing the drift of his remarks. The formality and propriety of their friendship up to this point is shown by his, "Mrs. Helmer." Its use here underlies the change that is to come shortly, when he will address her by her Christian name.

Considering Torvald's profession, Rank's use of business and banking terminology is apt, and in view of the nature of Nora's predicament it has ironic implications. His final sentence is deliberately harsh and repugnant. It accomplishes several things. For one, it reminds Nora of an ever-present, fearful fact: death and corruption are unpleasant truths which few people wish to face. In the Helmer household they have been glossed over, and buried under the surface of a happy domestic existence.

NORA: Oh! What an ugly way to talk.

RANK: The thing itself is so confoundedly ugly, you see.

An echo of the theme that pervades the four "social" plays in this series, A Doll's House, Ghosts, An Enemy of the People, *and* The Wild Duck, *that certain things in life are ugly and must be faced, not swept under the carpet in deference to social conventions.*

RANK: (*Cont'd*) But the worst of it is, so many other ugly things have to be gone through first. There is only one last investigation to be made, and when that is over I shall know pretty certainly when the breakup will begin.

Rank, in a way, is describing Nora's case as well as his own. Her "breakup" will begin when Helmer discovers the letter and learns of her forgery.

RANK: (*Cont'd*) There's one thing I want to say to you: Helmer's delicate nature shrinks so from all that is horrible: I will not have him in my sickroom—

Another parallelism. Both Nora and Rank wish to spare Helmer pain. We see little evidence in the play of Helmer's fastidiousness. His "delicate nature" seems rather to be a selfish reluctance to concern himself with the troubles of others. This is made clear in Act III.

NORA: But, Doctor Rank. . . .

What is Nora about to say? She, too, has a mistaken belief in Helmer's steadfastness, and is about to answer in rebuttal. Perhaps she is on the point of declaring her belief that Helmer's strength will not let him shrink from an ugliness where friendship with Rank is concerned.

RANK: I won't have him, I say—not on any account. I shall lock my door against him.

Why is Rank so insistent on this point? Would it be overinterpreting to suggest he has other reasons for wanting Helmer to keep away—possibly the desire not to be confronted on his deathbed with the sight of a man who enjoys robust health, and also the love and affection of Nora?

RANK: (*Cont'd*) As soon as I am quite certain of the worst, I shall send you my visiting card with a black cross on it; and then you will know that the final horror has begun.

Note that Ibsen establishes Rank's forthcoming dissolution first. Later he will explain the reasons for it. It is now clear that one of the three important functions Rank fulfills in the play is to introduce the harshest sort of reality into the little world of happy illusion that Nora has constructed for herself in her marriage.

Ibsen is conforming to the theatrical practice of his day in making good use of properties. The visiting card will be the second fatal missive dropped into the Helmers' letter box.

NORA: Why, you're perfectly unreasonable today; and I did so want you to be in a really good humor.

Ibsen's problem here is obviously to get the subject shifted to the causes of Rank's disease. In order to solve it he has had to make Nora appear insensitive and unfeeling, or else imperceptive. In any case he makes the point again that Nora's mind refuses to take in Rank's desperate plight. She apparently can think only of what she has decided to ask Rank to do to help her. Her line may even suggest that she has not heard what Rank has been telling her.

RANK: With death staring me in the face? And to suffer thus for another's sin! Where's the justice of it? And in one way or another you can trace in every family some such inexorable retribution—

No wonder Rank is flabbergasted at her seeming lack of comprehension. But his rage against his father whose immorality has caused all his trouble is strong enough to divert his attention away from it.

A father's excesses and "inexorable retribution" will form the subject of Ibsen's next play, Ghosts. *The cause of Rank's illness forms the subject of the third subscene.*

NORA: (*Stopping her ears.*) Nonsense, nonsense! Now cheer up!

Unless Nora is to be shown as an inane Pollyanna, she must read this line with an awareness of the seriousness of the circumstances. The tone must have sadness in it or a kind or rueful bantering. There must be a tragic intensity in the words, "Nonsense, nonsense," as if what Rank had said has brought to her mind what Torvald has asserted earlier, that an evil mother can plant the seeds of "moral ruin" in her family. The actress might try a pause after "Now . . ." accompanied by some gesture of an affectionate nature, to try and ease the awkwardness of the transition. Something of the sort is certainly necessary in order to explain Rank's willingness to adopt now a bitterly humorous view of his predicament.

RANK: Well, after all, the whole thing's only worth laughing at. My poor innocent spine must do penance for my father's wild oats.

For the first time we get a hint of the nature of

Rank's malady and its cause, congenital syphilis from his sire. Perhaps the description is as explicit as the mores of the time allowed, although the uproar caused by the play indicates that Ibsen was far too explicit on this point for public comfort.

NORA: (*At table, left.*) I suppose he was too fond of asparagus and Strasbourg pâté, wasn't he?

RANK: Yes; and truffles.

NORA: Yes, truffles, to be sure. And oysters, I believe?

RANK: Yes, oysters; oysters, of course.

NORA: And then all the port and champagne! It's sad that all these good things should attack the spine.

RANK: Especially when the luckless spine attacked never had any good of them.

NORA: Ah, yes, that's the worst of it.

The bantering tone brings some relief from the morbidity of the subject, although it is rather grisly humor, to be sure.

It is clear that Nora knows exactly what was wrong with Rank's father, and that Rank knows she knows. Nora's admission of knowledge places her relationship with Rank on a footing of frankness unfamiliar to polite society of that time.

It should be remembered here that her own husband has never talked to her as an equal. That she and Rank are in close intellectual association suggests the second dramatic use to which Ibsen has put the character of Rank. He serves in contrast to Helmer as a true companion for Nora. He goes on the assumption that she has a mind. From what develops in this study of an empty marriage, for that is what the play is, we know that Nora and Helmer have never had a serious conversation on a subject of importance. What Helmer has wanted in his wife is someone to dance and chirp and keep him amused, to bear children, run the house, and serve his appetites. Rank supplies the ingredient needed in a true union, now lacking in Nora's marriage. He recognizes Nora as an individual adult and treats her so; he respects her integrity as a thinking being.

RANK: (*Looks at her searchingly.*) H'm—

He must be wondering where, in Nora's circumscribed domestic existence, she has learned of these dark and forbidden subjects.

NORA: (*A moment later.*) Why did you smile?

RANK: No; it was you that laughed.

NORA: No, it was you that smiled, Dr. Rank.

Whoever started all this smiling and laughing, it is clear that Rank has thrown off his depression and has "cheered up," as Nora hoped he would.

RANK: (*Standing up.*) I see you're deeper than I thought.

Underlining further that Nora, in Rank's eyes, is far from being the scatterbrained doll of Helmer's imagination. Torvald will not discover this until the closing scene of the play.

Ibsen's direction is timely. It is the right moment to start on a new tack. The change of position befits the change of subject and serves also to introduce the new subject of the fourth subscene.

NORA: I'm in such a crazy mood today.

RANK: So it seems.

NORA: (*With her hands on his shoulder.*) Dear, dear Dr. Rank, death shall not take you away from Torvald and me.

The one opportunity Nora has had, so far in the scene, to express herself with deep seriousness and true emotion. Her gesture is openhanded, indicating womanly warmth and affectionate comradeship.

Any suggestion of coquetry or a reading which insinuates that Nora is exerting her charm for an ulterior purpose debases the character.

RANK: Oh, you'll easily get over the loss. The absent are soon forgotten.

His bleak mood returns.

NORA: (*Looks at him anxiously.*) Do you think so?

She cannot help reverting to the thought of her own straits, and wonders if her family will forget her after she has taken her life.

RANK: People make fresh ties, and then—

NORA: Who make fresh ties?

Another reminder that they are again speaking at cross purposes. Her mood is abstracted; Rank must bring her back to the original subject.

RANK: You and Helmer will, when I am gone. You yourself are taking time by the forelock, it seems to me. What was that Mrs. Linden doing here yesterday?

NORA: Oh!—You're surely not jealous of poor Christina?

"Oh" *and* "Ah" *are surely the most versatile words in the English language. They can be made to mean almost anything. Here the* "Oh" *indicates both Nora's realization that again Rank is following a different line of thought from her own, and relief that what he has been saying is not deliberately aimed at her.*

RANK: Yes, I am. She will be my successor in this house. When I am out of the way, this woman will perhaps—

NORA: Hush! Not so loud! She's in there.

Ibsen does not want us to forget the surrounding background. There are other people within hearing. They must keep their voices down, thus aiding the intimate feeling of the scene.

RANK: Today as well? You see!

Ibsen shows Rank's childishness and petulance in order to draw from Nora an assurance that he stands high in her favor. She is more than ready to do this in conscious preparation for the moment when she will ask him to help her.

NORA: Only to put my costume in order—dear me, how unreasonable you are! (*Sits on sofa.*) Now do be good, Dr. Rank! Tomorrow you shall see how beautifully I shall dance; and then you may fancy that I'm doing it all to please you—and of course Torvald as well. (*Takes various things out of box.*) Doctor Rank, sit down here, and I'll show you something.

Notice Ibsen's preparation for the introduction of the subject of the silk stockings. From Mrs. Linden, to her work on the costume, to the box where the stockings for the costume are. His ability to provide these natural associations of ideas marks him as a careful, and sometimes a superb, craftsman. But there is more to be said about the turn the scene takes. The contretemps about Mrs. Linden sounds not unlike a lovers' quarrel over a trifle. It evokes Nora's flattering remark about dancing which is said to please him. The afterthought that she will be pleasing her husband too sounds like a perfunctory concession to conscience and the amenities.

Nora here reverts to the personality of the little lark who exists to amuse, fulfilling one of the chief functions her husband wants of her. She now includes Rank along with her husband as one whom she wishes to delight.

The actress must walk a tightrope now. The problem is to preserve Nora's integrity as a respectable woman while at the same time making it clear that, whether she is deliberately leading Rank on by displaying her charms or not, the ultimate effect of her actions is to draw from Rank an offer to do anything he can for her sake.

It would be odd if Nora, in this scene of flirtation, had momentarily forgotten the purpose of her meeting with Rank, which is to use him as a means of escape from her dilemma.

RANK: (*Sitting*) What is it?

For the first time in the scene, except for the instant when Nora touched his shoulder in comradely fashion, they come into positions of intimate personal contact.

NORA: Look here. Look!

RANK: Silk stockings.

NORA: Flesh-colored. Aren't they lovely? It's so dark here now; but tomorrow—No, no, no; you must only look at the feet. Oh, well, I suppose you may look at the rest too.

A remarkable passage, and a very daring and suggestive one for that era. A lady with a man who is not her husband, sitting together in a darkening room, in an intimate exchange about personal objects which were not normally viewed as proper subjects for polite conversation between members of the opposite sex. The doctor's health may be poor but he is well enough to enjoy the experience.

RANK: H'm—

NORA: What are you looking so critical about? Do you think they won't fit me?

Nora, there is no doubt, is being provocative, as she directs the conversation and his attention to the size and shape of her legs.

RANK: I can't possibly give any competent opinion on that point.

What can she expect? She has tempted him into making this forward remark and he has made it.

NORA: (*Looking at him a moment.*) For shame! (*Hits him lightly on the ear with the stockings.*) Take that. (*Rolls them up again.*)

Ibsen carries Nora's display of flirtatious indiscretion as far as he dares without making Nora a cocotte. Few can doubt that she indulges in these provocations from an innocent sense of childish fun. Yet, considering the stakes at issue, her own life, her husband's reputation, the future of her family, can we blame her? If she uses guile and shows a faint lack of rectitude, it displays a fault of character; but this weakness will be totally excused when she is transformed in the end from doll to woman. Note the way Ibsen has used stage business rather than dialogue to terminate the segment.

RANK: And what other wonders am I to see?

NORA: You shan't see anything more; for you don't behave nicely. (*She hums a little and searches among the things.*)

Nora, playing at being the little girl again, marks time. Ibsen has to give Rank time to digest the meaning of the last portion of the talk, which will now more clearly than before develop into a love scene, at least as far as Rank is concerned. And who is to say that this is not what Nora wants it to do?

RANK: (*After a short silence.*) When I sit here gossiping with you, I can't imagine—I simple cannot conceive—what would have become of me if I had never entered this house.

Rank's instinctive gentlemanliness prompts him to disguise what they have been saying by referring to it as harmless gossip.

Ibsen uses Rank's feeling of gratitude to the Helmers to open the way for his offer of doing something to repay them.

NORA: (*Smiling.*) Yes, I think you do feel at home with us.

But beneath the smile must be the tension to indicate that she now awaits the crucial moment to arrive when she can ask him for the money.

RANK: (*More softly, looking straight before him.*) And now to have to leave it all—

NORA: Nonsense. You shan't leave us.

For the sake of variety, this should not be taken as a repetition of Nora's unwillingness to face up to cruel reality. She undoubtedly is sincere in her desire to cheer her sick friend, even though her remark must be cold comfort to Rank, in view of the known facts.

RANK: (*In the same tone.*) And not to be able to leave behind the slightest token of gratitude; scarcely even a passing regret—nothing but an empty place, that can be filled by the first comer.

Nora's applied psychology finally produces the result desired. The friend–lover makes manifest his anxiety to help her, and the "token of gratitude" will pay off the note and end her unhappiness.

NORA: And if I were to ask you for—? No—

RANK: For what?

NORA: For a great proof of your friendship.

RANK: Yes—Yes?

NORA: I mean—for a very, very great service—

RANK: Would you really, for once, make me so happy?

Ripeness abounds. His eagerness and willingness are established beyond the shadow of a doubt. Yet Nora hesitates, reluctant to state her problem. Part of her hesitation is due to Ibsen's never being in a hurry to exhaust the possibilities in a scene of suspense. Theatrically, the scene is too good to be rushed at the end. We are reminded of the popular formula for successful playwriting: "Make 'em laugh; make 'em cry; make 'em wait."

NORA: Oh, you don't know what it is.

The disclosure of her long-hidden guilty action, even to Rank, causes anguish.

RANK: Then tell me.

NORA: No, I really can't, Doctor

Rank. It's far, far too much—not only a service, but help and advice besides—

The suspense further prolonged by her last-minute reservations.

RANK: So much the better. I can't think what you can mean. But go on. Don't you trust me?

NORA: As I trust no one else. I know you are my best and truest friend. So I will tell you.

Revelation of the scene's main subject is announced.

NORA: (*Cont'd.*) Well then, Doctor Rank, there is something you must help me to prevent. You know how deeply, how wonderfully Torvald loves me; he wouldn't hesitate a moment to give his very life for my sake.

Indicating her unselfishness. It is really not herself she is thinking of but of Torvald. Her image of him, heroically taking the guilt upon himself for her sake, will prove to be a delusion.

RANK: (*Bending towards her.*) Nora—

For the first time he uses the intimate form of address.

RANK: (*Cont'd.*)—Do you think he is the only one who—?

NORA: (*With a slight start.*) Who—?

RANK: Who would gladly give his life for you?

NORA: (*Sadly.*) Oh!

The turning-point and climax of the French scene. Nora's provocations and now her obvious distress encourage the Doctor to plunge into this declaration of love.

RANK: I have sworn that you shall know it before I—go. I shall never find a better opportunity.—Yes, Nora, now I have told you; and now you know that you can trust me as you can no one else.

NORA: (*Standing up; simply and calmly.*) Let me pass, please.

Reversal. *Nora's plans misfire. She understands at once the extent of her miscalculation. Her coquettish naiveté, part of her play-acting of Nora, the little squirrel, has put her in a compromising position. As a woman of scruple, which of course she is, she cannot now ask Rank, as lover, for anything.*

RANK: (*Makes way for her, but remains sitting.*) Nora—

NORA: (*In the doorway.*) Ellen, bring the lamp. (*Crosses to the stove.*) Oh dear, Doctor Rank, that was too bad of you.

One of Ibsen's favorite metaphors, bringing light to dispel the darkness. Rank's usefulness as an easy way out for Nora was a delusion. She must now face the truth and the consequences on her own.

RANK: (*Rising*) That I have loved you as deeply as—anyone else? Was that too bad of me?

Ibsen spells it out lest the slow-minded miss the point. In a mass medium like the theatre, the successful dramatist is usually one who makes certain he is understood.

NORA: No, but that you should have told me so. It was so unnecessary—

No one can accuse her of immoral behavior, although contemporary critics found her final abandonment of husband, children, and wifely duties shocking and unacceptable.

RANK: What do you mean? Did you know—? (*Ellen enters with the lamp; sets it on the table and goes out again.*) Nora—Mrs. Helmer—I ask you, did you know?

How careful Ibsen is about little details, laboriously so, some may think. Rank returns to the formality of "Mrs. Helmer," putting the relationship back where it was at the start.

NORA: Oh, how can I tell what I knew or didn't know? I really can't say—

Remember Nora is as yet unenlightened, not the free, sentient being she will become. She is unsophisticated and not given to the mental exertion of analyzing her feelings.

NORA: (*Cont'd*) How could you be so clumsy, Doctor Rank? It was all so nice!

In her childish world of pretense, there was no place for deep personal entanglements.

RANK: Well, at any rate, you know now that I am at your service, body and soul. And now, go on.

If he understands her feeling, he chooses to ignore it. His main interest is to be of help.

NORA: Go on—now?

RANK: I beg you to tell me what you want.

With his unequivocal offer, Rank puts Nora's scruples to the hard test.

NORA: I can tell you nothing now.

This ends Nora's opportunity to escape the net. It also ends the scene's action. Little is left for the writer to do but to tidy up one or two points and go on to the next segment. Nora accepts her defeat bravely and pretends she really doesn't need his help. And there is a brief explanation of Nora's view of Rank's place in her life.—"There are people one loves, and others one likes to talk to." She does not realize, as yet, that in a true marriage, the person one loves and the person one talks to should be one and the same.

CHAPTER FIVE

Literary Style

POLONIUS: What do you read, my lord?

HAMLET: Words, words, words.

II, 2 *Hamlet*

High on the list of directorial qualifications must be placed a developed perception of what words mean, a sense of dialogue. And along with this must go a sensitive appreciation for hearing whatever music words make.

What is "good dialogue"? Here is another question which cannot be answered categorically. There is no hollower commentary in dramatic criticism than one which avers without supporting evidence, that a "play has good dialogue."

The Uses of Dialogue

Dialogue has to be judged in terms of context; it is futile to try and evaluate it in general. For while it may be true that dialogue is effective when it advances the story, in another case it can be equally effective when it retards it. It may be considered good when it clearly manifests the speaker's thoughts, or conversely, when it conceals them.

On one point there seems to be agreement. The style of expression, the vocabulary, and often the rhythms of speech should fit the character whether he be the Prince of Denmark or an American gangster. When there are discrepancies between the way a character speaks and his education, background, social status, profession, nationality, state of health, and his emotions, a confusion of effect follows, as may be seen, presently, in the case of *Winterset*.

Dialogue, catching the attention, should lead the mind to an understanding of what is going on, so that the listener may both follow the action and become emotionally a part of it. It may be said to fulfill its function more than adequately when above and beyond this it kindles the imagination with suggestions and overtones of meaning deeper than the surface words; when, as Stanislavsky writes, it leads from external fact to inner truth. When it does this and at the same time strikes the ear with a pleasing sound it provides satisfaction on both intellectual and esthetic levels.

We expect the dialogue to get somewhere, to fulfill a purpose. It should throw light upon a character, clarify the plot, underline a theme, add to suspense, create a mood. Of the latter, it should be noted that while dialogue supplies the materials for creating or sustaining a certain atmosphere, it does not have the power to create such moods unaided. The mood follows or is sustained from the way the lines are spoken as much as from the sense they contain. In many cases, if not most, the sense follows from the inflection, which itself follows from the emotional state of the speaker. This is why it is just as important for the director to know why a character speaks the way he does as it is for him to understand what it is that is being spoken. Hence his constant concern with the characters' attitudes, motives, and personal feelings at any given moment.

Dramatic speech ranges from the flattest unadorned prose to the most formal or most profusely ornamented verse, with countless gradations in between. How good it is depends on how well it suggests the direction the scene is taking. There must be a recognizable end in view and signals along the way to guide us.

Nothing could be drier, sparser, or more economical in its revelation of the bare facts than the opening of Ibsen's *John Gabriel Borkman:*

(*Mrs. Borkman sits for a time erect and rigid at her knitting. The bells of a passing sledge are heard.*)

MRS. BORKMAN: (*Listens; her eyes sparkle with enthusiasm and she whispers involuntarily.*) Erhart! At last!

(*She rises and draws the curtains a little aside to peer out. Seems disappointed, and sits down on the sofa, resuming her work. Presently the Maid enters from the hall with a visiting card on a small tray.*)

MRS. BORKMAN: (*Quickly*) Has Mr. Erhart come after all?

THE MAID: No, ma'am. But there's a lady . . .

MRS. BORKMAN: (*Putting aside her knitting.*) Oh, Mrs. Wilton, I suppose . . .

THE MAID: No, it's a strange lady . . .

MRS. BORKMAN: (*Taking the card.*) Let me see . . . (*Reads it; rises quickly and looks intently at the girl.*) Are you sure this is for me?

THE MAID: Yes, I understood it was for you, ma'am.

MRS. BORKMAN: Did she say she wanted to see Mrs. Borkman?

THE MAID: Yes, she did.

MRS. BORKMAN: (*abruptly, resolutely.*) Good. Then say I am home.

(*The Maid opens the door for the strange lady and goes out. Miss Ella Rentheim enters.*)

ELLA RENTHEIM: You are surprised to see me, Gunhild.

MRS. BORKMAN: Have you not made a mistake? The bailiff lives in the side wing, you know.

ELLA RENTHEIM: It is not the bailiff I want to see today.

MRS. BORKMAN: Is it me you want, then?

ELLA RENTHEIM: Yes. I have a few words to say to you.

MRS. BORKMAN: Well then, sit down.

ELLA RENTHEIM: Thank you. I can stand just as well for the present.

MRS. BORKMAN: As you please. But at least open your cloak.

ELLA RENTHEIM: (*unbuttoning her cloak.*) Yes, it is very warm here.

MRS. BORKMAN: I am always cold. . . .

ELLA RENTHEIM: Well, Gunhild, it is nearly eight years now since we saw each other last.

MRS. BORKMAN: (*coldly*) Since last we spoke to each other at any rate.

ELLA RENTHEIM: True, since we spoke to each other. I daresay you have seen me now and again—when I came on my yearly visit to the bailiff.

MRS. BORKMAN: Once or twice, I have.

ELLA RENTHEIM: I have caught one or two glimpses of you, too—there, at the window.

MRS. BORKMAN: You must have seen me through the curtains then. You have good eyes. (*Harshly and cuttingly*) But the last time we spoke to each other—it was here in this room—

ELLA RENTHEIM: (*Trying to stop her.*) Yes, yes; I know, Gunhild!

MRS. BORKMAN: —the week before he—before he was let out.

ELLA RENTHEIM: Oh, don't speak about that.

MRS. BORKMAN: (*firmly but in a low voice.*) It was the week before he was set at liberty.

ELLA RENTHEIM: Oh yes, yes, yes! I shall never forget that time! But it is too terrible to think of! Only to recall it for a moment—oh!

Without departing in the least from colloquial speech and using nothing but a basic vocabulary, Ibsen provokes an immediate interest in his opening situation. The characters are shown to have positive relationships toward each other. They have somehow shared in the humiliation suffered by, presumably, the bailiff. We want to know what it was, what the two women are to each other, and the reasons for Mrs. Borkman's coldness as well as Ella Rentheim's distress at the recollection of what went on in that very room. So even though the dialogue may be said not to have any pronounced literary "style" except compression and succinctness, it accomplishes what it sets out to do, and that is to create a lifelike reproduction of a meeting between two real people in a real place, two people furthermore who have together experienced some catastrophe. The air is charged with tension. Their emotional involvement in this experience even though it is as yet unknown to us and the swiftly drawn contrasts between their personalities seize the attention and pique our curiosity to learn more about them.

Now let us set these tight-lipped laconicisms against an earlier example of rhetorical prose stage speech in a work which tries to make an unashamed assault upon the emotions by showing the characters themselves laying their passions bare; George Lillo's *The London Merchant:*

BARNWELL: Trueman!—My friend, whom I so wished to see! yet now he's here, I dare not look upon him. (*Weeps*)

TRUEMAN: Oh, Barnwell! Barnwell!

BARNWELL: Mercy! Mercy! Gracious Heaven! For death, but not for this, was I prepared!

TRUEMAN: What have I suffered since I saw thee last!—What pain has absence given me!—But, oh! to see thee thus!

BARNWELL: I know it is dreadful! I feel the anguish of thy generous soul:—But I was born to murder all who love me. (*Both weep*)

TRUEMAN: I came not to reproach you; I thought to bring you comfort; but I am deceived, for I have none to give. I came to share thy sorrow, but cannot bear my own.

BARNWELL: My sense of guilt, indeed, you cannot know; 'tis what the good and innocent, like you, can ne'er conceive; but other griefs at present I have none but what I feel for you. In your sorrow I read you love me still; but yet, methinks, 'tis strange, when I consider what I am.

TRUEMAN: No more of that; I can remember nothing but thy virtue; thy honest, tender friendship, our former happy state, and present misery. Oh, had you trusted me when first the fair seducer tempted you, all might have been prevented!

BARNWELL: Alas! thou know'st not what a wretch I have been! Breach of friendship was my first and least offense. So far was I lost to goodness, so devoted to the author of my ruin, that had she insisted on my murdering thee—I think—I should have done it.

TRUEMAN: Prithee, aggravate thy faults no more.

BARNWELL: I think I should! Thus good and generous as you are, I should have murdered you!

TRUEMAN: We have not yet embraced, and may be interrupted. Come to my arms.

BARNWELL: Never, never will I taste such joys on earth; never will I so soothe my just remorse. Are those honest arms and faithful bosom fit to embrace and to support a murderer? These iron fetters only shall clasp and flinty pavements bear me. (*Throwing himself on the ground*) Even these are too good for such a bloody monster!

Among other things one trouble with this passsage is that it deals with vague generalizations about pain, sorrow, mercy, guilt and remorse, and it presents them in such quick succession and with such frenetic emotionalizing that they seem like a mere catalog of woes unrelated to real persons, a perfervid recital rather than an explicit personal illustration of the sufferings of Barnwell and his friend. The grammar is correct; the speeches have a not unpleasing rhythm, but there is nothing unexpected in the sense, nor unhackneyed in the way that sense is expressed. It is a dialogue of exclamation points, *about* passions, but so inflated and unspecific as to be funny rather than touching. The characters speak exactly alike; and it is difficult to perceive exactly where the scene is going.

The director is always concerned with what the dialogue means, the cognitive and connotative impact the words are having on the audience. He is also concerned with the sound, the song, the words make as they fall from the lips of the actors, and with the effect which these tunes and cadences are to have on the listener. It goes without saying that his duty lies in exploiting every evocative possibility the words present for stimulating the audience's interest and holding its attention. But if he is to have any success in this assault on the senses, the play must offer him the material to work with in its verbal texture and literary style. When a play has no style at all, or, conversely, where it has much style and little else, he should not waste time trying to capitalize on something that is not there in the first instance, or is so rigid and artificial as to discourage vocal experimentation with it in the second.

Verse Drama

Verse plays give the director his widest opportunities, for in them he can make use of the imagery, metaphor, meter, rhythm, synecdoche, parallelism, rhyme, alliteration, onomatopoeia or any and all the other devices used in conventional poetic expression. Not always, of course. In T. S. Eliot's *The Cocktail Party,* for example, the dialogue is set down in the form of verse, and it looks like verse on the page; but except for some meager attention to rhythmic principles, the result is as prosy as the excerpt from *John Gabriel Borkman* without any of the latter's forward-pushing tension or true dramatic interest:

> And so will you send me to the sanatorium?
> I can't go home again. And at my club
> They won't let you keep a room for more than seven days;
> I haven't the courage to go to a hotel,
> And besides, I need more shirts—you can get my wife
> To have my things sent on: whatever I shall need.
> But of course you mustn't tell her where I am.
> Is it far to go?

This passage stabs at meter without being metrical enough, and there is no song in it, no resonance; nor does it give the actor a chance to speak with the heightened inflection that comes so easily when he deals with genuine poetry:

> A good persuasion. Therefore hear me, Hermia.
> I have a widow aunt, a dowager
> Of great revenue, and she hath no child:
> From Athens is her house remote seven leagues;
> And she respects me as her only son.
> There, gentle Hermia, may I marry thee;
> And to that place the sharp Athenian law
> Cannot pursue us. If thou lovest me, then,
> Steal forth thy father's house tomorrow night;
> And in the wood, a league without the town,
> Where I did meet thee once with Helena,
> To do observance to a morn of May,
> There will I stay with thee.

Shakespeare leaves us in no doubt about where the accents come, as Eliot does. The matter in both is factual, yet the difference lies not only in the regularity of emphasis in the speech from *Midsummer Night's Dream*, it lies in the fact that Lysander has a plan for Hermia; it involves action; somebody has got to get somewhere. What Lysander is saying interests us. The other, listing rather drab alternatives between sanatorium, club, or hotel, does not. Lysander compresses in a small space a considerable amount of information unlike the other, which has little, and that little is conveyed in dull, bloodless prose. There are no surprises, delightful or otherwise in the vocabulary.

The actor in *The Cocktail Party* has no alternative except to read the lines as conversational prose.

Eliot's attempt to harness the ordinary conversation of contemporary people by this sort of quasi-versification recalls a similar experiment by Maxwell Anderson, who tried to blend, in *Winterset*, poetic dialogue in the Romantic tradition and characters of American life, specifically slum life. The teen-age hero, the gangsters, the Jewish heroine and her family, all, in moments of emotion, speak blank verse. The playwright justifies this usage on the grounds that prose is the language of information and verse the proper language of passion.

Neither Eliot's nor Anderson's experiment comes off, but Anderson's is on the whole a nobler failure, for his verse is unmistakably verse and can be read as such with full stress on the meter. Where his difficulties lie is in the vocabulary, for there is a fundamental violation of sense between the known social and educational backgrounds of the characters, and in particular those of the leading character, Mio Romagna, and the pedagogical language the characters are given to speak, to say nothing of the many learned classical allusions and poetic flights they use that jar with such discrepancy against the characters' condition of life.

Mio sounds more like a professor of English Literature than a seventeen-year-old rail-bird whose education stopped after one year at Hollywood High School. The same is true of Carr, his friend, another child of the pavements.

Mio's erudition leads him to employ such words as *circumnamb, legerdemain, dissolution, paucity, prerequisite, cerebrum, sleuthing, glauming, eviscerate;* and such expressions as *lux-et-lex putrefaction* and *presto-prodigioso*. He admires Carr for being able to follow him through "the driven snow of Victorian literature." He refers to Judge Gaunt's "Brahminical mouth," and accuses him of "running cascades of casuistry." When he recites, something like Cyrano, an improvised elegy on the death of Shadow, he comments thus on his own creation: "How I hate these identicals. The French allow them, but the French have no principles anyway."

What is the director to do when he is confronted with a problem like this? His job is not to criticize the writing but to try and make it palatable to the audience in any way he can. His only choice here is to get the actors to speak the lines and the words with bravura and with a sort of impertinent aplomb. Mio must be made to seem to enjoy, with wry humor, the extravagance of his expressions. When he and Carr match verbalisms as other boys might match pennies they must do so with an air of good-natured banter, and in a style which conveys to the audience that they realize the contradiction between what they are supposed to be and what they are saying. And the actor playing Mio must hold steadily in mind that he is intended to be two opposite things at once: a real young hobo and a poetic symbol of justice and revenge, a tenement-bred Orestes. Only thus can he hope to strike some sort of acceptable balance between the warring demands of poetic convention and realistic illusion.

The extremes to which the rigidities of poetic convention can go may be imagined in a play written entirely in heroic couplets, of which this one may serve as an example.

> Without unspotted, innocent within,
> She feared no danger, for she knew no sin.

The form here is so artificial that the actor encounters many difficulties if he tries much vocal experimentation with it. It is foolish to try and speak such lines with naturalness or with any attempt to obtain variety because of the very perfection of their mechanical regularity and the absolute monotony of their rhythm. Everything works against their acceptance as human speech, including the end rhymes, the alliteration, the symmetry with exact balance in the two iambic-pentameter lines, each not only divided into exactly matching halves but each half the antithesis of its twin. Perhaps it is just as well that the director and actor of today are not very often called upon to cope with plays written in this style.

Poetic Prose

It is in the texts of the middle range, that is, in prose plays which have some of the rhythmus and verbal richness of verse, and in verse plays which have some of the natural cadences of prose, where the director and the actor find the most plentiful and rewarding examples on which to work in their never-ending efforts to increase the auditory appeal of a production.

Any director with a sensitive ear knows that lines may be written out on the page as prose but actually possess some of the qualities of rhythm, balance, and often meter just as in verse. This is one of the reasons why we so often hear Tennessee Williams, Eugene O'Neill, John M. Synge and others referred to as writers of poetic prose.

As an example of this let us look again at a play we have been discussing, *The Doctor's Dilemma.* One cannot read very far in it without being impressed with the regularity of the beat in many of the speeches, particularly those of Sir Paddy Cullen. Sir Paddy, being Irish, might be expected to fall into a measured lilt more readily than the others, but Ridgeon, a distinctly Anglo-Saxon type, does so too. With a slight rearrangement in the way the speeches are set down on the page, we get blank verse or some other recognizable poetic form:

SIR PATRICK: In my early days, you made your man drunk;
And the students and porters held him down . . .

[1]

Nowadays you work at your ease;
And the pain doesn't come until afterwards,
When you've taken your cheque, and rolled up your bag,
And left the house. . . .

I tell you, Colly,
Chloroform has done a lot of mischief,
It's enabled every fool to be a surgeon. . . .

[1] Symbol indicates omission of one or more lines.

There's nothing wrong with your spine;
And there's nothing wrong with your heart;
But there's something wrong with your common sense. . . .

It's only fit for fools and savages. . . .

Put down your foolish pencil, man,
And think of your position. . . .

Let me put him back on the pillow, ma'am,
He will be better so. . . .

On occasion Ridgeon falls into the same speech patterns. When he does, he is usually reflecting Paddy's attitudes and admitting, unconsciously perhaps, the influence over him of his old friend and counselor, as in:

I see you don't believe in my discovery.
Well, sometimes I don't believe in it myself.

Once having detected these examples of poetic usage, what can the director do about them? How can he use them in performance?

The very least he can do is to see to it that the actors do not miss the beats, otherwise the metric understructure that adds shape and cadence to the sense of the lines is lost. Speaking in this somewhat formal way adds to Paddy's stature and underlines Shaw's notion of him as an oracular figure from the past. The measured sentences suggest gravity and dignity in the man, and give evidence of the orderliness and clarity of his mind. They lend to what Paddy says an old-fashioned ring, and set him even farther apart from his younger colleagues, whose theories he regards with the skeptical wisdom of old age.

The Irish dramatists have been more prone than others writing in English to capitalize on the lilt of ordinary speech. O'Casey, for instance, like Shaw frequently uses a regular iambic pentameter or tetrameter line although it is set down on the page as prose. In *Juno and the Paycock* all the characters save Bentham, the outsider, speak lines that sooner or later gather themselves into recognizable meter:

JUNO: For you an' me is middlin' old,
An' most of our years is spent. . . .

We'll have to keep it quiet,
Till we see what we can do. . . .

MARY: I haven't time to listen to you now. . . .

JOHNNY: Tay! tay, tay! You're always thinkin' o' tay.
If a man was dyin', you'd thry to make him
Swally a cup o' tay. . . .

Oul' Simon Mackay is thrampin' about
Like a horse over me head. . . .

MRS. TANCRED: Balanced by the bodies
Of our two dead darlin' sons. . . .

SALESMAN: You don't happen to want a sewin' machine?
BOYLE: No, I don't want e'er a sewin' machine!

It is significant that in most cases these characters resort to rhythmic utterance at times of considerable emotional stress, and this, as Maxwell Anderson has suggested, is in keeping with ancient English dramatic tradition.

The great John M. Synge was no stranger to this usage, and indeed may have been O'Casey's model. There are many lines in *The Playboy of the Western World* susceptible to regular scansion. And lest some may think that this usage is merely an echo from a distant past, listen to these lines from Brendan Behan's *The Hostage:*

PAT: Begod, the old leg's killin' me tonight.

and:

Tomorrow morning at the hour of eight
He'll hang as high as Killy-man-jaaro.

And could it be that our own Tennessee Williams has earned the appellation of poet in the modern American Theatre partially at least because of his use of meter? Here are some samples from *A Streetcar Named Desire:*

BLANCHE: And turn that over-light off! Turn that off!
I won't be looked at in this merciless glare!

Oh, my baby! Stella! Stella for star!

Your sister hasn't turned into a drunkard.

Why, that you had to live in these conditions!

I guess that is what is meant by being in love.

Hello, Stanley!
Here I am, all freshly bathed and scented,
And feeling like a brand new human being. . . .

Well,
I never cared for wishy-washy people. . . .

Yes, Stella is my precious little sister. . . .

Here all of them are, all papers!
I hereby endow you with them.

And Blanche is not the only character who falls into rhythmic speech:

EUNICE: We own this place so I can let you in. . . .

STEVE: I told you at breakfast—
And phoned you at lunch. . . .

STELLA: Blanche, you sit down and let me pour the drinks.
I don't know what we've got to mix with. . . .

They're having a—found some soda!—tournament. . . .

These are isolated examples, but I think they supply sufficient evidence of the persistent urge toward metrical expression in the theatre in spite of its heavy reliance on so-called realistic speech.

Using the Language

There are other instances in unexpected places of the effectiveness of poetic usage. Consider *The Importance of Being Earnest* by another

Irish stylist of the first rank. As is well known, this is a play of language whose comic life draws its sustenance as much from the way its people say things as by what they say, as in these lines for Algernon Moncrieff:

> My dear fellow, the way you flirt with
> Gwendolyn is perfectly disgraceful. It is
> almost as bad as the way Gwendolyn flirts with you.

It is obvious from the first sentence that Algy is taking a strongly moral, even sententious, stand against Jack's flirtatious inclinations. Notice that after the nominative of address, there ensues the familiar pattern of the iambic measure:

> ... Thĕ wāy/yŏu flīrt/wĭth Gwēn/dŏlȳn
> ĭs pēr/fĕctlȳ/dĭsgrāce/fŭl.

The cadence exactly fits Algy's hypocritically censorious attitude, and he can pound it out impressively just by staying with the beat. But Algy cannot hold this pretense of high morality for very long, and proceeds to puncture it with an absurd anticlimax which reasserts his normal air of careless worldliness. The inversion of the second sentence minimizes Jack's weakness for flirtation with the realistic admission that Gwendolyn's is equally reprehensible. The contrast in Algy's two attitudes is underlined by the change in the form of the two sentences, the first formally measured, the second written in uncadenced prose.

Balanced sentences, the use of antithesis, and regularity of rhythm give a poetic dimension to the prose dialogue of Arthur Miller.

Listen to these excerpts from *Death of a Salesman:*

> LINDA: ... Either he's your father and you pay him that
> respect or else you're not to come here.

> LINDA: Willie Loman never made a lot of money; his name was
> never in the paper; he's not the finest character
> that ever lived. But he's a human being, and a
> terrible thing is happening to him.

> CHARLEY: Why must everybody like you?
> Who liked J.P. Morgan? Was he impressive?
> In a Turkish bath he looked like a butcher. But
> with his pockets on he was very well liked.

CHARLEY: . . . He's a man way out there in the blue, riding on a smile and a shoeshine; and when they start not smiling back—boy, that's an earthquake. . . .

The nature of the vocabulary, the very choice of the words, have an important bearing on the quality of dramatic writing. There are those who believe Shakespeare's greatness was in part due to his taking advantage of the extraordinary opportunities offered him by the sudden enrichment of native English by the introduction of new words derived from classical sources, part of the widening intellectual influence of the Renaissance. This phenomenon is seen in some of the great speeches in Hamlet:

> . . . absent thee from felicity awhile,
> and in this harsh world draw thy breath in pain,
> to tell my story.

In an entirely different context, we see what comic effects can be obtained by this same usage, an elaboration of the vocabulary drawn again from classical sources:

LADY BRACKNELL: Rise, sir, from this semirecumbent position. It is most indecorous.

Thus through her choice of words and her propensity for the Latinist style of speech, Lady Bracknell displays both the impeccable grand manner of the ruling class and its traditionally unshakeable aplomb.

The Importance of Being Earnest is a good example also of a comedy that uses with effect another verbal device, the epigram. In this case, much of the amusement follows from the fact that the apothegms voice sentiments that are comic reversals of respectable or commonplace ideas, as in the following:

> Divorces are made in heaven.

> I hear her hair has turned quite gold from grief.

> In married life, three is company and two is none.

Christopher Fry, like Wilde, takes obvious delight in using language for its own sake. In *The Lady's Not for Burning* he follows literary tradition by writing in verse and achieves much comic effect by metaphor (which will be discussed separately later), and repetition, alliteration, hyperbole, the non sequitur, anachronisms, and incongruity. These, along with invective, are carried forward by the humorous employment of an archaic vocabulary in keeping with the medieval story, and much witty coupling of unexpected adjectives with polysyllabic nouns. Here are some examples:

Repetition:

RICHARD: O God, God,
God, God, God, I can see such trouble!

TYSON: I stare at you, Nicholas,
With no words of condemnation. I stare,
Astonished at your behavior.

TYSON: What is the meaning of this?
What is the meaning of this?

THOMAS: O Tedium, tedium, tedium: tiddy-um,
tiddy-um, tiddy-um.
The frenzied
Ceremonial drumming of the humdrum!

Alliteration:

THOMAS: . . . faintly festive hiccup [The diminishing effect of the adverb is characteristic also of another successful British writer of comedy, Noel Coward.]

ALIZON: You're hidden in a cloud of crimson
Catherine-wheels.

NICHOLAS: You slawsy poodle, you tike, you
crapulous, puddering pipsqueak!

MARGARET: O peaceful and placid heaven, are
they both asking to be punished?

THOMAS: . . . for the involving ivy, the briar,
The convolutions of convolvulus. . . .

TYSON: It probably went past
Perfectly preoccupied with some anxiety or another. . . .

THOMAS: The night's a pale pastureland of peace. . . .

Hyperbole:

ALIZON: . . . And the trees were as bright as a shower of broken glass.

MARGARET: Oh! It's bell-ringing practice! Their ding-dong rocks me
Until I become the belfry, and makes bright blisters
All along my nerves . . .

Non sequitur:

NICHOLAS: She wishes to be burned
Rather than sleep with my brother.
MARGARET: She should be thankful
She can sleep at all. For years I've woken up
Every quarter of an hour. . . .

Anachronisms:

RICHARD: *Sanctus fumus!*

THOMAS: The Last Trump
Is timed for twenty-two forty hours precisely.

Incongruity:

ALIZON: No father or mother?
RICHARD: Not noticeably.
ALIZON: You mustn't let it make you
Conceited. Pride is one of the deadly sins.

TAPPERCOOM: Quite. An excess of phlegm
In the solar system. It was on its way
To a heavenly spittoon.

Invective (with archaisms):

NICHOLAS: You dismal coprolite!

NICHOLAS: O blastoderm of injustice.

THOMAS: You bubble-mouthing, fog-blathering,
Chin-chuntering, chap-flapping, liturgical,
Turgidical, base old man! . . .

Elaboration of vocabulary:
TAPPERCOOM: . . . The whole thing's a lot of amphigourious
Stultiloquential fiddle-faddle.

Once he has recognized these literary devices, the director must contrive a way of matching the extravagancies they represent with a fitting exuberance in the playing and the speaking. The acting style must be heightened to gibe with the comedy's hyperboles.

Imagery and Metaphor

Professor Caroline Spurgeon and others have shown how an important light can be thrown on a play's meaning and atmosphere by the recurring use of images and connected metaphors. A good director is always aware of these and seeks ways to make them count with the audience. For just as there are subject—or theme—threads holding the weave of a play's meaning together in explicit fashion, as we have seen, there are often threads of metaphor working towards the same purpose although not perhaps in such direct manner. At one and the same time these metaphors and images enrich and enhance the play's significance as literature.

Two familiar works, one a comedy and the other a tragedy, will furnish the starting point for an analysis of how metaphor and imagery may be used, and further, how the director may make them work for him in the production.

The first is a play already mentioned, *The Lady's Not for Burning*, whose appropriateness in this connection is established at the very beginning when the hero, Thomas Mendip, cries, "O, what a wonderful thing is metaphor!" and proceeds to drop them like bright spangles all through the text.

The Lady's Not for Burning is a play of Spring, a blend of comedy and seriousness with a happy ending. The plot has to do with witch burning, which is used to set in motion the love story. As a subject witch burning is not exactly hilarious but it becomes the substance of high comedy because of the way the author approaches it, both as dramaturgy and as literature.

For one thing, the would-be witch-burners cannot be taken too seriously. They are absurdly irresponsible, even fatuous. Tyson, Tappercoom, and the Chaplain, standing as they do for government, law, and church, far from being representative of the implacable instruments of the forces of oppression and bigotry, are figures of fun. The sniffling mayor, the overstuffed judge, and the pixilated cleric are no match for the hero, Thomas, except at one point and that offstage. Mendip defends the beauteous heroine, Jennet, in true Elizabethan style, for he combines in himself a warrior's toughness and the sensibilities of a poet, or at least a poetaster. Expressive of the comic attitude of the playwright toward his characters is the general tone of the dialogue, full of metaphorical conceits and the stylistic verve usually associated with a much earlier tradition in English drama. All this turns the play toward comedy.

The metaphorical pattern is enclosed in a web of figures related to the play's setting and to the weather. It is filled with April sunshine, spring flowers, a beautiful sunset and a gorgeous spring night drenched with moonlight, hardly the atmospheric accompaniments to tragedy. The metaphors themselves recall Keats' view that poetry "should surprise by a fine excess."

The flower-image is introduced in the first scene when Thomas says to Richard:

> I'll just nod in at the window like a rose;
> I'm a black and frosted rosebud whom the good God
> Has preserved since last October. . . .

To underscore the image, Thomas carries a black rosebud in his belt, and he can use it, of course, for a bit of business. Later it is used symbolically as a gift offering of love and life to Jennet. But in this same scene with Richard it serves also as a means of indicating Thomas's ironical awareness of the ugliness of life and, for the moment, his somewhat acid view of romantic love:

> ALIZON: Men are strange. It's almost unexpected
> To find they speak English. Do you think so too?
> RICHARD: Things happen to them.

ALIZON: What things?
RICHARD: Machinations of nature;
As April does to the earth.
ALIZON: I wish it were true!
Show me daffodils happening to a man!
RICHARD: Very easily.
THOMAS: And thistles as well, and ladies'
Bedstraw and deadly nightshade and the need
For rhubarb.

Then there is Nicholas's description of Jennet:

If evil has a soul it's here outside,
The dead-of-midnight flower, Satan's latest
Button-hole . . .

But in the main, the play's blooms are sweet, from the daffodils that Humphrey carries on in his hand, through Margaret's likening Alizon, or rather unlikening her to a cowslip, to her more personal application of the image:

One day I shall burst my bud
Of calm, and blossom into hysteria.

One final instance comes in a key scene in which Thomas tries to correct Jennet's pragmatic view of life by maintaining that some truths exist unseen:

I can pass to you
Generations of roses in this wrinkled berry.
There: now you hold in your hand a race
Of summer gardens, it lies under centuries
Of petals. What is not, you have in your palm.

Nature supplies the bulk of the images, and while some may seem strained, like Jennet's:

That was the pickax voice of the cock, beginning
to break up the night,

most of them are original and striking enough to make a metaphorical field day reminiscent of the best tradition in Elizabethan comedy.

Imagery plays its part in tragedy also, perhaps even with greater effect than in comedy. For illustration we turn again to Maxwell Anderson's *Winterset* where it is one of the play's chief attributes. Indeed, without its metaphorical language *Winterset* would be just another gangster melodrama. As it is, the imagery clarifies, illuminates, and even ennobles the work, as used repetitively, just as do the themes and motifs in a symphony.

It is as if Anderson had taken his cue from Caroline Spurgeon, who had this to say about another tragedy of star-crossed lovers:

> In *Romeo and Juliet* we find a beautiful "running" or constantly recurring image which shows that Shakespeare there imaginatively conceives of love as light in a dark world.[2]

Winterset's four main images are drawn from the elements—light, fire, water, and darkness. More often than not they are juxtaposed in conflicting pairs, light against darkness, fire against water.

The images are reinforced and given concrete definition in the settings. The action passes in a night of wind and rain. The storm builds, like the play itself, to a climax at the end of the second act, and does not subside completely until the close.

In the street scene a single lamp cuts a small circle of brightness against prevailing shadows, just as inside the Esdras' tenement a single naked bulb provides the only illumination.

We see only faintly beyond the dark river in the background to the twinkling lights of the distant city.

All the major images are introduced by the old rabbi, Esdras. Early in the play he establishes the wind as an agency of separation:

> Let the wind/and fire take that hour to ashes out of time/
> and out of mind!

Mio echoes the thought at the end of the second act, adding the suggestion that he and his beloved Miriamne are in the grip of elemental powers larger than they:

> . . . but we're parted anyway, by the same dark wind
> that blew us together.

And the curtain line is:

> Let the winds blow, the four winds of the world,
> and take us to the four winds.

[2] Spurgeon, Caroline, *Shakespeare's Imagery*. New York: The Macmillan Company, 1936. p. 18.

The metaphor is used extensively and in a number of different guises:

TROCK: Shadow was just nobody, you see. He
blew away....

MIO: ...and all his words
are curses on the wind!

There are constant references to dampness, rain, tears, and the river and these appear more frequently than all the other images except those which have to do with light. It is obvious that the rain, the storm, and the river are associated with the evil forces operating against Mio and personify the harshness of the world he moves in. In the third act the water images replace the fire images except for Esdras's final speech. Mio's ironical apostrophe to the murdered Shadow is filled with them, even to the final line:

Time and his silence *drink* us all. Amen.

Here is a partial list:

TROCK: They've soaked me once too often in that vat
of poisoned hell....

TROCK: I'm all one liquid puke inside....

TROCK: Jesus, somebody tipped it over again!

MIO: ...No further than the moon takes the tides....

MIO: ...and [let] the city go out with the tide....

TROCK: His fuse is damp.

MIO: This is the burial of Shadow, then;
feet first he dips, and leaves the haunts of men.
Let us make mourn for Shadow, wetly lying,
in elegiac stanzas and sweet crying.
Be gentle with him, little cold waves and fishes ...

MIO: Now all you silent powers
that make the sleet and dark . . .
. . . let fall some mercy with the rain.

The warring clash of truth against lies, of good against evil, and of life against death, is caught in a series of images in which fire and water meet. Mio likens himself to a flame destined to burn away the lies which have darkened his father's name, and fire itself is used to express the truth of his father's innocence. And as in *Romeo and Juliet,* fire serves to describe Mio's love for Miriamne and hers for him. It is used to describe her personal appearance as well:

MIO: It lights from within—
a white chalice, holding fire, a flower in flame,
this is your face.

And Miriamne returns the compliment in the same terms:

And you shall drink the flame/and never
lessen it. And round your head/the aureole shall
burn that burns there now,/forever.

Intensive use of antithetical fire and water images is made at the climax, when Mio at last discovers the identity of the criminals who committed the murder for which his father was wrongly executed:

Let it rain!
What can you do to me now when the night's on fire
with this thing I know?

And:

Let the night speak fire
and the city go out with the tide, for he was a man
and I know you now, and I have my day!

Throughout the play, the contrasts between light and dark are made as vivid as possible. There are no halftones:

GAUNT: I have sent men down that long corridor
into blinding light and blind darkness!

MIO: That night the guards
walking in floodlights brighter than high noon. . . .

MIO: I tell you I've lived
by his innocence, lived to see it flash/and blind them all—

MIO: To be safe until he steps
from this lighted space into dark!

Following the lead the metaphors give him, the director can underline these contrasts vividly. He can see to it that the stage lighting is stark and harsh with no toning or blending to kill the shadows. He can put the characters in acting areas that are appropriately dark or bright in accordance with the purport of the lines and their own natures. He may even move them from dark to light areas, or vice versa, as the metaphors dictate. Trock and Shadow, for instance, can play their scenes in the gloomiest portions of the set; and he can give the key words of the image vocal emphasis to make sure they are projected with added strength.

The playwright makes further use of these images of darkness and light. Esdras expresses his concept of the unreality of guilt in these terms:

ESDRAS: The days go by like film,
like a long written scroll, a figured veil
unrolling out of darkness into fire
and utterly consumed. And on this veil,
running in sounds and symbols of men's minds
reflected back, life flickers and is shadow
going toward flame. Only what men can see
exists in that shadow. . . .

And later Mio describes his mission in life in much the same metaphorical terms:

Will you tell me how a man's
to live, and face his life, if he can't believe
that truth's like a fire,
and will burn through and be seen. . . .
While I stand up and have breath in my lungs
I shall be one flame of that fire;
it's all the life I have.

In the play's closing moments the images are used again, once to sum up Mio's discovery at the moment of revelation and finally in Esdras' closing requiem which gives the play a cosmic dimension:

ESDRAS: On this star,
in this hard star-adventure, knowing not
what the fires mean to right and left . . .
. . . in all these turning lights I find no clue,
only a masterless night. . . .

ESDRAS: . . . yet is my mind my own
yet is my heart a cry toward something dim
in distance, which is higher than I am
and makes me emperor of the endless dark
even in seeking!

As noted before, it is one thing for the director to recognize the threads of metaphors which hold the play together, but quite another to find some way to insure that the audience will recognize them. Even if he fails in this and the audience is not conscious of their effect, the metaphors may exert some response subconsciously, and this is usually worth trying for.

One thing should not be done and that is to cut them out as being merely repetitive. The repetitions in *Winterset*, as in many other dramas, are themselves part of the double process of evoking the right atmosphere and hammering home by repeated association the playwright's concept of the characters as not mere individuals but symbols standing for forces larger than themselves. In *Winterset* Mio stands for truth, Miriamne for love, and Trock for death. Perhaps it is not possible to do any more than give vocal emphasis to words that forward conflict between elemental opposites of the chief images, and spatial emphasis to the characters when they speak metaphors. Perhaps that is enough. The director certainly will avoid weakening the lines and will not allow the actors to throw them away or introduce movement or business that might distract from them.

That the cast should understand the web of metaphor goes without saying.

The imaginative use of language, most marked in plays written in verse, has but one object: to increase the listener's enjoyment of what he hears. The verbal effects which have been described are means to that end. They add one more dimension to a form of communication that can also appeal by means of interesting plots, significant themes, and characters human and engaging enough to enlist our attention and entangle us emotionally in what they feel and do. Taken together they give a play literary style, a quality that makes the dichotomy between the journeyman effort and the great play.

Dramatic Devices

It has been said that dialogue explains plot, describes theme, creates character and mood, and conveys emotion. Joined to actions and stage business, it is the play. Yet quite apart from its literary merit, dialogue is also the chief medium for the projection of certain devices which produce telling dramatic effects in the modern theatre just as they did in Greek drama 2500 years ago. They are irony, suspense, reversal, discovery and foreshadowing. A director must recognize them automatically when he finds them in a text, and be ready to exploit the special character they impart to a scene, an act, or even to an entire play.

IRONY

When made deliberately, an ironic utterance has a double meaning; the character speaking it says one thing but means something else; and the person to whom it is addressed may be aware only of the surface meaning. This may sound casual, harmless, and without derogatory or threatening implications, but in serious drama, the subsurface meaning is usually dire, as when Lady Macbeth tells her husband that "Duncan must be provided for." Often the irony lies in the difference between a literal and a figurative interpretation of what is said, as in Sophocles' *Electra.* Aegisthus asks where the two young strangers are who have just arrived at the palace. Electra replies that "they have found a way to the heart of their hostess," and, of course, means it literally.

The device is equally effective in comedy. Towards the close of *Arsenic and Old Lace,* the two old maiden ladies offer Mr. Witherspoon a glass of wine. He is not aware that they have spiked it liberally with poison.

WITHERSPOON: . . . You don't see much elderberry wine
nowadays. I thought I'd had my last
glass of it.
ABBEY: Oh, no . . .
MARTHA: (*Handing it to him.*) Here it is!

Irony occurs when there is a difference in the amount of knowledge the characters present may have of a given situation, as in the cases above, although there may be some uncertainty, as in the example just quoted, about whether or not the speaker understands and is conscious of producing an ironic effect. What is important here is that the audience recognizes it as such. The Messenger from Corinth tells Oedipus that Polybus is dead, and thinks to offer him consolation by adding that Polybus was not Oedipus' real father. But instead of consoling him, the news has the opposite effect, for what the Messenger did not know was that Oedipus had been staking his all on finding proof that his real father had not died by his hand as the oracle predicted.

Irony may be present in a situation or an action yet not be perceived as such until the conclusion, as when a character exerts his will to achieve a specific aim only to find in the end that he has miscalculated and an entirely unexpected and different result is obtained. Thus in Ibsen's *The Wild Duck,* Gregers Werle seeks to persuade little Hedwig to sacrifice her dearest possession in order to prove to her father that she loves him more than anything else. In Gregers' mind is the thought that she should destroy her beloved wild duck as this proof. Instead, she kills herself.

Irony in situation has comic as well as tragic possibilities. In Wycherley's *The Country Wife,* Mr. Pinchwife, trying desperately to shield his concupiscent wife from the attentions of importunate city rakes, entrusts her to the care of Mr. Horner, the most notorious roué of all, in the mistaken belief that Horner is no man. He thereby makes possible, through his mistaken appraisal of the situation, the very thing he hoped to avoid.

SUSPENSE

Deliberately prolonging the outcome of an action or the solution of a dilemma, and keeping in doubt the settlement of any important issue until such time as the emotions of the audience have been raised to the highest point of expectancy and anticipation, and sometimes even beyond its limits of endurance, have always been favorite devices in the popular theatre. Suspense is the chief attraction of the cliff-hanging school of melodrama. Desperate delays, new hazards, and unforeseen obstacles of all kinds are placed between the hero or heroine and the successful accomplishment of their purposes. The greater the odds against them and the more critical the dangers they are compelled to face, the larger the satisfaction of the onlooker at the moment of climax when issues are finally settled, dangers overcome, and tensions released. The element of surprise may play a large part in building suspense.

The director's problem is to calculate to a nicety every gradation of tension present so that the surge of expectancy does not spend itself prematurely.

Suspense is largely a matter of action rather than words and is sustained by physical actions and stage business more often than by dialogue. This may be one of the reasons why plays of suspense are regarded largely as minor literary types, unless they happen to be generously laced with poetic language and contain a major theme, as in *Macbeth*.

REVERSAL

If the progress of a play's action may be likened to a canoe containing the hero traveling on a stream in one direction toward a specific destination, and if that destination represents either triumph or disaster for the hero, any event or circumstance which causes the canoe to turn and proceed in an opposite direction is a dramatic reversal. It is a turn from good fortune to bad, or conversely from bad to good.

The reversal may be merely temporary, as if the canoe had been caught in an eddy and turned around for a moment before resuming its original course; or it may be a permanent turning point. Reversal may contain elements of discovery, irony, and suspense.

For illustration we take again Sophocles' *Electra.*

At a moment of climax, Aegisthus is led to believe that he is about to be shown the dead body of his enemy, Orestes. Instead, Orestes himself, in disguise, discloses the corpse of Aegisthus's consort, Clytemnestra. The shock this dicovery produces on Aegisthus involves some measure of suspense and irony, and of course it represents a reversal in his fortunes.

Reversal may affect groups as well as individuals. The fortunes of the whole Boyle family in *Juno and the Paycock* are disintegrating when an unexpected legacy snatches them from poverty and disaster. But in the end the inheritance is not forthcoming and the family's downward course is resumed.

A familiar pattern in farce is to set the hero's course toward failure and show him making one mistake or misstep after another. But always, as in melodrama, means are found in the nick of time to reverse the downward plunge and lift the hero to triumph at the close. The late George S. Kaufman was a past master at this technique. His *Merton of the Movies,* written with Marc Connelly, shows the hero pinning all his hopes on becoming a famous film star. After many setbacks, Merton finally gets a part, but his acting is catastrophically inept in his serious role, and before its release the picture is acknowledged a failure. Merton is about to return home in disgrace, abandoning all his hopes and dreams, when it is suddenly found that he has unwittingly scored a triumph as a comedian.

The escape of Fleance in *Macbeth* represents a different example of reversal. Its importance is not appreciated until the work is viewed as a whole. When it happens, it appears to be a minor miscalculation in Macbeth's plans to safeguard his throne, and Fleance drops entirely out of the play. But viewed in terms of Macbeth's personal fortunes it marks the beginning of a change. Up to this point Macbeth has not been thwarted in any way. He has fulfilled his ambition to become King, and the removal of Banquo has seemingly brought his good fortune to a crest. But from the time of Fleance's escape the tide turns against him; the forces of revenge and justice gather and finally bring about his downfall.

DISCOVERY

Like reversal, a dramatic discovery may be sudden or prolonged. It may be as straightforward and simple a matter as the apprehension of someonc's identity, as in *The Libation-Bearers* when Electra recognizes her long-lost brother, Orestes. It may also be complex and drawn out over the entire action as in *Oedipus Rex,* with the hero being led step by step toward the truth about his own identity.

Many plays of significance are voyages of discovery towards an answer to man's perennial search for himself. "Who am I?" and "Whence did I come?" are drama's perennial questions although they may be phrased as variously as Willy Loman's, "What's the answer, Ben?" and J.B.'s "What is my fault? What have I done?"

FORESHADOWING

> Don't touch the pistol, Hedwig! One of the
> barrels is loaded; remember that.

Ibsen's crude and old-fashioned use of this device in *The Wild Duck* may strike us as amusing now, but it should not be forgotten that some foreshadowing is better than none at all, unless the objective is not suspense but surprise. Here it is altogether too obvious as a signpost pointing the way to Hedwig's taking up the pistol later on; a modern director would have to do something to soften it. But even Ibsen could be more subtle about its use, as he was in *Ghosts*. Our first view of Pastor Manders in that play shows him trying to get in out of the rain. But when seen against the perspective of Ibsen's finished portrait of him, this initial action is expressive of the man's whole inner nature, for he is one who is unable or unwilling ever to face up to unpleasant realities, whether they be mere adversities of weather as at the start of the play or the truth about Captain Alving's dissoluteness or Mrs. Alving's ruinous marriage.

These more or less self-evident examples of fundamentals of writing technique are to the director as the scales to a pianist. He must learn what to do with them and to recognize how effective they can be with an audience when properly exploited.

Having gained through study a knowledge of the literary attributes and thematic aspects of the material he is to deal with, and having come to understand the play's structure, plot, subject, style, and the nature of its characters, the director is now ready to evolve his plans of presentation in terms of the medium, that is by means of actors set in motion on the stage and giving voice to words in the text.

PART TWO

The Director's Medium

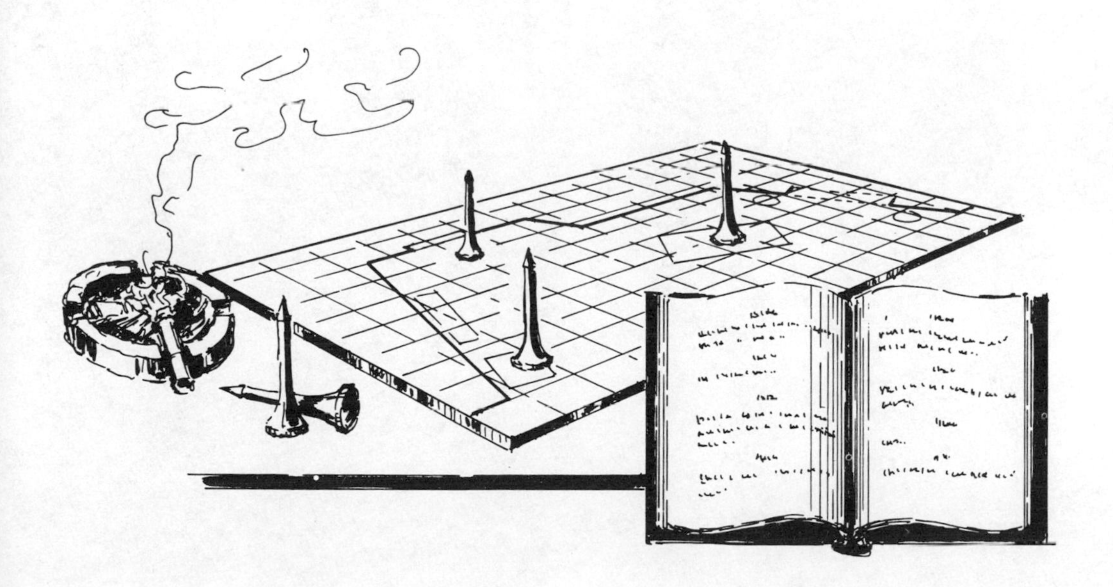

CHAPTER SIX

Blocking

People are beginning to understand in our day that exact localization is one of the first elements of reality.

VICTOR HUGO: *Preface to Cromwell*

There are wide differences of opinion about when the prompt book should be prepared and what it should contain, although most directors concede that there should be one. Indeed, there must be one if only to provide the stage manager with an authoritative source of reference for the physical details of the performance and as a ready guide to assist him in keying performances to the original standards during a run. Ordinarily the prompt book contains the time and place of actors' entrances and exits, every move and bit of business, pauses, cuts, notations about tempo and rhythm of speeches and their inflections and stresses, music and light cues, and sometimes the director's own interpretative notes. In short, the prompt book should contain any and all information about the production that is needed to show, clearly and completely, how the work is to be staged. The entries may be sketchy and rough, or detailed and precise, depending on the individual propensities of the director concerned.

When to Block

Of all the material included, the most important from the director's standpoint is the blocking, the maneuvering of characters around the stage, the theatrical action which unless managed correctly can mar the whole effect of the production. Basically, blocking consists of making decisions first about where individual scenes shall be played and, second, about where, why, and how characters shall move about in preselected acting areas. These decisions, of course, are noted down in the prompt book.

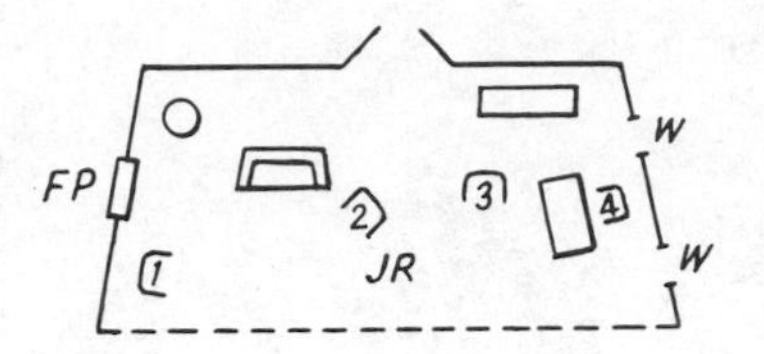

38 **The Doctor's Dilemma** ACT I

saving. ^ Oh, doctor, I married him just to help him to begin: I had money enough to tide him over the hard years at the beginning ~~to enable him to follow his inspiration until his genius was recognized~~. And I was useful to him as a model: his drawings of me sold quite quickly.

RIDGEON. Have you got one?

MRS DUBEDAT ^ [*producing another*] Only this one. It was the first.

RIDGEON [*devouring it with his eyes*] ^ Thats a wonderful drawing. ^ Why is it called Jennifer?

MRS DUBEDAT. My name is Jennifer.

RIDGEON. ^ A strange name.

MRS DUBEDAT. Not in Cornwall. I am Cornish. It's only what you call Guinevere.

RIDGEON [*repeating the names with a certain pleasure in them*] ^ Guinevere. Jennifer. [*Looking again at the drawing*] ^ Yes: it's really a wonderful drawing. ^ Excuse me; but may I ask is it for sale? I'll buy it.

MRS DUBEDAT. ^ Oh, take it. It's my own: he gave it to me. Take it. Take them all. Take everything; ask anything; but save him. You can: you will: you must.

REDPENNY ^ [*entering / with every sign of alarm*] Theyve just telephoned from the hospital that youre to come instantly—a patient on the point of death. The carriage is waiting.

RIDGEON [*intolerantly*] ^ Oh, nonsense: get out. [*Greatly annoyed*] What do you mean by interrupting me like this?

REDPENNY. ^ But—

RIDGEON. Chut! cant you see I'm engaged? Be off.

Redpenny, bewildered, vanishes.

MRS DUBEDAT [~~*rising*~~] ^ Doctor: one instant only before you go—

RIDGEON. ^ Sit down. It's nothing.

^ X1 Back to open up.

^ Puts portfolio on CH2 to steady it. Takes picture out of portfolio, Xing to R of Ch. 2 as she does so.

He looks at her.

Savoring them slowly. After P, he XR to below RC of sofa.

Re RJ X (loud)

^ X1R

^ Indicates sofa X1L

^ He X close to her L. She holds the picture for him.

He places his hand on the picture to hold it with her. They are close together.

Turns L to her.

^ She X to his L below sofa RJ

Opens both C doors. Slams in.

Redpenny X to UL Ch 2.

^ Puts drawing on R arm sofa, backing R1 to clear sightline.

^ XR1, hand out in appeal.

SAMPLE PROMPT BOOK. Pages from a published edition of *The Doctor's Dilemma* pasted shown. Warning signals and cues for actors' entrances and for sound effects should be

ACT I The Doctor's Dilemma 39

MRS DUBEDAT. ^ But the patient. He said he was dying.

^ *Indicate UL*

RIDGEON. ^ Oh, he's dead by this time. Never mind. Sit down.

^ *X1 DR*

MRS DUBEDAT ^ [*sitting down and breaking down*] Oh, you none of you care. You see people die every day.

She ⊗ L side sofa. Turn away to L. (Brokenly.)

RIDGEON [*petting her*] ^ Nonsense! it's nothing: I told him to come in and say that. I thought I should want to get rid of you.

^ *He ⊗ R of her. Pats her hand.*

MRS DUBEDAT [*shocked at the falsehood*] ^ Oh!

^ *Straightens. Looks at him.*

RIDGEON [*continuing*] ^ Dont look so bewildered: theres nobody dying.

^ *Offhand. Smiling.*

MRS DUBEDAT. My husband is.

RIDGEON [*pulling himself together*] ^ Ah, yes: I had forgotten your husband. ^ Mrs Dubedat: you are asking me to do a very serious thing?

^ *Withdraws hand. Expression sobers.*

Changes tone. Fresh attack.

MRS DUBEDAT. I am asking you to save the life of a great man.

RIDGEON. You are asking me to kill another man for his sake; ~~for as surely as I undertake another case, I shall have to hand back one of the old ones to the ordinary treatment.~~ Well, I dont shrink from that. I have had to do it before; and I will do it again | <u>if</u> you can convince me that his life is more important than the worst life I am now saving. But you must convince me first.

MRS DUBEDAT. ^ He made those drawings; and they are not the best—nothing like the best; ~~only I did not bring the really best: so few people like them.~~ He is twenty-three: his whole life is before him. Wont you let me bring him to you? wont you speak to him? wont you see for yourself?

^ *She again indicates the portfolio.*

RIDGEON. ^ Is he well enough to come to a dinner at the Star and Garter at Richmond?

^ *♂ after P. Thoughtfully (?). (May be too early for breaking the tête-à-tête, if so, wait until next page.*

MRS DUBEDAT. Oh yes. Why?

on leaves of a notebook. Script cuts, ground plan for French scene, blocking notes are added in red ink.

At what stage in the preparatory process the director elects to tackle the blocking is a matter of his own personal predilection. Several disparate methods are used but no one can say which one is best, in spite of vociferous arguments for or against one or another method. It is possible, however, and it may be helpful to consider and contrast two decidedly different ways of approaching the problem.

At one extreme is the director who would not dream of blocking before rehearsals begin lest, among other things, he give undue prominence to the merely mechanical aspects of his craft. He prefers to have his cast before him onstage before he starts to think about their positions and moves, for he regards the problem as one which can be solved best by close collaboration with the actors who are to assume the positions and make the moves. And it is the actors who can provide inspiration as he works out on the spot answers to the all-important question about where they shall be located at a given time.

It is assumed that his prerehearsal preparations have been confined to what he considers more weighty matters: the inner meaning of the play, the nature of the characters, and the subtle interplay of their motives, compulsions and complexities. In short his mind has been on high things, and not diverted into minor channels of traffic handling.

Not the least argument in favor of this view is that some of New York's outstanding directors use this technique, or at least say they do. Another is that this is the only way to avoid the risks and pitfalls of the opposite method, in which moves are all planned before rehearsals begin. The main objection to prerehearsal blocking is that it imposes an overly rigid pattern of placement and movement on performers before they have had a proper chance to get into their parts. When the director arbitrarily sets a fixed framework of moves, which they must follow in blind obedience to his will, an atmosphere is created that tends to stifle and inhibit the exercise of an actor's own inspiration and his own personal creative gifts. It is argued that the inevitable results of this procedure are performances that are mechanical, untrue, utterly lacking in spontaneity and qualities of naturalness.

It is further claimed that when a director blocks before rehearsals and sometimes even before the cast is selected, in the calm and privacy of his study, he cannot possibly take into account the special personalities and immense variations in playing styles of the people who will eventually play the parts. Not knowing their special skills or individual attributes, he cannot capitalize on them as he should; not knowing their weaknesses he cannot arrange the blocking in such a way as to conceal or minimize them. And what is the good of laboriously planning everything beforehand, if, when the director calls for a certain preset move, the actor feels he is not physically capable or psychologically prepared to make it, or deems it out of keeping with his own style or perhaps contradictory to his concept of the role? Conversely, the director may not have been aware that a particular actor has abundant grace in movement and is capable of making far more effective moves than those previously set down for him, and of making them more often. With the actors there before him, the director has the immediate advantage of seeing clearly and exactly what they can and cannot do, and can shape the blocking accordingly.

The subject of the actors' feelings always looms large in these arguments. And what makes it touchy is the implied conflict of authority between director and actor in areas where creative responsibility is difficult to define and limit categorically. Who will have the final say in these matters of placement and movement when the director's instructions run afoul of the actor's understanding of his part, a field in which he surely should enjoy some prerogatives of choice?

Let us take the case of a director who puts full confidence in the actor's judgment about where he should be on the stage at any particular time and the best way of getting there. If such confidence is absolute, there is no need to plan anything. For if the director has arranged for an actor to cross down right on a line, what is to be done except abandon the idea if the actor's intuition propels him down left? This sort of director feels strongly that his first function is to make sure that the actor is comfortable in what he is doing. He concludes that any move or position that "feels right" to the actor will automatically be the most effective and acceptable. He postpones blocking until the last moment for this very reason. Then the actor and director can attack the task jointly. The actor is given a meaningful share in the work of creation, particularly with respect to his subjective wishes. He is thus made happy, and a happy actor is a better performer than one who is unhappy, or so the theory goes. When inspirations conflict, as when Mr. A., the leading man, and Miss B., the leading woman, both feel an inner compulsion to sit down in the same chair at the same time, it becomes the director's function to arbitrate the issue between them and convince one of the parties that his or her instinct has erred.

What we have been considering is not one question, but two. The first is: should the director block before rehearsals or after they begin? The second: should he block at all?

The second question involves a school of thought, particularly prevalent among actors, which upholds this "free" system, whereby actors block themselves with the director acting as judge and referee of results.

The unacceptable feature of this theory, and one which in my opinion completely invalidates it, is this: it is not the primary purpose of stage placement and stage movement to make the actor happy or comfortable. An actor may feel as comfortable as a cat before the fire and still fail to register properly the attitude or the emotion his position or his move is intended to convey; or he may feel uneasy and discomfited in his position, even unhappy and rebellious, yet still express to the audience his character's attitude and emotion with clarity, force, and naturalness.

The Purpose of Blocking

The purpose of stage placement and stage movement is to help the audience understand the play's action. It can do this by stage arrangements which clearly indicate the psychological relationships between characters, in short by purposeful placement that shows what the characters are to each other, that makes necessary business viewable, that directs the audience's attention to the right target at the right moment. Also, in certain types of plays, the stage arrangement may be used for the esthetic purpose of creating a series of pictorial compositions pleasing to the eye and expressive of the play's artistic or historical tone.

The best way to fulfill these purposes is for someone to have a preconceived idea about what the placement and the movement are expected to achieve and then to put into operation a deliberate preconceived plan to attain those ends.

Another guiding purpose of blocking is to avoid visual monotony. Audience lassitude ensues when there is too little movement, when stage pictures are held too long, or when certain acting areas are overused while others are neglected or not used at all. For, if all the key scenes are played up center, eventually even that important and emphatic area will cease to hold visual interest. Likewise, it is important to avoid recognizably repetitive patterns in the sequence of acting areas used. Nothing induces a feeling of mechanicalness and artificiality more quickly than to have a series of scenes take place successively in right center, center, and left center, followed by another series using the same areas in the same order.

At the opposite pole is the fault of excessive movement, movement for its own sake. Meaningless changes of position convey an empty restlessness and are usually the results of weak directional control.

There is also the important matter of keying the emotional intensity of scenes to areas best suited to express that intensity.

It is common knowledge that a scene's "emotional carry" is directly connected with and influenced by the area of stage upon which it is played. Areas off to the sides and far upstage are weaker than those nearer the center and downstage. The reason for this is simple: the audience can see and hear the actors better when they are in these latter areas, provided there is equal light in all areas. An actor loses stature and force in proportion to his distance away from the spectators on a line running on an axis up- and downstage, and also in proportion to his distance from the center line of the set. To be sure, some of the carrying power of a weak area can be restored or increased by putting it in stronger light or by darkening surrounding areas, but it is not always possible to justify light changes that have to be made to do this, particularly in a realistic production.

There may be as many as forty or fifty French scenes in a full-length play and there are seldom two alike in importance or intensity, depending largely on their positions in the over-all structure of the work. Someone has to think about fitting each scene into the proper emotional relationship to those which have come before and to those which follow if a logical progression is to be obtained in the dramatic build of an act and an effective balance achieved between moments of intensity and moments of relaxation. This cannot be done by piecemeal selection of acting areas.

No single scene, whatever its importance, can be thought of as an isolated entity in itself. It is always part of a larger integrated whole, flowing in sequence with some sort of theatrical logic out of the scene which preceded it and on into the next. The placement must be geared to that sequential flow, and thus becomes a matter of directorial strategy rather than tactics. Each segment must fit into the larger picture. To control the flow and impose upon it a purposeful design requires a single mind with a grasp of the master plan. This is why one person with an objective view of the total effect to be obtained is needed in a position of command.

The successive acting areas have to be chosen *in relation to* each other, just as the moves of an actor within the area have to be *related* to the moves and positions of all the other actors in the scene. For it is only when the areas are chosen all together and in their proper sequence that they can be thought of as contributing a part to the purpose of the whole blocking operation, which is to employ the physical plan of the staging in such a way as to exert a calculated and varied assault upon the emotions of onlookers; an assault, furthermore, that produces a maximum response, whatever the nature of that response may be.

It is this *concerted* action which the director must think about, and which the actor concentrating on his part is in no position to think about.

Once this is understood it is clear that it is the director's responsibility to block, and no one else's. To let the actor block himself is as preposterous as permitting a musician in a symphony orchestra to decide at what point in the score he will start to play, and in what key and with what tempo.

When the Actor Blocks Himself

An actor left to decide for himself will gravitate toward the most emphatic area or into the strongest light. Who could blame him? It is asking too much of him to arrange his own blocking with due regard for the past and future uses to which each area of the stage is put.

Besides, if one actor is given such authority, there is little justification for not giving the same authority to each member of the cast. The confusion such a mistaken application of democratic principles would introduce into what has to be a controlled and highly contrived operation, as the production of a play must be, is too distressing to contemplate.

When an actor moves upon the stage he does not move in a vacuum, except in monodrama or when he has a soliloquy to speak. Under normal circumstances, other actors are present. An actor cannot move a muscle without effecting some visible change in his physical or psychological relationship to his fellow actor or to a whole ensemble. If he takes a position or makes a move because it feels comfortable to him, there is always the chance that in doing so he makes his fellow actors decidedly uncomfortable and unhappy, for they cannot help being affected by anything he does. And he is in no position to gauge what effect his position or move will have on the ensemble. The director, sitting out in front where he has an objective view of the picture in its full perspective, can; and it is this difference of perspective that gives the director his biggest advantage over the actor if there is a conflict between them about the rightness and effectiveness of relative positions.

While it is possible and even desirable to admit the value of an actor's feelings and the validity of his instincts when these are evoked as guides to enable him to find the way to the heart of his character, it is an altogether different matter to accept them as the foundation stones on which the architectonics of a scene are to be built. Feelings are unpredictable and transitory. They are determined in some measure at least by subjective pressures ranging from conditions in the actor's home life and the state of his gastrointestinal tract to the size of the type used in his billing or his struggles with his id. If he *feels* today that it is right and comfortable for him to play a scene down left, there is no way of knowing that he will not feel like playing it down right tomorrow. And the director who lets himself be guided in this same manner, by hunches and emotions, has only himself to blame if no clearly perceived and rationally executed plan is apparent in the production's choreography.

This is not to say that a director should be indifferent to an actor's feelings, or that he should go out of his way to make him unhappy by frustrating his legitimate desire to make creative contributions to common problems. If he must make minor adjustments in blocking to accommodate the actor's desire, he should do so. But the actor's reasons for wanting the change must be sound and the change itself should be an improvement, without altering the underlying design in any major detail.

Recently, I heard a director say that he "hadn't told his actors a single thing." He said it as though it were a matter of pride rather than shame. I might add that the results achieved by this "no-direction" method were nothing short of chaotic.

There is a school of directing that believes in conscientiously refraining from giving explicit instructions or positive orders to actors on the grounds that they should be encouraged to find their own means of expression, their own concepts of roles, and in some cases their own stage movement and business without help or hindrance from anybody. They believe the director's chief function is to stimulate the actor into a state of creative activity and then go to the side lines and judge the results. What is hoped to be gained by this abdication of directorial authority is spontaneity, truthfulness, and individuality in performance, as well as the full enlistment of the actor's enthusiasm, which is supposed to stem from his realization that he is doing everything himself.

It works something like this.

The director outlines to the actor the general mood and dramatic content of a scene, and shows him the locations of entrances and furniture on the ground plan. The two collaborators then discuss the character, his attitudes, his relation to the subject of the scene, his feelings toward himself and the other characters in the scene with him, his place in the play, his drives (both hidden and overt), his antecedent history, the surface meaning of his speeches and the inner meanings that lie above, below, or behind the lines, and anything else that may supply the actor with an avenue of approach to the creative process. The actor then departs to prepare the role, and returns only when he is ready to show the director the outlines of his character in form and motion onstage. The rehearsal, or perhaps we should say the demonstration which follows is submitted for the director's comments and criticism.

These comments may bear upon such matters as the means the actor used to arrive at his basic concepts, his emotion memory, the strength or aptness of his images, his freedom or restraint in employing his own feelings. Since in this directorial pattern the director is more or less honor bound not to impinge on the actor's creative sphere, he usually speaks in general terms. Reference at this stage to such details as mispronunciation of words, graceless posture, or lack of vocal projection is made somewhat casually and with considerable tact. The actor is then given additional time to evolve his characterization, and the process is repeated as many times as necessary until the director is satisfied with results. At this point, all actors in the scene are brought together and allowed to react to each other's concepts with little or no outlining from the director.

Some actors, particularly those who are potential directors, are much in favor of this system and enjoy the freedom they are given to explore roles and experiment. Others are bewildered by it and flounder around, lost without positive directorial guidance.

Sensibly applied, the technique has seemed to work, especially in plays of psychological realism, in scenes involving no more than two people whose personalities adjust easily to each other. But it is more adapted for a school of acting in which the demonstrations are given for the benefit of teacher and pupil than for public productions. There just isn't enough time for it under normal theatre conditions.

What seems wasteful as well as hypocritical is the case of the director who, while pretending to extend creative freedom and the privilege of self-direction to his players, has up his sleeve an already prearranged blocking plan, and gradually leads the actors to execute it after some weeks of wasted and misdirected effort.

The hardest way to achieve integration and interplay in any ensemble scene is to eliminate a dominant authority, or central control with supervision, to pull the diverse parts of the scene together.

On the other side of the coin, there is evidence to show that many actors welcome the sense of security that comes when the director precisely and conclusively sets the limits of their external activity. The reason for this is that they are then free to put their minds and imaginations to work on more important matters central to their craft and within their rightful areas of responsibility.

The Actor's Real Responsibilities

The actor has his own formidable tasks to perform. He must first discover the nature of the character he is to play and penetrate that nature deeply. He must understand the character's attitude toward every situation in the plot and toward every other character involved in each situation with him. He must understand what the character means in every word he utters, must identify correctly the emotions he is supposed to feel at every given moment, and somehow proceed to make those feelings seem his own.

In the next phase of his preparations, he must find the technical means to convey those emotions to the public. And this is only the beginning. He must test facial expressions, bodily carriage, postures, gestures, and physical attitudes until he finds a combination of these that seem most true and most effective. But the judgment as to what seems most true and most effective has to come eventually not from him, but from the director as he watches the results of the actor's experimentation from the outside.

The volume, pitch, inflection, tempo, rhythm, and timbre of his voice must likewise be adjusted to the character, to each emotion, and to each idea so that thought and feeling are projected together with the right force and timing.

These are major assignments calling for the utmost concentration of imagination and sense. To add to them others which fall naturally outside the actor's sphere of responsibility is to ask him to assume burdens with which he is physically unable to cope. He cannot leave the stage and look at himself from the front. And few actors possess the versatility to be simultaneously subjective creators of as complicated a thing as a blocking plan and at the same time objective critics of that same creation.

Prerehearsal Blocking

Let us now consider some of the objections we have noted to prerehearsal blocking. Does this method, if it is detailed and precise, really tend to destroy the naturalness and spontaneity of a scene?

I would answer that it does. But only if the blocking itself lacks spontaneity, naturalness, and logic. A good actor can make any reasonable and befitting move seem lifelike if he wants to, or he may make it seem awkward and unnatural if that is the intention.

Suppose a meticulous director at the first rehearsal asks the actor to sit down at the exact moment he speaks a certain word in a line, or even a particular syllable of that word. Assuming that the director has sound reasons for wanting the actor to make the move at that time, and also that he has made these reasons clear to the actor, what happens in actual practice in the theatre?

The good actor obeys the direction.

What happens then?

There are at least four weeks of rehearsal time. As the actor makes that move time after time it becomes second nature to him, so that when opening night arrives he will have succeeded in making it his own, provided of course it was a good move to begin with. By then he will also have produced the proper feeling or attitude to provide himself with ample justification for making it. He may even have hit upon better reasons for making it than the director gave him in the first place.

Should a director have to wait until he has studied the personalities and decided upon the physical and other capabilities of those who are to play the parts before deciding where they shall be at every moment in a scene, and when and how they get there?

It should not be necessary. Adjustments to fit individual styles can be made in rehearsal. The essential point, however, is that good basic blocking depends neither on the individual actor's personality nor upon his capabilities. Moves are blocked for characters, not for actors. Where a character goes and what he does is determined by the director's understanding of the relationships between the characters as found in the text, and by his fundamental concept of the dramatic ideas the placement and movement are supposed to express. It is Willy Loman crossing right, whether Lee Cobb or someone else is playing the role.

Basic blocking is just that, a base from which to start. One of the purposes of rehearsing is to correct, adjust, refine, and add to or subtract from preplanned movement. And there are few sensible directors who hold their homework in such esteem that they regard it as sacrosanct and unchangeable.

When all is said and done, the question about when the blocking should be done is of less importance than the quality of the results obtained. A good director in all probability will block as well in rehearsal as a poor one who works out all the moves beforehand.

But he will save much time, as well as much wear and tear on himself and his cast, if he does it beforehand. Some directors refuse to do this because prerehearsal blocking is an arduous, exacting, and lonely business; and many directorial temperaments are completely unsuited to the kind of concentration necessary to do it well.

Others find rehearsal conditions much too hectic to go through the kind of thoughtful and unhurried testing of possibilities that is needed to work out an effective staging plan. There are always distractions and interruptions even in the best-regulated sessions; and tensions born of uncertainty can lead to hysteria. Few directors are blessed with the power to make instantaneous and infallible judgments "as they go along," particularly when each separate judgment is supposed to mesh with all others to devise a design in staging that has a meaningful totality.

What usually happens when the director resorts to improvisation is that each placement and move as these are hit upon are tested by the trial-and-error method. This can be a very wasteful and inefficient process. The actors are kept waiting around while the director tries first one move and then another, and then a third and a fourth. The actors become confused, the director more so, and sooner or later he may begin to shout to conceal his shame or his incompetence. Eventually, and with luck, the company gropes its way toward some arrangement which may still fail to convey the true dramatic idea.

The surest way to make a cast lose confidence in itself as well as in the director is to adopt this fumbling approach.

But if the players are made aware that the director has taken the trouble to put his mind and imagination to work beforehand in order to hammer out a plan of the action, even though that plan may be inconclusive and faulty, they are reassured and sustained, as any explorers in unknown country may be thought to be, by the knowledge that they are in the hands of a guide who has a map, with the point of destination decided upon, and the main routes charted.

I for one would rather have it this way than to embark on a voyage of discovery in which everyone concerned is equally unsure and equally ignorant of where he is going and how he is going to get there.

How Detailed Should Early Blocking Be?

To what state of refinement should such blocking be carried?

Before he meets his cast is it enough for the director to set down in his prompt book merely rough indications of the acting areas and general, unspecific suggestions about moves, leaving the precise details until a later time? Or, should the early blocking be minutely annotated to account for every last half-turn or gesture fixed inexorably to its motivating syllable?

Two things determine the answers to these questions. The first is the experience and the temperament of the director; the second is the experience and the quality of the acting talent he deals with.

If the director is tidy, meticulous, and thorough, and wants his rehearsals to be well run and orderly, he will block the play in detail. If he isn't, he won't.

With able professionals, even the meticulous director will not have to cross every T and dot every I in his prompt book. He should have only to indicate, for instance, that a cross is to be made in a certain speech, and the actor who knows his craft will start the cross at the right moment, and with the proper foot. An actor with a developed technique can usually tell instinctively how far a cross should carry him without having to ask the director to measure it off in inches; and he can sense how close he should come to another character to supply the requirements of the scene. If he doesn't the director can adjust his position with a word.

Certain famous directors, at the outset of their careers, preplanned all movements with scrupulous attention to detail. With experience this exactitude was abandoned, as constant practice and a growing mastery of the craft made such spadework unnecessary. Perhaps this is the natural process of evolution in directing.

But whenever the blocking is done, common sense demands that a director working with an inexperienced group must give them explicit directions, and give them early if he hopes to achieve assurance and precision in the mechanical aspects of performance.

In plays which demand formal, stylized, or strictly rhythmic movement exact choreography must be supplied, as in ballet, with every step, turn, and gesture synchronized with the beat of the dialogue. Here it makes no difference whether the cast is made up of veteran professionals or untried amateurs; absolute precision in execution cannot be obtained without absolute precision in the plan. And because the blocking in such cases is complicated, prerehearsal blocking is recommended in the interests of time saving if nothing else.

CHAPTER SEVEN

Developing the Ground Plan

The eye of the master grooms the horse.

Old Saying

A director can do no accurate blocking at all until he has collaborated with the designer to bring into being a ground plan, drawn to scale, that will show the dimensions of every element of the setting, the location of the entrances, the heights of platforms or steps, and a tentative siting of the furniture.

The Director's Contribution

Before the director meets with the designer he must have some general as well as some specific ideas of his own about the layout of the set, the furniture placement, the number and size of the acting areas, and whatever special requirements there may be for the effective enactment of key scenes.

It is normal procedure for him to go first to the text to discover what the playwright has to say about the settings. These descriptions may range from vague hints about bare necessities to comprehensive and detailed instructions. Of the two, I prefer the first, having discovered to my regret, as will be shown shortly, that in too many cases the more dogmatic a playwright is about how he wants the setting to look, the more incomprehensible and ineffectual are his ideas likely to be when translated into terms of acting areas, sightlines, and architectural realities.

The unscaled line drawings in "acting editions" which show the ground plan, or something like the ground plan of the Broadway set, are not as helpful as they may seem to be at first glance, not because they are poor designs—few designers outside New York can compete with the professionals—but because the proportions may be all wrong for the physical conditions prevailing in the local theatre. The stage may be smaller, the auditorium larger, the sightlines altogether different, and complicated technical aids nonexistent. So, although a reasonable adaptation of the original design may be satisfactory, an absolute copy may be inappropriate, particularly if a set designed for a forty-foot proscenium is tried on a stage with a twenty-foot opening.

But a self-respecting designer or director is usually reluctant to accept completely someone else's concepts, no matter how excellent they may be. One's own artistic integrity demands a fresh look at the material; and this, coupled with pride or obstinacy, calls for a chance to set one's own personal stamp and signature on that material by means of a new and different approach. The results may not be as spectacular as those obtained in the New York production, but they are often more effective because the designs are conditioned and adapted to the possibilities and the disadvantages of the specific stage. If the first are exploited and the second avoided and if the new concept has merit and uniqueness of its own, there are rewards and personal satisfactions enough to compensate for the extra effort involved in trying to make a new statement about the play by means of design.

What, in general, are the things the director looks for in the script that will enable him to be of help to the designer?

First are the author's intentions, the play's meaning, the feel of the production. The director must make up his mind, if only at first in a general way, about the tone and style he will strike for in the playing. When the time comes he will endeavor to describe these in such a way as to provide clues to the designer for a graphic treatment that will express and supplement this tone and style. Sometimes a designer needs only a hint or a scrap of a suggestion, and will find this sufficiently meaningful to give him a germinal base from which to build the production's basic artistic metaphor.

After formulating his ideas about the esthetic impression the set is supposed to convey, the director usually finds himself concerned with problems of a very practical nature. How much room is needed for the acting space? How many people have to sit down? What pieces of furniture are required, and can they be so placed as to provide the right acting areas? Will the actors be able to circulate freely within the areas, and from one area to another? Will the furniture arrangement provide good sightlines for important scenes? or force all the action toward one area?

Is there variety in stage levels so that plastic compositions are possible? Is there logic in the architectural plan? Is it more important to have strong entrances or strong exits? How many exits must there be? Where do they lead?

These are far more important considerations for him than the decorative features of the set or the color scheme, although it may be the director's idea to play *Hamlet* in the Regency or some other period with backgrounds and costumes appropriate to it rather than in Elizabethan style. It is not essential for him to spend time trying to decide the most efficacious relationships between the set and the larger building of which it may be a part, or between the set and the surrounding countryside, if the scene is an exterior, unless there are references in the dialogue to specific landmarks that affect the staging. These problems are the designer's and should be left for him to solve.

In the director's pragmatic view the style of a doorway and its fittings are inconsequential compared to the doorway's potential effectiveness as an entering point for the characters, its position in respect to other entrances, and the amount of space around it that lets enterers turn in more than one direction. Likewise, from the director's viewpoint, it is not so important that a piece of furniture, say a sofa, should be in the authentic style of a period, but that it should have an arm for an actor to sit on in a certain scene and that it should be placed far enough away from the wall to let an actor play or cross behind it.

What specific staging situations confront him?

As stated earlier, he starts with the playwright's own description of the physical setting he had in mind when he wrote the work. But the following may indicate that he must be ready to face difficulties.

Let us assume he is about to stage Shaw's *The Doctor's Dilemma*, and turns first to what the author has to say about the set for the first act. Here is what Shaw tells him:

> The consulting-room has two windows looking on Queen Anne Street. Between the two is a marble-topped console, with haunched gilt legs ending in sphinx claws. The huge pier glass which surmounts it is mostly disabled from reflection by elaborate painting on its surface of palms, ferns, lilies, tulips and sunflowers. The adjoining wall contains the fireplace, with two armchairs before it. As we happen to face the corner we see nothing of the other two walls. On the right of the fireplace, or rather on the right of any person facing the fireplace, is the

door. On its left is the writing-table at which Redpenny sits. It is an untidy table with a microscope, several test tubes, and a spirit lamp standing up through its litter of papers. There is a couch in the middle of the room, at right angles to the console, and parallel to the fireplace. A chair stands between the couch and the windowed wall. The windows have green Venetian blinds and rep curtains; and there is a gaselier; but it is converted to electric lighting. The wall paper and carpets are mostly green, coeval with the gaselier and the Venetian blinds. The house, in fact, was so well furnished in the middle of the XIXth century that it stands unaltered to this day and is still quite presentable.

Reading this lively description, no one can deny that Shaw in his fine literary style suggests the chief features of the room. His little touches of detail convey a sense of the room's reality as well as its quality; and his assiduity in spelling out such minutiae as the flowers painted on the pier glass and the sphinx claws on the console bcspeaks both his humor and the closeness of his observation of the particulars which, when taken together, give the space its special atmosphere.

But it is absolutely useless to the working director in search of a ground plan in which he can stage the act effectively.

If translated graphically, Shaw's information produces this:

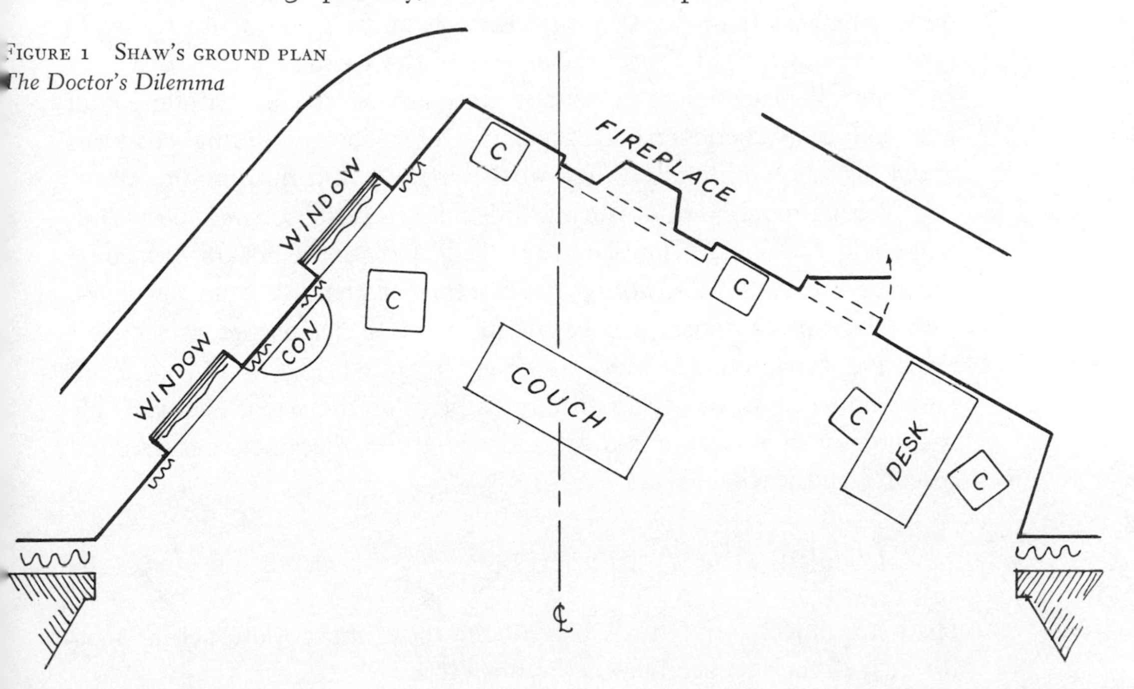

FIGURE 1 SHAW'S GROUND PLAN
The Doctor's Dilemma

Even if we cheat a little as has been done in the diagram and add a portion of the third wall on stage left in violation of Shaw's injunction to show only two walls of the room, the layout makes no sense at all, theatrically speaking.

The desk, one of the set's largest pieces of furniture, is squeezed into the narrowest part of the set and the weakest area. Whoever sits in what is presumably Ridgeon's important chair on stage left of the desk must face upstage. There is no opportunity for the actors to circulate around it to vary their positions, and there is only one restricted avenue of approach to this chair on the downstage side.

The awkward placement of the entranceway makes it necessary for all characters coming on to turn right, there being no space to allow an alternative cross left without colliding with the desk.

The three chairs on stage right bear no relationship either to each other or to the couch, which presents its back to the fireplace in most unlikely fashion. Anyone seated in the chair on the right of the fireplace would be effectively hidden from view of the audience. The angle of the couch prevents all interplay between those seated on it and others in the chairs both left and right.

There is no balance in the design. The weight of the couch and desk leans heavily to the Left, and there is nothing to anchor the wide open area down right center to the rest of the room.

Not all playwrights, of course, are guilty of the ineptitude found here, but long experience makes one wary of taking any dramatist's ideas about his sets too literally. They are a starting point, nothing more.

With a rough plan of the author's notion of the setting before him as a guide, the director must now proceed to break the act down into its separate French scenes, noting the number of characters involved, the psychological relationships between them, the exact nature of their actions and the amount of physical activity required. Listing the scenes in order, he will give to each a title descriptive of the scene's subject. He will note what furniture is used, and where the characters are required to enter and leave.

Locating the Acting Areas

His main objective in this is to find the most appropriate acting areas for each French scene. That is the first step.

An acting area is a unit of stage space usually demarcated and given limits either by articles of furniture or by other physical elements such as platforms, steps, ramps, or doors. An acting area may also be fixed arbitrarily by concentrating light on any selected space in the set, as in a poetic play which may contain little or no furniture. If a scene involves only one or two characters, the acting area may be a small island of isolation around a single center point like a sofa or a dining table. For scenes with several characters the whole set from wall to wall may be considered the unit.

One thing is certain: if a director aims at obtaining a purposeful blocking design which uses all available acting areas to best advantage, he cannot approach each scene separately and come to a final decision about where that one is to be played before going on to the next. All the French scenes in a single setting must be approached *en bloc*. He must see the whole flow and progression of scenes taken together before making a commitment about any single one, with the possible exception of the climactic scene. This may be the hinge on which all the others are hung, so he may rightly elect to block it first. It is his handling of the dynamic progression of stage activity as French scenes move from one area to another that will determine the strength, continuity, build, clarity, and emotional power of the whole act.

To think like a director means, in part, to visualize characters in action; to be drawn instinctively, when reading a scrap of text, toward consideration of the positions the characters must take in relation to each other to express the meaning of the total scene. And one of the first decisions to be made is whether that meaning can be best expressed by the characters sitting down or standing up. This is one of the several factors affecting his choice of acting area.

Another may be the director's subjective belief that certain areas, by virtue of their geographical position, possess certain psychological or emotional values to a greater degree than others. Alexander Dean felt that intimate love scenes went better if played down right, regardless, apparently, of the setting, furniture placement, or lighting. Being wholly subjective, feelings of this sort are difficult to assess and it is pointless to argue their validity. It should be noted, however, that another director may feel just as positively that his love scenes play better down left.

The fact is that any area of the stage can be invested with emotional values and atmospheric interest. It depends on setting, furniture arrangement, and the color and intensity of lighting. It should be clear, too, that in this same setting and with the same furniture arrangement, emotional values can be drastically changed by altering the lighting. An area that was once warm and inviting can be transformed into a dull and forbidding place merely by changing gelatins.

As helpful as these physical production elements may be, they are of secondary importance to the power of emotion and atmosphere that can be evoked by the actors. It is a mere matter of academic interest where a star like Audrey Hepburn might play a love scene, provided that we are able to see and hear her, and that the area used has not lost its attention-holding value by having had too many scenes played in it beforehand.

The Breakdown into French Scenes

Now concentrating on the one problem of assigning appropriate areas to French scenes, let us proceed to divide the first act of *The Doctor's Dilemma* into its basic ideational and motivational blocks, noting the progress of the act's dramatic idea as it develops from block to block, with a wary eye out for every opportunity the text presents to match the dramatic idea with its most expressive and appropriate locality. For a start, we shall adopt Shaw's general stage arrangement, at least as far as the main pieces of furniture are concerned, with the desk on the left and the couch on the right.

The list of French scenes follows:

1. *Emmy and Redpenny.* At rise, Redpenny is working at the desk, so the acting area will obviously be centered on that. Redpenny is stationary throughout; Emmy is mobile, dusting and pretending to work. Her moving about is the only physical activity in the scene.

What are the character's attitudes toward each other and the place in which they work? Emmy, from the eminence of age and with pride in her position acts as if she owns it. She looks upon young Redpenny as an upstart, although her condescension is not without friendliness. He tries to maintain a semblance of importance by the way he works at the desk. He is fond of Emmy.

TITLE: "Ridgeon's Success, and a Mysterious Visitor."

2. *Ridgeon and Schutzmacher,* following a short transitional scene between Emmy and Ridgeon. Schutzmacher is paying a somewhat formal social call. The two men are not close friends and have not seen each other for years. In his reserved way, Ridgeon is affable enough to his former classmate. Shaw has them seated through most of the scene.

TITLE: "Consultation Free, Cure Guaranteed."

3. *Ridgeon and Sir Patrick Cullen.* This, like scene 2, follows a brief covering scene between Ridgeon and Redpenny. Not one but two major subjects are presented: opsonin and its significance as a medical discovery, and Ridgeon's physical and emotional condition. Emmy's interruption in the middle of it serves as the excuse for shifting from the first subject to the second and is the dividing point between them. Because the tone of the discussion in the second section of the scene is more personal than the first, the placement of the two characters must be changed in order somehow to express this change.

This is a meeting between old friends and social equals, with Ridgeon showing deference to Paddy's age and wisdom. Paddy must be made to feel at home in contrast to the more formal reception of Schutzmacher. Shaw suggests that this be done by seating Paddy in the armchair upon entrance. There he can enjoy the comfort of the fireplace. Ridgeon sits center, on the couch. Now, it is clear that this arrangement is static and fails to take into account the change in subject midway through the scene. The director may wish to stage the start of the scene quite differently.

TITLE OF THE FIRST SECTION: "A Skeptical Sage."

In the second subscene, Paddy diagnoses Ridgeon's malaise as a sublimated sex urge and bids him to be careful of his behavior. At the very end, the subject shifts, for a third time, and has to do with Walpole who is about to enter.

TITLE OF THE SECOND SECTION: "Ridgeon's Complaint."

4. *Walpole, Ridgeon, Sir Paddy.* The scene contains preplot background material, expository shoptalk, and shows Shaw's penchant for *discussion* as a dramatic value. His intent, of course, is satirical, and the means he uses is to set the doctors arguing, usually in defense of their obsessions about the nature of sickness and their favorite cures. Walpole, advocating the extirpation of the useless nuciform sac, dominates the

scene. But along the way further information is forthcoming about the beautiful lady waiting below, which increases interest in her.

TITLE: "The Nuciform Sac."

5. *Sir Ralph Bloomfield Bonington, Ridgeon, Paddy, Walpole.* The discussion continues. The scene's comic import can be caught in the title: "How to Talk Your Way to Success in Medicine." B.B. prevails, carrying all before him by his volubility, his sonorous voice, and his commanding energy. He gradually reveals himself as a medical nincompoop.

Note is made that Shaw has Walpole sit down at the close of scene 4.

B.B. must clearly be in motion, the changes of subject as well as the bursts in his narrative supplying motivation for the moves. Advantage must be taken of his habit of addressing each of his successive auditors by name. He can cross to them as he does so.

6. *Blenkinsop, Sir Ralph, Ridgeon, Paddy, Walpole.* The scene contains the maximum number of characters, five, and it is more than likely that the whole stage, therefore, should be considered the acting area. The seedy but likeable Blenkinsop supplies the contrast to his rich and successful colleagues. The others may be characterized thus: Ridgeon —smug, proud of his accomplishments, but humbled by B.B.'s account of the reason why he got the knighthood; Paddy—a doubter, crusty, sagacious, with a saturnine sense of humor; Walpole—opinionated, dynamic, ridiculous; B.B.—irrepressible, theatrical, absurd.

The discussion continues and the conflicting points of view are aired further. Since it is all talk and no plot, the arguments must be conducted with energy, and movement must be imposed to compensate for the absence of dramatic action.

TITLE: "The Shams and Stupidities among Men of Medicine."

7. *Jennifer Dubedat and Ridgeon.* The scene marks the start of the plot's forward motion. Looking at it as a whole, it is seen that what begins as a professional consultation turns into something else, a personal, almost intimate encounter. This fact will provide a key to the division of the scene into two distinct acting areas. For the medical consultation Ridgeon should be behind his desk so the area will be some-

what the same as for scene 1. As the tone of the interview changes, the two characters may gravitate towards the warmer atmosphere of the other side where the fireplace is located.

TITLE: "A Woman's Plea."

Throughout the act the entrances are more important than the exits. This would indicate that the most likely and most practical place for the door is up center.

Eventually each of these unified blocks of textual material, insofar as any French scene is unified by its single dominant idea, must be matched with its own self-contained acting space, on the old and somewhat mechanical theory that each French scene should have its own acting area.

This cannot be done until the ground plan is fixed, and there is no better way to start on this problem than by first analyzing the use to which the setting is put. In *The Doctor's Dilemma* the key is the room's double function. It is a medical consulting room, but it serves as well as a sort of parlor where Ridgeon receives his friends. It follows that the ground plan should express this division. As a start it might be arranged in such a way as to suggest that roughly one-half the space constitutes the professional side, and the other the social side. Thus the plan would parallel the double function of the act itself, to show the series of social calls from Ridgeon's well-wishers and then the much shorter professional interview with Mrs. Dubedat.

So on the left, or consultation side, let us place the desk with Ridgeon's chair behind it, and a table for medical books, papers, and scientific apparatus. The desk will face onstage and be set between the two windows. The table will be left of the center door against the rear wall. On the opposite side will be placed the sofa, probably right center, with Paddy's armchair below the fireplace which itself will fit best into the right wall. There can be a side table in conjunction with the couch, possibly upstage of it, and a lamp or two to add to the atmosphere of domesticity and warmth. A bookcase along the wall on the right of the entrance door will balance the table on the other side. The door itself, as previously decided, is up center so that the characters may turn in either direction as they come in. The rough plan as developed to this point appears on the following page.

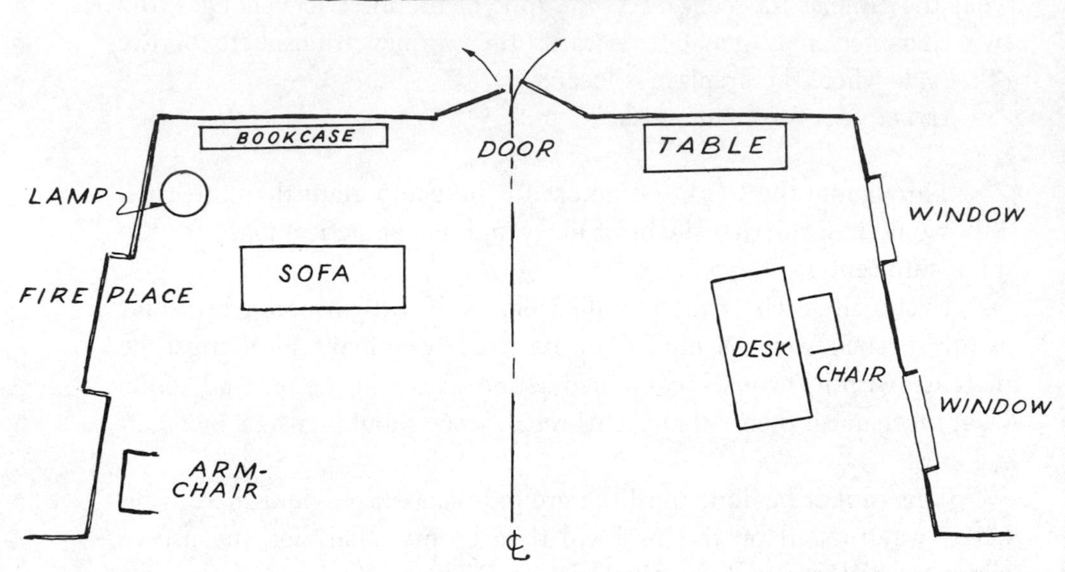

FIGURE 2 DIRECTOR'S ROUGH PLAN

The first and seventh scenes will be placed on the professional side, all the others in various areas but mainly toward the right or social side.

The director now returns to the task of placing the first five callers, knowing that for variety's sake each must have his own separate and appropriate location. What basis can be found for differentiating between their positions?

Since the tone of the room varies from the cool and businesslike impersonality of the left to the warmth of the right, it may be effective to separate the visitors and place them in accordance with the relative degree of intimacy and friendship each enjoys with Ridgeon, the more intimate the association the farther the character can penetrate into the warm side, and vice versa.

Thus, Paddy, as Ridgeon's oldest and closest friend, will be deep in the social side, in the most comfortable chair and nearest the fireplace. This automatically places the chair and the fireplace on the extreme side wall of that area.

Schutzmacher, not on close terms with his host, will stay somewhere near the dividing line between the two halves of the room, and a chair must be provided in that area to accommodate him.

Walpole, too full of his monomania to get on a very companionable footing with anyone, should be given an isolated space of his own, perhaps on the professional side.

The irrepressible B.B. has to take stage and cannot be confined to any one place, the very force of his personality not allowing him to come to rest for more than a moment at a time.

Blenkinsop, ailing and overawed, would not dare to invade the sanctum but would hover on its edges, possibly close to the door, as if unsure of his status.

Stage left has already been selected as the starting place for the final scene, but it is equally important that Ridgeon and Jennifer be placed in a relationship that will show his aloofness and impatience and her desperation and helplessness. When Ridgeon thaws, they can both be maneuvered to the opposite side.

It is by analyzing and dividing the act in such fashion that the director arrives at a working scheme, a motivating concept, which gives him a reason and a purpose for placing the characters where he does. Without such a scheme, the blocking process proceeds blindly from moment-to-moment expediencies, tending to produce results that are meaningless, irrational, or improvisatory. If movement and placement so produced have any effect on the audience at all it is the result of happy accident rather than design.

The director should now make a rough working plan of the layout of the act, with the acting areas indicated. He may then test-run one or two scenes to see how it works. He is then ready to meet with the designer.

Perhaps it should be said that this is but one way to proceed. Some directors prefer to let the designer do all this preliminary work, after which he adapts the blocking to the set as best he can. But if there is to be a directorial concept taking into account the interweave between placement and dramatic meaning, his collaboration with the designer will have to be extremely close, and the director must supply ideas at every stage of the plan's development.

Armed with whatever leads the director has been able to give him, the designer now works up a detailed ground plan, drawn to half-inch or one-inch scale, on graph paper, for the director's use. Some directors prefer that the furniture be omitted from this plan. The necessary articles can be represented by cardboard cutouts drawn to scale. These can be

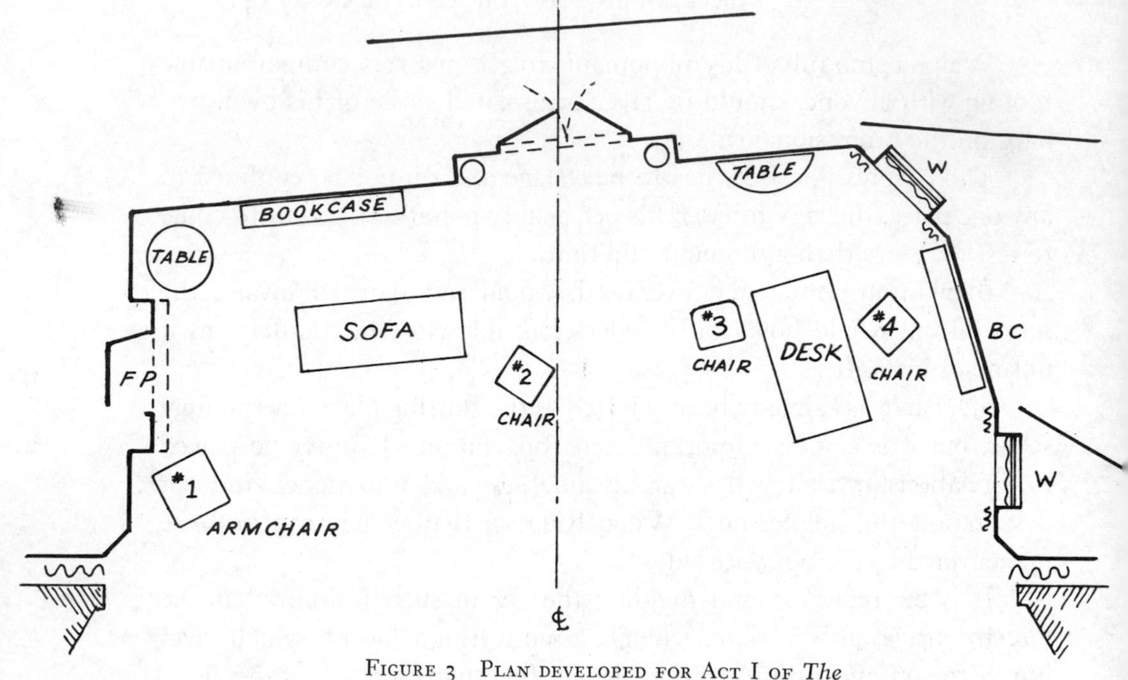

FIGURE 3 PLAN DEVELOPED FOR ACT I OF *The Doctor's Dilemma* BY PROFESSOR CHARLES E. ROGERS FOR THE AMHERST MASQUERS' PRODUCTION, AMHERST COLLEGE. SEE PHOTOGRAPH OF THE FINISHED SET ON PAGE 149.

moved around until the best locations are decided upon. The director can then pencil them in himself on the plan.

To complete the first phase of his work, the establishment of acting areas, the director now defines the limits of each area on the finished plan, first labeling the pieces of furniture and numbering the chairs to simplify the notations to be placed in the prompt book.

Scene 1. Emmy, Redpenny.

The acting area is shaded. Chairs are numbered from stage right to stage left as shown. As noted, Redpenny sits at the desk and remains there. Emmy remains for the most part within the shaded area, although her occasional forays with her duster may take her out of it momentarily as far right as the edge of the sofa.

Scene 2. Ridgeon, Schutzmacher.

Center area. Schutzmacher is held out of the social side. He may sit in chair 2 or 3 (Ch. #2 or #3). Since chair 3 was included in the scene 1 area, it might be better to shift the focus now farther to the

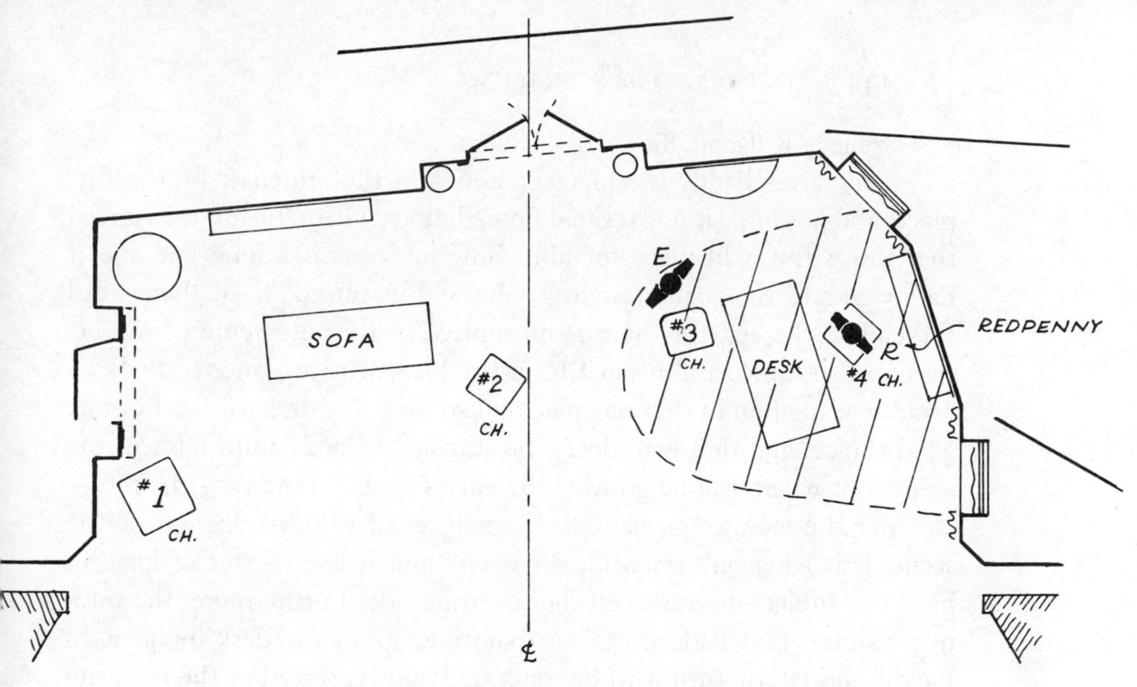

FIGURE 4 FRENCH SCENE 1

right. So chair 2 seems best for him. Ridgeon maintains something of his professional attitude if he plays to Schutzmacher's left on the professional side; and contrary to Shaw's directions, the tone of formality in the scene is preserved if Ridgeon remains standing most of the time.

FIGURE 5 FRENCH SCENE 2

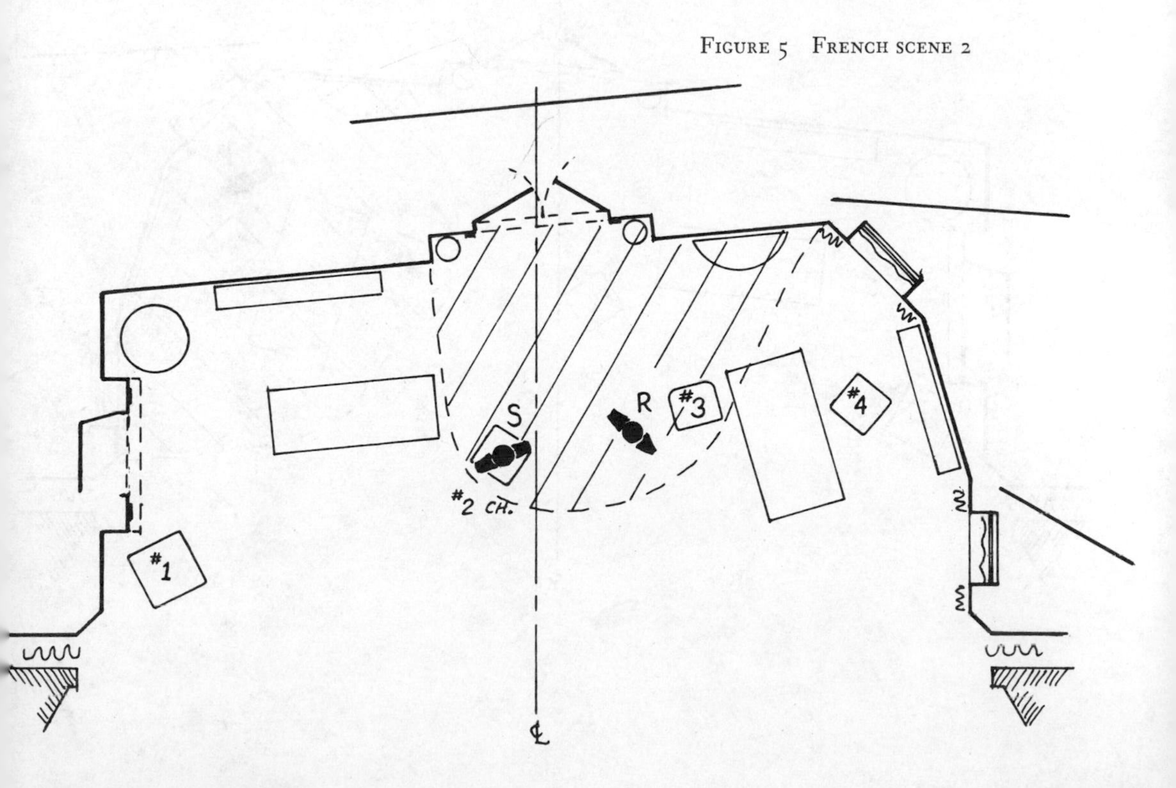

Scene 3. Ridgeon, Sir Patrick Cullen.

Shaw gives Paddy the place of honor in the armchair by the fireplace, and has him sit down there immediately. Theoretically it is agreed that this is the right place for him. But the scene is a long one and if Paddy goes to the chair straightway he will be immobilized there until the end of the act, for there is no motive in the intervening time between his entrance and his exit to justify his getting up once settled. To avoid freezing him in that one place for so long, the director has but one good choice, and that is to delay the seating of Paddy until later in the scene. But where will he go when he enters if not to the easy chair?

For the clue we go back to the subject of the first section of the scene. It is Ridgeon's scientific discovery, and it is a matter of logic to have this subject discussed on the scientific side. Furthermore, the business requires that Ridgeon take a pamphlet from the desk, hand it to Paddy, and later return it to the desk. If Paddy is seated at the opposite

FIGURE 6 FIRST PART OF SCENE 3

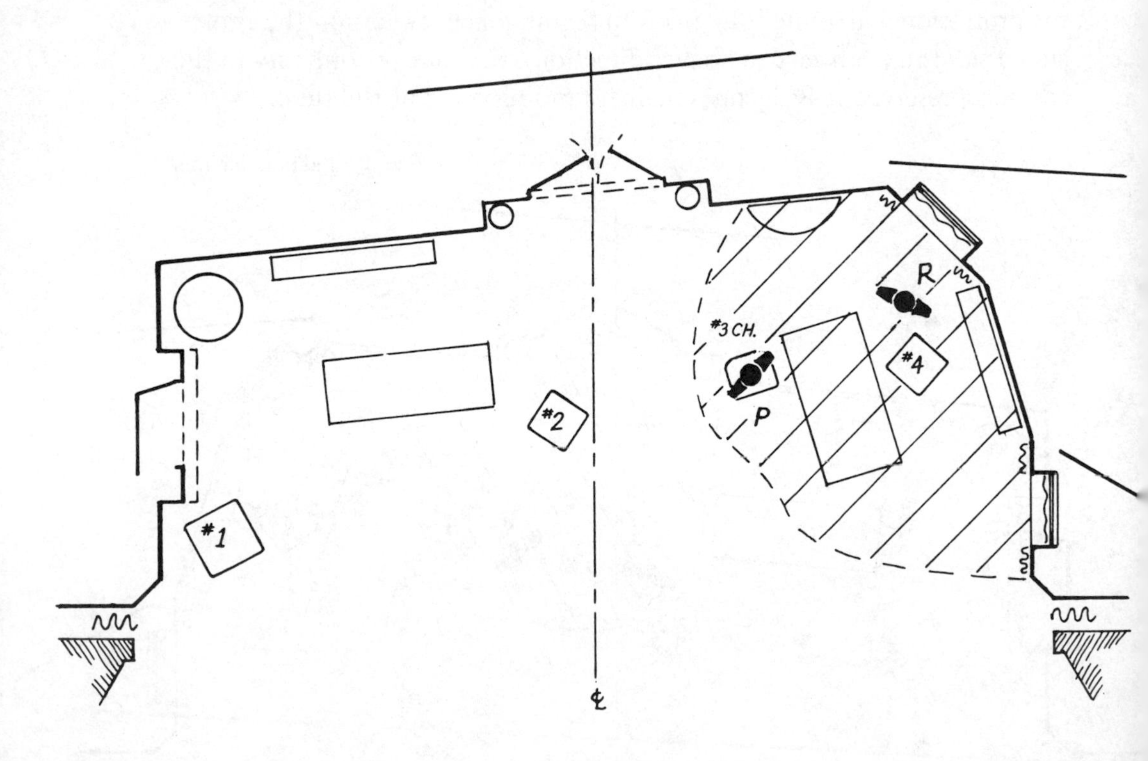

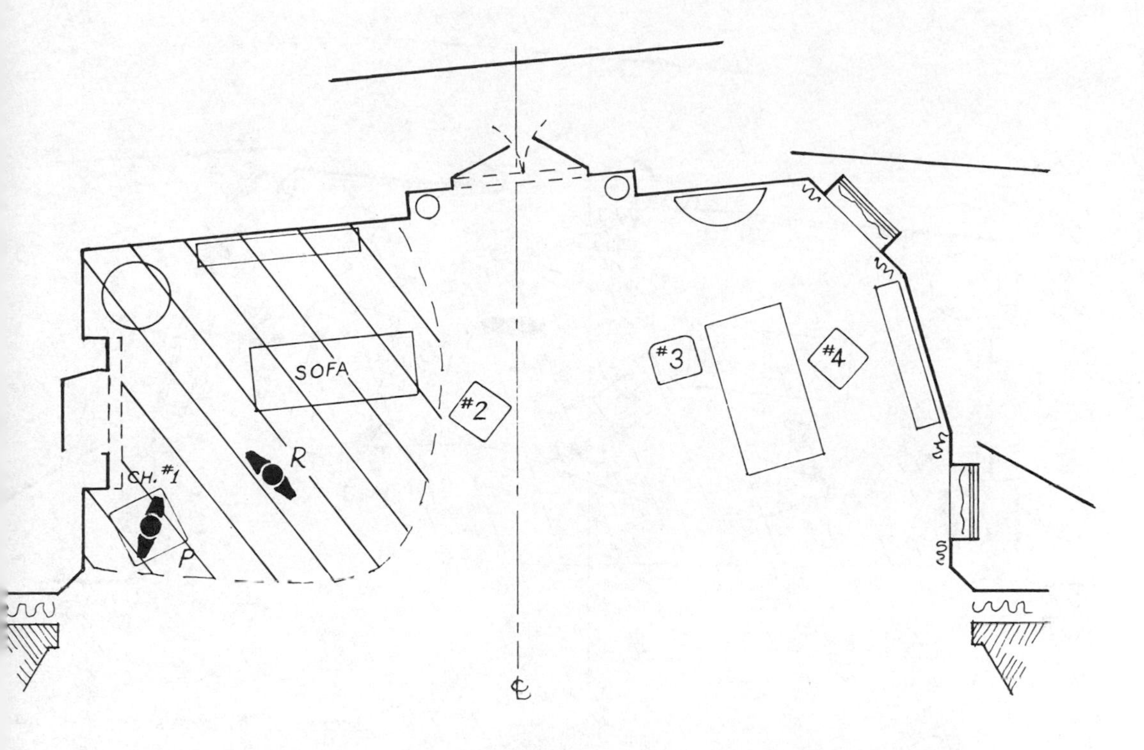

FIGURE 7 SECOND PART OF SCENE 3

end of the room, Ridgeon would be forced to make a long cross to the desk and back again to Paddy and the business is not important enough to warrant such an extended move. So the theory of placing this scene entirely on the social side must bow to expediency.

There are other arguments in favor of starting the scene on the left. When Ridgeon pontificates on the importance of his findings, he does so as a scientist. This leads to the choice of chair 3 for Paddy at the opening of the scene, with Ridgeon above or at left of the desk. Both may cross right at a later moment to be determined. It would do no harm to postpone Paddy's seating himself in the arm chair until the announcement of Walpole's entrance. So, the rough pattern would put Ridgeon on Paddy's right as the scene begins. He would then cross to the desk for the pamphlet, play above or below it, as the director sees fit, then cross right with Paddy following. Ridgeon could then sit on the couch to let Paddy cross unobstructed above it to his chair (1).

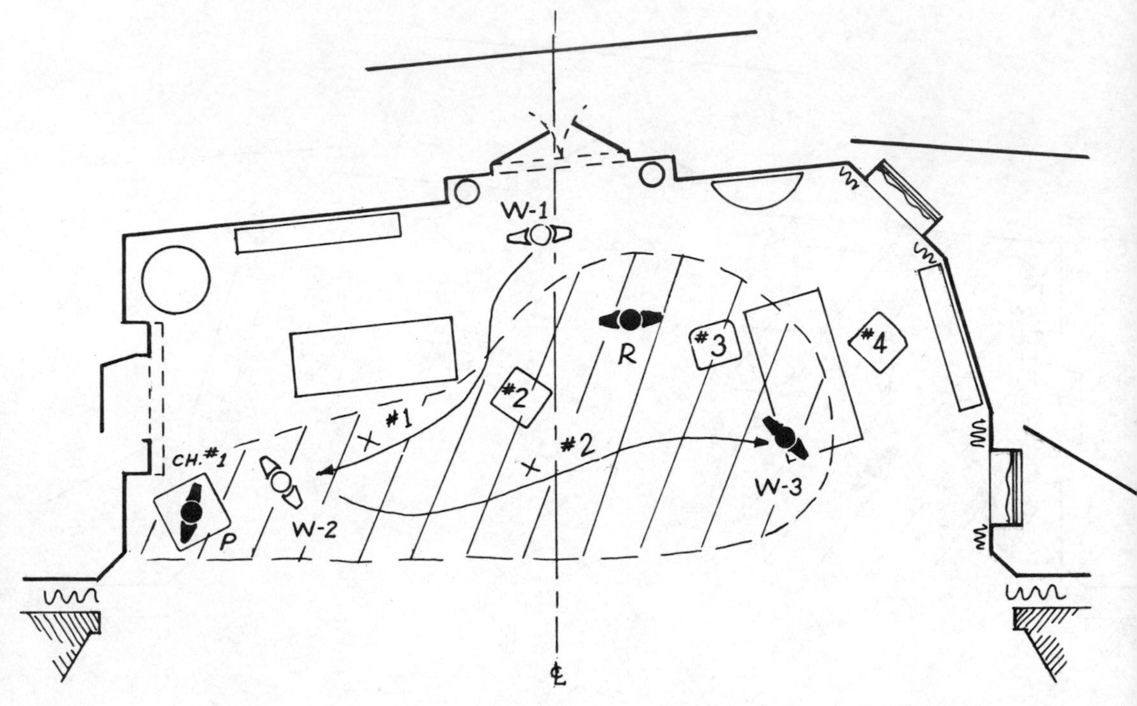

FIGURE 8 FRENCH SCENE 4

Scene 4. Walpole, Paddy, Ridgeon.

At this point, the director knows he must establish a locus for two more enterers after Walpole: Blenkinsop and B.B. He has already settled in his mind that Blenkinsop's relationship to Ridgeon is such as to keep him outside the circle of warmth and congeniality that spreads outward from the fireplace. Chair 2 is the likeliest choice for Blenkinsop, so Walpole must not be seated there. Decided, also, is the plan for keeping B.B. on the move. Yet Walpole, too, is a dynamic, rushing personality, hardly the type to come to rest early in his scene. It follows that he should be kept on his feet until at last he is forced to give way to the stronger personality, B.B. The text requires Walpole to cross to Paddy to shake hands with him. After Paddy rebuffs him on the subject of the "cabinetmaker's jimmy," he continues the scene with Ridgeon. Shaw has him sit on the couch just before B.B.'s entrance, but this presents awkward complications in the present setting. Two more characters must enter and go right or center, with ensuing crowding of that area. To relieve the possibility of future pressure on the right, Walpole may sit briefly on the sofa, then rise and cross to chair 3 or to the downstage edge of the desk, and sit there. He thus provides a good target for B.B. to cross to after the latter greets Ridgeon and Paddy, and serves also a useful function as anchor man in the composition.

Scene 5. Bloomfield Bonington, Walpole, Paddy, Ridgeon.

B.B. will move over the entire stage from Paddy on the right to Walpole on the left. To give him a series of dominant positions, Ridgeon should be seated on the left of the couch, so B.B. can be placed above it and to the right for an least one speech, and then be free to circulate in the upstage areas without being masked by a figure standing below him. If it seems advisable to bring B.B. to a halt somewhere, as when he expresses his views that germs, like men, imitate each other, the right arm of the couch provides the best choice.

FIGURE 9 FRENCH SCENE 5

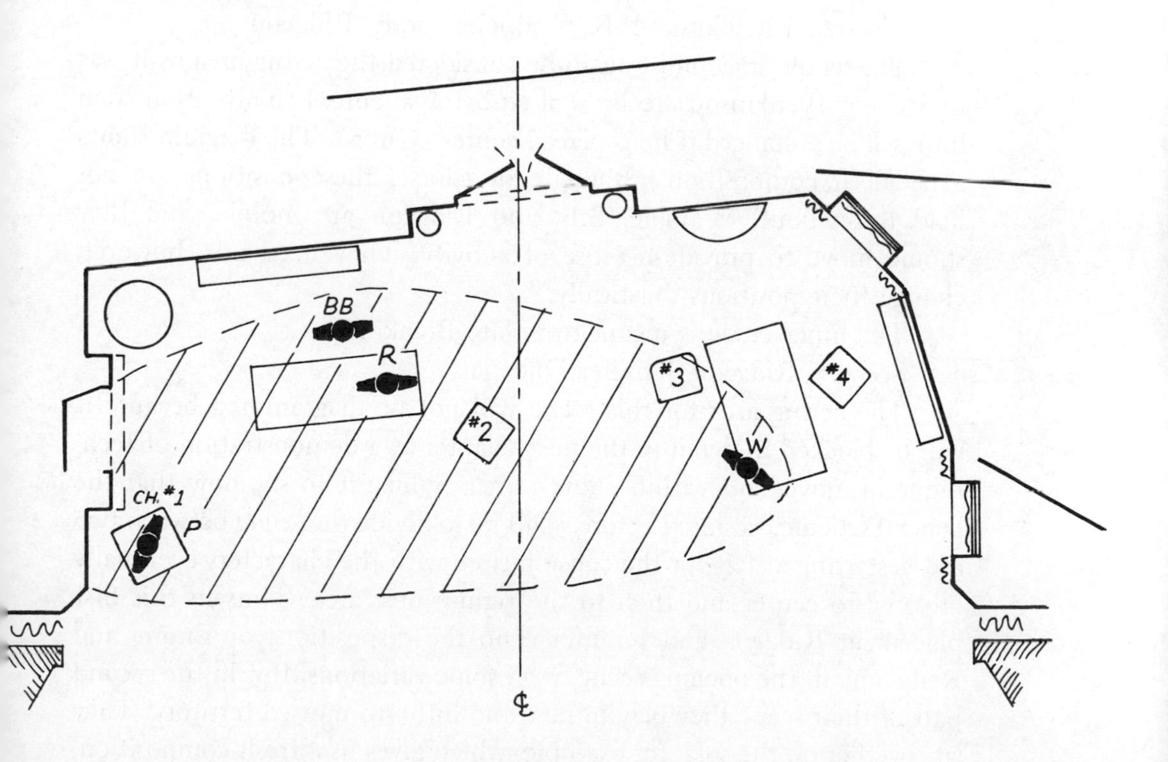

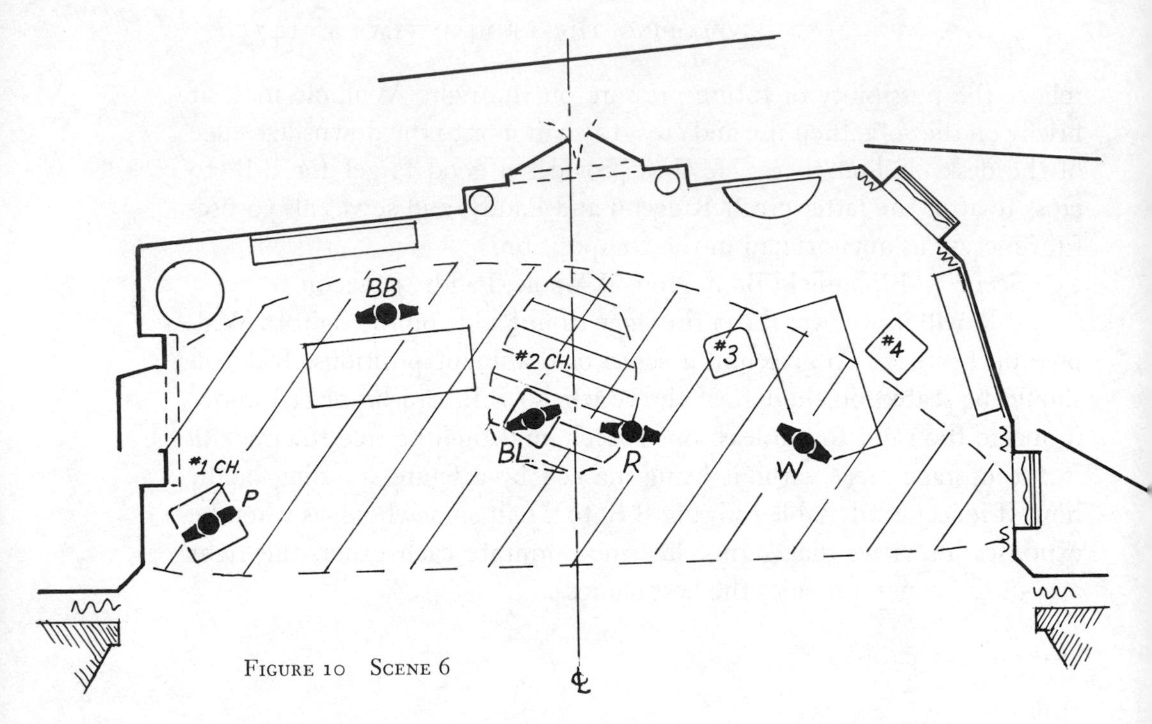

FIGURE 10 SCENE 6

Scene 6. Blenkinsop, B.B., Walpole, Paddy, Ridgeon.

The whole stage must again be considered the acting area as it was in Scene 5. Blenkinsop's feelings of embarrassment when attention is on him will be enhanced if he is placed center (Ch. 2). The diagram shows a balanced composition, although, of course, these positions are not held throughout. Walpole, B.B. and Ridgeon are mobile, and they should move to provide a sense of activity. They need not, however, change their positions drastically.

The inner circle is meant to isolate Blenkinsop.

Scene 7. Ridgeon, Jennifer Dubedat.

The acting area for this scene will not be diagrammed because it will be blocked in detail in the next chapter as a demonstration of technique in movement within a given area. Suffice it to say now that the general scheme, as stated before, shall be to divide the scene between two areas, starting at left for the consultation, with the characters eventually crossing to center and then to the right-center area. Thus in this first placement Ridgeon and Jennifer echo the dispositions of Emmy and Redpenny in the opening scene, with some variations. But in the second part of their scene they play in new and hitherto unused territory. They sit together on the sofa, for example, which gives us a fresh composition.

FIGURE 11 *The Doctor's Dilemma,* ACT I. AMHERST MASQUERS' PRODUCTION, DESIGNED BY CHARLES E. ROGERS

To sum up: By preselecting acting areas in some such fashion as has been described, guided by a basic tenet which establishes the *modus operandi,* the director aligns reasons for placement with basic meaning of the scenes and design of the setting, and by careful consideration insures a change of visual focus for each French scene.

If the process strikes some as mechanical, they should be reminded that it is just as basic to the director's craft as detailed plans are for a building prepared by an architect. Few in that profession, be it observed, make a practice of going to the site, studying the topography, the building materials as they lie strewn about, and then and there start deciding what sort of edifice shall be built.

Once the general acting areas have been fixed, the next step is to particularize exactly the moves of characters within each area.

Exterior Ground Plans

As in the case of interior settings, the director tries to establish in all exterior settings as many different acting areas as there are French scenes except that in exteriors the areas are not usually defined by objects of furniture but by trees, stones, other natural objects, or by varying levels. In a chairless and benchless outdoor set, the director must find appropriate substitutes for furniture in stumps, outcroppings of rock, or "natural" platforms. In bare formalized exteriors, he must sometimes depend entirely on steps and ramps to provide places on which the characters can sit down.

An exterior set also presents its own unique problem of geography. The ground plan must be made to conform logically to whatever lines in the text refer to specific locations in the topography. This is a problem to be solved either by the designer or the director, or jointly by both. But it is so often involved with and determined by the placement and movement of actors that the director with full knowledge of his craft usually prefers to tackle it himself, at least initially. His rough notes can be an invaluable guide to the designer.

Playwrights usually specify the number of required entrances in an exterior set and sometimes indicate their location, but few supply maps of the surrounding countryside. This the director should do for himself by following textual clues. A character, for instance, may have to point out a distant landmark or indicate a specified place offstage; another may make reference to compass directions. For the sake of consistency and to enable the audience to locate such indicated places easily, the director must decide where they are to be, and then point to their direction on the ground plan.

If a fundamentally sound approach to the problems of working up an exterior ground plan based on deductive reasoning can be established for a specific case, it should be possible to apply such a system or such a procedure for all cases. In that spirit, let us examine the outdoor setting in Maxwell Anderson's well-known *Winterset* and see what can be done with it.

We begin, as always, with the author's description:

> The scene is the bank of a river under a bridgehead. A gigantic span starts from the rear of the stage and appears to lift over the heads of the audience and out to the right. At the left rear is a wall of solid supporting masonry. To the right an apartment building abuts against the bridge and forms the right wall of the stage with a dark basement window and a door in the brick wall. To the left and in the foreground, an outcropping of original rock makes a barricade behind which one may enter through a cleft. To the rear, against the masonry, two sheds have been built by waifs and strays for shelter. The river bank, in the foreground, is black rock worn smooth by years of trampling. There is room for exit and entrance to the right around the apartment house, also around the rock to the left. A single lamp is seen at the right, and a glimmer of apartment lights in the background beyond.[1]

Procedure.

First pencil in the four entrances as the playwright has described them:

1. A door to the basement apartment right, labeled R. 1E. (right first entrance) on the ground plan.
2. A passage through a cleft in the rock down left. (L. 1E.)
3. Another around the rock up left. (L. 2E.)
4. An entranceway upstage of the apartment house right. (R. 2E.)

Two questions arise at once. Where, exactly, do these last three passageways lead to offstage? Where are places to sit down? As for the

[1] The directions "left" and "right" in the text have been reversed here in order to use them in terms of stage left and stage right, meaning to the left and right of an actor onstage facing the audience.

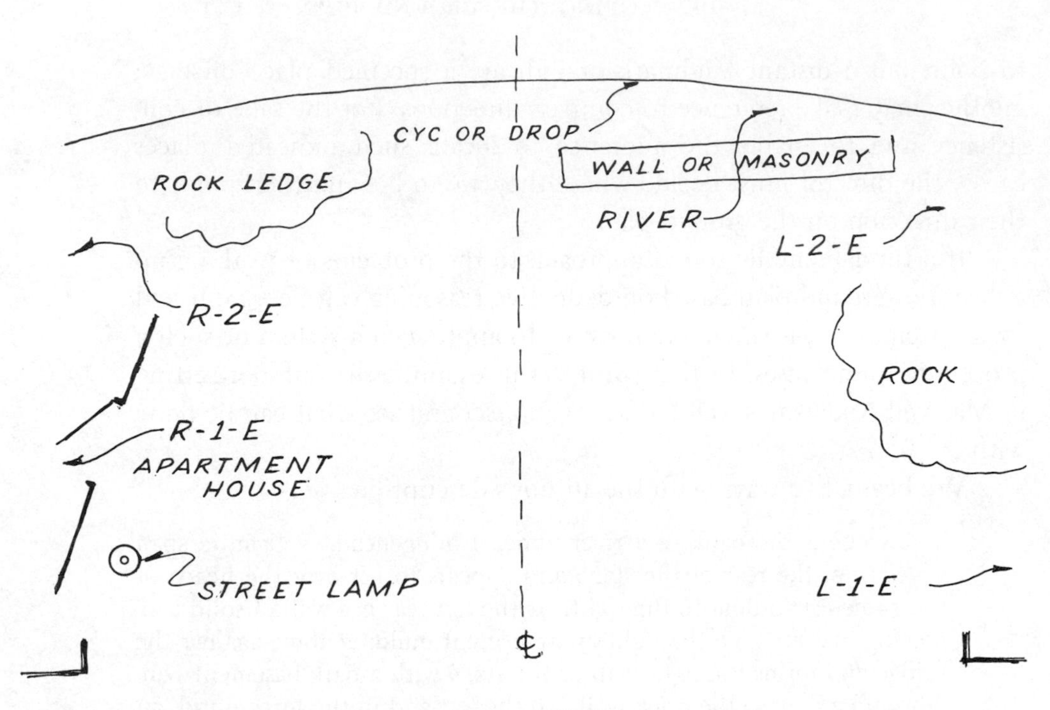

FIGURE 12 ANDERSON'S GROUND PLAN FOR *Winterset*

latter, there is only one mentioned in the printed directions. Miriamne is said to be seated on "the ledge at the rear of the apartment house" at the start of I, 3. This is up right, but probably too far upstage to make it the most desirable spot for the love scenes which are to come. There are several such scenes, and some are so protracted that additional seats must be found in other areas unless the lovers are to be forced to play them all in that one place, or standing up, which would be unfortunate.

For the moment let us accept the fact that Miriamne is seated up right on the ledge, that is to the left of R. 2E. The Hobo enters "through the rocks on the other side," that is from the left. After some business at the Apple Woman's hut, whose location is as yet undetermined, he curls up on his makeshift bed "in the corner," which can only mean up left.

The Two Girls then enter from "around the apartment house" (R. 2E.). They have to cross the stage and will go out on the left. Just before exiting they see "the sleeping Tramp," which produces a comment from one of them. The Judge then enters from "the right" and goes "up to the Hobo" to speak to him.

If the director tries to follow these directions he is at once in difficulty. The Hobo sees Miriamne when he enters from the left and she sees him, but there is no suggestion that she is seen by the Girls or by Judge Gaunt. Indeed she must not be seen by him. But if she is sitting up right and Gaunt enters up right he must cross directly below her to reach the Hobo, left. Reason dictates that Judge Gaunt, having lost his way and being anxious to discover where he is, will naturally speak to the first person he meets, in this case it is the Hobo. But the way his entrance is arranged he practically bumps into Miriamne and, ignoring her completely, crosses the stage to get to the Hobo. It strains credulity to use his condition of dazed bewilderment as an excuse for not noticing her. A correction in blocking is demanded. It would be far better to have Gaunt enter left, for the Hobo is on that side, then Gaunt will see him before he sees Miriamne.

If such reasoning is correct, which entrance shall Gaunt use, the upstage or the downstage? The upstage, of course. Otherwise, if he enters below the Hobo and on the same side, the audience will have at best a fleeting glimpse of his profile before he must turn upstage to address the Hobo. And he will have to make an awkward wide circular cross before he can get into a reasonably strong position from which to play the scene.

Yet it is not so simple as all that. The geography of the set argues against this arrangement. For according to the script, if R. 2E. leads to a street and L. 1E. also leads to a street, then L. 2E. must lead to the river. And what has Judge Gaunt been doing down there?

If reason is to prevail L. 2E. is not the right place for Gaunt's entrance after all.

A better solution is to obey the text and let Gaunt enter from the same common public-street entrance from which the Girls appeared (R. 2E.) but to change Miriamne's position to get her out of Gaunt's crossing path.

Before this can be done, the entrances themselves must be restudied.

As observed in Figure 12, there are two general entrances on the left and one upstage on the right. There is another exit right into the apartment house, but it is for private use. The absence of a general entrance down right makes it difficult to provide any logical reason for allowing the movement to flow in that direction (D R). Characters crossing that way are going nowhere except towards the dead end of the corner of the tenement, and have no "geographical" reason for doing so. Furthermore, all traffic moving to exit right will have to turn upstage, causing very weak exits on that side.

To remedy this two adjustments must be made in the playwright's plan: another entrance must be provided down right, and a place further downstage must be provided for Miriamne to sit down.

The ground plan is then revised as shown below.

Where shall Miriamne seat herself? The entrance to the basement tenement must go down a flight of steps. Some sort of railing will be needed around this entranceway, and it is in conjunction with this railing, specifically, and preferably downstage of it, that a box or a bench may be placed. Since Miriamne and Mio shall probably sit on it together, it must be wide enough to accommodate two people.

Now we have a bench on which Mio and Miriamne can play the love scene in the final act when they huddle together under the solitary street lamp that protects them from the surrounding dark. But if that

FIGURE 13 DIRECTOR'S REVISION OF PLAN

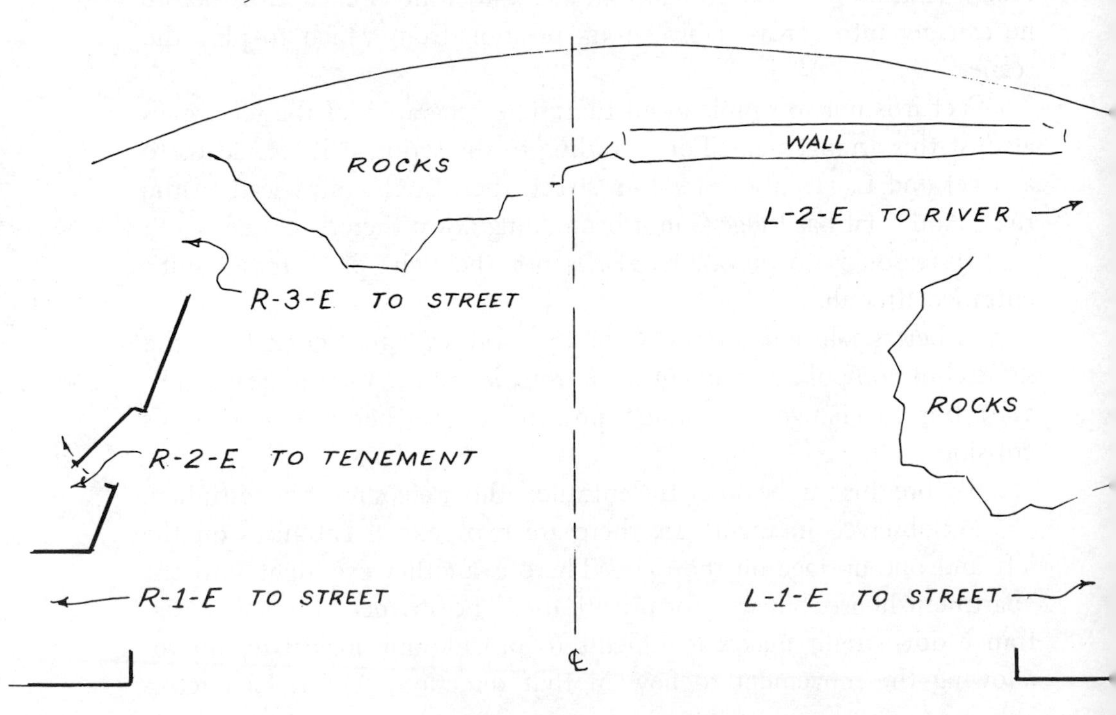

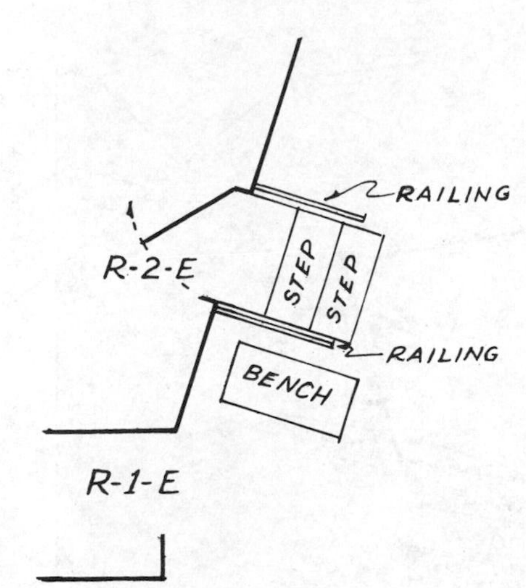

FIGURE 14 POSITIONING OF BENCH

lamp is to light them as they are seated down right center, it must be sited in relation to some sort of street. It will be remembered that Gaunt has a line which places the light "near the alley": "There, where the street lamps are." This gives us still another reason for an entrance down right. Trock can use it with advantage in Act III as an exit, permitting Mio to be placed in a strong position facing the audience as he sees him "hunched under the warehouse eaves." This is far better than having Trock exit up right, for then Mio would have to keep looking off upstage in order to refer to him and thereby lose audience contact.

Because it is important to suggest that the action passes in an isolated and depressed pocket overwhelmed by the bridge that towers above, it might be feasible to make the added entrance a ramped sidewalk which the characters could descend on entering. Another railing below this would give something for the characters to lean against as they played on the ramp or below it. Such a railing would isolate the area below the ramp from the rest of the set, and provide a good vantage point from which Mio and Carr could watch the dancers in I, 3 without being covered or pushed out of the picture—which would be the case if they stood upstage.

Moreover, since the downstage face of the apartment wall must abut the upstage edge of the ramp, the wall itself can now be brought further downstage, helping to close the set and adding to the feeling of

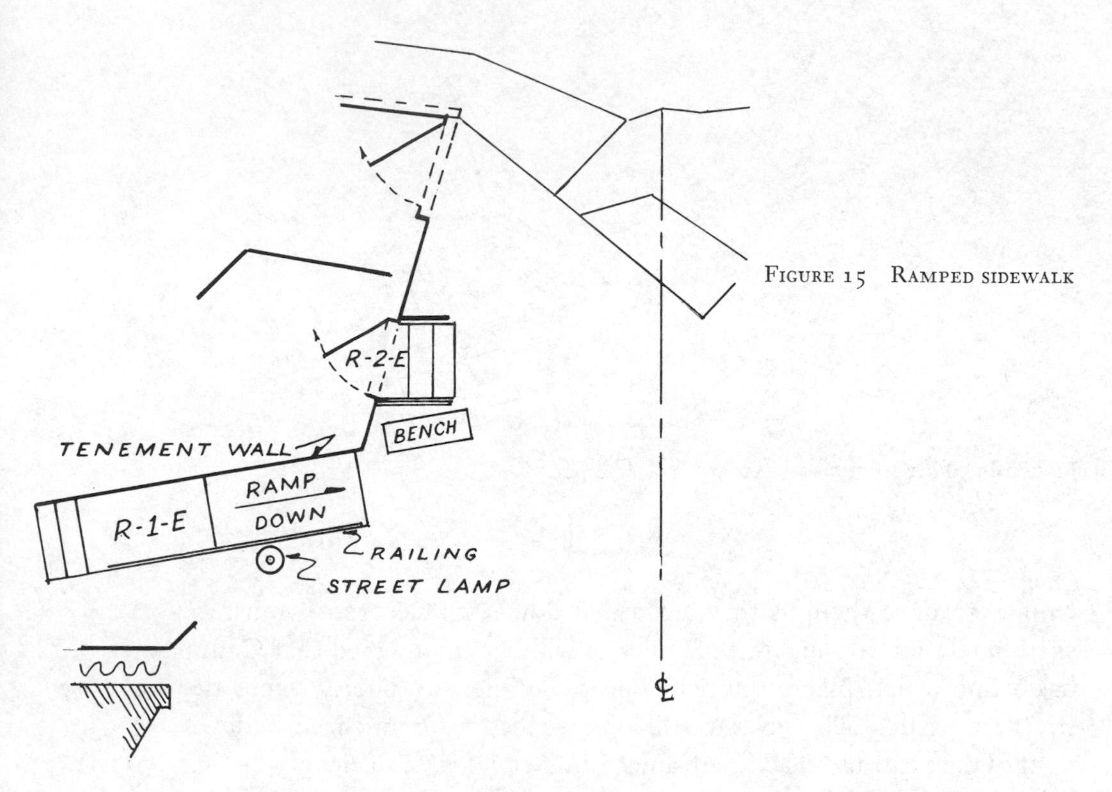

FIGURE 15 RAMPED SIDEWALK

restriction and confinement it should convey. All these matters supply powerful arguments for the inclusion of the down right entrance.

There is one drawback, though it can easily be remedied. Four exits at each corner of the stage make it more difficult to suggest in Act III that Mio is sealed up in this pocket with little chance to escape from the lurking Trock and his henchmen. A third gunman must be called in to stop the fourth exit, while Trock himself can guard the important one down right. Esdras can then enter down right when he is "kicked back" by Trock, and when Mio refers to Trock's presence off there he can speak the lines toward the front within an angle formed by his body and the tormentors.

What references in the text can be found that will help establish the geographical surroundings?

One occurs in the opening scene that contains Trock's ironic apostrophe to Manhattan. The scene is brief and somewhat static. Trock should be given a strong entrance and one that allows him some movement. The city he addresses should therefore be located toward the side opposite his entrance. The rocks and the river entrance have already been established up left, so Brooklyn, later pointed to by Mio, can be across the river, offstage up left. Manhattan is therefore in the opposite direction, or down right. Logic decrees that Trock should enter L. 1E, cross the stage, and deliver the key speech from a quarter-front right position in the down right area.

Geographically, the plan now looks something like this:

R. 1E is now designated as the "alley" and leads up the ramp to the warehouse and a street.

R. 3E is a wide path on the near side of the river bank, leading off to a street. It is the strongest entering point.

L. 1E is now thought of as part of the architecture of the bridge structure, possibly an arched masonry entrance. It leads to a street and will serve as a general entrance. Since Lucia must trundle his barrel organ offstage and on again, and inasmuch as the sloped rocky defiles of the two upstage entrances and the ramped exit down right are difficult to negotiate, L. 1E must be wide enough to let him get the barrel organ through easily.

L. 2E leads off and down to the river bank.

FIGURE 16 GEOGRAPHY OF PLAN

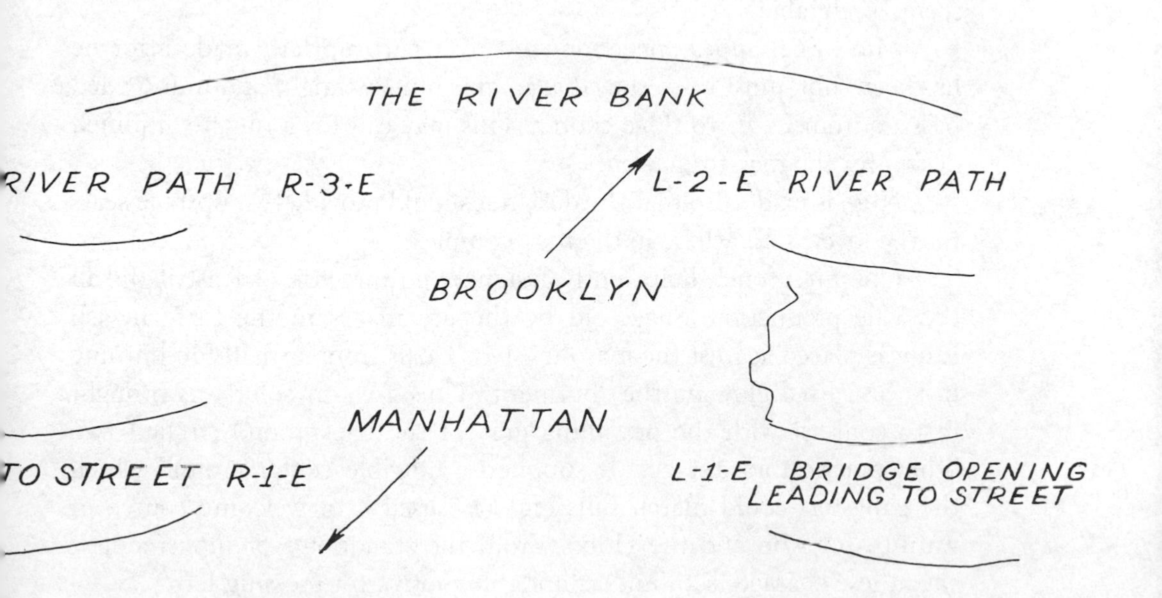

A few more details remain to be settled before the rough plan can be completed.

Two small structures are called for, Piny's hut and Lucia's shelter which houses the barrel organ. But these, no matter how cramped and unobtrusive, must occupy valuable upstage acting space. They may also clutter up the set. It may be possible to eliminate one of them altogether and hide the other so as to show only the door. There is space enough for a door and suggestion of a shack front between the upstage edge of the tenement house and R. 3E. So let us put it there. This forces Piny and Lucia to enter from what may appear to be a shared abode, but no harm is done if this suggests that these two characters live on somewhat more intimate terms than the script indicates.

Because the entrance is used only once there is no need to designate it by a separate number in the ground plan.

An emphatic spot must be found from which the Radical can harangue a crowd. The audience has to be able to see him over the heads of onlookers, yet he must be in a place far enough away from the Policeman to be able to elude his grasp when ordered to descend. Anderson has the Radical "leaping on the base of the rock at stage left." But these rocks are so far upstage that if he stood on them the Policeman and the crowd would be forced into weak positions as they sought to observe him. A level step or platform on bridge masonry farther downstage seems preferable.

Mio's final appearance from the river path up left, made after he has been shot, must be so staged as to give him a straight and unimpeded passage from L. 2E to stage center. This may call for a much simplified design for the rock formation.

Note is made also that the designer should provide two upstage seats for the lovers somewhere in the rock complex.

One final touch helps both designer and director, at least it did in the Yale production. Suggested by the fire-images in the text, an ash can was placed against the masonry, left. Coals from a small fire burning in it cast a red glow on the abutment. Thus a warm color was brought in to contrast with the prevailing gray of the background. It had two other practical advantages. It supplied a tangible center around which the gangsters could match bills and was used as a welcome source of warmth for Mio and the Hobo. From the standpoint of movement it gave these characters an understandable motive for crossing left.

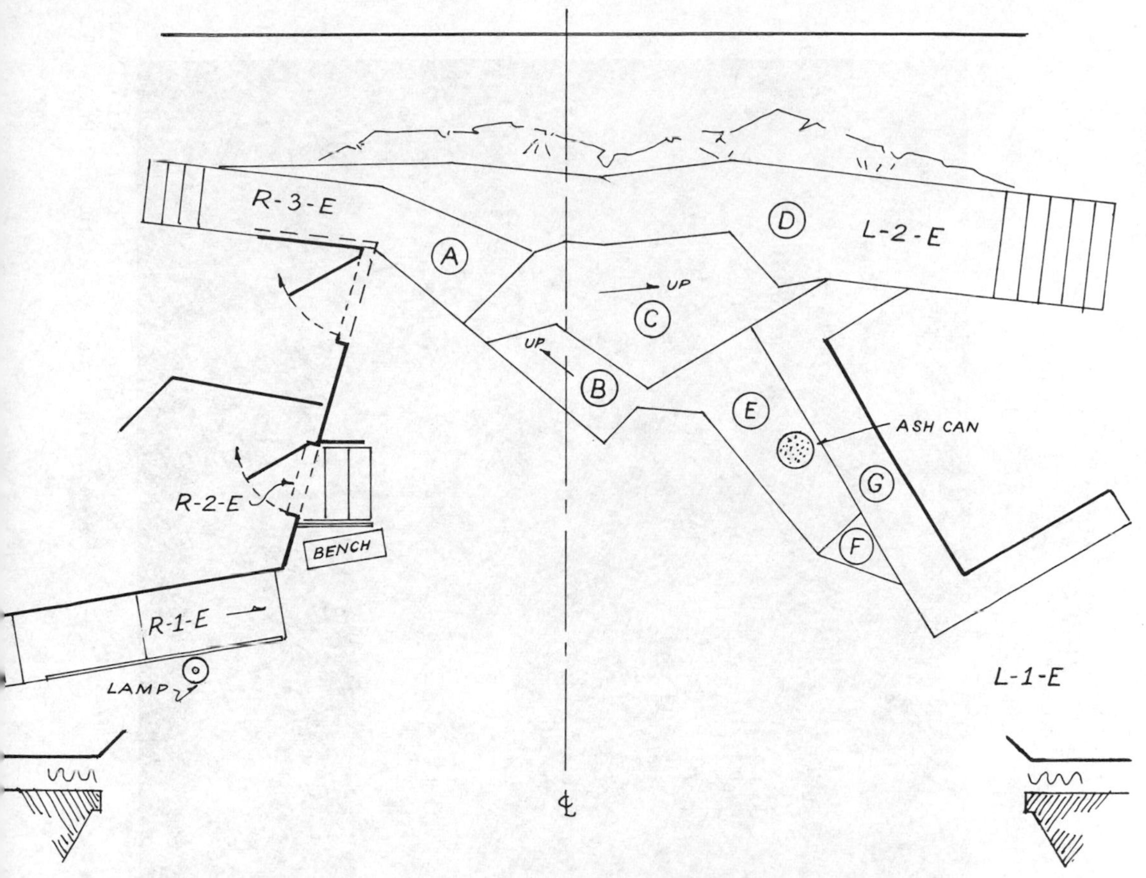

FIGURE 17 DESIGNER'S GROUND PLAN

From these hints, ideas, and rough sketches, the designer can proceed to refine and develop his ground plan. Here is the completed plan as used in the Yale Drama School production designed by Philip Eck.

The plan is seen to have four strategically situated seating places: the bench (D R C), large enough for two people; seat C (U C), eighteen inches high; seat D (U L C), thirty-six inches high: and seat F (D L C), twenty inches high. There are three objects which the actors can use to lean or rest against: the railing downstage of the ramp on the right, the guardrail downstage of the basement entrance; and the ledge of bridge masonry left. Also included is a small slightly inclined level rock ramp (U L C) B, upon which Judge Gaunt falls when pushed by the Policeman (I, 3).

All seats, ramps, entrances, and platforms are identified by numbers or letters on the ground plan. They should be similarly designated in chalk or paint on the stage floor when the ground plan is laid out on it.

Figure 18 *Winterset*, Act I, Scene 1. Yale Drama School production, designed by Philip Eck

CHAPTER EIGHT

The Director Blocks the Play

> Since things in motion sooner catch the eye
> Than what not stirs.
>
> *Troilus and Cressida* III, 3

Having made tentative selections of the acting areas for each French scene, the director now proceeds to place characters in position and set them in motion. In order to make sure he knows where they are at any given moment, he uses golf tees, chessmen, pushpins or some such device appropriately labeled with the initials of characters they are to represent, and moves these around on the scaled ground plan.

Each move is recorded in the prompt book or on the margin of the printed text if it is wide enough. To save space and time the moves and directions are usually expressed in symbols.

SUGGESTIONS FOR PROMPT-BOOK NOTATIONS:

X—cross
X3—cross three steps
XRT—cross right to table
XDL sofa—cross to down left of sofa
♂—rise
⊕—sit
⊕ Ch. 3—sit in chair 3
Ex R. 1E.—exit right first entrance
⤻—turns
P—pause

General Principles

Key scenes may be blocked first, then subordinate or transitional scenes. But if the work of preselecting the various acting areas has been sound, the director may prefer to start at the beginning and go straight through the act to maintain continuity of build in the sequence of French scenes.

The nature of the relationship between characters at the start of the scene must be clearly established first. Initial placement will tend to be meaningless unless it is based on an idea that gives expression to what the characters are to each other. Their attitudes, dispositions, or views of life may be identical and harmonious, or they may be utterly opposed. The original placement and, later, the moves must reflect that identity or that opposition.

Differences and likenesses between characters may be social, religious, philosophical, moral, psychological, ethnic, political, or emotional. They may hinge on age, sex, belief, appetite, basic interests and aims or, indeed, upon anything that brings people together or sets them apart. Whatever the relationship it must be deduced from the director's grasp of the play's theme, the essential subject, the nature of the characters, and their specific personal objectives.

What they are to each other at the start must then be contrasted with what they are to each other at the end. Then every step in the gradual evolution of that change or development must be noted and understood, whether subtle or overt, before anything is set down in the prompt book.

Only then is the director prepared to maneuver the figures in the allotted stage space with any sort of confidence, for the chief justification for moving them at all is to *illustrate* in action whatever psychological or other motion the dramatist provides in the words. It is the only way he can reach the one objective from which no director can legitimately escape, and that is to make every move suggest, point, or clarify every nuance of the interactions between characters, and to do it in a manner so clear and direct that an observer who could not hear the lines being spoken would still be able to follow the scene's basic idea by sight alone.

It does no damage to this contention to admit that some directors block entirely by instinct or by hunch, without being conscious of the operation of a guiding intellectual principle, and sometimes with acceptable results. But again, the theatre is a self-conscious art which deals for the most part in preordained effects, whether these be to alienate the audience or draw them into the life on the stage. If ever a method of communication needed superintendence to achieve its conscious goals, and to do so by the exercise of logic and common sense working to achieve the ideas set forth in a reasoned out plan, it is the theatre. One of the reasons why the theatre has ceased to be the popular art it once was is in the present failure to accept it as a relatively uncomplicated medium, and in the proneness on the part of some directors to dodge the normal routine and, yes, drudgery connected with their basic preparations, in the hope that success will be reached by attention solely to ineffabilities, the mystical and the superconscious aspects of the art. And all this when what is needed is a cool downgrading of the director's function to what it really is on its most effective level, a craft.

Contrary to much that has been said about the involvements and intricacies of character relationships in drama, it is not necessary in the staging to muddle and complicate them by oversubtlety. An audience responds favorably and quickly to simple, even obvious, ideas provided they are expressive of the principal differences or interconnections between personalities. And they respond because they can understand. The director's key in blocking may be nothing more complex than some physical arrangement or disposition which shows one character dominant and another subordinate. Opposition can be indicated merely by separating characters in space with a piece of furniture between them, and as differences between them are resolved they can be brought closer together. Whatever metaphor the director chooses to portray vividly the meaning of a scene must be graspable, like Bobby Lewis' staging of a moment in *My Heart's in the Highlands,* when the assembled crowd, listening below to the lovely notes of the trumpet above, were arranged to resemble a tree lifting up its leaves to be watered.

In a large theatre, in the majority of cases, the broad brush stroke counts more than the hairline pen scratch. Tiny variations in the composition, overdelicacy and smallness of gesture, faintly shaded facial expression or vocal inflection are all too easily lost as the action streams by, although they may be appreciated in a studio theatre or in any medium that uses the close-up.

Arrangement should follow the sense, however elementary it may seem. In Molnar's *Liliom,* for instance, Julie pleads with her husband not to go out with his confederate, Sparrow. Sparrow, on his part, is urging Liliom to join him in a robbery. Liliom, of course, is the center of interest with Julie and Sparrow in contention trying figuratively to pull him in opposite directions. The placement must mirror this situation literally.

Liliom, therefore, is rightly seen as the middle figure in the group, with Julie and Sparrow on opposite sides of him. Variations in movement of the figures in this basic triangular pattern must be made to reflect the progress of the struggle, with Liliom inclined first toward one and then the other until the end when Sparrow prevails and Liliom leaves with him, with Julie isolated and alone on her side of the stage.

Or, again, in a scene involving several characters where the dramatic progression moves from conflict to harmony the director may rely simply on the straightforward pictorial device of keeping the characters in a deliberately unrhythmic or unsymmetrical composition until the moment of reconciliation when it is made to assume a balance, just as a composer may construct a series of dissonances which finally terminate in a tonic chord.

Almost everyone is familiar with the old saw that there should be no move on the stage without a purpose. But one should add that it is never difficult to find *some* purpose for every action. The problem is to find a purpose that counts, one that directly contributes to the audience's understanding of what the scene means, while seeming at the same time to be in character and natural for the person making it.

Among all the many reasons for moves, the following are the most common, as well as the most acceptable:

1. Practical necessity.
2. For emphasis.
3. To express emotion.
4. To please the audience's sense of rhythm, proportion or balance, or to jar it.
5. To illuminate or underline character relationships.
6. To combat audience inattention.

Practical moves are those demanded by the text. A character must reach a door before he can open it, or a lamp before he can light it. These are the moves required by stage business. Under this heading also come moves which enable a character to get close enough to the person he is addressing to make sure the audience is not led to think that he is speaking to someone else; moves to relieve dangerous overcrowding in any acting area; to prepare for a prescribed action, as a cross to place a character near an exit point before his final line; and moves of adjustment designed to open up a group so that a particular actor may be seen and heard—unmasking.

The more ingenious and inventive a director can be in discovering reasons to make a move seem plausible, the better the results will be. The motivation may be supplied simply by planting a useable property such as a cigarette case, a purse, or a wine glass in a strategic place and then having the character cross to pick it up.

Moves for purposes of emphasis are both useful and commonplace. It should be noted, however, that while it is generally true that a moving actor catches attention, he does so only by contrast with those who remain still. He who remains motionless while others are moving about is also made emphatic by contrast. A movement designed to draw the audience's eyes may be a gesture, a turn of the head, the twitch of an eyebrow, or a cross. The nature and force of the move will be graduated, of course, to produce the explicit degree of emphasis desired.

One of the director's chief tasks is to search the text for "lines of motion." These are lines, phrases, or even single words which seem to him to demand some expenditure of physical energy as they are spoken and which appear to be more telling, more positive, more emphatic, and more "in character" with a move than without one.

A character may move for no other reason than that his emotion propels him. In such a case he does not necessarily have to have a specific object to cross to. If an intensification of emphasis or emotion is desired, a strong movement will be used, that is, a move toward the audience or from a weak to a strong area of the stage. Such moves add to speech an extra "carry," the weight of which is determined by the amount of physical energy expended in the move. Conversely, a weak move away from the audience or toward the wings disengages attention, subdues the "carry," and can even suggest an ironic contradiction between what a character is saying and what he really means.

When physical expressions of feelings—hatred, love, anger, hope, fear and the like—are called for, the director must decide whether they can be projected by body attitude alone, with the actor in repose but using his face and hands as instruments, or by the addition of some kind of physical effort involving a move. Not to be overlooked is the third possibility of using a combination of both.

Once the intensity of feeling has been fixed, the actor's muscular response may be modified or enlarged to correspond to the situation and the character's attitude toward that situation.

Vocal emphasis, the intensity with which the lines are spoken on a move, may be even more important than the move itself for conveying the desired degree of feeling. A move must always be considered in conjunction with speech. It is possible, for instance, to weaken a strong cross by an unemphatic delivery of the line accompanying it, or to strengthen a weak cross by punching the words. The combination of voice and movement that may be used simultaneously to express nuances of emotion and emphasis are infinite, and work on them constitutes one of the most laborious and fascinating aspects of rehearsal.

It goes without saying that hackneyed postures, gestures, or body attitudes should be avoided. Ham acting is nothing more or less than the employment of clichés, like placing the palm of the hand on the lifted forehead to express grief or thumping the breast to express passion. In good acting the emotion proceeds from a sense of truth within the actor himself about the emotion he is supposed to convey. He cultivates this sense by exploring the nature of the character in depth and then by attempting to transfer his own emotional reactions to the part into terms that seem to fit the character best. What he does with his body has to proceed from what he discovers about the character as he plunges deeply into the life of the role, and to do this he must call into play all his resources of concentration, understanding, and imagination. It is a major directorial function to guide and encourage the actor toward his understanding of the part and after that toward outward expressions of feelings that are true, original, and personal to the character's individuality while avoiding the stereotypes. More will be said about this relationship between the actor and the director in Chapter Ten.

Esthetic moves are those used to balance or to unbalance the stage picture, or to render the visual effects of a scene more striking by applying the rules of composition, balance, proportion, and symmetry to the arrangements of figures.

But for more than any other single reason, characters move in order to convey to the audience by their physical placement in relation to each other the nature of their psychological relationship to each other, as has already been pointed out. In any scene one character or set of characters may be dominant, and others subordinate, or one may be dominant at the start and subordinate at the end, or none may dominate. Either their aims and interests are parallel and similar or they are opposed and dissimilar. Or characters may begin a scene in harmony and end opposed, or begin opposed and end in harmony. Let me repeat once more that with the exception of certain covering or transitional scenes in which no dominance or subordination is present or is of minor importance, the director's craft, or part of it at any rate, is mainly applied to making certain that the juxtapositions of the characters reveal and point up as exactly as possible what they are to each other. This is known as picturization or pictorial dramatization.

Every play, indeed every scene, presents its own problems of how much movement and what types of movement are appropriate for it. The nature of the scene and the director's understanding of the people in it are his only reliable guideposts. Generalizations are not very helpful and always self-evident, as the one which asserts that there should be more movement in farce than in tragedy.

What the director must do is to decide *before* he starts blocking how much movement seems to be indicated for a particular scene, and then proceed to abide by that decision. If he makes mistakes, he can correct them in rehearsal, and if need be make further corrections in the light of what he sees in the first performances. Waning audience attention, a display of boredom or indifference, or unwanted audience reactions may in part be attributed to too much movement, or too little. The director must test variations until he has corrected at least this one cause of public indifference.

A good director never relaxes his efforts to undertake a continuing critical estimation of the length of time a stage picture may be held before it begins to lose interest for him. When that point is reached something must be done, for the chances are good that the audience's attention will begin to wane at that point also.

It should be unnecessary to note that there must be consistency between the number and type of moves a character makes and his age, temperament, physical condition, and state of feelings.

Before proceeding to demonstrate how a director might set about this blocking task, it may be advisable to set down some fundamental principles of stage movement. These are not "rules" but rather notations of what has been proved effective in practice:

1. Unless there are persuasive reasons for not doing so, an actor should cross, sit, or rise as he speaks his own lines.

2. An actor speaking should cross downstage of another rather than upstage. Otherwise, the upstage crosser momentarily hides himself behind the actor crossed, while the actor being crossed loses contact with the crosser. The former must either make a full turn upstage to follow the crossing character with his eyes, or swivel his head awkwardly through a 180-degree arc or make a full turn in order to maintain his position and still follow the cross. Exceptions to this practice are common, and many fast upstage crosses have been made without undesirable results.

3. In an ensemble scene those characters in whom dramatic interest subsides should be moved into downstage areas and toward the sides, otherwise they are in danger of being masked by the active characters and must awkwardly keep adjusting their positions to the right and left in order to be uncovered.

4. No move should be made on a plot line, particularly if it is essential that the audience hear it to keep abreast of the story, although it is common to provide a move immediately preceding the plot-line.

5. No actor should be placed upstage of another without cause. The actor downstage of another must turn up and away to play the scene, with resulting loss of contact and "carry" with the audience.

6. When an important character makes an entrance, it is usually desirable to let him cross well into a center area. His approach should not be blocked by furniture or by other characters in the entranceway.

7. A character leaving the scene should be given a position near enough to his point of exit so that he can finish his final line on the cross, unless for some reason the silence of the ensuing pause in the time between the end of the line and the exit is desirable. The stagy effect produced when, after a cross toward an exit, an actor makes a final onstage turn to finish his exit line should normally be shunned.

8. If a play is written in verse or strongly rhythmic dialogue, timing of the steps of a cross should be made to coincide with the rhythm beat of the lines unless a broken or arrhythmic effect is preferred.

Two Characters in a Single Scene

Purposeful blocking may be illustrated by following the text of two scenes, each involving two characters; the first from the final French scene of Act I of *The Doctor's Dilemma,* and the second from Maxwell Anderson's *Winterset.* In *The Doctor's Dilemma* the problem is concentrated in the space of a few pages, while in *Winterset* it extends over the whole play, a condition requiring considerably more preplanning on the part of the director.

Here again is the now-familiar ground plan of Act I of *The Doctor's Dilemma:*

FIGURE 19 DESIGNER'S PLAN
The Doctor's Dilemma

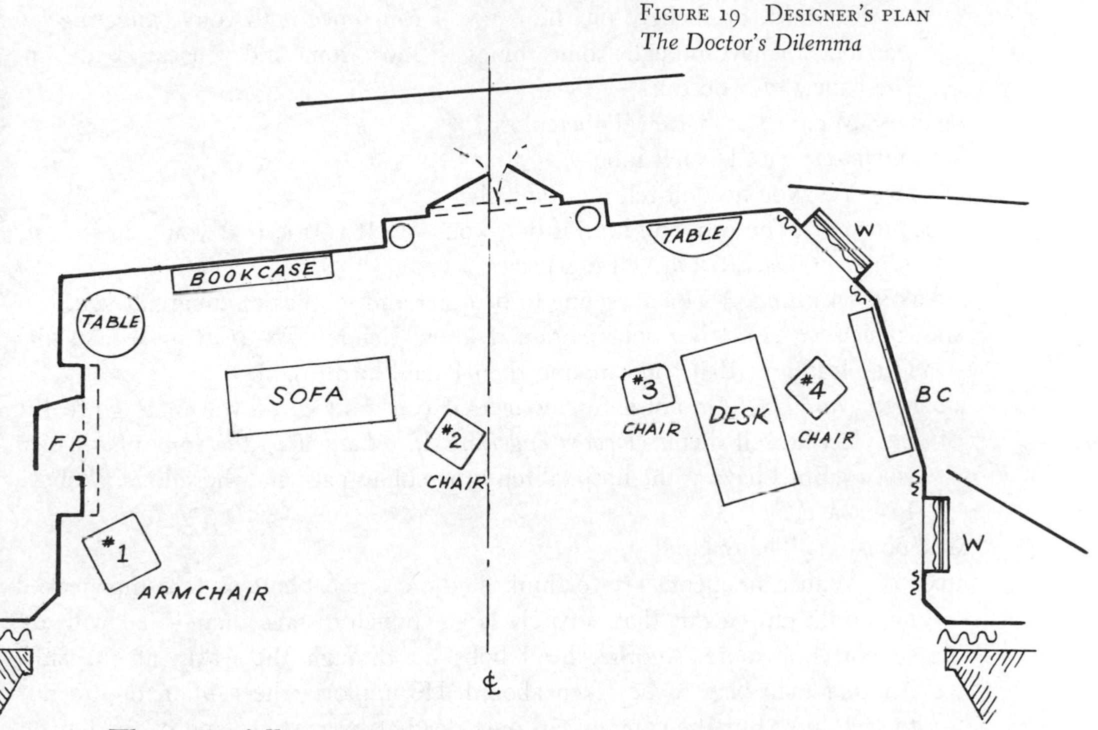

The scene follows:

EMMY: (*announcing*) Mrs. Doobidad (*Ridgeon leaves the glass and goes to the writing-table*).

The lady comes in. Emmy goes out and shuts the door. Ridgeon, who has put on an impenetrable and rather distant professional manner, turns to the lady, and invites her, by a gesture, to sit down on the couch.

MRS. DUBEDAT: (*in low urgent tones*) Doctor—

RIDGEON: (*curtly*) Wait. Before you begin, let me tell you at once that I can do nothing for you. My hands are full. I sent you that message by my old servant. You would not take that answer.

MRS. DUBEDAT: How could I?

RIDGEON: You bribed her.

MRS. DUBEDAT: I—

RIDGEON: That doesn't matter. She coaxed me to see you. Well, you must take it from me now that with all the good will in the world, I cannot undertake another case.

MRS. DUBEDAT: Doctor: you must save my husband. You must. When I explain to you, you will see that you must. It is not an ordinary case. He is not like anybody in the world: oh, believe me, he is not. I can prove it to you: (*fingering her portfolio*) I have brought some things to show you. And you can save him: the papers say you can.

RIDGEON: What's the matter? Tuberculosis?

MRS. DUBEDAT: Yes. His left lung—

RIDGEON: Yes: you needn't tell me about that.

MRS. DUBEDAT: You can cure him, if only you will. It is true that you can, isn't it? (*In great distress*) Oh, tell me, please.

RIDGEON: (*warningly*) You are going to be quiet and self-possessed, aren't you?

MRS. DUBEDAT: Yes. I beg your pardon. I know I shouldn't—(*Giving way again*) Oh, please, say that you can; and then I shall be all right.

RIDGEON: (*huffily*) I am not a curemonger: if you want cures, you must go to the people who sell them. (*Recovering himself, ashamed of the tone of his own voice.*) But I have at the hospital ten tuberculous patients whose lives I believe I can save.

MRS. DUBEDAT: Thank God!

RIDGEON: Wait a moment. Try to think of those ten patients as ten shipwrecked men on a raft—a raft that is barely large enough to save them—that will not support one more. Another head bobs up through the waves at the side. Another man begs to be taken aboard. Hc implores the captain of the raft to save him. But the captain can only do that by pushing one of his ten off the raft and drowning him to make room for the newcomer. That is what you are asking me to do.

MRS. DUBEDAT: But how can that be? I don't understand. Surely—

RIDGEON: You must take my word for it that it is so. My laboratory, my staff, and myself are working at full pressure. We are doing our utmost. The treatment is a new one. It takes time, means, and skill; and there is not enough for another case. Our ten cases are already chosen cases. Do you understand what I mean by chosen?

MRS. DUBEDAT: Chosen. No: I can't understand.

RIDGEON: (*sternly*) You must understand. You've got to understand and to face it. In every single one of those ten cases I have had to consider, not only whether the man could be saved, but whether he was worth saving. There were fifty cases to choose from; and forty had to be condemned to death. Some of the forty had young wives and helpless children. If the hardness of their cases could have saved them they would have been saved ten times over. I've no doubt your case is a hard one: I can see the tears in your eyes (*she hastily wipes her eyes*): I know that you have a torrent of entreaties ready for me the moment I stop speaking; but it's no use. You must go to another doctor.

MRS. DUBEDAT: But can you give me the name of another doctor who understands your secret?

RIDGEON: I have no secret: I am not a quack.

MRS. DUBEDAT: I beg your pardon: I didn't mean to say anything wrong. I don't understand how to speak to you. Oh, pray don't be offended.

RIDGEON: (*again a little ashamed*) There! there! never mind. (*He relaxes and sits down.*) After all, I'm talking nonsense: I daresay I am a quack, a quack with a qualification. But my discovery is not patented.

MRS. DUBEDAT: Then can any doctor cure my husband? Oh, why don't they do it? I have tried so many: I have spent so much. If only you would give me the name of another doctor.

RIDGEON: Every man in this street is a doctor. But outside myself and the handful of men I am training at St. Anne's, there is nobody as yet who has mastered the opsonin treatment. And we are full up. I'm sorry; but that is all I can say. (*Rising*) Good morning.

MRS. DUBEDAT: (*suddenly and desperately taking some drawings from her portfolio*) Doctor: look at these. You understand drawings: you have good ones in your waiting-room. Look at them. They are his work.

RIDGEON: It's no use my looking. (*He looks, all the same.*) Hallo! (*He takes one to the window and studies it.*) Yes: this is the real thing. Yes, yes. (*He looks at another and returns to her.*) These are very clever. They're unfinished, aren't they?

MRS. DUBEDAT: He gets tired so soon. But you see, don't you, what a genius he is? You see that he is worth saving. Oh, doctor, I married him just to help him to begin: I had money enough to tide him over the hard years at the beginning —to enable him to follow his inspiration until his genius was recognized. And I was useful to him as a model: his drawings of me sold quite quickly.

RIDGEON: Have you got one?

MRS. DUBEDAT: (*producing another*) Only this one. It was the first.

RIDGEON: (*devouring it with his eyes*) That's a wonderful drawing. Why is it called Jennifer?

MRS. DUBEDAT: My name is Jennifer.

RIDGEON: A strange name.

MRS. DUBEDAT: Not in Cornwall. I am Cornish. It's only what you call Guinevere.

RIDGEON: (*repeating the names with a certain pleasure in them*) Guinevere. Jennifer. (*Looking again at the drawing.*) Yes: it's really a wonderful drawing. Excuse me; but may I ask is it for sale? I'll buy it.

MRS. DUBEDAT: Oh, take it. It's my own: he gave it to me. Take it. Take them all. Take everything; ask anything; but save him. You can: you will: you must.

REDPENNY: (*entering with every sign of alarm*) They've just telephoned from the hospital that you're to come instantly—a patient on the point of death. The carriage is waiting.

RIDGEON: (*intolerantly*) Oh, nonsense: get out. (*Greatly annoyed*) What do you mean by interrupting me like this?

REDPENNY: But—

RIDGEON: Chut! can't you see I'm engaged? Be off.

(*Redpenny, bewildered, vanishes.*)

MRS. DUBEDAT: (*rising*) Doctor: one instant only before you go—

RIDGEON: Sit down. It's nothing.

MRS. DUBEDAT: But the patient. He said he was dying.

RIDGEON: Oh, he's dead by this time. Never mind. Sit down.

MRS. DUBEDAT: (*sitting down and breaking down*) Oh, you none of you care. You see people die every day.

RIDGEON: (*petting her*) Nonsense! it's nothing: I told him to come in and say that. I thought I should want to get rid of you.

MRS. DUBEDAT: (*shocked at the falsehood*) Oh!

RIDGEON: (*continuing*) Don't look so bewildered: there's nobody dying.

MRS. DUBEDAT: My husband is.

RIDGEON: (*pulling himself together*) Ah, yes: I had forgotten your husband. Mrs. Dubedat: you are asking me to do a very serious thing.

MRS. DUBEDAT: I am asking you to save the life of a great man.

RIDGEON: You are asking me to kill another man for his sake; for as surely as I undertake another case, I shall have to hand back one of the old ones to the ordinary treatment. Well, I don't shrink from that. I have had to do it before; and I will do it again if you can convince me that his life is more important than the worst life I am now saving. But you must convince me first.

MRS. DUBEDAT: He made those drawings; and they are not the best—nothing like the best; only I did not bring the really best; so few people like them. He is twenty-three: his whole life is before him. Won't you let me bring him to you? won't you speak to him? won't you see for yourself?

RIDGEON: Is he well enough to come to a dinner at the Star and Garter at Richmond?

MRS. DUBEDAT: Oh yes. Why?

RIDGEON: I'll tell you. I am inviting all my old friends to a dinner to celebrate my knighthood—you've seen about it in the papers, haven't you?

MRS. DUBEDAT: Yes, oh yes. That was how I found out about you.

RIDGEON: It will be a doctors' dinner; and it was to have been a bachelors' dinner. I'm a bachelor. Now if you will entertain for me, and bring your husband, he will meet me; and he will meet some of the most eminent men in my profession: Sir Patrick Cullen, Sir Ralph Bloomfield Bonington, Cutler Walpole, and others. I can put the case to them; and your husband will have to stand or fall by what we think of him. Will you come?

MRS. DUBEDAT: Yes, of course I will come. Oh, thank you, thank you. And may I bring some of his drawings—the really good ones?

RIDGEON: Yes. I will let you know the date in the course of tomorrow. Leave me your address.

MRS. DUBEDAT: Thank you again and again. You have made me so happy: I know you will admire him and like him. This is my address. (*She gives him her card.*)

RIDGEON: Thank you. (*He rings.*)

MRS. DUBEDAT: (*embarrassed*) May I—is there—should I—I mean—(*she blushes and stops in confusion*).

RIDGEON: What's the matter?

MRS. DUBEDAT: Your fee for this consultation.

RIDGEON: Oh, I forgot that. Shall we say a beautiful drawing of his favorite model for the whole treatment, including the cure?

MRS. DUBEDAT: You are very generous. Thank you. I know you will cure him. Good-bye.

RIDGEON: I will. Good-bye. (*They shake hands.*) By the way, you know, don't you, that tuberculosis is catching. You take every precaution, I hope.

MRS. DUBEDAT: I am not likely to forget it. They treat us like lepers at the hotels.

EMMY: (*at the door*) Well, deary: have you got round him?

RIDGEON: Yes. Attend to the door and hold your tongue.

EMMY: That's a good boy. (*She goes out with Mrs. Dubedat.*)

RIDGEON: (*alone*) Consultation free. Cure guaranteed. (*He heaves a great sigh.*)

ANALYSIS OF THE SCENE

What is the relationship between the two characters at the start of the scene? Mrs. Dubedat, "in mortal anxiety," is in the position of supplicant, appealing desperately to Ridgeon to use his medical discovery to save her husband's life. Ridgeon, coldly detached, is like a rock on which her fervent and pathetic appeals at first make no impression. Mrs. Dubedat is the active force and motivator at this point. It is a scene of persuasion, with Jennifer's will projected in assault on Ridgeon's adamantine position, a position conditioned by his irritation at Mrs. Dubedat's persistence in seeking the interview and the real problem of his being unable to accept any more than the specific quota of patients on whom to use his serum. She conducts the struggle; Ridgeon resists. Notice the course of conflict between them.

Before Jennifer can speak two words Ridgeon confronts her with a refusal: "Before you begin, let me tell you that I can do nothing for you." This is followed almost immediately, after a passing reference to Emmy which serves as a link between the scene of transition and this one, by a second refusal, ". . . with all the good will in the world, I cannot undertake another case."

This negative attitude is maintained through Ridgeon's detailed explanation of the circumstances which make it impossible to listen to Mrs. Dubedat. His refusal is repeated yet a third time with, "You must go to another doctor." Shaw has correctly had Ridgeon state his ample reasons for not complying with her wishes *before* the counterattack, only then does he allow Jennifer to show Ridgeon proofs of her contention that her husband should be saved.

Two lapses in Ridgeon's adopted attitude of huffiness and heartlessness should be noticed:

> I am not a curemonger: if you want cures, you must go to the people who sell them. (*Recovering himself, ashamed of the tone of his own voice.*) But I have at the hospital ten tuberculous patients whose lives I believe I can save.

And a moment later the crack in his armor is shown again:

RIDGEON: I have no secret: I am not a quack.

MRS. DUBEDAT: I beg your pardon: I didn't mean to say anything wrong. I don't understand how to speak to you. Oh, pray don't be offended.

RIDGEON: (*again a little ashamed*) There! there! never mind. (*He relaxes and sits down.*) After all, I'm talking nonsense: I daresay I am a quack, a quack with a qualification. . . .

These mitigating lapses in his posture of aloofness reveal Ridgeon's humaneness and a wry humor. They are enough to make his ultimate capitulation seem probable. And they serve another purpose. The very fact that he is unapproachable and testy evokes much sympathy for Jennifer. Her apology, when it should be Ridgeon's for his stern treatment of her, her admission of wrong when it is he who is behaving rudely, melts us, as it eventually melts him and makes him want to kick himself for behaving like a prig.

Still another rejection is forthcoming:

RIDGEON: And we are full up. I'm sorry; but that is all I can say. (*Rising*) Good morning.

The lines of the relationship seem to have been fixed by this fourfold iteration, although Ridgeon's "I'm sorry" marks a difference between his original curt dismissal and this touch of forbearance, however slight. Ridgeon's move to rise appears put to a period on the interview, and this, of course, represents the lowest point in the scene as far as the fortunes of Jennifer are concerned.

The dramatic reversal starts immediately, when in final desperation Jennifer shows him the portfolio (another motive for a movement). But, for good measure, Shaw has the doctor make one last effort of resistance: "It's no use my looking."

Ridgeon is overwhelmed by the beauty of the drawings and certainly not unaffected by Jennifer's portrait among them. His fond savoring of the music of her name, "Guinevere. Jennifer.", represents the extent of his entrancement and gives us a foretaste of the coming capitulation. Shaw extracts more fun from the situation by delaying the denouement with Redpenny's entrance and his now mistimed announcement of the concocted emergency.

The delay in reaching the scene's conclusion shows Shaw at his craftsmanlike best. First, Ridgeon consents to the possibility that he may take Dubedat's case even though it means sacrificing the life of one of the patients already chosen. He then agrees to let his fellow doctors judge the case after they have had an opportunity to meet Louis. This is followed by his willingness to accept as his fee a drawing of Jennifer, showing his gallantry as well as his admiration for the subject. His positive affirmation that he will cure her husband ends the scene.

The burden of action is thus seen to be:

1. A woman seeking to bend a man to her will.
2. The man equally determined not to be bent.
3. Variations in the type of assault made by the protagonist, all equally unsuccessful.
4. Introduction of a "persuasive element."
5. The sudden reversal of the antagonist's position, and his capitulation.
6. The woman succeeds in getting what she wants.

Note should be made that the reversal is accomplished with the use of concrete, visible stage properties (portfolio and drawings) around which the conversation is made to center. Business with the pictures can be exploited to make the reversal telling. Since it is an important part of the director's craft to deal effectively with properties, he will want to settle the matter of that portfolio at the very start. Obviously Jennifer cannot hold such a bulky object in her hands or in her lap for the whole scene. Nor can she be so forward as to place it on top of all the scientific papers and paraphernalia that cover the desk. The portfolio has to become the center of interest at the exact point when the antagonist begins to retreat from his position, actually shaken from it by his realization that the husband Jennifer is pleading for is a rare genius, capable of creating exquisitely beautiful things. The drawings, of course, are the tangible means by which he is drawn to this discovery.

Remembering the scenic concept which divided the room into two parts, this scene of reversal can be made pictorially vivid if the characters can now move from the scientific side to the social side, illustrating the change in Jennifer's status vis-à-vis Ridgeon and his new regard for her.

What is the business? Shaw has Ridgeon rise to effect Jennifer's dismissal on his "Good morning." Jennifer then takes the drawings from the portfolio, shows them to him, and he in turn takes one of them to the window in order to be able to see it in better light. He then "looks at another and returns to her." He asks her if she has a drawing of herself, and she gets that one from the portfolio and shows it to him. He looks again at the drawing as he repeats her name, upon which Redpenny interrupts.

When Ridgeon rises to indicate that the interview is concluded, it is presumed that Jennifer is seated in the chair at right of the desk. Naturally, Ridgeon has been seated behind the desk. Now if the portfolio has been placed beside Jennifer's chair, on the floor, she can reach for it from her chair and hand it to Ridgeon across the table without rising. But the moment and the business itself are so important that Jennifer would never remain seated for it. She must rise. If Ridgeon takes the drawing from across the desk, he needs only to turn left slightly to get the light from the window on it. But it is readily seen that this involves only a series of small, insignificant moves without changing positions materially. They are certainly not emphatic or *long* enough to add to the excitement of Ridgeon's discovery of Dubedat's genius. This is sufficient reason for rejecting the site beside Jennifer's chair as the best place for the drawings to be laid. This leaves chair 2 in the center as the most likely place for them. They can be deposited there by Jennifer on entrance. Her cross on "Look at these" changes the focus of attention by opening the view on a new acting area, nearer the social side. Ridgeon can now be drawn toward the center, attracted there and away from his stand on the left of the desk by what he sees. His subsequent substantial cross to the window and return to Jennifer's left, which must follow the move, supply the motion that is needed to match his growing excitement. Then, as he gazes intently at the next picture she hands him, he can cross her to below the sofa. This carries him well into the social side, and gives Jennifer a natural motive for following in order to show him the picture of herself.

What the director has done here is to settle the fairly simple matter about where Jennifer should put the portfolio down, but on the way to a solution of that problem has been able to pencil in the rough blocking of the whole reversal scene.

Now let us return to the scene's beginning. First question: should Ridgeon be sitting down or standing up when Jennifer enters? The answer is found in a glance at their attitudes. Jennifer is agitated, he composed. Planted solidly in his chair, Ridgeon would certainly present a figure of ensconced authority, but the picture would also carry the suggestion that he was prepared to admit the interview and was even awaiting it, when the intent of the scene is to show him as actively rejecting the notion of an interview. If he stands, however, his physical presence continues to be formidable, perhaps even more so than if seated. In this position there is no suggestion that he is ready to sit back and listen to Jennifer's case. It seems best then to have both characters standing at the start, Ridgeon below the downstage edge of the desk and Jennifer to the right of chair 3, right of the desk.

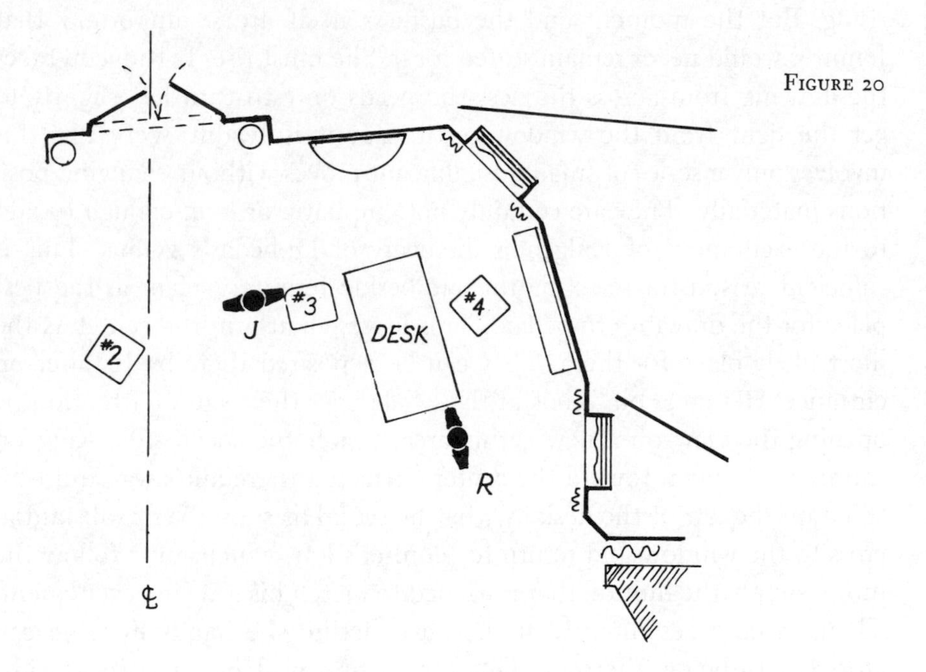

FIGURE 20

MRS. DUBEDAT: (*In low urgent tones*) Doctor—

RIDGEON: (*curtly*) Wait. Before you begin, let me tell you at once that I can do nothing for you. My hands are full. I sent you that message by my old servant. You would not take that answer.

MRS. DUBEDAT: How could I?

RIDGEON: You bribed her.

MRS. DUBEDAT: ^ I—

^ *With a half-gesture toward the door.*

RIDGEON: That doesn't matter. She coaxed me to see you. Well, you must take it from me now that with all the good will in the world, ^ I cannot undertake another case.

^ *A move is called for here, but if Ridgeon crosses up toward his chair the weak move will belie his resolution. One step D L may be enough.*

MRS. DUBEDAT: Doctor: you must save my husband. ^ You must.

^ *Any opportunity to express Mrs. Dubedat's anxiety and agitation by movement must be seized. Immobility would belie her tension. Ridgeon's previous slight move away is reason enough for her to step toward him, to below Ch. 3. Because of the circumscribed playing area, previously set around the desk, the moves have to be small, a step or two at most.*

FIGURE 21

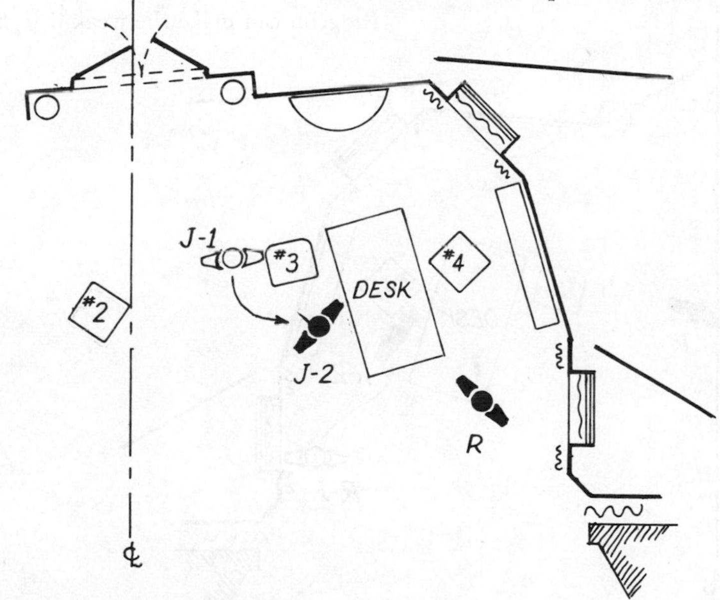

When I explain to you, you will see that you must. It is not an ordinary case, not like any other case. He is not like anybody in the world: ^ oh, believe me he is not. I can prove it to you: (*fingering her portfolio*) ^

^ *The repetition is intensive.* X1 *L to D R corner desk.*

^ *As previously noted, Mrs. Dubedat has left*

the portfolio on Ch. 2 at C. There is much to be said for not bringing it into prominence before the psychological moment of the climax which comes later. It will be enough for her now to X2 *backward (toward R) with a half-turn and gesture toward Ch. 2 to indicate the portfolio. This will free the area below the desk slightly and allow Ridgeon to move in a moment.*

MRS. DUBEDAT: (cont'd) I have brought some things to show you. And you can save him: the papers say you can.

RIDGEON: What's the matter? Tuberculosis?

For all Ridgeon's rigidity, he is at least curious enough about her husband's case to ask what it is. To make the inquiry properly casual, Ridgeon can make the weak X *to below Ch. 4.*

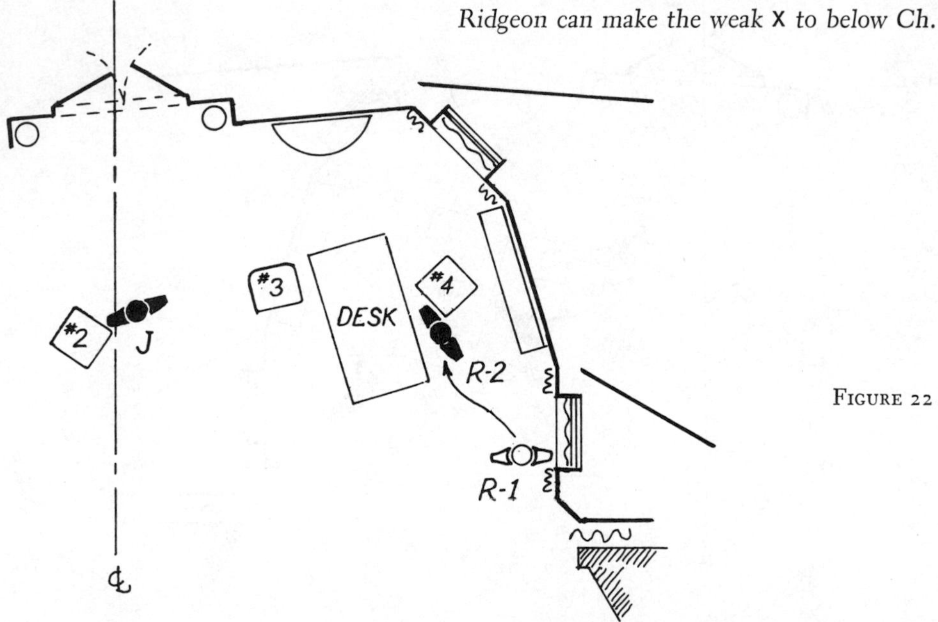

FIGURE 22

MRS. DUBEDAT: Yes. His left lung—

RIDGEON: Yes: you needn't tell me about that. ^

^ *This is, on second thought, a better moment for Ridgeon's* X *than the one above. His inquiry about the nature of Dubedat's ailment could be purely instinctive, a doctor's natural reaction. If he moves now to below his chair, the* X *will have in it a measure of impatient dismissal and a suggestion that he is a little annoyed that he had asked the question. This change is noted in the prompt book.*

MRS. DUBEDAT: You *can* cure him, if only you will. It is true that you can, isn't it? (*In great distress*) Oh, tell me, please.

She beseeches him pitifully. Another move is desirable. But she has already confronted Ridgeon from below Ch. 3 and she cannot X *to* D L *which would put her below him. The director chooses a* X *to above Ch. 3, giving her the advantage of the upstage position for a moment.*

FIGURE 23

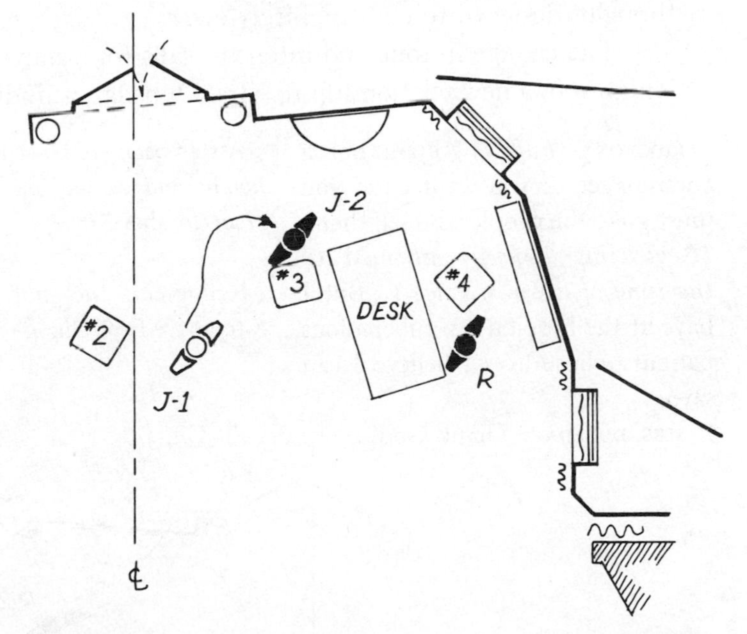

RIDGEON: You are going to be quiet and self-possessed, aren't you?

Typical British antipathy toward a "scene."

MRS. DUBEDAT: Yes. ‸[1] I beg your pardon. I know I shouldn't—(*Giving way again*) ‸[2] Oh, please, say that you can; and then I shall be all right.

‸[1] *Jennifer makes an effort to control herself. She can turn away to do so,* X*ing to R of Ch. 3. But her feelings overwhelm her and so she* ‸[2] *turns left to again address him directly.*

Now, Ridgeon has three long speeches coming up, after the expression of pique in the next. It is clear that he must have the dominant position while all that Mrs. Dubedat has to do is to listen without protest or interruption. They have both been standing, and it is time to vary the picture. The director must watch, therefore, for an opportunity to seat Mrs. Dubedat since Ridgeon must be free to move for his speeches. It comes, most opportunely, on her expression of relief, "Thank God!"

As the director studies the page it becomes clear that Ridgeon's explanation of his position is divided into two parts. The first describes why it is impossible for him to take any more patients; the second explains how rigorous was the process for selecting those who were to have the opsonin treatment, and that the final say was based on Ridgeon's own evaluation of the worth of the life to be saved. The first section, spoken seriously enough to be sure, is different from the second in which the speaker is even sterner and more implacable and ends with still another thought, designed to end the interview.

The change in tone and intensity calls for a move which will place Ridgeon in a new relationship to Mrs. Dubedat, as indicated below:

RIDGEON: (*huffily*) ∧ I am not a curemonger: if you want cures you must go to the people who sell them.

∧ *A step back (to L) will let him rise to his full height and enable him to* X *next behind his chair to above it.*

(*Recovering himself, ashamed of the tone of his own voice.*) ∧ But I have at the hospital ten tuberculous patients whose lives I believe I can save.

∧ *Reinforcing the guilty feeling with a move,* X *to above R of Ch. 4.*

MRS. DUBEDAT: Thank God! ∧

∧ *Sit Ch. 3*

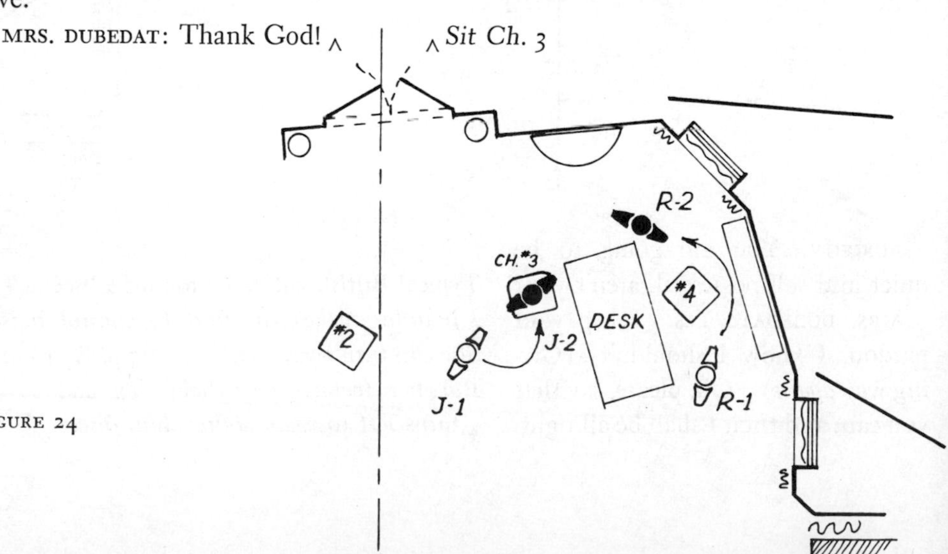

FIGURE 24

RIDGEON: ^ Wait a moment. Try to think of those ten patients as ten shipwrecked men on a raft—a raft that is barely large enough to save them—that will not support one more. Another head bobs up through the waves at the side. Another man begs to be taken aboard. He implores the captain of the raft to save him. But the captain can only do that by pushing one of his ten off the raft and drowning him to make room for the newcomer. ^ That is what you are asking me to do.

^ The word of caution designed to quell her rising hopes demands emphasis by a change of position, so Ridgeon may X *to L and above Ch. 3. This position, however, is somewhat unsatisfactory for Jennifer, though good for him. In order for her to keep him in view, she must twist her head upstage and toward the back. At the first opportunity, then, Ridgeon should* X *to a shared position. Because he has already assumed a variety of positions on her left, this time he should be brought around to her right.*

^ Because it marks the end of the speech, this seems to be the right moment for Ridgeon to X *to R of her chair.*

FIGURE 25

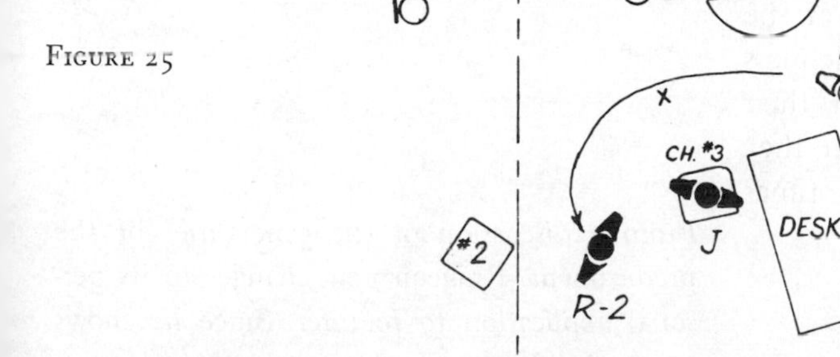

MRS. DUBEDAT: But how can that be? I don't understand. Surely—

Ridgeon's placement on her R allows her to speak this from profile position.

RIDGEON: You must take my word for it that it is so. My laboratory, my staff and myself are working at full pressure. We are doing our utmost. The treatment is a new one. It takes time, means, and skill; and there is

These short, choppy sentences give evidence of Ridgeon's nervousness and impatience. They should be accompanied by extremely small changes of position, a gesture toward his laboratory, etc. And for still another time he confronts her with refusal.

not enough for another case. ∧[1]

A change of subject follows in the same speech: to a consideration of the fact that the cases have already been chosen with care in accordance with the value of the patient. This should be prepared for at ∧[1] *with a slight* X1R *and a turn back at* ∧[2].

∧[2] Our ten cases are already chosen cases. Do you understand what I mean by chosen?

MRS. DUBEDAT: Chosen. No: I can't understand.

RIDGEON: (*sternly*) ∧ You must understand. You've got to understand and to face it. In every single one of those ten cases I have had to consider, not only whether the man could be saved, but whether he was worth saving. There were fifty cases to choose from; and forty had to be condemned to death. Some of the forty had young wives and helpless children. If the hardness of their cases could have saved them they would have been saved ten times over.

∧ *If the previous move has put him a step away to her R, he must now* X *L a step to close the gap and reinforce the urgency of the case.*

From a discussion of the generalities of the predicament, Ridgeon now changes to its personal application to Jennifer. Since he shows some consideration for her in what he says next, this slight change of approach and idea can both be suggested by a move. Perhaps a turn away and a step R will suffice, as if he were motivated by embarrassment at seeing the tears in her eyes.

RIDGEON: (cont'd) I've no doubt your case is a hard one: I can see the tears in your eyes ∧ (*she hastily wipes her eyes*) ∧ I know that you have a torrent of entreaties ready for me the moment I stop speaking; but it's no use. ∧ You must go to another doctor.

∧ *Turn R.*

∧ *A gesture as if to stop an interruption.*

∧ *This is the next to last statement of rejection. Ridgeon should break contact. To give her an*

Figure 26

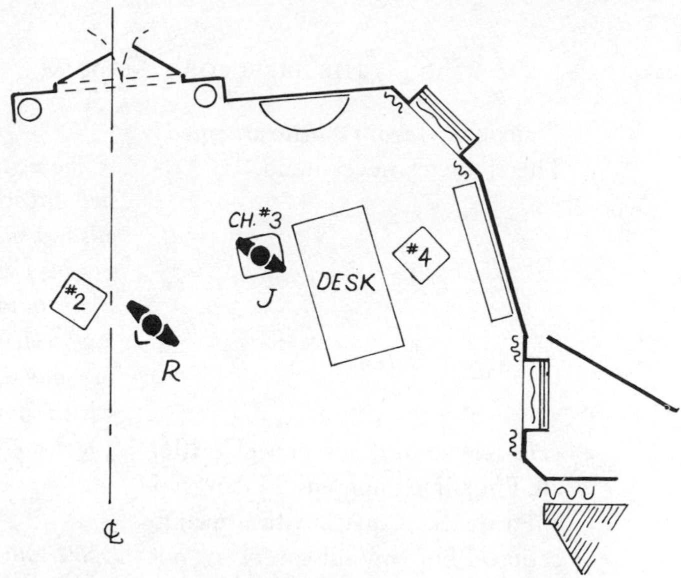

emphatic position for her next speech, he should turn down and to the R a step, possibly two.

MRS. DUBEDAT: But can you give me the name of another doctor who understands your secret?

RIDGEON: I have no secret: ∧ I am not a quack.

A minor outburst, set off by Mrs. Dubedat's inadvertent and pathetic faux pas. The contretemps gains if characters are separated even farther in space, the physical matching the psychological distance.

∧ *Ridgeon X2 D R.*

MRS. DUBEDAT: I beg your pardon: I didn't mean to say anything wrong. I don't understand how to speak to you. Oh, pray don't be offended.

Does this sentiment call for a move on her part? Possibly. She has remained in her chair for a relatively long time. But looking forward we find that Shaw wants Ridgeon to sit again in the next speech, presumably to indicate a relaxation from tension and to express shame for the sharpness of his last speech. If Jennifer rises now, she will block Ridgeon's return to his seat at the desk, at least by the upstage route; and it is too early to allow him to sit anywhere but at the desk. In view of this, Mrs. Dubedat should remain seated.

RIDGEON: (*again a little ashamed*) There! there! never mind.

A moment of consolation. He must address her directly, and because he is human, after all, and susceptible to her attractiveness, it may not be a violation of decorum if he pats her on the shoulder. He melts but slightly, however, and perhaps as if surprised at his own mellowing mood, continues the X *to his chair in what follows.*

(*He relaxes and sits down*) ^ After all, I'm talking nonsense: I daresay I am a quack, a quack with a qualification. ^ But my discovery is not patented.

^ X *above Ch. 3 to Ch. 4.*

^ *Sits Ch. 4.*

MRS. DUBEDAT: Then can any doctor cure my husband? Oh, why don't they do it? I have tried so many: I have spent so much. If only you would give me the name of another doctor.

RIDGEON: Every man in this street is a doctor. But outside myself and the handful of men I am training at St. Anne's, there is nobody as yet who has mastered the opsonin treatment. And we are full up. I'm sorry; but that is all I can say. (*Rising*) Good morning.

The final refusal. Her effect on him blunts its certainty, however, and supplies the reason for her making one last effort to convince him. The subject seed becomes the drawings, and it is a tribute to Shaw's instinctive sense of dramaturgy to use in place of verbal argument these viewable "things" as instruments of Ridgeon's conversion. The scene becomes animated here, and it is right that Mrs. Dubedat, having been immobile and subdued for so long should now become active and forceful.

MRS. DUBEDAT: (*suddenly and desperately taking some drawings from her portfolio*)

The portfolio has been left on Ch. 2 at C. She must X *there to get it, taking one or two pic-*

tures from it back to R of desk. Ridgeon, upon rising, will have stepped down to below C of the desk to free himself for the move to the D S window.

JENNIFER: (cont'd) Doctor, look at these. You understand drawings: you have good ones in your waiting-room. Look at them. ∧ They are his work.

∧ *Mrs. Dubedat will time her* X *L to thrust two of the pictures toward him on the line. This last expression of indifference makes the reversal all the more effective.*

RIDGEON: It's no use my looking. (*He looks all the same*)
Hallo! ∧ (*He takes one to the window and studies it*).

∧ *He will take two pictures with him, eliminating the need for a double* X *to her and back to the window again. He goes to the D S window, of course. To prepare for the change in the acting area which is to come, Jennifer may back a step or two to C as he examines the first picture.*

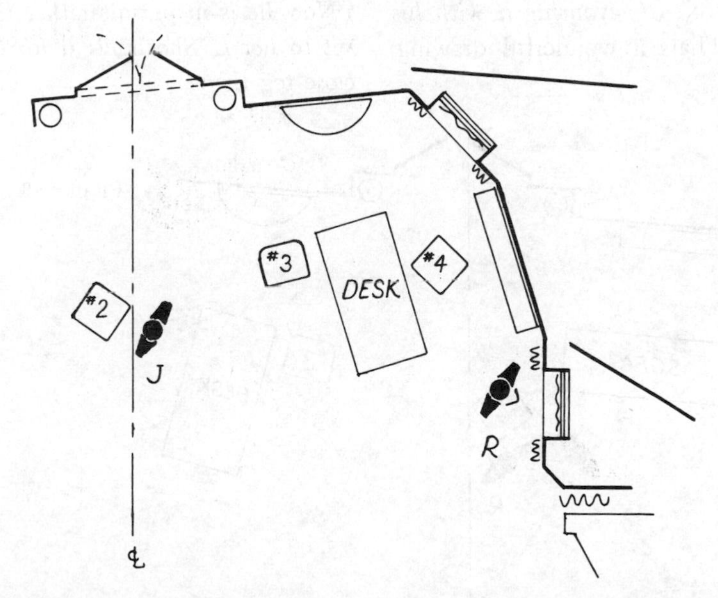

FIGURE 27

RIDGEON: (cont'd) Yes: this is the real thing. ∧ Yes, yes. (*He looks at another and returns to her.*) ∧ These are very clever. They're unfinished, aren't they?

∧ X *R2 to cut down length of the return* X.

∧ X *R to her L.*

MRS. DUBEDAT: He gets tired so soon. But you see, don't you, what a genius he is? You see that he is worth saving. ^ Oh, doctor, I married him just to help him to begin: I had money to tide him over the hard years at the beginning—to enable him to follow his inspiration until his genius was recognized. And I was useful to him as a model: his drawings of me sold quite quickly.

^ *X1 back toward R to open up a little.*

RIDGEON: Have you got one?

MRS. DUBEDAT: (*producing another*) ^ Only this one. It was the first.

^ *She will place the portfolio on Ch. 2 to steady it, and also to make it useless as a seating place in what follows. Her X carries her to the R of this chair when she turns to hand the picture to him.*

RIDGEON: ^ (*devouring it with his eyes*) Thats a wonderful drawing.

^ *Now he is in pursuit rather than in retreat; Xes to her L. She holds it for him. They are close together.*

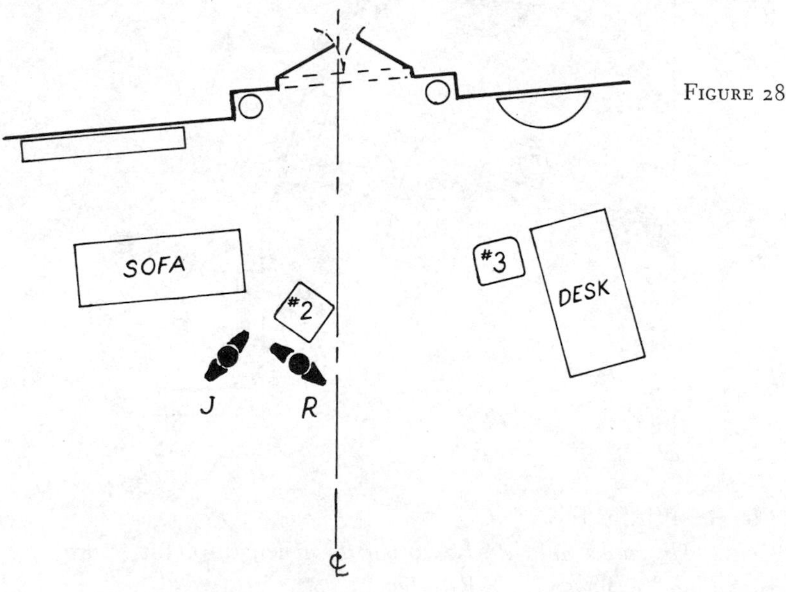

FIGURE 28

Why is it called Jennifer?

MRS. DUBEDAT: My name is Jennifer.

RIDGEON: A strange name.

He places his hands on the drawing, so that they both hold it together.

MRS. DUBEDAT: Not in Cornwall. I am Cornish. It's only what you call Guinevere.

RIDGEON: (*repeating the names with a certain pleasure in them*) Guinevere. Jennifer. (*Looking again at the drawing.*)

He looks at her deeply before returning his gaze to the portrait. We must now take the opportunity to shift to the social side. There is no reason for Jennifer to X R, so Ridgeon must originate the move. The moment for him to X R is now as he looks entranced again at the drawing, his interest more in the subject than the execution, perhaps.

^ Yes: it's really a wonderful drawing. ^ Excuse me; but may I ask is it for sale? I'll buy it.

^ *Xes her to R to below R C of sofa.*

^ *Turns L*

MRS. DUBEDAT: ^ Oh, take it. It's my own: he gave it to me. Take it. Take them all. Take everything; ask anything; but save him. You can: you will: you must.

^ *X to his L below sofa.*

FIGURE 29

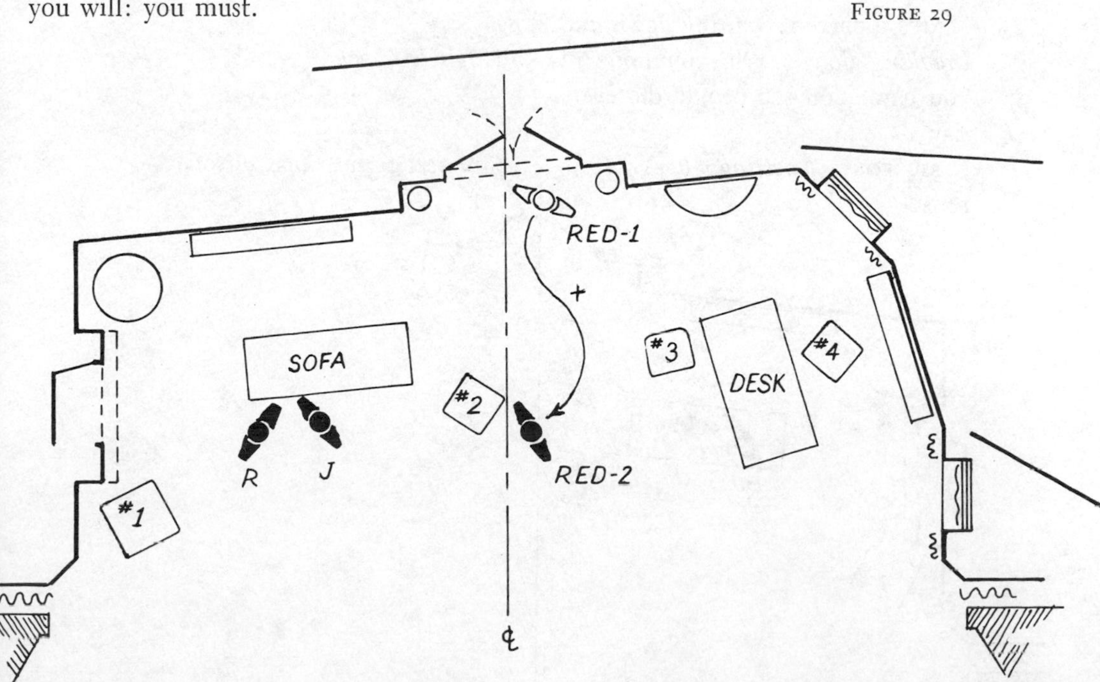

Ridgeon is now ready to succumb to her climactic appeal. Redpenny's entrance supplies the temporary check.

REDPENNY: (*entering with every sign of alarm*) They've just telephoned from the hospital that you're to come instantly—a patient on the point of death. The carriage is waiting.

RIDGEON: ^ (*intolerantly*) Oh, nonsense: get out. (*Greatly annoyed.*) ^ What do you mean by interrupting me like this?

^ *Puts drawings down on R arm of sofa, backing R.*

^ X *down and to R a step to clear sightline to Redpenny, who remains L Ch. 2.*

REDPENNY: But—

RIDGEON: Chut! Can't you see I'm engaged? Be off.

(*Redpenny, bewildered, vanishes.*)

MRS. DUBEDAT: ^ (*rising*) Doctor: one instant only before you go—

^ *We have not seated her yet, there having been no good reason to do so.*

RIDGEON: Sit down. It's nothing.

MRS. DUBEDAT: But the patient. He said he was dying.

RIDGEON: ^ Oh, he's dead by this time. ^ Never mind. Sit down.

^ X1 *D R to help the laugh with a move.*

^ *Turns back on her.*

MRS. DUBEDAT: (*sitting down and breaking down*) Oh, you none of you care. You see people die every day.

Sits L side of sofa.

RIDGEON: (*petting her*) ^ Nonsense!

^ *Sits next to her on R of sofa.*

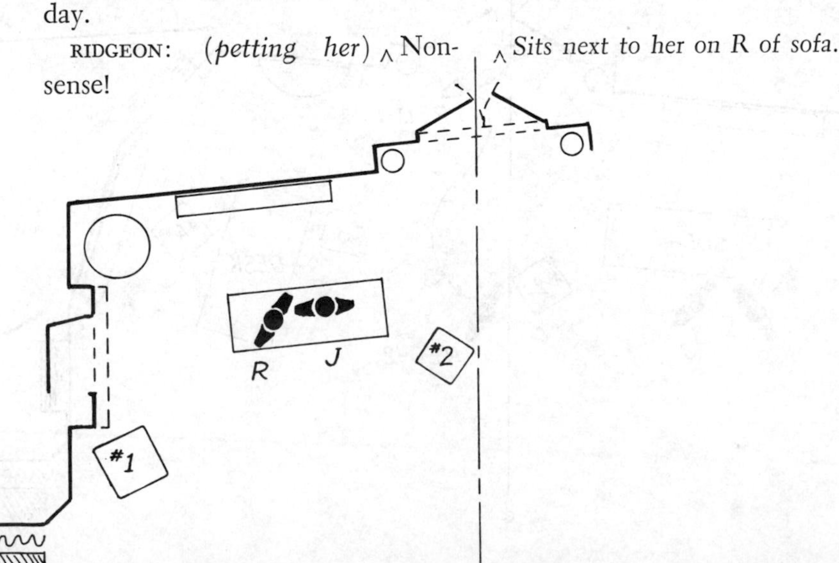

FIGURE 30

RIDGEON: (cont'd) It's nothing: I told him to come in and say that. I thought I should want to get rid of you.

MRS. DUBEDAT: (*shocked at the falsehood*) Oh!

RIDGEON: Dont look so bewildered: theres nobody dying.

MRS. DUBEDAT: My husband is.

RIDGEON: (*pulling himself together*) Ah, yes: I had forgotten your husband. Mrs. Dubedat: you are asking me to do a very serious thing.

From a wholly negative attitude toward her problem, he now weighs the possibilities of accepting her husband as a patient.

MRS. DUBEDAT: I am asking you to save the life of a great man.

RIDGEON: You are asking me to kill another man for his sake; for as surely as I undertake another case I shall have to hand back one of the old ones to the ordinary treatment. Well, I dont shrink from that. I have had to do it before: and I will do it again if you can convince me that his life is more important than the worst life I am now saving. But you must convince me first.

Statement of the condition; posing the test. No reason to break the scene on the sofa.

MRS. DUBEDAT: He made those drawings; and they are not the best —nothing like the best, only I did not bring the really best: so few people like them. He is twenty-three: his whole life is before him. Wont you let me bring him to you? wont you speak to him? wont you see for yourself?

RIDGEON: Is he well enough to come to a dinner at the Star and Garter at Richmond?

The search now is for a fitting place to have Ridgeon rise. Since he wants a reply to his question, he has no reason to get up until it is answered, and after he has explained the nature of the dinner. It is meet to keep the conversation on a pleasantly intimate basis, which a break in the tête-à-tête would not do.

MRS. DUBEDAT: Oh yes. Why?

RIDGEON: I'll tell you. I am inviting all my old friends to a dinner to celebrate my knighthood—you've seen about it in the papers, haven't you?

MRS. DUBEDAT: Yes, oh yes. That was how I found out about you.

RIDGEON: It will be a doctors' dinner; and it was to have been a bachelors' dinner. I'm a bachelor. Now if you will entertain for me, and bring your husband, he will meet me; and he will meet some of the most eminent men in my profession: Sir Patrick Cullen, Sir Ralph Bloomfield Bonington, Cutler Walpole, and others. I can put the case to them; and your husband will have to stand or fall by what we think of him. ^ Will you come?

^ As host, Ridgeon should initiate the change of position, but without giving the impression of hastening the end of the interview. Looking ahead, it is seen that he must ring for Emmy, and the bell-pull must be in a convenient place; R of the door seems best. And Mrs. Dubedat must retrieve her portfolio. The most logical moment to do this is at the mention of the drawings in her next speech. Consequently, they should be standing before she Xes to Ch. 2 which argues for Ridgeon's rise on this line. He will back a step to R of sofa as he does so.

MRS. DUBEDAT: ^ Yes, of course I will come. Oh, thank you, thank you.

^ The plan is settled. She rises. Her thanks might be accompanied by a handshake, but Shaw saves this until the "Good-bye" a little later.

^ And may I bring some of his drawings—the really good ones?

^ Let the business furnish the motive for the shift of subject to the drawings. This can be

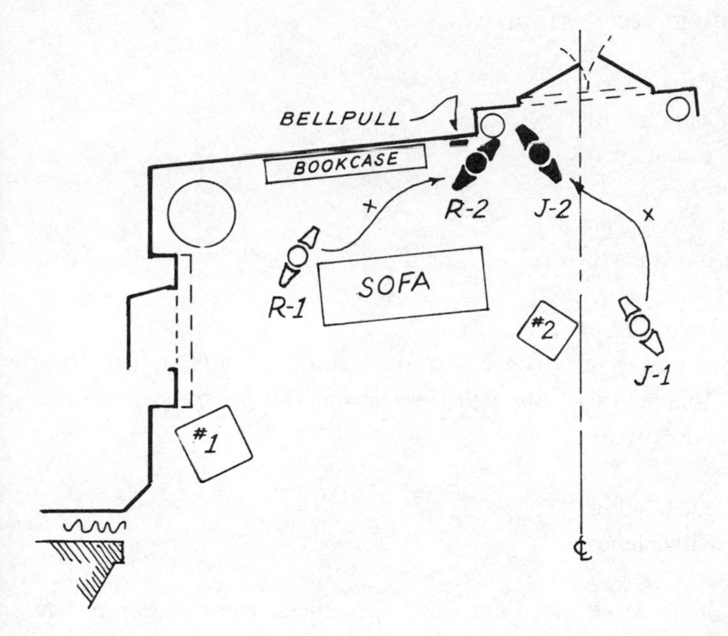

FIGURE 31

done by having her start X *for the portfolio a split second after she starts the line. It should carry her beyond Ch. 2 to L of it for her subsequent* X *to the doorway.*

RIDGEON: Yes. I will let you know the date in the course of tomorrow. Leave me your address.

An unimportant detail, dramatically speaking, and therefore a good line for his weak X *to the bell-pull, R of doorway.*

MRS. DUBEDAT: ∧ Thank you again and again.

∧ X *to C of doorway to his L. She must manage to get a card from her handbag and carry the portfolio at the same time.*

You have made me so happy: I know you will admire him and like him. ∧ This is my address. (*She gives him her card.*)

∧ X *close to him on R of doorway in order to clear it for Emmy's entrance.*

RIDGEON: Thank you. (*He rings.*)

Having rung once there is no need for him to ring again. Instead let him drop down a step to give Mrs. Dubedat the U S position for the next.

MRS. DUBEDAT: (*embarrassed*) May I—is there—should I—I mean —(*she blushes and stops in confusion*).

Hand gestures and perhaps a turn L and a turn back to him will help underline her feeling.

RIDGEON: Whats the matter?

MRS. DUBEDAT: Your fee for this consultation?

RIDGEON: Oh, I forgot that. Shall we say a beautiful drawing of his favorite model for the whole treatment, including the cure?

MRS. DUBEDAT: You are very generous. Thank you. I know you will cure him. Good-bye.

RIDGEON: I will. Good-bye. (*They shake hands.*) By the way, you know, don't you, that tuberculosis is catching. You take every precaution, I hope.

Ridgeon should continue holding her hand through the remainder of his speech.

MRS. DUBEDAT: I am not likely to forget it. They treat us like lepers at the hotels.

EMMY: ∧ (*at the door*) Well, deary, have you got round him?

∧ *Emmy will open the L door and step in two or three feet L of it.*

RIDGEON: ∧ Yes. Attend to the door and hold your tongue.

∧ X1 *down to clear sightline between Emmy and himself, if need be.*

EMMY: That's a good boy. (*She goes out with Mrs. Dubedat.*)

To manage the exit neatly, Emmy will hold the doorknob, standing L of door as Mrs. Dubedat exits. Emmy follows.

RIDGEON: (*alone*) Consultation free. Cure guaranteed. (*He heaves a great sigh.*)

Ridgeon should not close the scene at the doorway. The line suggests a return to his role as physician. There is time for him to get the picture from the sofa and make a X *toward the desk as he meditates on it and pauses to grasp the ironic reversal the scene has taken. The sigh should be given from a seated position for an extra touch of weariness and self-mockery. In consequence, let him* X *to L above desk before the line; speak it from there; and then* X *to sit at his old place in Ch. 4 for the curtain.*

Two Characters in Successive Scenes in a Single Set

Regardless of how widely they may be separated in the text, successive scenes between the same characters in the same setting should be studied *en bloc,* and blocked consecutively if variety of acting area and purposeful placement are to be achieved. The need for variety increases in direct proportion to the length of time the same characters operate in the same space.

Three separated major scenes between the two young lovers in Anderson's *Winterset* present us with a nice example of this technically complicated problem, and the first step toward its solution is to set down as clearly as possible the nature of the psychological, emotional, and dramatic relationships between the characters in each of the scenes and note in what respects these vary from one scene to another. But before proceeding to do this, we must look at the fleeting moment in I, 3 when Mio and Miriamne first come into contact with one another. It is an overture, a brief introduction to the more important scenes to come, yet it too must be thought of in terms of the full perspective of the major encounters to follow and as a part of the whole interlocking weave of the scenes they must play together.

Only three people are involved and the scene is presumably not a difficult one to stage, although as the lovers' first meeting it must be handled with care. What appears just below is the prerehearsal blocking scheme for a production at the Yale Drama School. It furnishes an

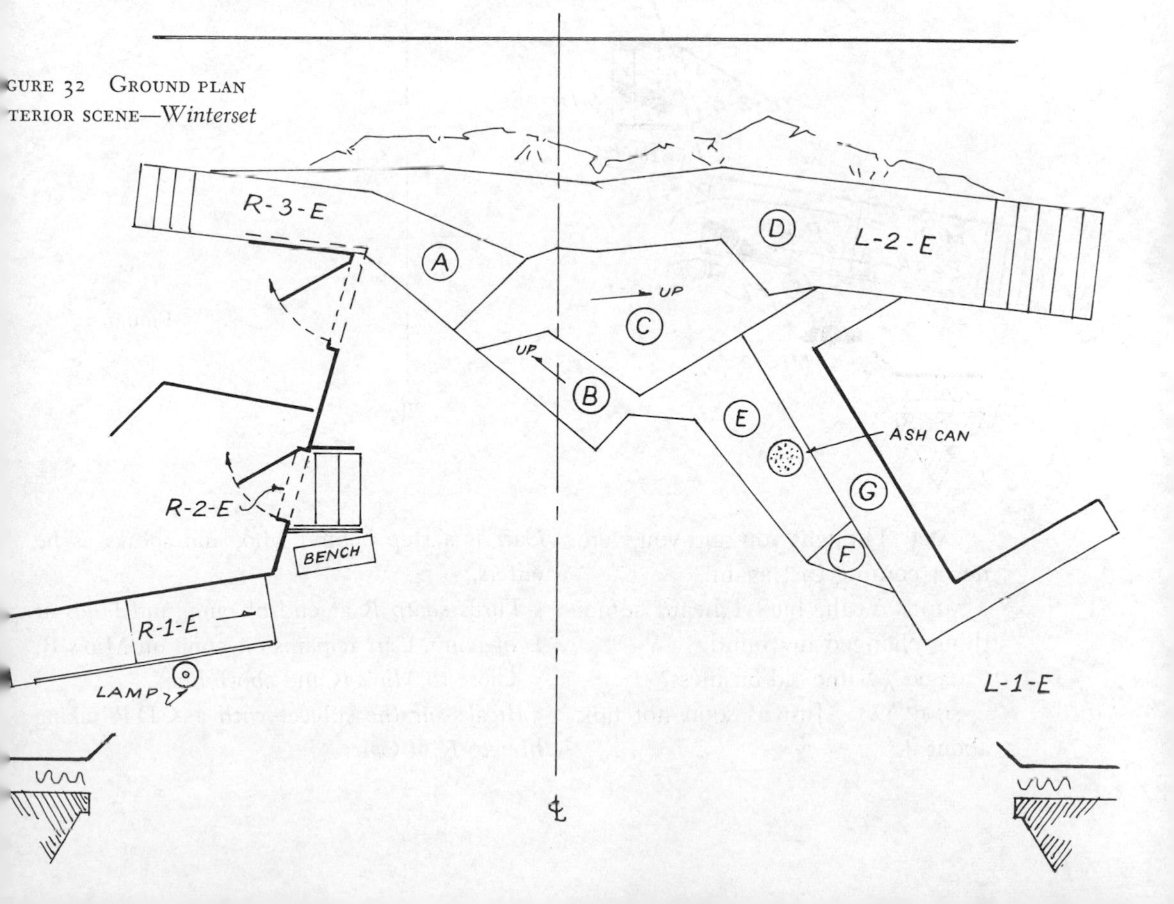

GURE 32 GROUND PLAN
TERIOR SCENE—*Winterset*

object lesson, a reminder that first thoughts are not always the best, and that no director is infallible.

In the Yale production, Miriamne was seated on the bench downstage of the basement entrance. The playwright states that Mio and Carr enter "around the apartment house," but since they would surely see her as they come downstage, they entered R 1E. To remove Miriamne from their field of vision, she has been made to make a prior cross to the basement steps, and to stand on the top step, pausing there to dry her eyes.

The preselected acting area for the scene between Mio and Carr was D R on the ramp and in the area below it.

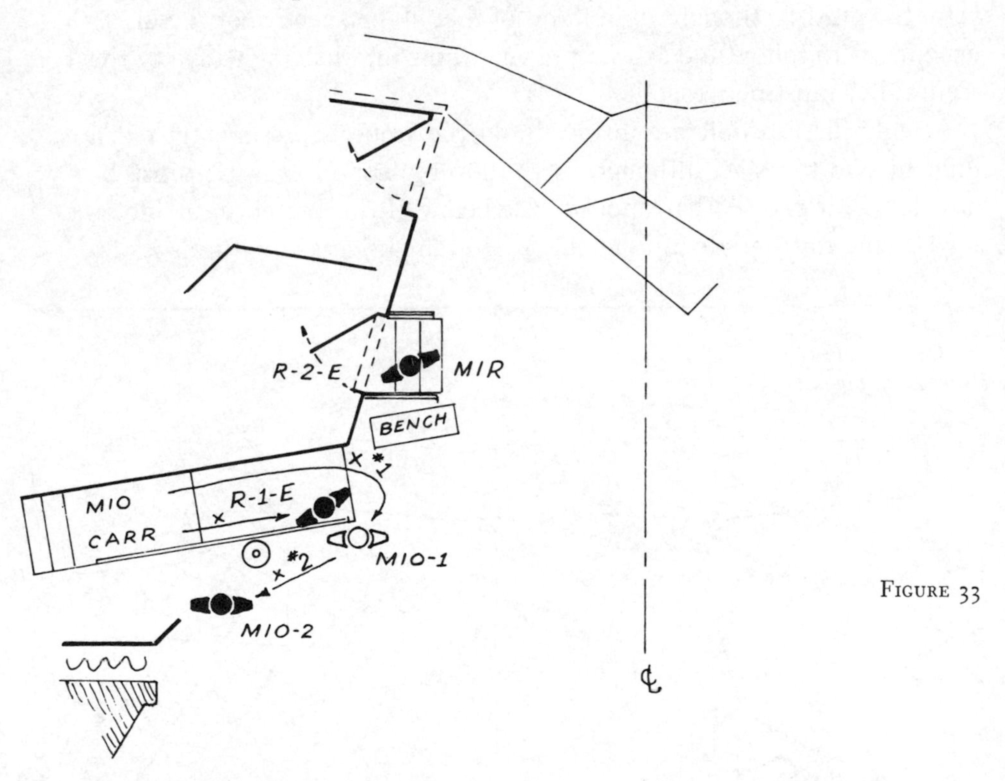

FIGURE 33

CARR: Thought you said you were never coming east again.

Carr is a step behind Mio, and speaks as he enters.

MIO: ‸ Yeah, but—I heard something changed my mind.

‸ Turns sharp R at end of ramp and holds at L of ramp. Carr remains on ramp on Mio's R.

CARR: ‸ Same old business?

‸ Close to Mio's R and above him.

MIO: Yes. ‸ Just as soon not talk about it.

‸ Breaks off the subject with a X *D R taking him to R of Carr.*

CARR: ^ Where did you go from Portland?	^ X *to end of ramp.*
MIO: Fishing—I went fishing. God's truth.	
CARR: ^ Right after I left?	^ X*1 to level with Mio.*
MIO: Fell in with a fisherman's family on the coast and went after the beautiful mackerel fish that swim in the beautiful sea. Family of Greeks—Aristides Marinos was his lovely name. He sang while he fished. Made the pea-green Pacific ring with his bastard Greek chanties. Then I went to Hollywood High School for a while.	
CARR: I'll bet that's a seat of learning.	
MIO: It's the hind end of all wisdom. ^ They kicked me out after a time. ^	^ X *D R1.* ^ *Miriamne* X *to top step R. @ E.*
CARR: For cause?	
MIO: Because I had no permanent address, you see. ^ That means nobody's paying taxes for you, so out you go. ^	^ X *L to R of C line.* ^ *Finish arc* X *and see her.*
(*To Miriamne*)	

FIGURE 34

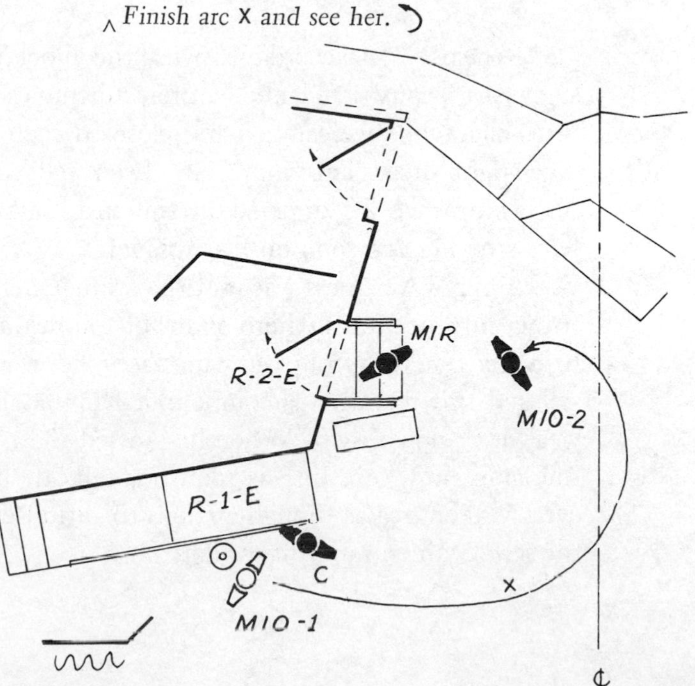

MIO: (*cont'd*) What's the matter, kid?	*Mio holds position. Carr drops down a step to anticipate Miriamne's exit* X *U ramp.*
MIRIAMNE: ∧ Nothing. (*She looks up at him, and they pause for a moment.*) Nothing.	∧ X *to L of bench.* Count of 3 for the P.
MIO: I'm sorry.	
MIRIAMNE: It's all right. (*She withdraws her eyes from his and goes out past him. He turns and looks after her.*)	*In this arrangement, if Miriamne is to* X *past Mio to exit, she will have to* X *the whole stage to exit L. Obviously, this will not convey the sense of Mio's coming line that she "vanished." The director chose to have her exit R. 1 E instead. On her exit Mio* X *R to L of bench.*
CARR: Control your chivalry. ∧	∧ X *to below C of bench, slightly above Mio.*
MIO: A pretty kid. ∧	∧ *Looking across Carr to R. 1 E.*
CARR: ∧ A baby.	∧ *Looks R. 1 E*
MIO: Wait for me. ∧	∧ X *Carr and exits R. 1 E. Carr gets out a cigarette.*
CARR: Be a long wait? ∧	∧ *Shrugs.* X *L to R of C line.*
MIO: ∧ She's gone.	∧ *Re-enters R. 1 E and* X *in to L of ramp.*
CARR: Think of that.	
MIO: No, but I mean—vanished. ∧ Presto—into nothing—prodigioso.	∧ *Looks off R.*

Rehearsed in accordance with the blocking above, the scene was stagy, stiff, constricted and entirely unconvincing. For one thing, the three characters were much too close to each other, crowded into the down-right area. This may have been relieved by placing Miriamne further upstage, as directed in the text, but then Mio would surely have seen her too soon on his cross left.

A major weakness was that the arrangement did not provide a good strong entrance for the hero on his first appearance in the play. Mio had to halt a few feet from the wings as if he were ashamed to show himself and this feeling was compounded by having to play the scene in a weak area, down right. When he crossed right from the ramp to left of the lamp post, on "Just as soon not talk about it," he moved into an even weaker area as though anxious to shrink into the farthest corner of the set. As an entrance it was flat.

The fundamental error lay in failure to think of the entrance as something much more than the advent of an actor on to the set. The blocking gave Mio no *motive* for coming into this particular place where he had presumably never been before. As it was, Mio seemed to enter for the purpose of standing under a lamp post. The entrance was ineffective and wrong because it did not convey, as it should have, that Mio had come into this part of the world for a most compelling reason, and that was to find the place where Garth Esdras lived. To make that all-important fact clear Mio should have been looking for Garth's address when he entered, even though he happened to be talking to Carr about something else at that moment.

The error was corrected by ignoring the direction in the text that Mio and Carr should enter around the apartment house, for even if they had used R. 3E they would have seen Miriamne at once. The point of entrance was placed on the opposite side (L. 1E). To guard against Mio discovering Miriamne prematurely, she stayed huddled against the tenement wall and the light was held down in that area. Mio entered first, crossed to up center, *looking up at the tenement*, as if intent on identifying it. He gave a momentary flash of recognition before turning left to face Carr, who remained down left. He turned after the word, "Fishing," in response to a grunt of disbelief from Carr, which gave a motive for his repeating the line: "I went fishing. God's truth." The first awkward curved cross was replaced by a straight cross from left to right with a turn back to Carr at the end of it. This arrangement had the further advantage of leaving Miriamne free to exit R. 1E without the necessity of crossing Carr.

The lesson to be learned here is that prerehearsal blocking should in no way be considered absolute and final. Every director makes mistakes and must always be willing to correct them. This one arose because too much initial attention was given to the *form* of the scene rather than to its *substance.*

The second meeting, in Act I, Scene 3.

(*After a pause Mio comes back from the L, alone. He stands at a little distance from Miriamne.*)

MIO: Looks like rain.

(*She is silent.*)

You live around here?
(*She nods gravely.*)
I guess
you thought I meant it—about waiting here to meet me.
(*She nods again.*)
I'd forgotten about it till I got that winter
across the face. You'd better go inside.
I'm not your kind. I'm nobody's kind but my own.
I'm waiting for this to blow over.
(*She rises.*)
I lied. I meant it—
I meant it when I said it—but there's too much black
whirling inside me—for any girl to know.
So go on in. You're somebody's angel child
and they're waiting for you.

MIRIAMNE: Yes. I'll go.
(*She turns.*)

MIO: And tell them
when you get inside where it's warm,
and you love each other,
and mother comes to kiss her darling, tell them
to hang on to it while they can, believe while they can
it's a warm safe world, and Jesus finds His lambs
and carries them in His bosom.—I've seen some lambs
that Jesus missed. If they ever want the truth
tell them that nothing's guaranteed in this climate
except it gets cold in winter, nor on this earth
except you die sometime.
(*He turns away.*)

MIRIAMNE: I have no mother.
And my people are Jews.

MIO: Then you know something about it.

MIRIAMNE: Yes.

MIO: Do you have enough to eat?

MIRIAMNE: Not always.

MIO: What do you believe in?

MIRIAMNE: Nothing.

MIO: Why?

MIRIAMNE: How can one?

MIO: It's easy if you're a fool. You see the words

in books. Honor, it says there, chivalry, freedom,
heroism, enduring love—and these
are words on paper. It's something to have them there.
You'll get them nowhere else.

MIRIAMNE: What hurts you?

MIO: Just that.
You'll get them nowhere else.

MIRIAMNE: Why should you want them?

MIO: I'm alone, that's why. You see those lights,
along the river, cutting across the rain—?
those are the hearths of Brooklyn, and up this way
the love-nests of Manhattan—they turn their points
like knives against me—outcast of the world,
snake in the streets.—I don't want a hand-out.
I sleep and eat.

MIRIAMNE: Do you want me to go with you?

MIO: Where?

MIRIAMNE: Where you go.
(*A pause. He goes nearer to her.*)

MIO: Why, you god-damned little fool—
what made you say that?

MIRIAMNE: I don't know.

MIO: If you have a home
stay in it. I ask for nothing. I've schooled myself
to ask for nothing, and take what I can get,
and get along. If I fell for you, that's my look-out,
and I'll starve it down.

MIRIAMNE: Wherever you go, I'd go.

MIO: What do you know about loving?
How could you know?
Have you ever had a man?

MIRIAMNE:
(*After a slight pause.*)
No. But I know.
Tell me your name.

MIO: Mio. What's yours?

MIRIAMNE: Miriamne.

MIO: There's no such name.

MIRIAMNE: But there's no such name as Mio!
M.I.O. It's no name.

MIO: It's for Bartolomeo.
MIRIAMNE: My mother's name was Miriam,
so they called me Miriamne.
MIO: Meaning little Miriam?
MIRIAMNE: Yes.
MIO: So now little Miriamne will go in
and take up quietly where she dropped them all
her small housewifely cares.—When I first saw you,
not a half-hour ago, I heard myself saying,
this is the face that launches ships for me—
and if I owned a dream—yes, half a dream—
we'd share it. But I have no dream. This earth
came tumbling down from chaos, fire and rock,
and bred up worms, blind worms that sting each other
here in the dark. These blind worms of the earth
took out my father—and killed him, and set a sign
on me—the heir of the serpent—and he was a man
such as men might be if the gods were men—
but they killed him—
as they'll kill all others like him
till the sun cools down to the stabler molecules,
yes, till men spin their tent-worm webs to the stars
and what they think is done, even in the thinking,
and they are the gods, and immortal, and constellations
turn for them all like mill wheels—still as they are
they will be, worms and blind. Enduring love,
oh gods and worms, what mockery!—And yet
I have blood enough in my veins. It goes like music,
singing, because you're here. My body turns
as if you were the sun, and warm. This men called love
in happier times, before the Freudians taught us
to blame it on the glands. Only go in
before you breathe too much of my atmosphere
and catch death from me.
MIRIAMNE: I will take my hands
and weave them to a little house, and there
you shall keep a dream—
MIO: God knows I could use a dream
and even a house.
MIRIAMNE: You're laughing at me, Mio!

MIO: The worms are laughing.
I tell you there's death about me
and you're a child! And I'm alone and half mad
with hate and longing. I shall let you love me
and love you in return, and then, why then
God knows what happens!

MIRIAMNE: Something most unpleasant?

MIO: Love in a box car—love among the children.
I've seen too much of it. Are we to live
in this same house you make with your two hands
mystically, out of air?

MIRIAMNE: No roof, no mortgage!
Well, I shall marry a baker out in Flatbush,
it gives hot bread in the morning! Oh, Mio, Mio,
in all the unwanted places and waste lands
that roll up into the darkness out of sun
and into sun out of dark, there should be one empty
for you and me.

MIO: No.

MIRIAMNE: Then go now and leave me.
I'm only a girl you saw in the tenements,
and there's been nothing said.

MIO: Miriamne.
(*She takes a step toward him.*)

MIRIAMNE: Yes.
(*He kisses her lips lightly.*)

MIO: Why, girl, the transfiguration on the mount
was nothing to your face. It lights from within—
a white chalice holding fire, a flower in flame,
this is your face.

MIRIAMNE: And you shall drink the flame
and never lessen it. And round your head
the aureole shall burn that burns there now,
forever. This I can give you. And so forever
the Freudians are wrong.

MIO: They're well-forgotten
at any rate.

MIRIAMNE: Why did you speak to me
when you first saw me?

MIO: I knew then.

MIRIAMNE: And I came back
because I must see you again. And we danced together
and my heart hurt me. Never, never, never,
though they should bind me down and tear out my eyes,
would I ever hurt you now. Take me with you, Mio,
let them look for us, whoever there is to look,
but we'll be away.
(*Mio turns away toward the tenement.*)

MIO: When I was four years old
we climbed through an iron gate, my mother and I,
to see my father in prison. He stood in the death-cell
and put his hand through the bars and said, My Mio,
I have only this to leave you, that I love you,
and will love you after I die. Love me then, Mio,
when this hard things comes on you, that you must live
a man despised for your father. That night the guards,
walking in flood-lights brighter than high noon,
led him between them with his trousers slit
and a shaven head for the cathodes. This sleet and rain
that I feel cold here on my face and hands
will find him under thirteen years of clay
in prison ground. Lie still and rest, my father,
for I have not forgotten. When I forget
may I lie blind as you. No other love,
time passing, nor the spaced light-years of suns
shall blur your voice, or tempt me from the path
that clears your name—
till I have these rats in my grip
or sleep deep where you sleep.
(*To Miriamne.*)
I have no house,
nor home, nor love of life, nor fear of death,
nor care for what I eat, or who I sleep with,
or what color of calcimine the Government
will wash itself this year or next to lure
the sheep and feed the wolves. Love somewhere else,
and get your children in some other image
more acceptable to the State! This face of mine
is stamped for sewage!
(*She steps back, surmising.*)

MIRIAMNE: Mio—
MIO: My road is cut
in rock, and leads to one end. If I hurt you, I'm sorry.
One gets over hurts.
MIRIAMNE: What was his name—
your father's name?
MIO: Bartolomeo Romagna.
I'm not ashamed of it.
MIRIAMNE: Why are you here?
MIO: For the reason
I've never had a home. Because I'm a cry
out of a shallow grave, and all roads are mine
that might revenge him!
MIRIAMNE: But, Mio—why here—why here?
MIO: I can't tell you that.
MIRIAMNE: No—but—there's someone
lives here—lives not far—and you mean to see him—
you mean to ask him—
(*She pauses.*)
MIO: Who told you that?
MIRIAMNE: His name
is Garth—Garth Esdras—
MIO:
(*After a pause, coming nearer.*)
Who are you, then? You seem
to know a good deal about me.—Were you sent
to say this?
MIRIAMNE: You said there was death about you! Yes,
but nearer than you think! Let it be as as it is—
let it all be as it is, never see this place
nor think of it—forget the streets you came
when you're away and safe! Go before you're seen
or spoken to!
MIO: Will you tell me why?
MIRIAMNE: As I love you
I can't tell you—and I can never see you—
MIO: I walk where I please—
MIRIAMNE: Do you think it's easy for me
to send you away?
(*She steps back as if to go.*)

MIO: Where will I find you then
  if I should want to see you?
MIRIAMNE: Never—I tell you
  I'd bring you death! Even now. Listen!

(*Shadow and Trock enter between the bridge and the tenement house. Miriamne pulls Mio back into the shadow of the rock to avoid being seen.*)

Studying the scene the director perceives that its essential rhythm consists of the lovers' gradually making contact with each other and then losing that contact. In a series of swings Mio is drawn toward Miriamne who offers him peaceful refuge from his bitter loneliness. But he withdraws from involvement with her as he becomes mindful of his duty towards his father. Thus a possible key to an underlying operative idea on which to base the blocking is this very simple one: bring the lovers closer together whenever they are in sympathy with each other, that is, on the lines of approach, and place them farther apart on the lines of separation. The placement would then echo the two opposed forces—attraction and repulsion—working in Mio.

Miriamne's feelings for Mio are constant; his for her are variable. So Mio as the dominant personality must initiate most of the moves, whatever their implication.

The lines of approach and the lines of separation are not difficult to identify:

Approach

MIO: I lied. I meant it—
  I meant it when I said it—

MIO: Do you have enough to eat?

MIO: When I first saw you,
  not a half-hour ago, I heard myself saying,
  this is the face that launches ships for me . . .

MIO: My body turns as if you were the sun, and warm . . .

MIO: I shall let you love me
and love you in return . . .

MIRIAMNE: What hurts you?

MIRIAMNE: Do you want me to go with you?

MIRIAMNE: Wherever you go, I'd go.

Separation

MIO: I'm not your kind. I'm nobody's kind but my own.
I'm waiting for this to blow over.

MIO: You see the words in books. Honor, it says there, chivalry, freedom, heroism, enduring love—and these are words on paper. It's something to have them there.
You'll get them nowhere else.

MIO: I don't want a hand-out.
I sleep and eat.

MIO: If I fell for you, that's my look-out,
and I'll starve it down.

MIRIAMNE: Then go now and leave me.

MIO: Only go in before you breathe too much of
my atmosphere. . . .

The flow of the scene is as follows. At the start Mio conceals his interest in Miriamne under a show of indifference. The conflict of feeling within him is caught and stated clearly in the first speech, when he tells her he doesn't want to see her again, only to deny this a moment later. Miriamne's sudden offer to go away with him thaws Mio's apparent coldness and marks the moment when he begins to lose his strained reserve. Twice in his long speech on p. 202 he admits being attracted to her, and twice overcomes this feeling as desire and longing contend with his sense of mission and the knowledge that he is engaged in what may be for him a fatal undertaking. The pendulum continues to swing until the kiss obliterates all distance between them, physical as well as psychological. They declare their love for one another, and this commitment seems final until Mio with a special effort of will recalls his father's execution. He then renews his pledge to let nothing interfere with his determination to clear his father's name. The scene reaches its climax with his peremptory and intentionally brutal dismissal of Miriamne:

> Love somewhere else,/and get your children in some other image
> more acceptable to the State!. . . .

This breaks the connection between them, and the love theme disintegrates as the scene takes another tack with the entrance of Trock and Shadow.

The key points are Mio's two long speeches, the first beginning,

> So now little Miriamne will go in,
> and take up quietly where she dropped them all
> her small housewifely cares.

and the climactic speech beginning, "When I was four years old . . ." which ends in his rejection of Miriamne. It is climactic because in it Mio's conflict is resolved. He eschews love and embraces duty—at least for the time being. This speech addressed to his father's spirit furnishes the best starting point for the blocking, because it contains the hero's unequivocal resolution: ". . . no other love . . . shall tempt me from the path that clears your name." To deliver it with the greatest effectiveness the actor must not only be in a dominant position, but must also have whatever background support he can get from the scenery. And he must be in a downstage area where there is plenty of light.

Now the best tangible support available in the ground plan developed in the previous chapter is the downstage wall of the tenement, above the ramp, and this is certainly preferable to any upstage position. Mio up center would seem to be delivering a set speech. But from down right center he can place his back against the wall and look up and out for his invocation to "this sleet and rain."

If the director decides that this is the right place for him to say these lines, the preceding speech can be given from a somewhat different area, and the problem during the speech itself will be to maneuver both characters into effective positions for the climax and final separation.

Once he has a clear notion of the alternating magnetic and repellent forces at work in Mio, the director can proceed to translate those forces into a graduated series of steps, crosses and turns to give them forceful illustration in terms of concrete stage positions. This must be done without forcing upon the actors a rigid and mechanical pattern of moves which might easily appear ludicrous. The lovers will not walk away from each other a certain number of steps on the lines of separation, nor walk toward each other the same number of steps on the lines of approach. A turn of the head, a meeting or an averting of the eyes, a single step backwards or forwards or a slight change of body position will be sufficient at times to convey the general attitude the characters have for each other at a given moment.

One thing is obvious. The whole scene is *active*. It is not one that can be played sitting down. From a tentative and uncertain relationship toward each other, expressed in a series of feints, the lovers move toward one which is certain. They come together. But before the end they separate. This gives the director his first and most important clue as to the difference between this love scene and the final love scene in Act III. In the latter, all the differences that stood between them are eliminated. The characters are at one in attitude and there is no longer a conflict between them. In consequence, and in contrast to the first love scene, the last can be played with much less stir and restless activity. Some of it may even be played with the characters seated.

In the following demonstration of detailed blocking, the subject is the familiar and classical conflict between love and duty. It is primarily a conflict within the hero, but before the end Miriamne, too, is involved in it, her growing love for Mio coming into opposition with her love for her brother, Garth, and her sense of duty towards him.

It may be helpful if the reader can follow the blocking by using golf tees in conjunction with the ground plan on p. 195.

At the end of the previous French scene Miriamne has seated herself in the shadows on the ledge, "G," left center.

Mio enters L. 1 E. X to L of Miriamne.

MIO: Looks like rain.
(*She is silent.*)
You ∧ live around here?

∧ *Mio Xes her to U R (L of C line) on "You," turning back to face her before completing the sentence. On X he indicates the tenement, thus supplying the motive for X.*

(*She nods gravely.*)
I guess
you thought I meant it—about
waiting here to meet me.
(*She nods again.*)
I'd forgotten about it till I got
that winter
across the face. ∧ You'd better
go inside.

∧ *Indicates basement door.*

I'm not your kind. I'm nobody's
kind but my own.
∧ I'm waiting for this to blow over.

∧ *To anticipate her coming rise, and in order to have space to move toward her on his next line, which is a "line of approach," he Xes 2 steps D R. There is room now between them for Miriamne to X a step or two R in the direction of the basement door.*

(*She rises.*)

He turns and sees her approaching him.

∧ I lied. I meant it

∧ *Mio Xes two steps L toward her.*

—I meant it when I said it— ∧ but
there's too much black

∧ *Half-turn away from her.*

whirling inside me—for any girl
to know.
∧ So go on in. You're somebody's
angel child
and they're waiting for you.

∧ *Faces her.*

MIRIAMNE: Yes, I'll go.
(*She turns.*)

On the line she completes her X to R of him. The text's direction provides no motive for this turn. Mio's next line does so.

MIO: And tell them ∧

∧ *His hand comes up. He means to interrupt her X. On his line Miriamne then can turn back.*

FIGURE 35 PHILIP ECK'S GROUND PLAN FOR I, 3

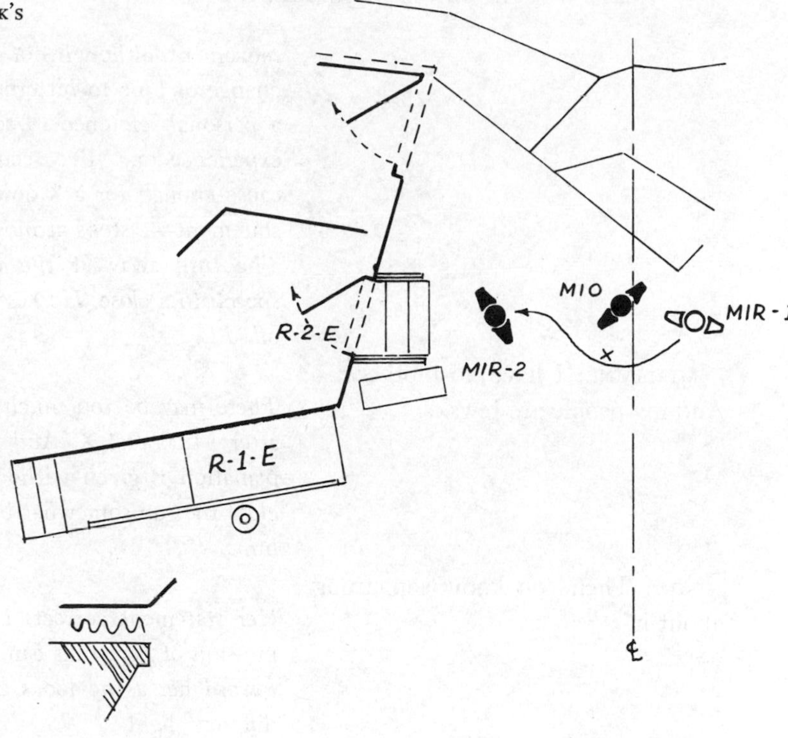

MIO: (*cont'd*)
when you get inside where it's warm
and you love each other,
and mother comes to kiss her darling,
tell them
to hang on to it while they can, believe while they can
it's a warm safe world, and Jesus finds His lambs
and carries them in His bosom.—I've seen some lambs
that Jesus missed. If they ever want the truth
tell them that nothing's guaranteed in this climate
except it gets cold in winter, nor on this earth
except you die some time.
(*He turns away.*)

A fairly long speech to be spoken without

movement, although not much is needed. The change of tone to bitterness, when Mio makes a personal reference to something in his own experience on, "I've seen some lambs . . ." is cause enough for a X *down—for it is a strong statement—2 steps at most.*

The turn away at the end helps bring the speech to a close. He X*es up on "B" and looks off U L.*

MIRIAMNE: I have no mother.
And my people are Jews.

There may be too much space between them after Mio's last X*. And since Miriamne's explanation is given without bitterness, she can close the gap somewhat by* X*ing 2 steps toward him.*

MIO: Then you know something about it.

Her statement corrects his first erroneous impression of her. This can be caught in his turn toward her as he looks at her in a somewhat different light.

MIRIAMNE: Yes.

MIO: ∧ Do you have enough to eat?

∧ *His sympathetic attention should be underlined with a move.* X*2 toward her, close to her L.*

MIRIAMNE: Not always.

MIO: What do you believe in?

MIRIAMNE: Nothing.

MIO: Why?

MIRIAMNE: How can one?

Her attitude is one of tired resignation, not of active rebellion. Spoken quietly. Both are subdued. No moves are needed, for there is no call for emphasis.

MIO: It's easy if you're a fool. You
see the words
in books. Honor, it says there,
chivalry, freedom,
heroism, enduring love—and these
are words on paper. It's something
to have them there.
You'll get them nowhere else.

The scene started with Mio on her L. He then Xed R and she in turn has Xed to his R. Mio's bleak outlook should be accompanied by an intensification of his feelings here. He is deeply hurt, as Miriamne's next line shows. A strong move is indicated to point his restlessness. Xes L and stays down of her on, "You see the words in books." His image places the books in his hand, and he can gesture toward them on the X with his hand.

MIRIAMNE: What hurts you?

Her concern is real, and tender.
Line of approach. Xes close to his R.

MIO: Just that.
You'll get them nowhere else.

He has knowledge of her tenderness, doesn't want to encourage it, although he would like to. To indicate his uneasiness and his conflicting feelings, he Xes to her R, going below her, of course.

MIRIAMNE: Why should you want them?

She naturally turns R toward him.

MIO: I'm alone, that's why. ∧ You see
those lights,
along the river, cutting across
the rain—?
those are the hearths of Brooklyn,
∧ and up this way
the love-nests of Manhattan—they
turn their points
like knives against me—outcast of
the world,
snake in the streets.— ∧ I don't
want a handout.
I sleep and eat.

∧ *Staying on her R, he leads her a step or two U L to point off U L.*

∧ *He Xes away from her to the basement entrance R C, indicating with a gesture the direction of Manhattan where Trock has already established it in I, 1.*

∧ *A return of his sullen defiance, though more subdued than at the start of the scene. Xes another step away from her toward D R.*

MIRIAMNE: Do you want me to go with you?

She should halve the distance between them on this emphatic line of approach.

MIO: Where?

They are now in D R C area.
Mio should speak as though he did not fully realize what she is saying. He can turn his head away to R.

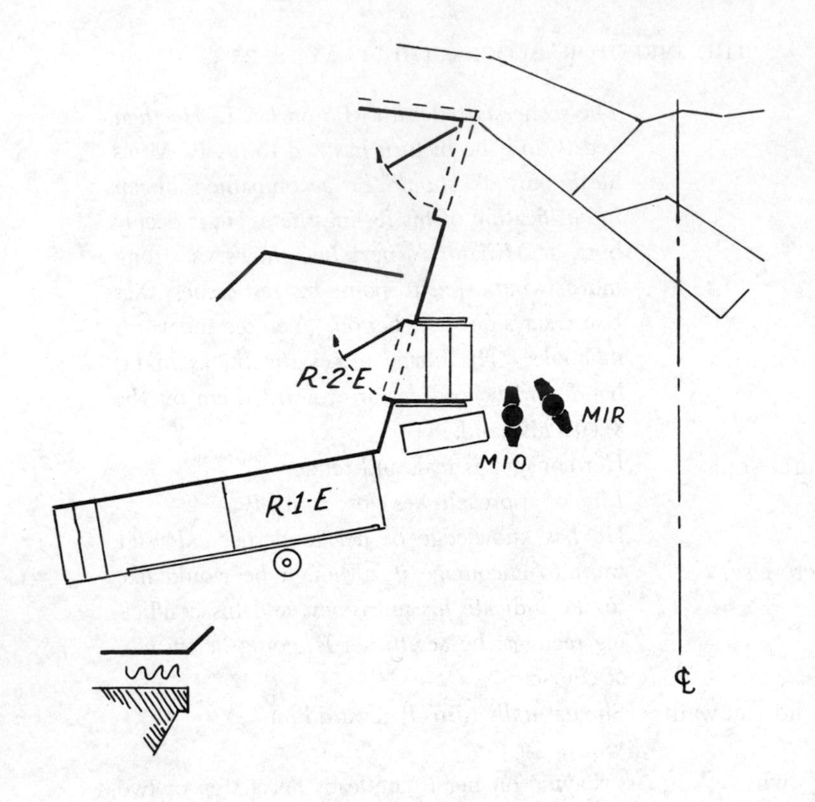

FIGURE 36

MIRIAMNE: Where you go.
(*A pause. He goes nearer to her.*)

MIO: Why, you god-damned little fool—what made you say that?

We must interrupt the blocking for a moment to call attention to a problem the playwright had to face here. He must convince us that a young girl can fall deeply in love with a stranger, and on top of that for the young man to fall in love with the girl, after one brief meeting and a short dance. The director's stint is to do all he can to make this seem plausible. His weapon is the pause. Miriamne's first utterance of the proposal can be delayed to show that she takes some time to consider it. And Mio will give himself plenty of time to react to it, even showing some initial incredulity at its suddenness, which would certainly be natural. Thus:

MIO: . . . I sleep and eat. ^ — ^ *He* Xes *away. Miriamne watches him go. Pause. She* Xes *a step toward him. Stops.*

MIRIAMNE: ^ Do you want me to go with you?	^ *Xes to within two steps of him. Blurting it out.* *Mio can then turn very slowly toward her. They hold the look between them, 4 seconds. He Xes slowly toward her. When he reaches her R side, he pauses again.*
MIO: Where?	
MIRIAMNE: (Pause) Where you go.	
MIO: Why you . . . ^ (Pause) . . . you god-damned little fool— what made you say that?	^ *Tone of bewilderment. With a half-gesture.*
MIRIAMNE: I don't know.	
MIO: If you have a home stay in it. I ask for nothing. [2 *lines cut*]	
^ If I fell for you, that's my look out, and I'll starve it down.	^ *As noted, a separating line. He is determined to suppress his growing feeling for her, and a move is called for. There follows a change in Mio's tone, a new tenderness. And there is the necessity of getting them near the D R area for the warmth of the street lamp, in preparation for the climactic placement, with Mio's back against the tenement. He will X, therefore, all the way to the railing of the ramp.*
MIRIAMNE: ^ Wherever you go, I'd go.	^ *Miriamne Xes a step or two on this obvious approach line to give force to the repetition. This places both in the D R area, where they can use the bench, the ramp, and the space below it as the focus for what ensues.*

The love duet is about five minutes long, and the characters have been standing up for almost two minutes, slightly less than half the scene. This is a long time, as time is reckoned onstage. So the director must be on the alert for an opportunity to break the picture by finding a line in the text for one or both of them to sit. The director knows that for at least one scene in Act III they will huddle together on the bench, their little lighted island of security, and that arrangement should not be anticipated now. There is another reason why *both* should not be seated. Mio is in a state of tormented indecision. To sit down and thereby manifest repose, acceptance, and inactivity would belie his attitude. But there is no good reason why Miriamne should not sit. Putting her thus in a position of stability would heighten Mio's indecision by contrast. So having decided that Miriamne shall seat herself, it becomes a question of finding the best place in the text for her to do so.

Since the law of variety demands that there be a new composition for Mio's two long speeches, there may be some virtue in seating Miriamne for his first speech and having her stand for the second. But there is no valid acceptable cue strong enough to warrant the move before Mio's line, "So now little Miriamne will go in . . ." She must show an eager interest in what is being said. And if she sat on "Tell me your name," the effect would be coy. Besides, Mio's, "So now little Miriamne *will go in* . . ." infers that she is standing and ready to go in.

So it appears that she will have to stand during Mio's first speech. And for a time after he begins the second also, because her last line before Mio begins it is, "Take me with you, Mio . . . ," a speech of active pleading that cannot be made convincing from a seated position. If there is to be any pictorial variation Mio will have to move to make it, possibly aided by slight changes in Miriamne's body position.

The acting area for the first speech can be below the ramp, right of the bench, and even up on the ramp itself so long as Mio stays away from the wall.

So we resume:

MIO: What do you know about
loving?
How could you know?
Have you ever had a man?
MIRIAMNE: (*After a slight pause.*)
No. But I know.
Tell me your name.
MIO: Mio. What's yours?
MIRIAMNE: Miriamne.
MIO: There's no such name.

Mio manages a smile here, for the first time. They relax.

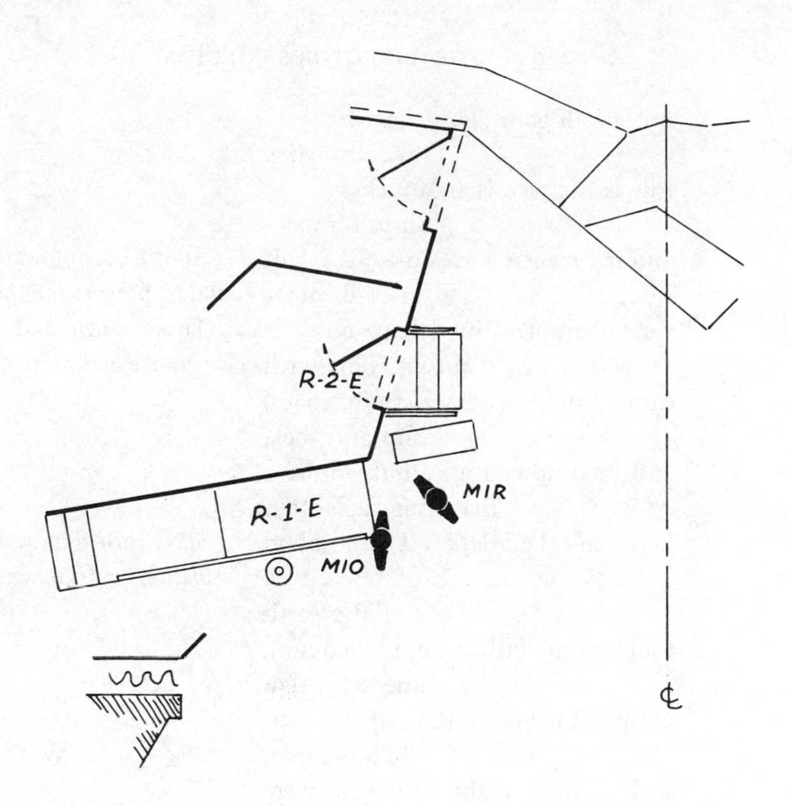

FIGURE 37

MIRIAMNE: But there's no such name as
Mio!
M.I.O. It's no name. ^ — ^ X *a step to him.*

MIO: It's for Bartolomeo.

MIRIAMNE: My mother's name was Miriam,
so they called me Miriamne.

MIO: Meaning little Miriam?

MIRIAMNE: Yes.

MIO: So now little Miriam will go in,
and take up quietly where she dropped them all
her small housewifely cares—

The scene has become quiet and intimate. No need for moves up to now. But the thought changes, and some motion is necessary to mark it.

^ When I first saw you, — ^ *Mio* X *U slightly for emphasis.*

not a half-hour ago, I heard myself saying, this is the face that launches ships for me—	
and if I owned a dream— ∧ yes, half a dream—	∧ *Another step toward her to deepen his feeling and to prepare for the break to follow.*
we'd share it. ∧ But I have no dream. This earth came tumbling down from chaos, fire and rock, and bred up worms, blind worms that sting each other	∧ *Turns down and* Xes *D R 4, to point the severance and break contact.*
here in the dark. ∧ These blind worms of the earth took out my father—and killed him, and set a sign on me—the heir of the serpent—and he was a man such as men might be if gods were men— but they killed him—	∧ *Stays turned away from her to emphasize his isolation, until now when he faces her.*
∧ as they'll kill all others like him till the sun cools down to the stabler molecules [4 *lines cut*]	∧ *Breaks visual contact with her, faces D L for the generalization, head raised.*
∧ Enduring love, oh gods and worms, what mockery!—	∧ *This outburst is violent enough to demand visual punctuation—another move away from her. But all Mio's* Xes *so far have been R. Try now for a* X *in the opposite direction, to reverse their positions. The* X *will be fast, carrying him to her L, and end on the last word, "mockery."*
∧[1] And yet, ∧[2]	∧[1] *The counterfeeling comes immediately and demands a turn back to her.* ∧[2]
I have blood enough in my veins. ∧ It goes like music, singing, because you're here.	∧ Xes *to her L (about 2 steps away). She should make a backward* X *to compensate for his* X*ing her on "Enduring love," which now gives him a longer* X *to her.*
My body turns as if you were the sun, and warm.	*He suits the action to the words and closes the gap between them by a step R.*

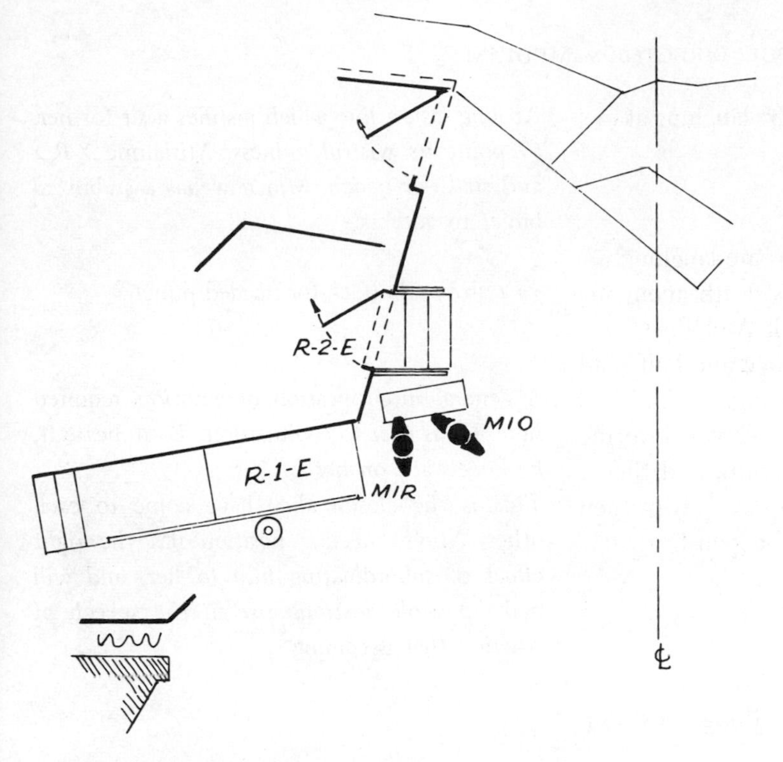

MIO: (*cont'd*) This men called love
in happier times, before the Freudians
taught us
to blame it on the glands.

The alternation between Mio's warm and cold moods continues at an accelerated pace. He swings from tenderness to sarcasm in the space of a sentence. The speech ends on a note of urgency as Mio tries to break off the liaison.

^ Only go in
before you breathe too much of my atmosphere
and catch death from me.

^ *A backing* X, *not yet used in the scene, will give some variety. Mio* X *L. backing 2 steps, gesturing toward R. 2 E.*

MIRIAMNE: I will take my hands
and weave them to a little
house, and there
you shall keep a dream—

Miriamne, facing him, can X *in the speech 2 steps toward him.*

MIO: God knows I could use a dream
and even a house.

MIRIAMNE: You're laughing at me, Mio!

At long last, a line which justifies a sit for her, to point its wistful sadness. Miriamne X *R 2 and sit C of bench. Mio now has a stabilized target to address.*

MIO: The worms are laughing.
∧ I tell you there's death about me and you're a child! And I'm
alone and half mad
with hate and longing.

∧ Fresh vocal attack for needed punch.

∧ I shall let you love me
and love you in return, and then,
why then
God knows what happens!

A general intensification of emotion required here. He is near to capitulation. To indicate it, he kneels at ∧ on her L.
This is the closest they have come to each other. Mio's kneeling position has the right effect of subordinating him to her, and will make possible a strong rise in the speech of reaction that is coming.

MIRIAMNE: Something most unpleasant?

MIO: ∧1 Love in a box car—love among the
children.
∧2 I've seen too much of it. ∧3 Are
we to live
in this same house you make with
your two hands
mystically, out of air?

Mio can withdraw in 2 distinct moves. Rise at ∧1, and X *R to R ∧ of her at ∧2. Turns for direct address at ∧3.*

MIRIAMNE: No roof, no mortgage!
Well, I shall marry a baker
out in Flatbush,
it gives hot bread in the
morning!

Rueful humor, calm acceptance. No move needed.

∧ Oh, Mio, Mio,
in all the unwanted places and
waste lands
that roll up into the darkness out
of sun
and into sun out of dark, there
should be one empty
for you and me.

∧ A heart-felt appeal. Gesture needed. R hand on his L arm.

MIO: No.

However reluctantly, her appeal is refused. Mio backs R 1 to give it some, but not too much, weight.

MIRIAMNE: ^ Then go now and leave me.

Accepting his decision, she should take the initiative to break away. ^ *Rises, backs away L to L of steps. Must be standing for kiss to follow.*

I'm only a girl you saw in
the tenements,
and there's been nothing said.

MIO: Miriamne.

Line of approach. X *1 L. He must initiate the reconciliation. Puts his hands out towards her.*

(*She takes a step toward him.*)

Text direction obeyed. She should respond with a move. X *to D L of bench.*

FIGURE 39

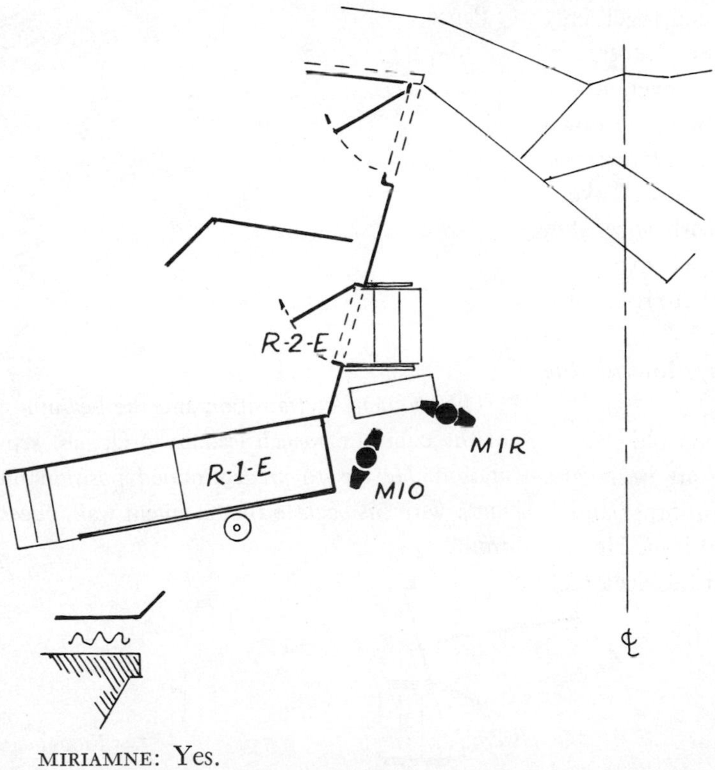

MIRIAMNE: Yes.

(*He kisses her lips lightly.*)

Must close the distance between them for business.

MIO: Why, girl, the transfiguration on
the mount

was nothing to your face. It lights from within—
a white chalice holding fire, a flower in flame,
this is your face. — *They hold the embrace.*

MIRIAMNE: And you shall drink the flame
and never lessen it.

[5 *lines cut*]

Why did you speak to me
when you first saw me?

MIO: I knew then.

MIRIAMNE: And I came back
because I must see you again. And we danced together, ^ — ^ *Pause.*
and my heart hurt me. Never, never, never,
though they should bind me down and tear out my eyes,
would I ever hurt you now. Take me with you, Mio,
let them look for us, whoever there is to look,
but we'll be away.

MIO: (*Turns away toward the tenement.*) ^ — ^ *The moment of transition and the beginning of the climactic speech leading to farthest separation. He* Xes *to predetermined position on ramp with his back to the tenement wall. Faces front.*

When I was four years old
we climbed through an iron gate, my mother and I,
to see my father in prison. He stood in the death-cell

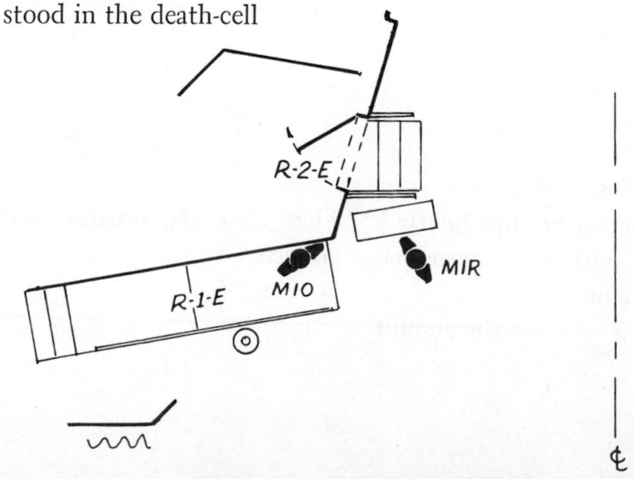

FIGURE 40

and put his hand through the bars
and said, My Mio,
I have only this to leave you, that
I love you,
and will love you after I die. Love
me then, Mio,
when this hard thing comes on you,
that you must live
a man despised for your father. That
night the guards,
walking in flood-lights brighter than
high noon,
led him between them with his
trousers slit
and a shaven head for the cathodes.
∧ This sleet and rain

∧ *Head up.*

that I feel cold here on my face
and hands
will find him under thirteen years
of clay
in prison ground. ∧ Lie still and
rest, my father,

∧ *Change head position to D L for invocation. No other move.*

for I have not forgotten. When I
forget
may I lie blind as you. ∧ No other
love,

∧ *With growing force.*

time passing, nor the spaced light-
years of suns
shall blur your voice, or tempt me
from the path
that clears your name—

The proposition, and statement of hero's purpose.

till I have these rats in my grip ∧

∧ *Change head direction to D R.*

or sleep deep where you sleep.
(*To Miriamne.*)
∧ I have no house

The end of the oath. Break positions. ∧ X *down ramp close to her.*

nor home, nor love of life, nor
fear of death,
[*4 lines cut*]
∧ Love somewhere else,

∧ *The dismissal is absolute now. To point it Mio* X*es her to R of C line, half-way U S.*

Moment of greatest separation. Away from the love area and out of her sphere of influence.

and get your children in some
other image
more acceptable to the State!
This face of mine
is stamped for sewage!
(*She steps back, surmising.*)

Text direction disobeyed, X *should be toward him. The moment is too tense for a calm appraisal on her part. She is most anxious to know now who he is.* X *2 L.*

MIRIAMNE: Mio—
[*3 lines cut to sustain momentum*]
What was his name—
your father's name?
MIO: Bartolomeo Romagna.
I'm not ashamed of it.
MIRIAMNE: Why are you here?
MIO: For the reason
I've never had a home. Because I'm
a cry
out of a shallow grave, and all roads
are mine
that might revenge him!
MIRIAMNE: But, Mio—why here
— ^ why here?

^ X *closer to him to intensify the repetition.*

MIO: ^ I can't tell you that.

^ X *2 down to emphasize uneasiness.*

MIRIAMNE: No—but—there's
someone
lives here—lives not far—and
you mean to see him—
you mean to ask him— ^

^ *Broken speeches suggest staccato breathlessness. Rising alarm.* X *L 1 step.*

(*She pauses.*)
MIO: ^ Who told you that?

^ *Sharp turn toward her.*

MIRIAMNE: His name is Garth—
Garth Esdras— ^

^ *Thunder roll.*

MIO: (*After a pause, coming nearer.*)

Obey text. But the move must convey suspicion and should be aggressive.

Who are you, then? You seem to know a good deal about me.— Were you sent ^	
to say this?	^ X *a backward step U, as though to regard her from a new viewpoint.*
MIRIAMNE: You said there was death about you! Yes,	
but nearer than you think! ^ Let it be as it is—	^ X *close to him, urgently appealing.*
let it all be as it is, never see this place nor think of it—forget the streets you came	
when you're away and safe! ^ Go before you're seen	^ *Gesture to indicate R. 1. E.*
or spoken to! MIO: Will you tell me why? MIRIAMNE: As I love you I can't tell you—and I can never see you—	
MIO: ^ I walk where I please—	^ X *1 L.*
MIRIAMNE: Do you think it's easy for me	
to send you away? ^ (*She steps back as if to go.*)	^ *He turns* ⤸ . *She* X*es R. One step only.*
MIO: Where will I find you then if I should want to see you? MIRIAMNE: Never—I tell you	
I'd bring you death! ^1 Even now. ^2 Listen!	^1 *Hears noise off R. 1 E. Looks R.* ^2 *Steps to him.* X*es L of him and pulls him off L. 1 E. Trock and Shadow enter R. 1 E.*

End of French scene

It is not necessary to continue the demonstration by a detailed blocking of succeeding scenes between the two lovers which take up most of the final act. But it may be helpful if the deductive logic behind the selection of the acting areas for this extended scene were explained, and the directorial procedure outlined.

It will be recalled that at the end of Act II Mio discovers that the real murderers of the paymaster were Trock and his henchman, Shadow. He now has the information which can clear his father's name. But a serious complication has arisen. If he reveals his knowledge that Trock and Shadow are guilty, he will implicate Miriamne's brother, Garth, who drove the getaway car. He is thus caught in the classical dilemma between his love for Miriamne and his duty to clear his father.

The French scenes may be listed:

1. *Mio and Miriamne.* Subject: he discovers that Trock and his hoods have sealed off the exits. He knows they are determined to kill him to prevent him from going to the police. Miriamne tries to help him escape.

2. *Mio, Miriamne, Shadow's cortege.* Subject: the burial of Shadow, killed by order of Trock.

3. *Mio, Miriamne, Esdras.* Subject: a possible way out for Mio. Esdras offers to summon aid, hopeful that if he does this Mio will not tell the police anything to implicate his son. Mio gives him no assurance he will cooperate.

4. *Mio, Miriamne.* Subject: they confess their mutual love, but Mio again reminds her that they are separated by Garth and Mio's debt to his father.

5. *Carr, Mio, Miriamne.* Subject: Mio reaches the point of no return. Carr can inform the police of Mio's predicament and help will be sent. But Mio, even though he knows this may be his last chance for survival, decides against enlisting Carr's help. Ominously, he bequeaths Carr all his worldly goods.

6. *Mio, Miriamne.* The turning point. A scene of discovery and the grand climax. Subject: as a human being, Mio cannot pursue vengeance if "it falls on his beloved." He appeals to her to "teach him how to live and forget to hate." She reminds him that his sainted father would have forgiven his enemies. This unlocks his understanding and his spirit emerges free from the "long trauma of hate and fear and death."

7. *Esdras, Mio, Miriamne.* Subject: Trock has intercepted Esdras and driven him back. Esdras leaves to seek a possible way out for Mio across the roofs.

8. *Mio, Miriamne.* Subject: a desperate chance. After invoking

help from the ironic gods, Mio decides to make a break for it. They bid each other farewell. Mio runs down the river path but the gangster's machine gun cuts him down. To prove her love Miriamne defies the assassins and is shot.

9. *Esdras, Garth, Mio, Miriamne*. Subject: Requiem. Esdras apostrophizes both Mio and his daughter for their courage to die for something believed.

The act is seen to be a prolonged love scene interrupted briefly by Esdras and Carr. If possible the repetitious use of I, 3 acting areas is to be avoided. These, it will be remembered, were chiefly R C, D R C, bench, ramp, and D R. Care must be taken also to mesh the staging with the new attitudes the principals have toward each other. Mio is still caught in his dilemma between love and duty. He is no longer the pursuer but the pursued, and in danger of his life. The playing must reflect the high level of emotional intensity this situation produces.

FIGURE 41 GROUND PLAN BY PHILIP ECK FOR EXTERIOR SCENE—*Winterset*

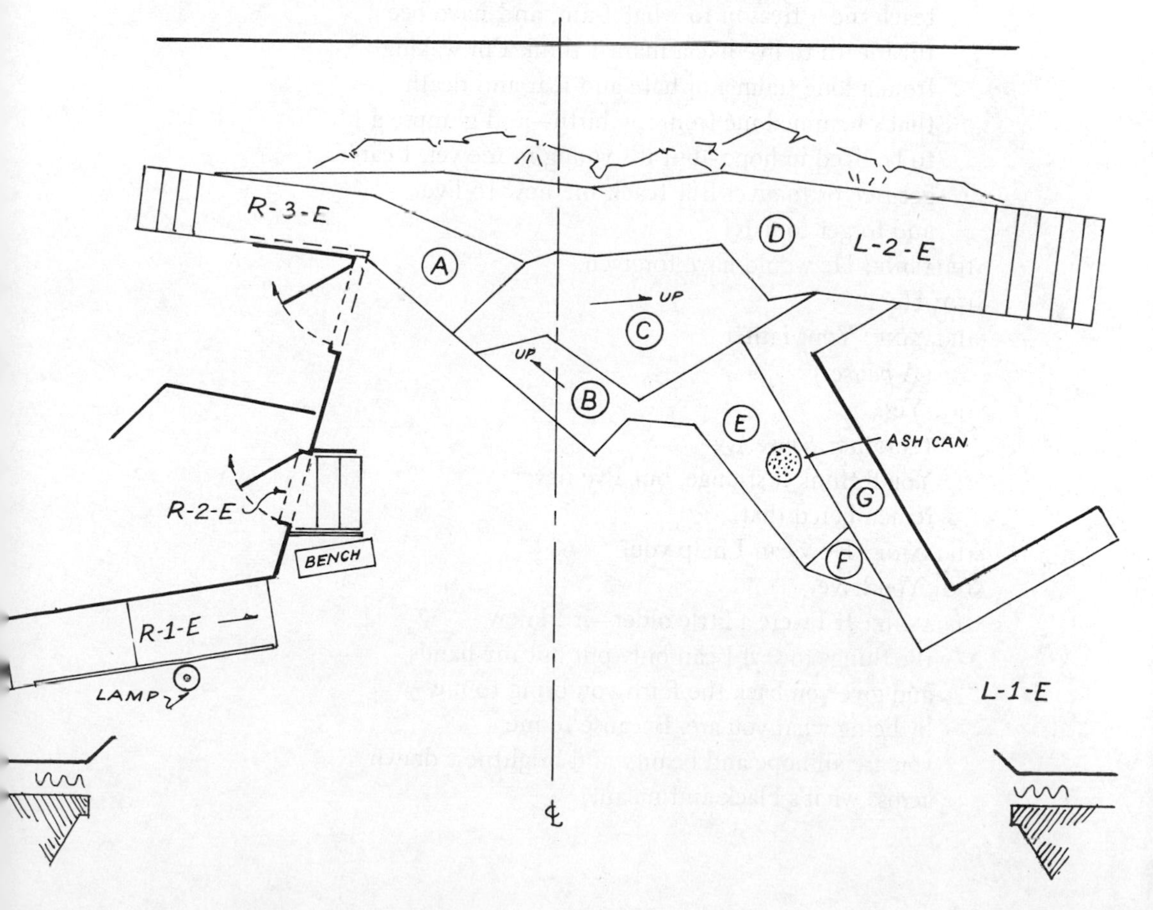

The director starts with the key scene, number 6, for once having determined the right acting area for that, those surrounding it will fall into place. The available areas are U C, U R C, the "B" and "C" platforms U C, the "E" platform L C, the seat at "F" (hitherto unused), D L C, and D L. He already knows that scene 4 must be played under the lamp light; and since Shadow's body is carried off U L by way of the river path, Mio's apostrophe in scene 2 must be spoken U C with L. 2E as the reference point. He knows also that in scene 5 Carr begins by pointing to the gangsters' presence off U L, so that scene will be somewhere on the U S platforms. Finally, it is noted that Esdras enters twice from R. 1E. so that the scenes in which he is featured (3 and 7) can most practically be played R. Thus by a process of elimination, the most emphatic unused areas for the crucial scene are on "E" platform and the seat at "F."

The moment of revelation comes in the following:

MIO: Miriamne, if you love me
teach me a treason to what I am, and have been,
till I learn to live like a man! I think I'm waking
from a long trauma of hate and fear and death
that's hemmed me from my birth—and glimpse a life
to be lived in hope—but it's young in me yet, I can't
get free or forgive! But teach me how to live
and forget to hate!
MIRIAMNE: He would have forgiven.
MIO: He?
MIRIAMNE: Your father.
(*A pause.*)
MIO: Yes.
(*Another pause.*)
You'll think it strange, but I've never
remembered that.
MIRIAMNE: How can I help you?
MIO: You have.
MIRIAMNE: If I were a little older—if I knew
the things to say! I can only put out my hands
and give you back the faith you bring to me
by being what you are. Because to me
you are all hope and beauty and brightness drawn
across what's black and mean!

MIO: He'd have forgiven—
Then there's no more to say—I've groped long enough
through this everglades of old revenges—here
the road ends. —Miriamne, Miriamne,
the iron I wore so long—it's eaten through
and fallen from me. Let me have your arms.
They'll say we're children—Well—the world's made up
of children.

MIRIAMNE: Yes.

MIO: But it's too late for me.

MIRIAMNE: No.

(*She goes into his arms, and they kiss for the first time.*)

We start at a key point of the scene rather than at its beginning. This is at Mio's point of discovery which comes on the single word, "Yes," after Miriamne tells him his father would have been forgiving. It is a moment of such importance that a strong move is mandatory, preferably a rise from a seated position. Mio must, then, be seated before he says it, and on seat "F." We find a suitable sitting line after Carr's exit. It is, "I might have known you'd win in the end." Sitting here rightly expresses Mio's rueful surrender to the inevitable, that he should finally cast the die in favor of Miriamne. The urgency and intimacy of the revelation call for the characters to be close together with their heads on the same level. For this, and to underline Miriamne's desire to help her lover in every way, it is fitting that she kneel at his side, on his right, with her arms around him. Mio then rises on the "Yes." But he lacks freedom of movement there on her left, and should take a stronger central position for the summing up. He has the opportunity on "this everglades of old revenges," and can cross Miriamne to up center on the line as he indicates the tenement with a gesture. The kiss is given center stage and from there Mio exits L. 2E.

The areas for these French scenes may now be fixed:

1. On Mio's first entrance he must cross freely L and R scrutinizing all the exits to see where Trock and his men are. Miriamne keeps urging him to come back into the house and it is best that she remain near the entranceway at R. 2E. So the scene is played R C and U R C where they wait on the R platforms for the funeral party to pass from R. 2E to L. 2E.

2. U C platform, "C," where Mio can observe the departure of Shadow.

3. U L C to U R C then transfer to D R C because Esdras must exit D R.

4. Taking cue from Mio's

> Only suppose
> this circle's charmed! To be safe until he steps
> from this lighted space into dark!

the lovers will be seated, for a time at least, on the bench under the lamp light. So—D R and D R C.

5. As explained, the first subject in this Carr scene is the gangsters' return to their posts on the river bank. This places it in the U C and U L C areas. Carr will exit R. 1E. leaving Mio U L C from whence he can cross to "F" for the start of scene 6, which moves from U L C to U C.

6. Already noted.

7. Esdras returns from R. 1E. They would naturally go to him. Played D R C.

8. Mio can deliver his prayer, "Now all you silent powers," from the "circle of light" D R. On Mio's question, "How many floors has this building?" he can back to U L C to get better perspective on the building's height. Miriamne can then cross to him, and the farewell can be given on the rock platforms U C. Mio returns, wounded, and falls on stage floor, U C, and they are there for the final tableau in scene 9.

They have thus "used the stage," at least as far as the large acting areas are concerned. The next step is to proceed to detailed blocking within these areas. This, as seen in the staging of I, 3, is wholly a matter of probing deeply into the details of the text, for the only clues lie there, and of setting the imagination to work in a relentless effort to match every nuance in the dialogue with a clear, truthful, and if possible, inevitable physical arrangement to reveal every facet of meaning that can be found.[1]

The foregoing has been concerned primarily with matters of direc-

[1] In some exceptional cases it may be more effective to play repeated scenes between two or three characters in the same acting area rather than to try and obtain variety by using several different areas. Thus, in a recent production at Yale, two comic characters engaged in plotting a robbery always gravitated to the same area to pursue their muddled schemes. This area, in consequence, was clearly established as the plotting place, and each time the characters approached it the audience could anticipate and enjoy what they knew was to come.

torial technique in handling mechanical problems of placement, and movement. Nothing has been said about the equally important problems of the acting itself—the search for the equivalency between the character's and the actor's emotions, the search for appropriate mental images on which to peg the portrayal concept of each character, matters of the actor's concentration and his sources of inspiration, to say nothing of the means whereby his thought and emotion are to be transferred to the audience. All these and connected subjects will be discussed in Chapter Ten.

Traffic Problems—Several Characters in a Small Set

Moving many characters around a cramped set demands precision in blocking so that the characters may find themselves in the right places at the right time, without bunching, masking, or colliding with each other. Being at the right place at the right time includes among other things a face-to-face confrontation between the character speaking and the character addressed, and avoidance of the confusion that always follows if there is much open space between them or if remarks have to be projected over the heads of several intervening characters. When the stage is full of people, the actors, if left to themselves, tend to line up in military fashion against the back wall. And unless the director is zealous in his preparation and anticipates the problems caused by new entrants upon a crowded scene, he will fall into the common error of settling on one single tasteful grouping and then leaving everybody in it without change—with inevitably dull results.

To demonstrate one way to handle a serious traffic problem we turn again to *Winterset*, which provides in Act II all the necessary ingredients —a tiny basement room filled with people in a situation requiring a lot of movement. Here is the scene:

(*There is a heavy knock at outside door. Miriamne opens it, at a glance from Garth. The Policeman is there in oilskins.*)

POLICEMAN: Evening.
(*He steps in, followed by a Sergeant, similarly dressed.*)
We're looking for someone
might be here. Seen an old man around
acting a little off?

POLICEMAN: (*To Esdras.*)
You know the one
I mean. You saw him out there. Jeez! You've got
a funny crowd here!
(*He looks round. The Hobo shrinks into his corner.*)
That's the one I saw.
What do you think?

SERGEANT: That's him. You mean to say
you didn't know him by his pictures?
(*He goes to Gaunt.*)
Come on, old man.
You're going home.

GAUNT: Yes, sir, I've lost my way.
I think I've lost my way.

SERGEANT: I'll say you have.
About three hundred miles. Now don't you worry.
We'll get you back.

GAUNT: I'm a person of some rank
in my own city.

SERGEANT: We know that. One look at you
and we'd know that.

GAUNT: Yes, sir.

POLICEMAN: If it isn't Trock!
Trock Estrella. How are you, Trock?

TROCK: Pretty good,
Thanks.

POLICEMAN: Got out yesterday again, I hear?

TROCK: That's right.

SERGEANT: Hi'ye, Trock?

TROCK: O.K.

SERGEANT: You know we got orders
to watch you pretty close. Be good now, baby,
or back you go. Don't try to pull anything,
not in my district.

TROCK: No, sir.

SERGEANT: No bumping off.
If you want my advice quit carrying a gun.
Try earning your living for once.

TROCK: Yeah.

SERGEANT: That's an idea.
Because if we find any stiffs on the river bank
we'll know who to look for.
MIO: Then look in the other room!
I accuse that man of murder! Trock Estrella!
He's a murderer!
POLICEMAN: Hello. I remember you.
SERGEANT: Well, what murder?
MIO: It was Trock Estrella
that robbed the payroll thirteen years ago
and did the killing my father died for! You know
the Romagna case! Romagna was innocent,
and Trock Estrella guilty!
SERGEANT: (*Disgusted.*)
Oh, what the hell!
That's old stuff—the Romagna case.
POLICEMAN: Hey, Sarge!
(*The Sergeant and Policeman come closer together.*)
The boy's a professional kidder. He took me over
about half an hour ago. He kids the police
and then ducks out!
SERGEANT: Oh, yeah!
MIO: I'm not kidding now.
You'll find a dead man there in the next room
and Estrella killed him!
SERGEANT: Thirteen years ago?
And nobody smelled him yet?
MIO: (*Pointing.*)
I accuse this man
of two murders! He killed the paymaster long ago
and had Shadow killed tonight. Look, look for yourself!
He's there all right!
POLICEMAN: Look, boy. You stood out there
and put the booby sign on the dumb police
because they're fresh out of Ireland. Don't try it twice.
SERGEANT: (*To Garth.*)
Any corpses here?
GARTH: Not that I know of.
SERGEANT: I thought so.
(*Mio looks at Miriamne.*)

SERGEANT: (*To Mio.*)
Think up a better one.
MIO: Have I got to drag him
out here where you can see him?
(*He goes toward the inner door.*)
Can't you scent a murder
when it's under your nose? Look in!
MIRIAMNE: No, no—there's no one—there's no one there!
SERGEANT: (*Looking at Miriamne.*)
Take a look inside.
POLICEMAN: Yes, sir.
(*He goes into the inside room. The Sergeant goes up to the door. The Policeman returns.*)
He's kidding, Sarge. If there's a cadaver
in here I don't see it.
MIO: You're blind then!
(*He goes into the room, the Sergeant following him.*)
SERGEANT: What do you mean?
(*He comes out, Mio following him.*)
When you make a charge of murder, it's better to have
the corpus delicti, son. You're the kind puts in
fire alarms to see the engine!
MIO: By God, he was there!
He went in there to die.
SERGEANT: I'll bet he did.
And I'm Haile Selassie's aunt! What's your name?
MIO: Romagna.
(*To Garth.*)
What have you done with him?
GARTH: I don't know what you mean.
SERGEANT: (*To Garth.*)
What's he talking about?
GARTH: I wish I could tell you.
I don't know.
SERGEANT: He must have seen something.
POLICEMAN: He's got
the Romagna case on the brain. You watch yourself,
chump, or you'll get run in.
MIO: Then they're in it together!
All of them!

MIO: (*To Miriamne.*)
Yes, and you!
GARTH: He's nuts, I say.
MIRIAMNE: (*Gently.*)
You have dreamed something—isn't it true?
You've dreamed—
But truly, there was no one—
(*Mio looks at her comprehendingly.*)
MIO: You want me to say it.
(*He pauses.*)
Yes, by God, I was dreaming.
SERGEANT: (*To Policeman.*)
I guess you're right.
We'd better be going. Haven't you got a coat.
GAUNT: No, sir.
SERGEANT: I guess I'll have to lend you mine.
(*He puts his oilskins on Gaunt.*)
Come on, now. It's getting late.
(*Gaunt, the Policeman and the Sergeant go out.*)

It is clear that the Policemen take charge. They are ambulatory and free to move about as they please. No one else will stir except Mio who provides the thrust that sends the action forward. The others remain still because of fear, reticence or feigned indifference as in the case of Trock. The feeling of the scene is one of suspended animation, a tense waiting to see if the officers will discover Shadow's body. Technically it is a scene of persuasion with Mio as protagonist in a position of dominance. It ends in anticlimax when Shadow's body is not found. Mio fails to prove his charge; the emotional surge of the scene recedes and Mio is left in a position of defeat.

Following standard procedure a synopsis of the action is set down to serve as a guide line.

1. The policemen enter and identify Gaunt.
2. They recognize Trock and warn him to behave himself.
3. Mio accuses Trock of the payroll murder and of killing Shadow.
4. The Policeman recognizes Mio as the smart aleck who baited him earlier in the evening.
5. Mio declares that Shadow's body is in the next room.

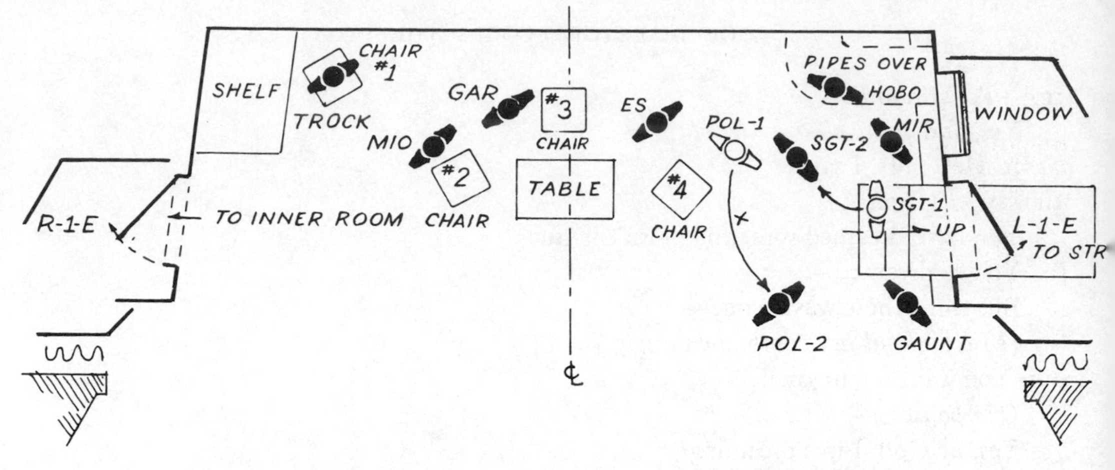

FIGURE 42 *Winterset*, ACT II. AMHERST COLLEGE MASQUERS PRODUCTION, DESIGNED BY CHARLES E. ROGERS

6. The policemen fail to find the body.
7. The Sergeant is half-persuaded that something is wrong. Miriamne urges Mio to admit he was mistaken. He does so.
8. The policemen take Gaunt away.

Certain obvious facts appear that bear directly on the blocking plan:

1. The Policeman addresses Esdras first, so Esdras should be close to the point of entrance to make this plausible.
2. Once Gaunt has been identified, he drops out of the scene until the end, so he should be placed in a weak area and in an inconspicuous position.
3. Trock's position must be such that the Policeman doesn't see him until after the discovery of Gaunt.
4. Mio must be given a dominating position for his accusation, and a weak one when he fails to make it stick.

After the policemen enter, the figures are arranged as shown in Figure 42.

Gaunt is D L below the steps so that the Policeman, entering, will sweep past above him. Once they recognize him he can remain there out of the way. Miriamne, having opened the door, backs down the steps and crosses to U L, with the Hobo on her R upstage near the pipes. Esdras, above Ch. 4 furnishes a target for the Policeman's cross to his L and gives him a reason for coming into the room. The Sergeant holds on the steps just inside the door. Garth is U R of Ch. 3 above the table; Mio U R of Ch. 2, R of table. Thus both Mio and Garth block off the policemen's view of Trock who sits Ch. 1 U R.

POLICEMAN: Evening.	*Policeman* X *to bottom of steps on entering. Sergeant closes door and stands top step.*
We're looking for someone might be here. ∧ Seen an old man around	∧ X *to L Ch. 4.*
acting a little off? ∧ You know the one	∧ X *U 1 toward Esdras. Sergeant descends 1.*
I mean. You saw him out there. ∧ Jeez! You've got	∧ *He* X*es to level with Esdras, turns L, looks at Hobo, who is U L of him.*
a funny crowd here! ∧	∧ *Hobo disappears under the pipes. Policeman steps down 1, sees Gaunt D R.*
∧ That's the one I saw.	∧ *Policeman* X *down 2, holds R of Sergeant who* X*es U R of Gaunt.*

FIGURE 43

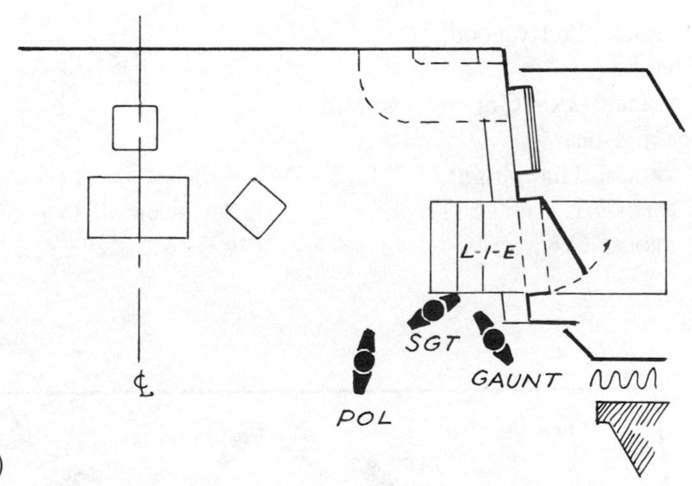

POLICEMAN: *(cont'd)* What do you think?	
SERGEANT: That's him. You mean to say you didn't know him by his pictures? ∧	∧ X *step close to Gaunt. Miriamne* X*es to above C of table. Her move motivated by fear that Garth may be implicated. Her move is toward Garth.* X *needed to relieve crowding stage L.*

^ Come on, old man
You're going home.

^ Puts a friendly hand on Gaunt's arm.

GAUNT: Yes, sir. I've lost my way.
I think I've lost my way. ^

^ Mio sits Ch. 2 to open Trock to view of Policeman. Mio must maintain attitude of tense watchfulness to counter weak move.

SERGEANT: I'll say you have.
About three hundred miles.
Now don't you worry.
We'll get you back.

Policeman backs 1 to R. ←

GAUNT: I'm a person of some rank
in my own city.
SERGEANT: We know that. One
look at you and we'd know that.

Policeman turns R. Trock rises.

GAUNT: Yes, sir.
POLICEMAN: If it isn't Trock!

To relieve C, Esdras backs L to U of door, above steps.

^1 Trock Estrella. ^2 How are
you, Trock?

^1 To Sergeant. ^2 Turn R.

TROCK: Pretty good,
Thanks.
POLICEMAN: Got out yesterday,
again, I hear?
TROCK: That's right.
SERGEANT: ^ Hi'ye, Trock?

^ Xes below all to R of Mio.

TROCK: O.K.

FIGURE 44

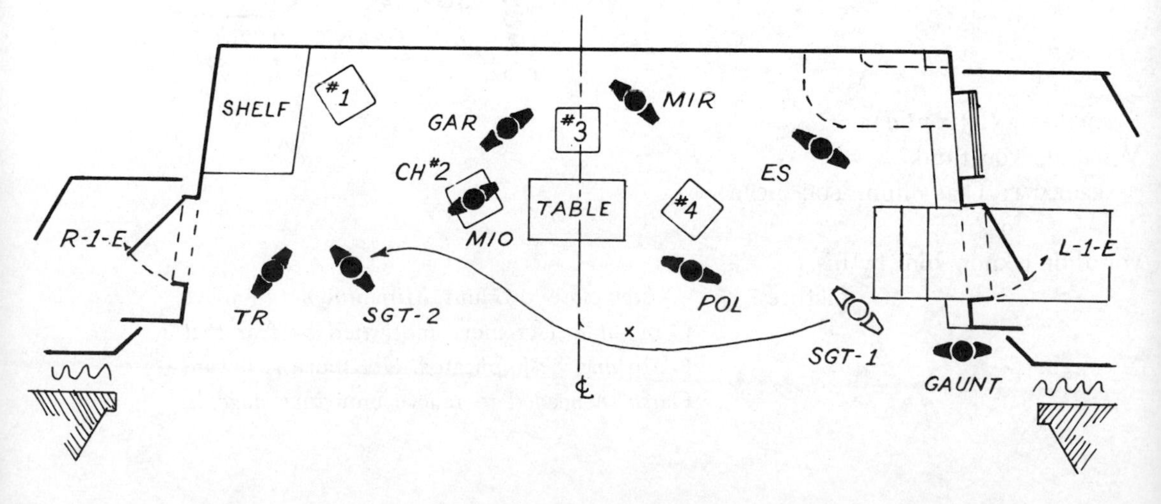

SERGEANT: You know we got orders to watch you pretty close. Be good now, baby, or back you go. Don't try to pull anything, not in my district.	
TROCK: No, sir.	
SERGEANT: No bumping off. If you want my advice quit carrying a gun. Try earning your living for once.	
TROCK: Yeah. ^	^ *X down a step anticipating Mio's rise.*
SERGEANT: That's an idea Because if we find any stiffs on the river bank we'll know who to look for.	
MIO: ^ Then look in the other room! I accuse that man of murder. Trock Estrella! He's a murderer! ^	^ *Springs up from chair.* ^ *Some movement in response to this is justified, and the coming placement can be anticipated. Miriamne X to U R, Ch. 3. Garth X to U L of her. Gaunt X to above steps. Esdras back 1 step U R.*
POLICEMAN: ^ Hello. I remember you.	^ *X to below Ch. 4.*

FIGURE 45

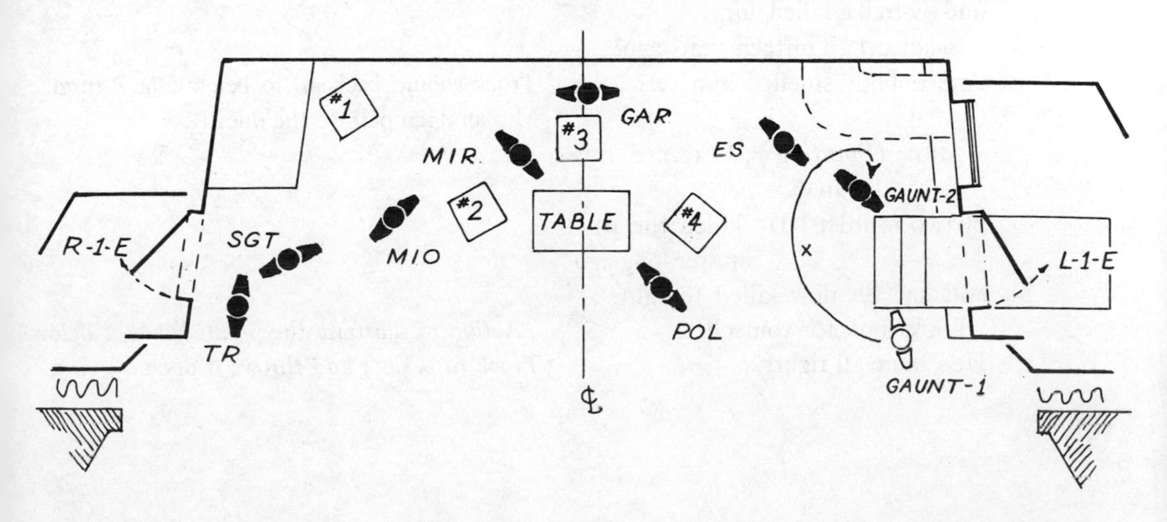

SERGEANT: Well, what murder?
MIO: It was Trock Estrella
that robbed the pay roll thirteen years ago
and did the killing my father died for! You know
the Romagna case! Romagna was innocent,
and Trock Estrella guilty!

SERGEANT: (*Disgusted.*)
Oh, what the hell!
That's old stuff—the Romagna case.

Preparation must be made for the Policeman to talk directly to Mio. Stage R is crowded. The Sergeant should relieve the pressure there. This speech gives him the opportunity. He Xes L to R of the Policeman, who stands below Ch. 4, for what follows between them.

POLICEMAN: Hey, Sarge!
(*The Sergeant and Policeman come closer together.*)
The boy's a professional kidder. He took me over
about half an hour ago. He kids the police
and then ducks out!

SERGEANT: Oh, yeah!

Sergeant turns to look at Mio. The audience should follow his eyes to Mio who speaks next.

MIO: I'm not kidding now.
You'll find a dead man there in the next room
and Estrella killed him!

SERGEANT: Thirteen years ago?
And nobody smelled him yet?

Trock should back up to below Ch. 1 to give Mio an open path to the door R.

MIO: (*Pointing.*) I accuse this man
of two murders! He killed the paymaster long ago
and had Shadow killed tonight.
^ Look, look for yourself!
He's there all right!

^ *Action to illustrate the point. Mio Xes below Trock to R door and throws it open.*

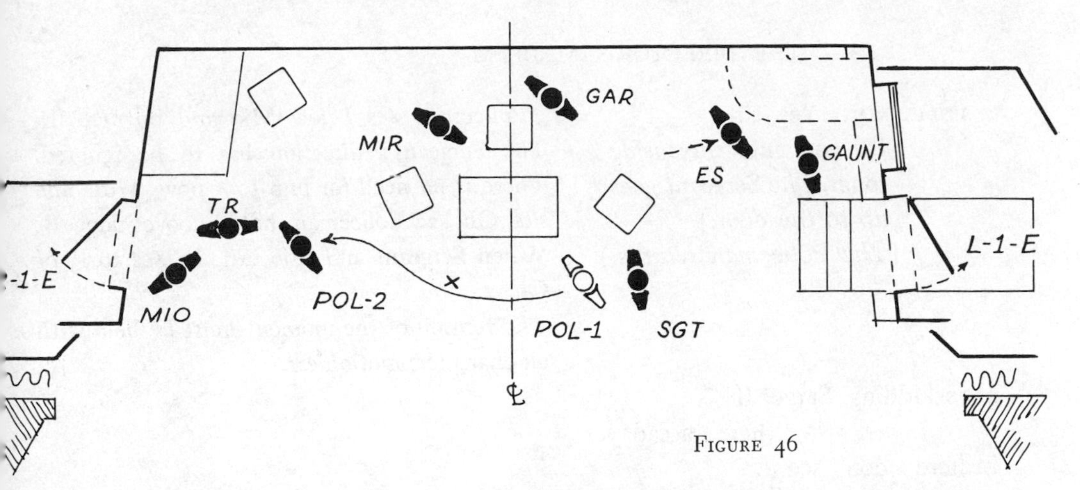

Figure 46

POLICEMAN: ∧ Look, boy. You stood
out there
and put the booby sign
on the dumb police
because they're fresh out of
Ireland.
Don't try it twice.

∧ Direct confrontation is necessary. Policeman Xes R to below R of Ch. 2. Sergeant backs to below Ch. 4.

SERGEANT: (*To Garth.*)
∧ Any corpses here?

∧ Circles to U L, Ch. 4.

GARTH: Not that I know of.

Trock backs a step to allow Mio and Miriamne to exchange glances.

SERGEANT: I thought so.
(*Mio looks at Miriamne.*)
(*To Mio.*) ∧ Think up a better one.

∧ Sergeant Xes down a step.

MIO: Have I got to drag him
out here where you can see him?
(*He goes toward inner door.*)

X R 1 step.

Can't you scent a murder
when it's under your nose?
∧ Look in!

∧ Mio X toward Policeman, Xing Trock. Gestures toward door.

MIRIAMNE: No, no—there's no one—
there's no one there!

Xes down a step to between Ch. 2 and table.

SERGEANT: (*Looking at Miriamne.*)
Take a look inside.

POLICEMAN: Yes, sir. ^
(*He goes into the inside room. The Sergeant goes up to the door.*)
(*The Policeman returns.*)

^ Policeman Xes below Mio and out R. 1 E. The Sergeant's direction has to be ignored. There is no need for him to X now. Miriamne sits Ch. 2. Policeman holds above door R. When Sergeant and Mio exit, he Xes to R of Ch. 2.
The tension of the moment must be held with all characters motionless.

He's kidding, Sarge. If
there's a cadaver
in here I don't see it.

MIO: You're blind then!
(*He goes into the room, the Sergeant following him.*)

SERGEANT: What do you mean?

Said while crossing.
To relieve pressure up Right, Trock now Xes to L. Ch. 3 going above table. And Garth Xes to L of Ch. 4 watching the door.

(*He comes out, Mio following him.*)
When you make a charge of
murder, it's better to have
the corpus delicti, son. ^ You're
the kind puts in
fire alarms to see the
engine!

^ *Sergeant should point the fact of his disbelief by getting away from the R area, besides, it's overpopulated. Tone of sarcastic dismissal in the line makes it a good one to X on. So, Sergeant Xes to L of table, below Ch. 4. To ready exit, Gaunt Xes up on step.*

FIGURE 47

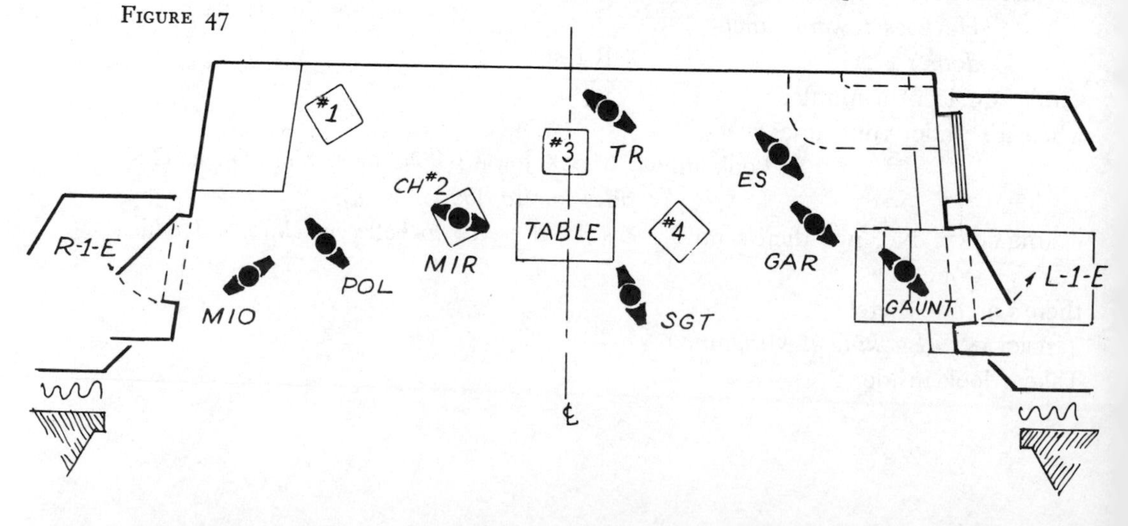

MIO: ∧ By God, he was there!
He went in there to die.

∧ X in 1 step.

SERGEANT: I'll bet he did.
And I'm Haile Selassie's aunt!
What's your name?

MIO: Romagna.
(*To Garth.*)
∧ What have you done with him?

∧ X in 1 step. Neither possible, nor necessary for him to be next to Garth for this line.

GARTH: I don't know what you mean.

SERGEANT: (*To Garth.*)
What's he talking about?

GARTH: I wish I could tell you.
I don't know.

SERGEANT: ∧ He must have seen something.

∧ X 1 step closer to Garth.

POLICEMAN: He's got
the Romagna case on the brain.
∧ You watch yourself,
chump, or you'll get run in.

∧ X 1 step to Mio.

MIO: Then they're in it together! ∧
All of them! (*To Miriamne.*)
Yes, and you! ∧

∧ Mio backs 1 step to R.

∧ Miriamne rises and Xes below Policeman to L of Mio. Her X motivates Garth's line.

GARTH: He's nuts, I say.

MIRIAMNE: (*Gently.*)
You have dreamed something—
isn't it true?
You've dreamed—
But truly, there was no one—
(*Mio looks at her comprehendingly.*)

MIO: You want me to say it.
(*He pauses.*)
Yes, by God, I was dreaming.

Garth, on this, Xes up to clear exit L as Mio Xes D R 1. Miriamne, with relief, may now sit again in Ch. 2.

SERGEANT: (*To Policeman.*) ∧
I guess you're right.

∧ Apparently a printer's error. The Sergeant's first line should be spoken to Mio, the second

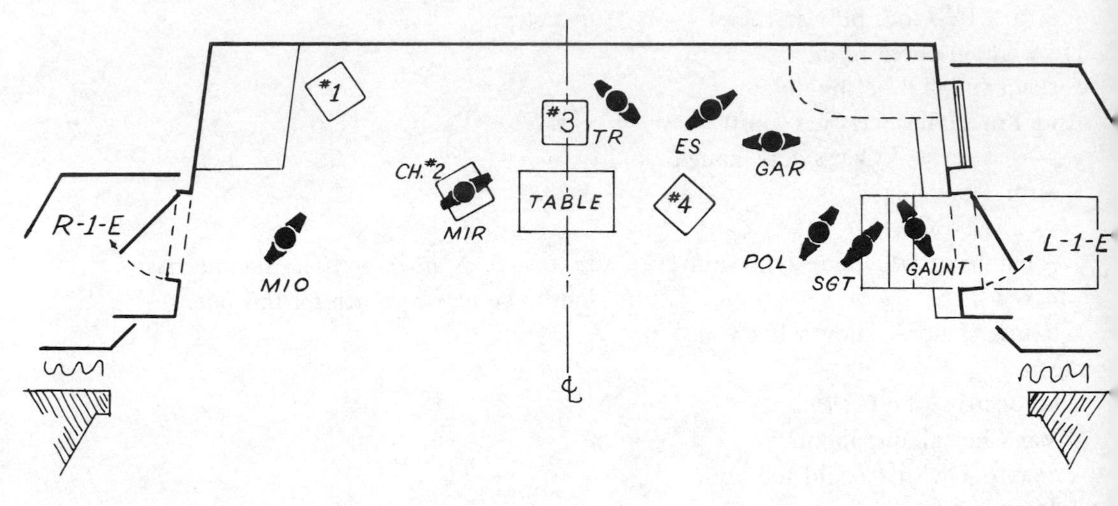

FIGURE 48

SERGEANT: (*cont'd*) We'd better be going.	*to the Policeman. On the line, Sergeant Xes to Gaunt, the Policeman following to make triangle D L.*
Haven't you got a coat? GAUNT: No, sir. SERGEANT: I guess I'll have to lend you mine. (*He puts his oilskins on Gaunt.*)	*Gaunt steps down to stage level for business.*
Come on, now. It's getting late. (*Gaunt, the Policeman and Sergeant go out.*)	

CHAPTER NINE

Cutting, Casting, First Reading

Prolixity is just as bad, when you must say with Plautus:
"My legs ache with sitting and my eyes with looking."

JULIUS CAESAR

Cutting

As has been pointed out, law decrees that the playwright owns his play; the words are his property, and not one may be cut nor any added to the text without his express permission. But in collegiate or community theatres and in stock, since the dramatist normally is not on the ground to protect his rights, the law is sometimes more honored in the breach than in the observance.

It is usually up to the director to initiate changes in the manuscript, to suggest to the playwright why cuts should be made and where they should be made. If he presses for them too assiduously or fails to offer persuasive reasons for them, he extends the area of potential conflict with both the playwright and the actors. Every request for a cut calls the judgment of the playwright into question and some writers are very sensitive on the subject. What the director should establish early in the game is the commonality of interests both he and the writer share, and the end to which they both aspire—a successful production. He must also gain the playwright's confidence by giving him demonstrable proof of the validity as well as the necessity for any change he proposes. Tact is needed. The wrong road to persuasion is to press the point that large chunks of material should come out because they are hopelessly confusing, extraneous, or downright dull. The director's critical language must be couched in gentler terms, and there must be an appreciation of the playwright's feelings. Some, it is true, welcome suggestions and comply readily when shown their value; others guard their words like a tigress guarding her cubs and howl with pain at the very thought of expunging a single one.

One basic reason for cutting is to bring performances to within customary time limits. On Broadway, the eleven o'clock curtain is almost mandatory if train and bus schedules are to be met. And there is the matter of the audience's attention span. The director is usually more mindful than the playwright of the numbing effect which a protracted period of sitting on a hard seat can have on the spectator. To this the playwright may reply by citing king-size plays and operas through which audiences have sat happily and without complaint—Maurice Evans's full-length *Hamlet,* O'Neill's *Strange Interlude, Mourning Becomes Electra,* and *Long Day's Journey into Night,* Wagner's *Ring.* This puts the director in the awkward situation of either having to withdraw his suggestions or making it clear to the author that his play may not be in the same class with these masterpieces, which happened also to have been acted or sung by stars of the first magnitude.

The fact remains that in the American theatre today the dramatic masterpiece is a scarce commodity. So is the acting talent necessary to sustain audience interest unflaggingly for more than two and a half hours, particularly in the amateur theatre and the professional theatre below the first rank. There is much to be said for the director who insists on taking the precaution to hold down the acting time to two hours. How many of us have had to suffer through long-drawn-out productions where judicious (and extensive) cutting would have been an act of mercy not only for the audience but for the cast as well.

The whole subject is touchy, perhaps the touchiest there is in the director-playwright relationship, because it does challenge the author's fitness in matters on which he is supposed to be the authority. This is why many directors refrain from approaching the subject at all until their own opinions can be supported by the responses of a paying audience.

Yet, when there is a question about the theatrical value of a line, a speech, or a whole section of dialogue, it is the director's duty to question the advisability of retaining them. He cannot, in conscience, avoid his responsibility for the success of the production with the public. It helps if he can offer his objections in a candid, objective, and helpful manner. The politest course is to try and persuade the playwright with the strength and rectitude of his argument, and to have the generosity of spirit as well as the humility to acknowledge the possibility that his own judgment may be in error, particularly with respect to cuts made before rehearsals begin.

One acceptable method of procedure is for the director to phrase his suggestions as questions and put them to the playwright as questions rather than demands. "Doesn't the audience already know that the hero was born in Pittsburgh?" "Does the heroine have to explain in such detail that she is filled with grief? Can't she show this in action?" "Would the juvenile, who graduated *summa cum laude* from Harvard, say 'Ain't,' and 'I feel like a Harvard graduate should'?" This approach at least reassures the playwright that the director shares with him the same uncertainty about a line's real effectiveness.

The most sensible course is for the director to postpone major cutting until he has heard a complete read-through by the cast. This gives him rough timing and suggests the dimensions of cutting that may be necessary. It is easy to miscalculate from his own solitary study of the script the true effectiveness of all the lines, even those which obviously repeat something that has been said before. The director must remember that there is some validity in Galsworthy's rule of three: the need to tell the audience that something is about to happen, that it is in the process of happening, and that it has happened. In any carefully written and already compressed work something of importance, although it may be a mere overtone, is bound to disappear with every excision; and how is the director to know that what reads as redundancy in his study may not exert a powerful cumulative emotional response in the theatre where repetitions, like recurring themes in a symphony, may contribute heavily to the continuity, naturalness, and build of the scene as is so often the case in the long works of Eugene O'Neill?

There is this to be said, however, about the advisability of doing some cutting before the first reading: it minimizes one cause of wounded feelings among the cast. Deep cuts in an actor's role, when he has gone to the trouble of memorizing it, is certainly wasteful of his time and can be a source of discouragement. It is hard to convince some actors that the cuts in their parts have not been made because of their own personal inadequacies. So in the amateur theatre especially, for the sake of morale, as many major cuts as possible should be given at the first reading. Subsequently some lines and speeches may be restored, if necessary, with attendant good feeling all around.

What in general should be cut?

Nothing in general. Only in particular. Every play presents its own special case. The problem is to find what can be culled with the least harm to the plot, the characterization, the mood, and the literary texture —in that order of importance. What can be omitted with the least damage are slight nuances of feeling that might be lost anyway in the hurlyburly of the playing, prolonged extensions, and convolutions or elaborations of any dramatic idea. The likeliest material for the scissors are passages that are peripheral or subordinate to the main subject and theme, which interfere with the intensity and flow of action, interrupt continuity, or seem too complex or difficult to be grasped as the words flash over the footlights. In some cases, subplots can be reduced or eliminated along with the characters in them without destroying the impact of main action.

Digressions, however interesting in themselves, can also be pruned. In Act V of *The Doctor's Dilemma,* for example, Jennifer Dubedat makes a long and eloquent plea against animal vivisection. This, as everyone knows, was the subject of one of Shaw's favorite crusades and he could not resist an opportunity to argue its cause. It is a fine passage but off the point of the scene, and it comes late in the play when such disquisitions yield diminishing returns.

Lines which add no more to the understanding of a character or a mood, or any interpolation in narrative form which recapitulates attitudes or events already known, must be given ruthless scrutiny. The surest guide is the director's own estimation of his audience's intelligence. When the sense of any passage is obscure and neither the actor nor the director can find a satisfactory interpretation for it, that passage should come out for there is little doubt that what is incomprehensible to them will also fail to be understood by the audience.

It has become the custom in the professional theatre to let the audience itself cut the play. It works this way. The director, producer and playwright prepare the uncut version although they are well aware that it is overlong. It is said that *Camelot* ran for over five hours at the Toronto opening. In the pre-Broadway tryout, which may last from two weeks to a month, an intensive study is made of the audience's reactions. What the public responds to with enthusiasm is kept in; what leaves the public cold and indifferent is taken out. The process is wasteful and expensive, but with the present high costs of production few directors are willing to take the responsibility of using the blue pencil before having a chance to test the public's judgment.

What must come out are lines or selections that evoke unwanted responses. There is no real test for these outside of actual performance. Most of the time they are in the form of laughs coming in the wrong places—at the players rather than with them. They usually occur in scenes of tension and may be more hysterical than derisive, although nonetheless unnerving for actors. Sometimes the fault is the dramatist's for maintaining a scene too long in one tone without variation; sometimes it may be the director's for insisting that a scene be played at a relentless emotional pitch without giving the audience a chance for relaxation. What must be remembered is that the spectators defend themselves, if they have to, against overinvolvement in scenes of horror or distress, particularly if the acting is exaggerated in any way. In a production of O'Neill's *Homecoming* at the Yale Drama School the first-night audience, whose emotions had already been considerably wrung by the intensity of *Agamemnon* which preceded it on the same bill, tittered in the last act when Christine Mannon, lifting her stricken husband upright in bed, gave him a poison pill as directed by the text, pressed a glass of water to his lips and said, "Now drink!" No words were needed; the pantomine had made all too clear what was taking place. When the line was eliminated in subsequent performances the undesirable response went with it.

Winterset, as we have seen in the previous demonstrations, is not what one could call an underwritten work. Even the present acting version takes over three hours to perform uncut. One passage from it has been chosen to illustrate the kind of elaboration found, and a possible working method for approaching the cutting problem follows. Since no one can be sure his cuts are good until the production faces the test of performance, the reader shall have to decide for himself if the cuts shown help or harm the play.

The passage occurs in Act II. Mio enters the basement tenement, explains who he is to Garth and Garth's father, Esdras, then asks Garth if he knows anything at all about the payroll robbery and murder for which his father was executed.

> MIO: . . . You may not care
> whether he was guilty or not. You may not know.
> But I do care—and care deeply, and I've come
> to ask you face to face.
> GARTH: To ask me what?
> MIO: What do you know of it?

But before Garth can reply, old Esdras interrupts with a counter-question, the answer to which has already been made unmistakably clear to the audience in Act I.

> ESDRAS: This man Romagna,
> did he have a son?
> MIO: Yes, sir, this man Romagna,
> as you choose to call him, had a son, and I
> am that son, and proud.
> ESDRAS: Forgive me.

Esdras' superfluous query has the effect of pushing Mio off the track and away from the main object of his visit. Esdras' derogatory phraseology spurs him to defend his father, but what he says is merely an unsupported assertion of a vague generalization:

> MIO: Had you known him,
> and heard him speak, you'd know why I'm proud, and why
> he was no malefactor.
> ESDRAS: I quite believe you.
> If my son can help he will. But at this moment,
> as I told you—could you, I wonder, come tomorrow,
> at your own hour?
> MIO: Yes.

Why Esdras should want to stall for time is understandable, but it is a long act, playing well over an hour, with most of it given over to a debate between Mio and Judge Gaunt which contains little dramatic motion except the flow of ideas. In any case, Esdras' appeal for delay gets nowhere and is really too half-hearted to evoke much actual suspense.

ESDRAS: By coincidence.
we too of late have had this thing in mind—
there have been comments printed, and much discussion
which we could hardly avoid.

This interjection by the old man, like the others, is unimportant; and coming as it does from a subordinate character in the scene is an annoyance, although it serves the purpose of giving Garth time to prepare himself for his answer. Mio now tries to get back to the point and turns to Garth again:

MIO: Could you tell me then
in a word?—What you know—
is it for him or against him?—
that's all I need.

But again the old rabbi butts in:

ESDRAS: My son knows nothing.

When Garth finally does respond to the question in the next speech, he includes a comment on yellow journalism:

GARTH: No.
The picture-papers lash themselves to a fury
over any rumor—make them up when they're short
of bedroom slops . . .

And then he comes to the point:

GARTH: (*cont'd*) This is what happened. . . .

Now it is submitted that the continuity of the dramatic idea in this scene, reduced to its essentials, is:

MIO: What do you know of it?
GARTH: This is what happened. . . .

If everything else between question and answer were cut, what of value would be lost? Garth's guilty reluctance to reply would not have been established, and Esdras would be removed completely from the scene. Perhaps the head of the household should not be so summarily overlooked. Garth could express his unwillingness with a move and Esdras' presence could be made to count sufficiently if a speech or two were retained. And these values would be suggested without being spun out at such length, thus:

ESDRAS: This man Romagna,
did he have a son?
MIO: Yes, sir, this man Romagna,
as you choose to call him, had a son, and I
am that son and proud.
ESDRAS: Forgive me.
MIO: (to Garth) Could you tell me then
in a word?—What you know—
is it for him or against him?—
that's all I need.
ESDRAS: My son knows nothing.
GARTH: No.
This is what happened....

The following points have been omitted: (1) Mio's assertion that but to know his father was to love him; (2) Esdras' fumbling attempt to delay the proceedings; (3) his feeble explanation about why they know something of the case; and (4) Garth's parenthetical criticism of the tabloids. Is the loss of momentum toward the main point, with whatever suspense is created by it, worth the not inconsiderable thirty-five seconds of playing time? This is the sort of question the director must be prepared to answer when he sets out to cut a script.

There are two different ways of cutting. One is to snip phrases and sentences here and there in the text while preserving the gist of the scene intact. The other is to undertake major surgery and remove whole blocks and sections of material or even entire scenes and acts. *Peer Gynt*, for instance, can be brought down to workable size only by omitting the whole fourth act. The consequences of this are dire, of course, but one must make the choice between a four-hour performance and one that lasts for six hours.

Of all playwrights whose extant works supply the richest ore to be mined and set aside, Shakespeare stands supreme. Except for one or two shorter plays, *Macbeth* among them, few people in the modern audience have had the opportunity to see any of them in entirety. It is not our purpose here to offer laments for this loss, but to give an example or two of what can be done in the way of cutting and stitching to accommodate audiences now too impatient or too busy to listen to everything our greatest dramatist has to say.

The first scene of Act II of *King Henry IV, Part One,* takes place in an inn yard at Rochester. Present are Two Carriers, Gadshill, who is one of Falstaff's party, and a Chamberlain, minor characters all. The Two Carriers are packing their goods on horseback. They have spent a miserable night at the uncomfortable inn and grumble at the fate which has put them on the road at two in the morning. Their failure to raise the ostler to lend them a hand increases their comic discomfiture. After refusing Gadshill the loan of their lanterns, they take themselves off. Now, aside from establishing the time of day, or rather night, and the meanness of their surroundings, the scene serves little purpose save as an example of the crusty way of menials and the earthiness of their talk. The meat of the scene follows when the Chamberlain tells Gadshill, and for the second time, that a franklin loaded with gold is ready to set forth from the inn. Gadshill sees the opportunity for a strike. To the Chamberlain's hint that robbery brings the hangman, Gadshill in a long speech hints that their highway gang contains some highborn members who could "make all whole" should they run into trouble, and after a few pleasantries takes his leave. He reappears in the following scene to tell Falstaff and Prince Henry that the franklin and his men are coming.

The first scene is a lively bit of preparation for the second, but strictly for its contribution to the plot it offers nothing that is not made apparent in Scene 2, and for this reason it can come out.

One more example: the second scene in the opening act of *Macbeth* gets the play off to a somewhat shaky start with two long speeches of narration, and is often omitted. The bleeding Soldier's description of the valor of Macbeth as he unseamed Macdonwald from the "nave to the chaps" is no doubt helpful as a preview of the hero, but his continuing description of the battle, of the retreat of the kerns, and the new onslaught by an entirely different foe—the Norwegians under Sweno—adds a whole new dimension, all too suddenly, to the amount of information we must digest in a short space. Ross then resumes where the fainting Soldier left off and adds more details to the story—of the treason of Cawdor and the final victory of Macbeth over him and the invading Norsemen. Inasmuch as Ross recapitulates much of this material to Macbeth himself in Scene Three, and gives him the further news that

Cawdor has turned traitor to the King and will be deprived of his title and life, it may be in the best interests of the performance to bring Macbeth and Banquo on immediately after the first Witches' scene (I, 1) and omit everything in their speeches at the start of I, 3 including "Aroint thee, witch! the rump-fed ronyon cries" which always draws a laugh, except "A drum, a drum," and the roundabout spoken in unison that winds up the charm just as Macbeth enters.

Perhaps the day will come when playgoers will have the leisure and the inclination to take Shakespeare whole, an eventuality devoutly to be wished. But in the meantime the director must face the unpleasant task of amputating much beauty. A necessity which must have been painful for Maurice Evans in his "*G.I.*" *Hamlet* was eliminating the entire Gravediggers' scene. The director must learn to accept as inevitable the howls of the purists, whose favorite passages seem always to be the ones to go, and comfort himself with the thought that he has as conscientiously as possible marked for deletion what harms the play least.

Casting

Few phases of theatrical production are more subject to windy chance than the assembling of a good cast, and none is more crucial to the success of the enterprise. Fortunately, one quantity in the casting equation need not remain unknown for long, and that is the exact nature of the characters to be played. The director can come to know them as he knows the palm of his hand, and armed with this knowledge he must be, before he can even begin the process of selection. Some directors make a point of preparing detailed sketches of each character in order to keep in mind the image seen by the playwright. Such notes may include mention of physical appearance, mannerisms, habits of mind, typical responses, essential motivations, reactions to the play's situations and the reasons for them, together with any other clues about the character's social, educational, or psychical background that may help to catch the essence of that personality. Whether the information is written down or not, the director's insight into the character must be complete.

The next step, which may sound simple but isn't, is to try and find an actor whose physique, personality, and acting style fit the director's image of the character, and whose stage age and physical appearance can be made to fit it.

In the search for talent to fill a specific role, there is no better guide for the director than his own knowledge of what the candidate has already done in action before an audience; but unfortunately even this is not always infallible. The circumstances of each play differ and there have been instances where an actor, successful in a specific type of part, has been a failure as a similar type in another play.

Almost any competent professional director can cast well if budgetary considerations are not a factor. But budget is always a factor in the New York theatre, and the director may not have the funds to command his first or second choices for a part—or even his third or fourth.

There is also the problem of availability. Producers and directors have been known to wait for two or three years before casting a play until their first choices work free of prior commitments. When conditions prevent them from postponing operations, they must do their best to find outstanding alternates.

Lack of familiarity with the work of actors, restricted budgets, or the engagement of the right people elsewhere often force the director to call upon casting agencies or actors' representatives for help. If this fails, he resorts to the "open call," a device that brings hundreds of actors—good, bad, and indifferent—to auditions.

Needless to say, the director rarely has to carry on this activity alone. The producer shares with him the responsibility and, often, the authority; and the playwright's contract gives him the right to veto any candidate.

Preliminary screening of aspirants in an open call is usually handled by the stage manager. Selected candidates may be given a copy of the script and permitted to return in an hour or so to audition, or even asked to read at sight.

Procedures differ with different directors. Guthrie McClintic claimed that he never asked an actor to read, no doubt in the belief that it would be discourteous thus to show any skepticism about the actor's ability. He preferred to talk about the part and get the actor's reactions to it. Ordinarily, however, the actor reads—first, alone for the producing team; then, possibly with other actors; finally, if he passes these tests, with the tentative cast.

In the amateur theatre, the number of candidates the director can draw upon is limited and he must make do with whatever material he has on hand. This disadvantage is offset by his continued exposure to the capabilities of his acting personnel and the resulting knowledge of what they can and cannot do. This often leads him to choose plays to fit his best talent, a condition which does not exist in the professional theatre. When a play succeeds on the collegiate stage, it is not so much the result of the director's having cast it well, although that is the common view, but because he has shown resourcefulness and skill in training and teaching actors who may not have been the right types at all. Unlike the professional director, he cannot cast to type except for juveniles and ingenues. All the characters, regardless of age, must be played by students between sixteen and twenty-four. He must therefore cast according to type potential, as indicated by height and weight. The casting of heavy, mature characters is his most critical problem. To give these any sort of acceptable reality the make-up box must be plundered of its supply of crepe hair, liquid white, and crimson-lake liner in order to supply the visible lineaments of age. And all too often these are supplemented by a style of acting which exaggerates the stereotype—the stooped back, the feeble gait, palsied hands, and the grossly altered voice hopefully simulating the cracked pipings of senility. That director is fortunate who is able to find young men and women (and there are such) with the looks and natural gift for playing character parts, who can reproduce the essentials of maturity without resorting to caricature.

Tryout procedures are more or less standardized in school and amateur theatres.

Copies of the play are made available in the library or wherever else those interested may easily consult them. Notices of the time and place of auditions are posted, together with lists dividing tryout hours into five- or ten-minute intervals so that the candidates can sign up for specific appointments.

Newcomers are usually asked to come prepared to read two short selections (one serious and the other comic) from plays of their own choosing to illustrate their acting range. Because a new actor may be nervous and unsure of himself, it is often better to give him a private interview in the director's office or study instead of a formal audition on the stage. The main object of the meeting should be to break the ice, to let the director become acquainted with the candidate and to determine his type as well as the extent of his interest and experience. If the student is outgoing, and prepared and willing to read something, he should be permitted to do so, but it is often better to postpone the actual reading until the second meeting, which may be the actual tryout. All newcomers should be asked to appear on the first day, while those whose work is known may be called on the second or third day. The director should give all candidates, new and old alike, his suggestions about what part or parts he would like them to read.

It is a simple matter to have a batch of three-by-five cards printed up to record the pertinent facts about each candidate. These may be filed alphabetically for future reference.

Appropriate entries should include the candidate's age, height, weight, and coloring—his theatrical type—the quality and range of voice, and a note about his muscular coordination. A list of important roles previously played is usually included, and space should be left for any additional comment the director wishes to make. The director should avoid making the tryout an ordeal. The atmosphere should be one of friendly informality where the task itself is taken more seriously than the people concerned. Since the auditioner is in a sense the director's guest, he should be treated with courtesy and given the director's complete attention. Whispers or covert glances to the stage manager, who may be present, poorly stifled yawns or other indications of boredom, impatience, or incredulity can turn the tryout into a shattering experience for the auditioner. And the director who only half-listens may miss something that might have been helpful to him.

If there are other people present besides the director and stage manager, they should be inconspicuous. In the professional theatre, the playwright and the producer are directly concerned and should be on hand, but seated in the house, if the tryouts are onstage, so as not to give the appearance that the candidate is facing a drumhead court-martial.

It is important for the director to talk to the candidate first, describing briefly the personality of the character to be read, his position in the play, and what physical or other features are being sought. The candidate should be encouraged to ask questions about the role. For it is only by hearing the actor talk and by observing his reactions and responses that the director can get some hints about what the actor possesses in the way of singularity of personality that sets him off from others. An intelligent estimate of these somewhat intangible expressions of individuality may prove of more use than the audition itself. After the talk, the candidate may go up on the stage in order that the director from half-way back in the house may judge his vocal projection and facial expression, as well as his ability to move.

An experienced director learns not to expect too much from a first tryout. He uses the occasion to weigh the candidate's good points against his bad, beginning with the physical features—size of head in proportion to body, set of eyes, characteristic carriage, presence or poise, and nature of temperament. He may even give the actor a simple direction or two to test his physical responses, his coordination and grace.

Above all, he will listen to the voice—its timbre, range, and expressiveness, the force of attack on words and the rhythm and tempo of sentences. He will try to detect regional dialects, and observe if breath sustains tone. He will listen to hear if the actor makes sense of what he reads, and whether or not he manages to convey an emotional compatibility with the lines.

The director must be on his guard against overestimating the staying power of the natural extrovert whose self-assurance may carry him over the hurdles of a first reading with flying colors. Some actors fail to improve in rehearsal and may never be as good in performance as they were at the audition. It is just as easy to underestimate the potential of someone who is shy and tense at the outset but who may be transformed into a real performer once he is sure of his part and in the presence of an audience.

Those who already have some rudiments of technique are often most adept at concealing all semblance of what sort of people they really are inside—and it is for what they *really* are that most directors look. Exaggerated vocalization, mannerisms, and readily generated but shallow emotionalism tend to conceal their real natures, and when an actor resorts to them it may be the result of shyness or overtension. Faults like these can be corrected. The director should ask the aspirant not to act but to be himself in the reading and to approach the character honestly and simply without recourse to acting clichés or trumped-up feelings.

It is helpful if the director can say something constructive about a reading. Adverse criticism is of little use to an actor who is not to be given another chance, and it may be humiliating.

In the amateur theatre where good morale is always an important consideration, the director should tell unsuccessful candidates why they were not cast. This should be done tactfully and sympathetically in a private interview before the cast is announced, and the director should be careful to confine his remarks to technical rather than personal deficiencies. College students are too intelligent to be dismissed with the stale excuse that they are "not the type." There are many legitimate, and, from the candidate's view point, understandable grounds for rejection. He may have a provincial accent or faulty projection, or even a slight speech defect which may be corrected in time. Or the physical characteristics of the individual may not mesh with those of the other members of the cast. A boy may not be tall enough to play opposite the leading woman or he may fail to provide some physical contrast needed for the part. Lack of experience may be the deciding factor. Whatever the cause, the applicant who shows some talent should be encouraged to try again the next time.

Prior to auditions, the careful director will have penciled in a possible cast drawn from actors with whose work he is familiar. All such precasting has to be tentative, and preaudition choices should never be disclosed to anyone. The tryout may uncover better material. What the director has to do is to measure the qualifications and abilities of a new possibility against his memory of the strength and attributes of the preselected candidate. This gives him a concrete comparison. Later in the tryout period his first prechoice can be pitted against all the new possibilities in face-to-face competition.

Having heard the new people, he then calls the veterans. These may have already decided what parts they wish to try for, and they should be heard in them. Naturally they will be interested most in the leading roles. But among actors as elsewhere, the reach oft exceeds the grasp, and the director may eventually be compelled to suggest that one in his seasoned group may be more suitable for a minor or supporting part rather than a lead. The importance of such a role in the production should be stressed, and the candidate further reminded that there are no small parts, only small actors. If the morale of the group is high, such candidates usually agree to read whatever part the director suggests.

When everyone has had his chance, the director will study his card file and discard first all who are obviously unqualified. The remaining cards will be sorted and all the candidates for each separate part will be considered together, beginning with the leads. After careful weighing of each prospect, the director will then list the candidates in preferential order for each part. The leads should be chosen first because the second and third choices for these may well be the best for supporting parts. Thus, the runner-up for Thomas Mendip may play Humphrey Devize; the second J.B., a Comforter; and the loser for Willy Loman may be the logical first choice for Charley or Uncle Ben.

Before he comes to any firm decision about any of the roles and sets aside the cards for a minimum number of candidates, perhaps two or three for each part, the director exerts his memory and imagination to visualize the various contenders in combination with each other, thinking always in terms of what physical and stylistic relationships the several assortments may produce when considered as an enemble. He will speculate on how they match, blend, contrast, or clash in terms of height, weight, coloring, voice, and personality. This, of course, is only the test run. Whatever hunches he has at this point must be put to the proof in the final group tryout, the "call-back," when the final three or four choices for each part read in many combinations. Every effort should be made to limit the number of recalls to those who are really in contention. If the director is absolutely sure one candidate is clearly superior to all others for a particular role, that person alone should be recalled. It is not fair to obviously weaker candidates to be kept in suspense and made to read in the call-back if the director already knows they really stand no chance. Whenever he has some doubt, however, he should call back as many as half a dozen, if need be, in the search for the right actor.

The list of candidates for the ensemble audition is then posted, along with the specific parts they are to read. If possible, the actual scenes that are to be worked on should be indicated in order that the group may prepare them.

Call-backs are held onstage with the director seated in the house.

The stage manager is in charge of details, distributes the parts, and summons the readers in proper turn, leaving the director free to concentrate on what is being revealed as the various combinations read.

Physical discrepancies, mismatching, and differences in vitality or force of personality are thrown up in high relief once the groups are seen together from the front. The director should proceed by a process of elimination. As soon as it becomes apparent that one candidate is less suited than another for a role, he should not be allowed to continue reading for it, although he may well read for another part later.

Auditioners should be required to move around a little, to sit down for some scenes and stand for others. Some directors even try to stage a scene in rough fashion, although this has always struck me as being designed to impress onlookers rather than to accomplish any helpful purpose except perhaps to show whether or not the actors are quick at picking up directions and cues.

If an actor should misconceive his character or mistake the sense of a scene, the director should not let the misreading continue. He should call the actor aside, briefly explain the error, and make a positive suggestion about the proper approach.

Often there is a choice between a candidate who is close to the required physical type and another who is less like the type but a better all-around actor. On the average, I think it is better to choose the better actor, and leave to the costumer and make-up man the problem of closing the gap between the actor's appearance and the physical requirements of the part.

The director should so work toward the assembly of his final choices that at the end of the tryout those final choices are onstage. This should be done even though it becomes obvious to the other contenders what the choices will be. There is no point in prolonging suspense about the final selections, although some directors with a misplaced sense of the dramatic delay the announcement until everyone's nerves are awry.

The First Reading

With the cast chosen and the list posted, the usual procedure is to call everyone together on the following day for a first reading. This should not be considered as another tryout with several contestants reading for each role. It is a reading by the cast, although the director may wish to explain that his selections are tentative, being founded on his fallible judgment, and that he must reserve the right to change his mind about any part if the reading offers convincing proof that he has made a mistake.

There are several ways of handling the reading.

Some directors prefer to read the play entirely themselves to the listening cast. This is a pleasant custom because it gives the director an opportunity to show how well he can read. But unless he has great gifts for it and a developed acting technique that lets him do justice to every role, both male and female, and as long as everybody understands that the real purpose of the occasion is to celebrate the director's skill in acting and interpretation, the experience is likely to be unfruitful for all concerned. If the director's object in reading himself is to provide something for the actors to imitate, there is danger that all the parts will sound alike. Besides, there is always the possibility that his inflections and intonations may be wholly misleading and present a handicap to the actors which time alone may overcome.

Sometimes the playwright is brought in to read his own script. This is laudable as an act of courtesy toward the author but of no practical use otherwise. The playwright's skill is usually confined to writing the words, not reading them. If the objective is to reveal to the cast how the playwright thinks the lines should be spoken, the results are invariably embarrassing unless as is rarely the case, the playwright is an expert at stage speech. Besides, any sensible playwright is far more interested in discovering how the actors are going to speak his lines than he is in demonstrating how well he can read them himself. The sensible director should feel exactly the same way.

If the playwright can be present at the first reading, it is much more helpful if he does not read at all but talks briefly about the meaning of the work, his ideas of the characters, and the gist and tone of the whole. What should be borne in mind is that the final test is neither how well the playwright reads nor how well the director acts. The final test is the actors' performances.

If the director wishes, he can follow the playwright's remarks with some of his own, concentrating on the aim of the production. He can show designs, ground plans, or models of the settings, and with the help of the designer explain their nature and purpose. The first meeting is not the most propitious time for lengthy explications of acting problems or for extended discussions of the details of characterization. Prolonged around-the-table arguments are not much help either. Invariably, some actors will be too tense and preoccupied to take in what is being said, and these will refrain from participation in the discussion. Others will take the floor to compound the obvious or shine in forensics. Either way not much is proven except the point that brilliance in debate and excellence in acting are not always one and the same thing.

Another waste of time is for the director to use the first meeting to explain exactly what he wants from his actors before they have had a chance to demonstrate what they have to give. A few years ago, Mr. Yuri Zavadski, the director of the Mossoviet Theatre in Moscow, was invited to direct a professional off-Broadway company in *The Cherry Orchard. The New York Times* reported that he spent five hours of the first rehearsal discoursing on the meaning of Lopahin's first speech, "The train is in at last, thank God. What time is it?" Considering the short time allowed for rehearsals for the production, this display of directorial vanity and arrogance was, of course, preposterous. The assumption was made that the actors had never heard of the play before, nor of the author, nor of the Stanislavsky method which he wished imitated; and all this before anybody in the cast had had a chance to open his mouth!

The fact is that at such a time actors are anxious to do one thing more than anything else, and that is to read their parts aloud. I doubt that many have much interest in voicing their ideas and opinions about their parts, or the play, or anything else, and even less in hearing somebody else read their parts for them. Most of them being strangers to each other, the one sensible way to start things off is not to try to set them arguing but to let them give voice to the text. The director should begin with a few remarks about the work and a brief outline of the main aspects of each character. It is assumed that he has already discussed their parts in detail with each actor. If he hasn't, he may find a player embarking upon a reading wholly at variance with the director's idea of the character, and will be forced to interrupt the reading to make the actor revise his concept on the spur of the moment.

Interruptions in the reading should be kept at a minimum. The director should not stop to make corrections. Instead, he should take notes of faults and misconceptions, and give them privately to the individuals concerned at a later time.

First readings are usually bad, but this should not discourage anyone, least of all the director. His common sense should tell him that the cast is facing unfamiliar material and, probably, unfamiliar company. Under these circumstances even the more experienced in the group will show little polish. He, himself, must maintain an air of cheerful confidence if only to banish inner qualms. He may also find consolation in the thought that if they all gave marvelous renditions at the initial meeting there would be very little left for him to do in the weeks of rehearsal ahead.

If it should become obvious in the course of the reading that a particular actor is all wrong for the part, the director should not reach an immediate decision to replace him then and there. He may ask the readers to switch parts around for a scene or two in the hope that a better distribution of roles may result. If this does not work, the director should sleep on the problem and then re-examine his card file. The next day, he can recall one or two of his other choices for that part and give them a rehearing. If, on the basis of this audition, he decides that one of these is better than his original selection, or let us say, not as bad, he should go ahead and make the change, explaining as tactfully as possible to the one replaced his reasons for making it.

Occasionally but not often it is impossible to decide between two actors for the same role, and the director may dodge the issue by casting them both with a view to letting them alternate in performances. This seldom works and can harm the production. It makes double rehearsals necessary. If this severe measure is adopted one of the players will be skimped in rehearsal or neither given enough time for thorough preparation. In addition, two sets of costumes have to be made. If the two actors differ somewhat in style or take the moves and speeches at different tempos and rhythms, the other players may find it difficult to set their performances in adjustment with both. And there is always the possibility that one of the performers will far outdistance his rival in rehearsals and as the opening night nears will clearly demonstrate his superiority. In such a case the director is forced at last to come to the decision he should have made at the beginning. His only alternative is to accept a poorer performance every other night. This unhappy predicament can be avoided by not double casting at any time, or perhaps, if there is little to choose between two players, by designating one of them as an understudy.

CHAPTER TEN

Through Rehearsals to Performance

Produce! Were it not the pitifulest infinitesimal fraction of a product, produce it in God's name.

CARLYLE: *Sartor Resartus*

Various Procedures Examined

The rehearsal period is divided roughly into four main sections with considerable overlapping: a time for discussion and analysis, a time for actors to learn their parts and their moves, a time for polishing, and final concentration on perfecting synchronization between playing and the technical aspects of production.

AROUND THE TABLE

There is little uniformity of opinion among directors about the proper amount of time to spend at the outset around the table before actors get on their feet and start moving. Sometimes a full week or more may be given over to discussion and analysis, although George Abbott and other consistently successful directors begin blocking after a single fast read-through.

Actors who are keen on debating and have a gift for probing into the psychological or esthetic sinuosities of their roles enjoy these sessions enormously. So do directors with the same bent. Yet as suggested in the previous chapter an actor's fluency in discoursing on the philosophical niceties of his part is not necessarily an index of his ability to act it successfully. And a director may be full to the brim with theories about what the play means and still not have the technical apparatus to stage it well.

From prolonged discussions about interpretation, inner meaning and inner motivation, the director may gain much information about his cast's intellectual prowess and imaginative power. Nevertheless, he must remain in the dark about the kind and quality of performance the players are capable of giving until such time as they stop talking and start acting.

Complicated literary plays with baffling themes certainly need more time around the table for an interchange of ideas than straightforward "shows." So do symbolic dramas with hidden meanings and period pieces whose archaic language may demand considerable explication. Few can quarrel with any system that gives the director as much time as may be needed to see that his cast has a working knowledge of what the play is all about and the significance of their respective parts in it. But extending the seminars and directorial lectures beyond this point is a waste of time. Two or three such sessions are usually sufficient for the groundwork.

When the main problems of interpretation, approach, and characterization have been settled in a general way, attention is given to readings, to matters of vocalization, word emphasis, tempo, rhythm, tone blending, and the like. Such study will be more meaningful if these subjects are approached in relation to meaning, motivation, and mood. Now further consideration may be given to matters discussed in the earlier sessions: psychological attitudes, character relationships, and nuances of feeling as expressed by the voice. In fact, while the cast remains seated, the whole acting mechanism can be set going with the exception of motion and total body response.

What tends to be forgotten by those who insist on long drawn-out meetings of this sort is that the natural locus of the actor is the stage. It is his chosen habitat, and I suspect that in general he feels more at home upon it than he does in the atmosphere of the classroom which the seated rehearsals suggest. When the seminar approach is prolonged unduly, which would seem to be the case if, say, a quarter or a half of the entire rehearsal time were to be given over to it as has been done in some productions, there is bound to be exaggerated and one-sided emphasis on the verbal and intellectual aspects of performance. This in turn can be a primary cause of strained and unwanted self-consciousness in playing.

Difficulties arise when the actor is asked to read with feeling from his seat at the table. The effect of emotion on inflection, as everyone knows, is profound. More often than not an emotion follows in direct response to a physical attitude, to muscular tension or a body reflex; not the other way around. A true feeling is rarely evoked if the actor's whole instrument is not engaged. This is why an actor after four or five days of sitting still finds himself itching to get on his feet and act, particularly if the theoretical discussions have centered mainly on someone else's role rather than his own.

ON THEIR FEET

I happen to be one (among many, I hope) who believes in holding as many rehearsals as possible on the regular stage of a theatre, and in moving as quickly as is expedient away from the table in order to set the play in motion. The build of a play should be gradual, and so should the actor's progress toward mastery of his characterization, lines, and business. Movement is a crucial factor in this build and must be connected to it very early in the learning process, not hastily and peremptorily tacked on to it at the end. Good movement resulting from good blocking will not save a bad play, but if the positions are right it means that the characters are always in the right physical relationships, if nothing else. To start from any other technical base than one which sees to it that the positions are unassailable and, if possible, inevitable, can easily lead the director to unforgivable ineptitudes in interpretation.

Memorization goes better this way, too. As a mnemonic device, the seated rehearsal is unsatisfactory. It is always easier to remember lines when they are associated with moves, business, and explicit stage areas.

When he is on the stage, the actor can be encouraged to project instead of mumbling his lines into his chest. There is something of a challenge about those empty seats. They remind everyone of the ultimate target toward which all their labor is being aimed. It is possible, too, that in the stage environment, the players' awareness will be more easily quickened to consider the part the audience will play when the time comes for actors to share the fruits of the creative process with them. The actor may be a little more mindful of the importance of the spectators, and they are all-important. When they are not there the reason for the actor's being ceases to exist. It is healthy to work in conditions which bring this truth home.

When the actors do get on their feet, the director usually starts with the rough blocking, taking each act as a unit. On the ground plan drawn to scale on the rehearsal floor and with the furniture and entrances exactly sited, he gives them their positions and crosses in a general way. The players make the moves and note them in their books or "sides." Blocking rehearsals should be concerned with blocking alone. There is no point, at this time, in burdening the cast with minute details of business, with subtleties of characterization, or with precise readings. This comes later. The director should take pains to explain precisely the reasons for each move, and enough time should be allowed for the actors to test them and to try alternatives, if need be. They should even be encouraged to think of more effective moves if they can.

With a three-act play, it is customary to block one act at a time and to let the cast give it a quick run-through during the last hour, with the director correcting obvious mistakes. The fourth session will be a complete run-through of the entire play with the cast holding books. This may have to be repeated once or twice more with the whole play as a unit until the actors are fairly sure of where they are going.

The next stage is memorization. The single act is again the unit and the daily schedule is much the same as that for rough blocking, one act per session without books for three days and on the fourth a full run through without books. Memorization of lines and positions is a matter of drill. The director, to get results fast, may have to act as drillmaster. There is no reason for actors to object to this, and those who do are usually impatient at any show of authority, or incapable of doing anything with precision.

It is often difficult to avoid giving some consideration to line readings, characterization, responses, attitudes, motives, and character interactions in the blocking and memorization sessions. But the director should try to remember that progress in these areas will be much faster once the cast has mastered the lines. Full attention to these subjects should be left until the ensuing period, which follows immediately.

It is only natural that up to this time the actor's concentration has necessarily been on his own lines, his own part, and his own moves. Individual coaching sessions tend to bend his gaze even further inward. Now arises the necessity to shift the emphasis to work on his relationships with the other characters and to try and fit his performance with theirs. Particular attention has to be paid to the alternations of intensity and relaxation as the scenes move from climax to anticlimax. There is a paradoxical motion in the rehearsals of this important period: increased attention must be given to the ensemble playing, but at the same time there has to be a narrower and narrower concentration on individual scenes, beginning with the most difficult. So as the segments of scenes treated tend to get smaller and smaller, as they should, and the refinement and polishing of fine points of movement, interpretation, and light and shade are given closer and closer scrutiny, there arises the danger that the full perspective of the play will be lost in a welter of details. To avoid this at least two complete uninterrupted run-throughs should be scheduled in each of the polishing weeks, in order that the "finish" of all the acts may be maintained at a fairly constant and relatively uniform level.

While this outlines a general procedure, the actual rehearsal schedule must be a flexible affair to take cognizance of the special problems each play always, and uniquely, presents. If there are crowd scenes, for example, they must be handled separately first without the principals, who in turn are rehearsed separately. When each has a grasp of its assignments they are brought together. Duels, love scenes, or other scenes requiring complex business are also rehearsed separately. Some directors even like to take scenes out of order, perhaps in imitation of movie technique, and then hold special sessions for melding them together in their proper places in the play. There seem to be few advantages in this, and it works for irregularity of pattern and raggedness of continuity, both of which may be avoided by rehearsing scenes in textual sequence.

There are other methods of rehearsing which do not follow at all the one I have described. I have been told about one in which the director confines himself to two or three pages of text per rehearsal, and sets them completely without further review until the dress rehearsal. While such procedure would seem to place an unbearable burden on the poor actors who are not given opportunity for drill or the benefits of repetition, no one can condemn it without first viewing the results in performance, however unpromising such a method may sound.

Directing the Individual Actor

FINDING THE RIGHT APPROACH

As has been said, when the director rehearses an individual player he functions as a coach. His object is twofold: to help the actor toward an understanding of his part and to explore with him the most effective technical means of objectifying that understanding. *How* he approaches each actor, what means he employs to stimulate the actor's imagination and evoke his enthusiastic cooperation so as to draw from him a full, solid, and rounded performance depend entirely on the nature of the personality he is dealing with. Some actors respond readily to the slightest suggestions; some wish to be shown explicitly what is wanted. One may have to be cajoled, another browbeaten (in rare instances). There are actors who resent frank criticism and those who are discouraged by it. It is the director's business to criticize and make corrections. But he should be at pains to do both in as objective a fashion as possible. His attitude should be one of friendly detachment, not cold or hostile. It should bespeak a sincere desire to be helpful and constructive. Actors are quick to sense this posture and under it will normally react to correction with grace. What is essential is that the director establish very early a footing of mutual confidence. He must not talk about it but show by his actions and his whole bearing that he respects the actor's abilities, is considerate of his feelings and judgment, and when the chips are down is on his side. There is nothing so detrimental to morale, so inhibitory to the creative atmosphere and eventual success of a production as a state of war between the director and the members of the cast. If it is true that only strangers can be enemies, then the director must make certain that his actors are not strangers to him. He must learn to know their temperaments, their favorite methods of work, their strong and weak points as players, and tailor his approach to each one on the basis of this knowledge.

This does not mean that rehearsals have to be simpering love feasts. Gifted people seriously intent on first finding the truth, and then on one honest way among a multitude of choices to express it, may differ strongly with each other and with the director both as to what the truth is and the best means of projecting it. There should be healthy clashes of opinion, and full "gloves-off" discussions of differences. It is best if these can be conducted without any suspicion of personal rancor, with both parties aware of their common goal and all concerned striving for effectiveness in performance.

WHAT TO LOOK FOR

Coaching the actor, the director will take one scene at a time, let the actor walk through it on his own, and conscientiously scrutinize and make note of every detail—the voice, the use of the body, facial expressions, gestures, moves, indeed every and all outward manifestations of feeling and intention being expressed. And even though it is a hackneyed phrase, one of the most helpful things he can do is to see that the action suits the word and the word the action. He will check appropriateness and consistency in the character's psychological attitude in every line and examine whatever progressive change there may be in the attitude to align it with the dynamics of the action. Brought under review will be the propriety and aptness of the basic attack on the character—is it right with respect to the age, sex, disposition and background of the person portrayed? Does the reading of the lines reveal the personality? The execution of the moves? The moves themselves? The actor will be encouraged to experiment with his voice until he and the director are satisfied that the desired shade of meaning is being registered. Nor will the director be so concerned with subtleties of inflection as to overlook the need of insisting that the words be pronounced in accordance with the preferred reading in Webster's *New International Dictionary*, a book no director should be without.

The force of the emotions will be regulated to fit the need of the scene; and criticism will be aimed at eliminating mannerisms, vocal tricks, or any other manifestations that ring false or seem stagy, trite, or unconvincing. All such matters of technique will form the basis of the drill in the coaching sessions and will be subject to attentive review later in the regular rehearsals with the ensemble.

Perhaps the most important aspect of the coaching rehearsal, however, is the opportunity it presents to the director to exploit and capitalize upon the actor's strong points, and to minimize or hide his weaknesses—the same procedure, incidentally, that he applies to the text of the play. If an actor has unusually expressive eyes, the director must invent occasions for their use. If he is skilled in pantomine a way must be sought to bring that gift to the foreground. If there is a capacity for much grace and style in movement, the blocking must be made to reveal them.

Concealing defects is no less a part of his responsibility. The habit of starting a line on the same note as the cue and reading it in the same rhythm or tempo of the speech preceding it is to be avoided, and so is the use of repetitive and meaningless gestures, a common failing among amateurs. For the actor who moves awkwardly, the blocking may have to be revised to keep him seated much of the time. For the actor who does not know what to do with his hands the director may have to resort to drastic measures. A start can be made by asking the actor to hold his hands naturally at the sides, neither dangling them loosely nor exerting too much muscular control because this produces rigidity. If the actor can stand up straight without stiffness, it will be found that the arms fall naturally in a line with the seams of the trousers. The fingers should be slightly curled, and the thumbs should not be extended. For variation of posture one arm may be bent at the elbow, the forearm held parallel to the floor with the fingers lightly touching the jacket.

It is obvious that an actor cannot go through an evening with his hands mechanically set in these formal positions, even if they do convey a certain air of naturalness and relaxation. Hands are meant to be used, and on the stage they must be used expressively. The director may have to suggest specific gestures at designated points in the action. The actor may even learn to make these easily and give the impression that they are unstudied. With luck they may suggest the moment's emotion and seem to be in keeping with the character. But the odds remain long that such gestures imposed from the outside will be mechanical or mannered. With an awkward actor the director must start by teaching him to use his body as a single entity. Unease of stance and the unconvincing use of hands, arms, and legs begin from a failure to realize that these members are not disassociated from the trunk but function as essential components of a single structure. The muscles which move the arm and hand must work in conjunction with the larger muscles of the shoulder and the back in such a way as to engage the whole mechanism. Once the actor begins to think of his whole physical being as an integrated instrument in which the meshed parts move together, some of the awkwardness should disappear. It helps, too, if he can be made to think of his body balance, beginning with the feet. Once he learns to place his feet in a position natural to him and curl his toes under as if to grip the floor, his body will have a solid, muscular set, and his arms should fall into natural positions of rest.

If this fails, the director must find things for the hands to do. Lighting and handling cigarettes or a pipe, managing a teacup or a cocktail glass; manipulating a handkerchief or a fan are commonplace devices, as are sewing or knitting. Clasping the hands behind the back or keeping them hidden in pockets is an admission of failure.

A good actor can appear relaxed and in repose without seeming to be indifferent or inattentive. This is a calculated effect and can be learned. It involves good muscular coordination, control of the breath, physical balance and inner composure. Manifestations of nervousness and tension can be consciously suppressed, and even such minor reflexes as nictation can be controlled so as to occur only at designated times. The back must be straight, the shoulders squared, and the trunk should rest solidly on the pelvic bones. Most importantly, the legs must take the body weight without effort. Of the actors who have mastered the problem of how to stand still on the stage without stiffness, I would hazard a guess that most of them began by learning to be aware of the line the legs make. The classic stance is obtained by putting the feet about five or six inches apart with one foot drawn back about half its length and slightly turned out at the toes. The knee of that back leg is held straight or flexed slightly backwards, with the other bent slightly forward. Most of the weight is carried by the back leg, otherwise the body will seem to be falling forward. Placing the feet further apart changes the pose from one of ease to one of stolidity, and this can be effective when the aim is to heighten the style. If the feet are too close together, the weight may appear to be placed on a single unsteady balancing point offering too little resistance to a push, with the body in danger of toppling over.

Bodily relaxation can be vitiated by excessive concentration of the gaze and any stiffness in the facial muscles. For an actor to look too intently at another without sufficient cause is almost as bad as not looking at him at all. Directed to the audience the piercing stare is simply a form of overacting. Where the actor looks and the intensity of it must be calculated in terms of the sense of the scene at that moment and its emotional content. An actor can be a good listener without summoning up an expression of avid eagerness which makes the listener seem equal in importance to the speaker, if not more so. The director must watch for such distractions and correct them.

A beginning actor usually has to be taught how to start a cross from a position of rest. It is not an easy matter to do it correctly. First the weight must be shifted to the foot opposite the one the actor is to step off with. The body must move as a single articulated unit, always in balance and with a contained arm swing. The amount of swing depends on the purpose of the move and the emotions of the mover. But however large or small the arm swing is, it should begin at the shoulder and the muscles must be under control all the way down the arm to the tips of the fingers.

The actor may also have to be taught to time his steps to fit the rhythm of the crossing line, with each step taken on the beat of a long syllable, if this can be done without seeming to be artificial or mechanical. If there is no relationship between the steps and the line, the timing will seem eccentric and the move itself unrelated to the line's meaning.

Beginners also have to learn how to maintain balance as well as to help motivate a move by making a gesture with the hand or arm simultaneously with the first step of a cross or the beginning of a rise. Nor should they be left unaware of the fact that one can cross backwards as well as forwards. Many a snarl in an ensemble can be unraveled by having an actor back up a step or two.

These, of course, are all rudimentary matters which mainly concern the director of amateurs. Of far greater importance both to the amateur and professional director, and for both a fundamental responsibility, is the search for unhackneyed and appropriate physical responses which accurately express specific emotions.

FINDING THE RESPONSE

On the highest level, the problem for the director is to get the actor to use his body as a metaphorical vehicle for the expression of a dramatic idea. Success in finding original and effective physical responses marks the difference between a journeyman director and a master of stagecraft. And because the actor himself is directly concerned in the search and may conduct much of it on his own, the degree of his success in the search marks the difference between a stock actor and a star. The imposed gesture, the imitative stance and the timed cross are all childish matters of abecedary technique and it has to be assumed that the experienced actor will not have to be given them. What is significant is that the gesture, the stance, the cross, and any connected stage business must arise from a complete understanding of the character at the moment he puts these instruments of expression into effect, his emotional attitude in the scene, the essence of the scene itself, the depth of his participation in it—both emotional and psychological—and the whole history and background of the character in relation to the moment.

Needless to say, the prime object is to find responses which fit the character. What must be avoided are the stale stereotypes that seem like parodies of emotion, such as these described in *Reflections upon Theatrical Expression,* published in London in 1755, which, if adopted, would reduce acting to a simplified set of rules and at one stroke eliminate both the problem of searching for responses and the director himself.

> In astonishment and surprise arising from Terror, the *left* leg is drawn back to some distance from the other; under the same affection of the mind, but resulting from an unhop'd for meeting with a beloved object, the *right* leg is advanced to some distance before the left. Impatience and regret at being detected in an iniquitous design may be heightened by shuffling of the feet without moving from the spot.

One of the principal purposes of rehearsing with the actor individually is to settle what he will *do* at any moment in the play when some palpable manifestation of feeling must be shown. To say what *he* will do is perhaps misleading. More correctly, it is what he, *as the character,* will do.

What does Hamlet do when he first sees his father's ghost? What does J.B. do upon being told that two of his children have just been killed in an automobile accident? And how will these characters look at such moments of tension?

What they will do and how they will look must follow inescapably from what they *feel.* The emotions that seize them before, during, and after the event must first be defined before they can be expressed. When the playwright is too explicit about the emotions his characters are feeling at any given moment, the director must be on his guard, for this is a sign that he is dealing with inferior dramatic material as in the following:

> SIR PHILIP: You there behold his father—my brother—
> (*Weeps*)—I've not beheld that face in twenty years. Let
> me again peruse its lineaments. (*In an agony of grief.*)
> Oh, God! how I loved that man!—

Or:

HANDY, JR.: (*Starting with horror, then recovering.*) What followed? [1]

Good dramatists supply clues, but in a different way from the above, as for example:

QUEEN: But, look, where sadly the poor wretch comes reading.[2]

The line tells us what Hamlet's mood is and what he is doing. The clues are not always as explicit as this and, more often than not, how a character "takes" a situation and how he reacts to it must be deduced from the background facts of the situation and our knowledge of what sort of person he is.

What the actor should do when, as Hamlet, he sees the ghost of his father offers a good problem on this point.

His first utterance is:

Angels and ministers of grace defend us!

and this is followed by an expression of determination to speak to the apparition whether it be a messenger from heaven or hell. In the first place, it must be remembered that his sight of the Ghost is not wholly unexpected. Horatio and Marcellus have already identified it and have told Hamlet what to expect, so whatever shock of surprise is to be heard in Hamlet's invocation must be somewhat softened by the realization that the Prince is not unprepared for what he now sees. To be sure, he has to be startled at the moment of confrontation, but he can recover swiftly. What follows "Angels and ministers of grace . . ." has not a little recklessness in it. Come what may, Hamlet will risk daring the powers of evil, if that is what the Ghost represents, by addressing it boldly. This, of course, he does. So it should be obvious that his call to heaven for help is not the cry of a terrified man, but one who is ready for danger and composed enough to face it without flinching. If, in general, it has already been decided that this Hamlet is spirited and courageous, not a melancholy neurotic, the actor will certainly not shrink in terror and fall to the floor in a fit.

Under the circumstances, what, then, shall his physical response be?

[1] Morton, Thomas, *Speed the Plough*. Act IV.
[2] Hamlet, II, 2.

Personal testimony of how other people may have reacted on similar occasions is scant, seeing ghosts not being a common human experience. So there is no point in seeking expert advice on the subject. Even if some authority could be consulted, the general instance would be of absolutely no use to us. What is wanted is the specific and likely reaction of this one person, the man Hamlet is supposed to be.

The answer must be found in the light of the special circumstances of the scene itself and with due consideration of the actor's own personal and physical endowments as these are related to the concept of Hamlet's character already decided on. The special circumstances include the design of the setting, the lighting, Hamlet's costume, and his properties, if any.

The director and actor, having decided between them that at the moment of discovery Hamlet is startled but not afraid, struck but not stunned, now proceed to work out something expressive of these attitudes in terms of the exact physical conditions of the set. Hamlet may try taking a step backward with his hand raised as if to protect his eyes, but the move should not in any way suggest a retreat. If the actor is already standing on a step or a ramp he may descend slightly, backing away from the Ghost. Since the Ghost has not yet been clearly identified, Hamlet would not be likely to kneel even if in a position to do so, there being no call at this moment for such a gesture of obeisance. If there is a pillar or some other architectural element nearby, he may use it to support himself and check his backward move. Since he carries his sword some use may be made of that. He might raise it by the blade and hold the hilt outthrust before him as a symbol of the Cross, giving visual representation of the heavens he invokes to stand between him and what he sees. If he does this, the gesture should end with the line, and the sword returned to a position of defense as if in readiness against anything that may come.

The business and the move may then be rehearsed in detail until the actor feels secure in them. He will then try it with the speech. Repetition and experiment may extend and elaborate the response. Later, if the moves appear too strong or too studied or do not register as they should to the eye of the director as he watches from out front, they may be modified, enlarged, or even scrapped and something else substituted.

How J.B. should react to the awful news of the deaths of his two children presents a somewhat different problem in that the experience, if not exactly common, is one that unfortunately can and does happen. Children die in traffic accidents every day, and parents have to be told. This is not to suggest that the imagination has to be exercised in Hamlet's case and not in J.B.'s. Far from it. But while no one in the audience can criticize Hamlet's reaction on the basis of contrary findings from personal experience, the same cannot be said of J.B. Nevertheless the sort of testimony based on arguments *ad hominem*, or on evidence supplied by someone who may have been present somewhere when a similar situation occurred, is of little or no help to the director or actor, and for the simple reason that such a witness is not J.B. What must be discovered is how J.B. reacts to the news, and the reaction must not only fit him but be conventional enough to register his emotions with the audience.

Let us examine the scene:

(*J.B. and Sarah* (*his wife*), *arm in arm, walk slowly into the first circle of light. . . .*)

GIRL: (*Crossing to meet them with an affected walk, the First Messenger screening himself behind her, the Second following.*)
Good
Evening! What a pleasant evening!
Back from the theatre so soon?
We're neighbors, don't you know? You've met my
Miffkin walking me each morning:
You know Muff, my purple poodle . . .
Isn't it a pleasant evening!

SECOND M.: I'm from the press. There's been an accident . . .
(*He falters.*)

FIRST M.: Four kids in a car. They're dead.
Two were yours. Your son. Your daughter.
Cops have got them in a cab.
Any minute now they'll be here.
(*He raises his camera over the girl's shoulder.*)

GIRL: (*In her own voice, screaming.*)
Don't look! Cover your face!

SARAH: (*With scarcely the breath to say it.*)
Mary . . . Jonathan . . .

(*The flash. J.B. throws his elbow up as if to ward off a blow. Sarah does not move.*)

J.B.: You bastards!

I'll beat your god damned brains out . . .

(*He lunges after them blinded by the flash as they scatter.*)

Where have you

Gone?

(*Sarah moves like a sleepwalker through the circles of light, one after the other, touches a chair, goes down on her knees beside it, clinging to it.*)

J.B.: Answer me!

(*Silence.*)

Answer me!

(*Silence.*)

SARAH: (*Her voice dead.*) It wasn't

They that did it . . .

(*J.B. comes slowly back out of the darkness, sees her, crosses to her . . .*)

J.B., the reader will recall, is a strong, hearty, outgoing American businessman, tough enough to beat down competitors, yet withal a man with a sturdy belief in God's goodness. From the directions the playwright has provided, the character does not respond immediately to this appalling news. The response is a delayed reaction, triggered when the camera flash explodes in his face. This makes him raise his elbow and lunge after the departing messenger.

In the Yale production of the play, the scene was tried exactly as called for in the script, but something seemed to be missing. The moment was not as effective as it should have been. The difficulty appeared to be that after hearing that his children had been killed, J.B. had nothing to do while waiting for the Girl's line, "Don't look! Cover your face!", for Sarah's following line, "Mary . . . Jonathan . . . ," and then for the flash before he could react. That static pause had to be filled, and because J.B. himself was the key character, it had to be filled by something he did himself. It was suggested that the actor on first hearing the news should react as though someone had hit him in the stomach with a baseball bat, after a full swing. The blow was to seem enough to cripple him and double him up, but not to bring him down—that would come later under added jolts of fate. There was a slight pause to let this effect register with the audience and was followed by a bit of business showing him making an effort to recover and straighten up. A split second later his thoughts turned toward his wife, and he made a feeble gesture as if to try and protect her. This was done during the Girl's warning line. The next step was to extend the physical effect of the imaginary blow to the solar plexus until his cue came to say, "You bastards! . . ." on which he made his lunging cross. What had to be shown was his rage and hatred of the world, vented in speech, but rendered ineffectual by the blow the news had given him. This was done by coupling a strong reading of the line not with a powerful lunge after the reporter but with a weak, stumbling, and uncertain cross into the darkness at the edges of the set, as if the blow had robbed him of his strength and made pursuit futile. The actor's image was that of a mortally wounded animal biting at the spear while the hunter stands unscathed. Played this way, J.B. seemed to be in the scene every second and the long unfilled hold was eliminated.

Thus in *Hamlet* and *J.B.* alike the procedure for determining the response is the same. The problem is always to discover how *that particular character* might react to a given situation, to establish and identify the nature of his emotion at that given moment, to visualize the physical response in terms of the scene's environment—the costumes, props, set, and lights—and dovetail that response precisely with what the character says and when he says it, linking the sense of the speech and the physical response to everything that has preceded the event and comes after it. Having done this, what must ensue is a testing of the results of the director's findings to insure that what has been decided on registers as it should with the audience.

FINDING THE INFLECTION

Making the green one red

I will speak daggers to her but use none

There are more things in heaven and earth, Horatio, than
are dreamt of in our philosophy.

Needless to say, the sense of these familiar lines can be drastically altered by stressing different words. Thus the green sea may be made one universal red, or the particular one that is already green may be made red. Hamlet may intend merely to speak daggers to his mother, but not put a single one to use, or he may use daggers to speak with. And in the third quotation Hamlet may mean his own and Horatio's particular philosophy or just philosophy in general.

Such textual ambiguities as these are commonplace in the theatre, and while most of them including those above yield to common sense and logical deduction when weighed in relation to character and context, they occur frequently enough to be a continuing directorial problem. Assuming that the director is intelligent enough to know what meaning a line should have and able enough to choose the proper stress to make that meaning clear, the next problem is to find a workable and acceptable method of communicating his wishes to the actor. This is not always easy, particularly if the director is sensitive to the actor's prerogatives, not wishing to interfere with the actor's own efforts to come upon the meaning and the right inflection for it by himself. He may be loath to impose an arbitrary reading, which is done by actually speaking the line himself. So he adopts the procedure preferred by most actors and attempts, by suggestion and paraphrase, to guide the actor to an understanding of what is wanted.

Yet let it be said, in spite of widespread opinion to the contrary: if an actor is misreading the sense of a line, the most direct, efficient, forthright and time-saving way to get him to say it correctly is for the director to read the line aloud and have the actor repeat it after him.

This simple procedure, however, causes much fluttering in the dovecotes and is looked on as a demeaning infringement of the actor's rights, an insult to his dignity, and even as a plot to reduce his status to that of a trained ape or parrot.

The opposition to this procedure can be so strident that some directors prefer to go to absurd lengths to get a correct reading without actually seeming to put the lines into the actor's mouth—as illustrated in this imaginary but by no means fanciful scene:

ACTOR: *I* will speak daggers to her, but use none.

DIRECTOR: No, that's not quite it, I'm afraid. Try it once again, old fellow.

ACTOR: Iwillspeakdaggerstoherbutusenone.

DIRECTOR: Well, that's a lot better, but I still feel it's not essentially a matter of tempo. And if you run the words together like that, it may seem to make you too impetuous and out of control. Besides, no one will be able to understand a thing you're saying.

ACTOR: Slower?

DIRECTOR: Yes, I think so. A little slower. Hamlet has calmed down quite a lot at this point in the speech and doesn't really want to drink hot blood. While that thought may very well be in his subconscious mind, I feel it is not, as yet, in his conscious mind!

ACTOR: I agree. He's just said, "Soft! now to my mother." So I might even whisper the next. Shall I try it?

DIRECTOR: By all means.

ACTOR: Splendid.

(*He reads the line again, his voice barely audible.*)

DIRECTOR: The feeling is there, I'm fairly certain of that. But do you think the line will project if you whisper it as softly as that?

ACTOR: But that's the way I feel it.

DIRECTOR: I see. Well, let me sit out front and see if I can catch it.

ACTOR: Please do.

(*The Director takes a seat in the auditorium.*)

DIRECTOR: Go ahead.

ACTOR: (*Whispering.*) *I* will speak daggers . . .

DIRECTOR: (*Shouting from his seat.*) No, no! Can't hear a word.

ACTOR: (*Raising his voice slightly.*) *I* will speak daggers to her . . .

DIRECTOR: Much better. *Much* better. (*He mounts to the stage.*) The only thing is, when you read it that way, you somehow suggest that you, rather than somebody else, are going to speak to your mother.

ACTOR: Really! I certainly didn't mean to convey that. You mean it suggests that many other people wish to speak daggers to her but that I alone of many will get her ear?

DIRECTOR: Yes, that's what seemed to come across. Why not try something a little different. You know, of course, that it is you alone who are going to . . . er . . . converse in a harsh way with her—that is, to speak . . . you know what . . . to her. Try it once again. It's a difficult passage.

ACTOR: I *will* speak daggers to her . . .

DIRECTOR: Excuse me, old boy, for interrupting again, but do you think it's a matter of Hamlet's resolution? I mean is he suddenly determined to . . . er. . . . Is anybody trying to stop the coming interview?

ACTOR: Polonius?

DIRECTOR: But he's left the stage.

ACTOR: He may be hanging about, as he did in the Ophelia scene.

DIRECTOR: It's possible, of course, but even if he were, I don't think the Prince would take any interference from him very seriously, do you?

ACTOR: Well, he's under considerable strain.

DIRECTOR: Perhaps you wouldn't mind trying it once more.

ACTOR: Not at all. "I will speak *daggers* to her, but *use none* . . ." (*Pause.*) Is that more like what you want?

DIRECTOR: It's a difficult speech. You see, I don't believe he wants to show his mother anything of the murderous spirit of the mad Roman emperor . . .

ACTOR: Oh, I agree. Absolutely. ". . . let not ever the soul of Nero enter this firm bosom" . . . and so on . . .

DIRECTOR: Right. Nero stabbed his mother Agrippina. It says so here in the footnote. And undoubtedly that was in Hamlet's subconscious mind at the time. But he doesn't want to go that far. He's mad at her—but not that mad. And I don't think it is a matter of the choice of weapons, swords or spears or . . . er . . . dag—

ACTOR: Brinkmanship?

DIRECTOR: Exactly.

ACTOR: I think I've got it. The image of Foster Dulles.

DIRECTOR: I knew it would come to you. Once again?

ACTOR: Right you are. "Once more into the breach!" (*He pauses for thought, then reads the line rapidly several times under his breath. Then—*) I will *speak* daggers to her, but use *none*." . . . I think I've got it.

DIRECTOR: Much better, Much, much better. But it still needs a little something. Suppose we break for lunch and tackle it again, when you're not so tired.

ACTOR: (*Wearily.*) Yes, perhaps that would be best. (*Curtain.*)

FINDING THE GESTURE

Confusion of the same sort is likely to arise when a director wants an actor to make a particular gesture but is unwilling to show him exactly how he wants it made. A fumbling period of trial and error follows while the rest of the cast sits idly by waiting for their harassed colleague to wind his way through indirections before he stumbles, usually by accident, on what the director wants of him.

Such rehearsals are more likely to be guessing contests than sessions of mutual creativity, yet they may be less wasteful of time and effort than some I have observed. In one I witnessed some time ago, the director explained to a young actor in a minor role the kind of gesture he wanted in order to express a feeling of resignation approaching despair. He went so far as to *show* the actor how to make it. Both arms were to be brought up and outward from the sides with the fingers curled just so, and then brought down sharply against the sides with a slap. After several tries, the actor did it to his own and the director's satisfaction. Then the director told the mystified actor that the gesture was to be invisible. He was not to move a muscle but just to imagine he was making the gesture, meanwhile concentrating on what he should be feeling if he did.

To say the least this director failed to discriminate between what was important in a rehearsal and what was not, for there were many more pressing things to be done with the production than to spend this amount of time on a circuitous method of evoking in the actor some sort of subjective emotional response, particularly when the attention of the audience at that moment was going to be focused on someone else anyway. Besides there was also the question about the actor's own attention, which at that moment, should not have been on himself and his own soul state but on the scene that was going on around him. Absorbed in the fascination of his own feelings, he neglected to react to the outward event, as he should have done. If the director had merely told him to show a restrained feeling of resignation at that particular point, the chances are that the actor would have achieved the same visible result in twenty seconds. As it was he spent twenty minutes heading for a psychological dead end.

FINDING THE RHYTHM

The changing seasons, the sea tides, the beat of the pulse, the reflexive act of breathing, all these remind man that he not only lives in a rhythmic world but that he himself is a creature of rhythm. Almost any physical action, if the motion is repeated more than once in succession, whether it be running, walking, typing, pitching hay, felling a tree, or using a rocking chair, is easier to perform and seems more natural if done in a regular cadence.

Body rhythms of men at work reflect an intuitive selection of the right muscles for the job plus a timing in coordination based on the estimated time the job will take and the time the worker has to do it in. To do a thing rhythmically is to exercise a nice economy in the amount of physical energy expended. What is conveyed is a physical harmony, a synchronization of muscles plus an easy balance of body weight, in which the whole organism is used as a unit. Certainly part of our admiration for the fine performance of a skilled athlete is based on our appreciation of the rhythm with which he serves a tennis ball, swings a baseball bat, or lets go a countering one–two punch.

A rhythmic pattern in a move or an action appeals because it carries the suggestion that needless effort and motion have been eliminated. But even more important, any action done in a perceptible rhythm since rhythm is so closely associated with balance is easy for us to catch and unconsciously imitate. An action performed without rhythm evokes little empathic response.

In the same way absence of rhythm or inconsistencies in rhythm contribute to disorderliness in the style of a production.

The rhythm of a performance is detectable in several ways: by any regularity in the beat of the spoken lines—auditory rhythm; by any regularity in the moves and sequence of moves made by actors, or a rhythmic line in a static stage composition—visual rhythm. Steps may be timed to a definite beat, as may turns and gestures. The very number of moves a character makes may fit into a rhythmic pattern, as indeed do many forms of stage business like sweeping, counting, fanning, and so on.

The opening of Rouben Mamoulian's production of *Porgy and Bess* had a beautiful example of the effective use of rhythm. As a woman swept the dust from her doorway, the swing of her broom was adjusted to the lines and the timing of other stage business. Her motions, executed with ease and sureness of control, caught the whole slow but somehow inexorable beginning of another day in Catfish Row. This gave at least one onlooker the comfortable sense of security that comes whenever sound evidence is shown on the stage, as it was here, that the production is safely and surely in the hands of someone with imagination and authority, who, moreover, is using both delicacy and restraint. This device, for that is what it was, was not used again, but it set the whole rhythmic key of the production.

Yet there are dangers in stressing rhythm unduly, for unless one is dealing with a dance drama, a pantomine with music, or a ritualistic ceremonial, maintaining set speech- or action-rhythms for any length of time is one of the sure ways of inducing boredom from monotony. The ultimate effect of any sustained rhythm is mesmeric, and must be used sparingly.

It is not necessary for a director to set an absolute beat for every passage in a play, nor is this desirable. A drama is not a symphony, and its timing need not be defined in precise terms like a muscal composition. Imposing arbitrary physical rhythms puts a severe limitation on the actors' freedom of movement and chokes off the opportunity for rhythmic variety so closely associated with representations of man in action.

Verse plays supply their own rhythm. There is little reason not to stress the cadence in a good poetic line if this can be done without destroying the sense. To chop the beat for the sake of obtaining some casual, prosy, or spuriously natural effect is to rob the verse of one of its absolute essentials, its *time*. This is emphatically true in blank verse, which falls easily on Western ears. Shakespeare, along with many other fellow dramatists, wrote it with enough irregularity to allow it to be spoken without sing-song.

The director wherever possible should supply counterrhythms in movement as well as speech to avoid monotonous regularity.

The flat prose in realistic plays offers little opportunity to establish interesting cadences in sound, but the lack of aural rhythm may be compensated for by imposing rhythm in movement if this can be done with restraint. Too much of it can weaken a play's reality and make the enactment seem precious.

Instead of searching for a basic rhythm to which all parts of a play must adhere, it may be better to find out what characteristic speech rhythms each separate character possesses, and then build these into a series of rhythms, contrasting or harmonizing with one another as the case may be. The same applies to rhythms of gait, gesture, or any physical action.

Once a characteristic rhythm has been decided upon for a role, care should be taken to maintain it even though the tempo may be increased or decreased for the sake of variety.

Telling effects can be obtained by rhythmically blending dialogue and action with music and offstage sounds. In the opening scene of *Carousel*, the crowd moved in the rhythms supplied by the carousel itself. In *Uncle Vanya*, the chirping of the cricket in the last act can be made to supply the basic rhythm with which the measures of stage action and speech can be attuned. The shouts of a mob can be made more vivid and natural if they are held under some sort of rhythmic control. Mass entrances and exits, likewise, will look less awkward if the separate units into which the crowd is divided can move rhythmically.

Disparate and jarring rhythms add much to scenes of conflict and can sharply point up differences in characters, as when Polonius's rhythm of speech and gait is made to contrast with Hamlet's.

Advantage should be taken of all opportunities to use contrapuntal rhythms in offstage music for heightening a discordant stage atmosphere. Not many dramatists are so helpful in employing this device as was Strindberg in *The Dream Play* where during the scene at the Casino at Fairhaven, strains of a waltz played in the wings clash with the playing of a Bach fugue onstage.

ANTECEDENT ACTION

To start a scene correctly in its proper mood and tempo, and to supply the proper motivation for the characters, it is often necessary to reconstruct what a character has been doing before the scene begins, and to take cognizance of all the pertinent background circumstances of that antecedent action. If the dramatist does not provide specific material, the preceding situation may have to be re-created imaginatively. Sounder results are obtained if such histories can be deduced from related evidence in the text and not wholly fancied. Normally the problem is a straightforward one and may be solved by answering a few simple questions: Where has the character been? What has he been doing? Where has he come from? What is he seeking? What state of mind is he in? How does he feel? What are his primary and secondary reasons for entering? Or, if he is already onstage, what has been happening prior to the rise of the curtain? The failure to answer these fundamental queries was the reason for the lack of conviction in the staging of Mio's first entrance in *Winterset*. (See page 194 *et seq.*)

It is easy, for example, to reconstruct Mrs. Dubedat's immediate antecedent actions. She has read that morning in the newspaper about Ridgeon's discovery of opsonin, and realizing that her husband is wasting away with the disease which opsonin can now cure, is seized by the impulse to place Louis under Ridgeon's care. Eagerly and in some desperation she has thrown a few of her husband's drawings into a portfolio to offer Ridgeon as proof, if proof be needed, of the importance of saving him. She has come to the doctor's office posthaste to plead Louis' case. The long delay after her early arrival has not outwardly tried her patience. She has endured it without complaint, yet she must have had some misgivings that in the end Ridgeon might not see her at all. When she does get in, she experiences a feeling of profound relief at having at last succeeded in gaining an interview. But her original attitude of eager hopefulness is somewhat rudely squelched by Ridgeon's negative attitude.

This procedure for reconstructing a character's precedent actions and emotions is not limited to considerations of opening scenes alone. At any point in the play it may be necessary for the director to review with the actor what has happened, not only in the antecedent action before the play begins, but within the body of the play itself in order that there be consistency of bent and motive in the character's attitude in the bridges between one scene and another. The more vivid the actor's sense of the imagined immediate past is, and the more thorough his comprehension of what it is he is entering upon the scene to do, the better will be his chances of staying on the right track toward consistency of characterization and performance.

In order to help the actor create a fully rounded and completely realized character, some directors carry this idea to elaborate lengths, even to the extent of inventing a detailed case history of the character's remote past. Not only that, but much time may be spent in speculating on the way the character might behave in imaginary situations completely outside the framework of the play. The purpose of this is laudable insofar as it is aimed at strengthening the actor's grasp of the full personality of the individual he is trying to portray; and it is helpful if it enables him more clearly to envision the character as a three-dimensional human being. But it can easily be overdone.

How far such forays into the fancied psyche of the character should go depends on the character's complexity, for one thing. Discrimination is needed to restrict the reconstruction to matters which are wholly relevant to what the character is *in the play*. Extended psychical biographies which include the tabulation of imagined infantile repressions and complexes are a waste of time unless they lead directly to the kind of knowledge the actor can translate into concrete theatrical terms, such as an understanding of the character's ingrained habit of mind or his peculiarly individual way of looking at life. It must illuminate the reasons why he behaves as he does in the play's action. Only then can the actor use this extra-textual information as a solid frame of reference on which to build his part.

THE ACTOR'S FEELINGS

As a general rule, specialists in art tend to overcomplicate the nature of the medium in which they work and hedge it around with an arcane jargon few can penetrate. Much of this lies in that tantalizing twilight zone between sense and nonsense. Shaw was not far off the mark when he observed that all professions are conspiracies against the laity. The acting profession and the profession of teaching acting offer no exceptions to Shaw's theory. For beginning with Stanislavsky, the modern approach to acting has stressed its mysteries and difficulties, demanding that the actor qualify not only as a mime but as a philosopher and poet also. The overintellectualization of what, in essence, is a comparatively simple art, is centered in the actor's feelings. And much in modern teaching seems to be more concerned in making the actor himself happy rather than the audience. The theory seems to be that if the actor feels the emotion truly and honestly, his performance will be effective.

Successful acting depends on the skill and power with which a sensitive and in some ways remarkable human being can convey emotions and ideas to other human beings watching him. Whatever the actor does to cause the spectators to feel these emotions and understand these ideas profoundly and deeply in themselves is good acting. So long as these emotions and thoughts are transferred, it does not matter a particle whether they are being truly felt at the moment by the actor or are mere externalizations of that emotion being feigned. The actor's skill is measured only by the persuasiveness of his artifice, not by the truth of his feelings. There is no known way to perceive by optical or aural observation from one's seat in the theatre the state of the actor's soul. One can only judge the character and the character's emotions through outward manifestations expressed by technique.

Robert Morley was once asked by an eager student what it was he thought about while playing an emotional scene in one of his own plays. He replied, "The size of the house." Our empathic response to an actor who is thinking about the number of unsold seats can be just as warm and pleasurable, as it obviously was to the student watching Mr. Morley, as it could be to one who was busy making invisible gestures or inwardly calling up memories of his mother's funeral.

It is the actor's duty and privilege to use whatever means he can find to identify himself with his part so that he may play it truly and honestly. If he is the type who uses "associative memory" to sharpen and define the emotion he is trying to express, as when he tries to recall a mood of murderous rage by remembering how as a boy he smashed a wasp that was stinging him, then the director should not interfere with the process but encourage it and then objectively study the results. If he is dealing with an actor who believes he can vivify feeling and action by carrying in his mind a dominant image or some metaphor leading to an intensification of expression; if, for instance, he is convinced that he can register, say, unpleasant bewilderment with conviction by picturing himself fighting his way through a forest of wet spaghetti, then the director should accept this sort of metaphorical language and use it to stimulate the actor's imagination. For a good metaphor, like a burr, sticks in the memory.

Nevertheless, the thing the director must bear in mind is that he is there to pass judgment on *results,* whether arrived at by the Stanislavsky method or by some other. He must judge by what he sees the actor doing on the stage, not only in terms of his individual performance but in relation to all the other performances in the play. He is there to give shape and consistency to the whole, to correct whatever violates or disturbs the main design, to eliminate haphazard or meaningless inspirations whatever their source. He must also replace improvisation with calculation if there is to be discipline and order in the end result and a constant high standard of performance during the run.

Directing the Ensemble

LEADING THE ATTENTION

Much of the work of polishing is devoted to the attunement of one performance with another in consonance with style. Above and beyond that there is continuing stress on deftness of movement, economy of gesture, the display of authority in the actor's attack on words, and constant refinement of vocal nuances all working together to produce in the spectator the feeling that the cast knows exactly what it wants to do and how to do it. Not to be neglected is the director's responsibility to see that each act taken as a unit has its own unity, flow, and consistency of effect; and that this same unity and flow are detectable from act to act when the play is viewed as a whole.

Good dialogue, as we have seen, is always purposeful, with one speech following another as a result of some causal connection between them. It is the director's duty to see that such connections or associations are made clear. Any response to a line should seem to be evoked as the natural result of the speaker's having heard and understood whatever has been said beforehand, and should flow out from that. This desired effect can usually be achieved by centering the actors' attention properly and by judicious use of the pause.

There is also the important matter of directing the audience's attention to the right actor at the right time, and this is something that can only be done in ensemble rehearsals. Good direction leads the eye of the spectator to the character who is about to speak and keeps it always shifting from moment to moment to the most emphatic character in the scene. Ralph Richardson, the British star, paid the highest possible compliment to his director, John Gielgud, when he wrote, "Under him I have always found, maybe after small experiment, that I have ended up in a good position for my best speech and have faded mysteriously out of focus when not wanted, and I ask no more." [3]

STYLISTIC CONSISTENCY

To attune acting styles to a consistent unity the director first determines where, in the spectrum between artifice and naturalism, the most appropriate style lies for the work in hand. No choice can be absolutely precise in such an inexact medium, but obvious or blatant variations can certainly be avoided. An overly subjective performance by one actor when everyone else is playing in overt, straightforward fashion will be both out of key and out of style. It would probably represent also an illegitimate attempt to take stage. Stylistic inconsistencies can be detected in an actor's failure to attune the volume of his voice to the general level of his fellow players, and thus, by speaking louder or softer than

[3] *The London Times,* July 10, 1960.

they do, call attention to himself by contrast. The same applies to the speed in which cues are taken up. Registering emotion or prolonged thought between cue and speech, with its ensuing monopoly of attention, may throw unwanted emphasis on a minor character. And, finally, if an actor indulges in "front-playing," as though aware of the audience's presence, while the others do not, all stylistic uniformity is lost. Consistency in the manner of speech and the elimination of incongruous dialects or provincialisms is also a must. A single lapse into American inflections when the rest of the cast is speaking Oxford English is a grave stylistic error.

It is somewhat pedantic and usually unnecessary to explain to the players in an ensemble scene that the scene itself is, in nature, expository, transitional, parallel, conflicting, climactic or anticlimactic. The director, naturally, must know which it is and set the key according to the scene's function in the play and its relationship to those which precede and follow it. The climactic scenes establish the upper limits of tempo, pitch, and intensity, and the expository scenes establish the lower limits. Once these are set, the others can be regulated up or down from the median, so that if it were possible to draw a chart describing the intensity and speed in which different speeches are to be played, the variations in such a chart would be in rough conformity to the varying tensions contained in the text.

HANDLING CROWDS

A crowd can be directed in one of two ways. The director can treat each person in it as an individual and give him separate blocking, which is complicated, or he can divide the group into sections, give each section a leader, and have each group follow its leader in moves, reactions, and vocal responses. If the latter method leads to routine or mechanical results, individual directions may be given to two or three members of each section, thus relieving some of the sameness in response.

If a crowd has to make several entrances and take up a variety of positions, time will be saved in blocking if a rubber stamp of the ground plan can be made up. This will relieve the director of the burden of having to draw the plan on his prompt book for every disposition of the crowd. Another time-saving device is to run off multiple copies of the ground plan on mimeograph, numbering them to correspond with the crowd's entrances, and setting down the positions and changes on each as required.

A phalanx of forty supers huddled into a solid mass will register as a much smaller crowd than half that number judiciously spaced in strategic areas and in knots of three or four people each. Care must be taken to provide connecting figures to merge the groups together, and a wide variety of body positions must be sought. As soon as such groupings have been set, the designer should be called in to study the arrangement. He may then blend and correlate the colors of the costumes in accordance with the placement of each actor, or set them clashing if that is the intention. Color and light can unify a crowd or break it up into a series of unrelated segments.

For swift and clear-cut entrances not one but several means of access to the stage should be used, and the same holds true of exits, with particular attention being given to stragglers.

When the crowd is an important part of the action and onstage much of the time, as it is in *Julius Caesar*, it is often effective to place the figures in a series of formal compositions with a distinguishable pattern. This is usually just as convincing as realistic arrangements and simplifies cueing, although it does not always work with plays which call for strictly lifelike effects.

HANDLING THE CHORUS

There are two schools of thought about directing choruses in classical drama and in some modern plays in which a chorus plays a major part, as it does in Eliot's *Murder in the Cathedral*.

One method is to stress the archaic and ritualistic nature of choral responses and movements by eliminating intrusive naturalistic technique. This is done by treating the chorus as a single unit, indeed as a single character, with all the people in it dressed alike, made up alike, and responding uniformly and without individual differentiation to the stimuli of the scene. The chorus in such cases gesture together, move together, and even breathe together. Thus the Chorus of Theban elders become one Theban elder duplicated ten or twelve times.

Applying uniformity and precision to moves and speeches may evoke admiration for the efficiency of the choreography, as in the case of the Rockettes, but in a full evening, the interest of the spectator may demand something more than absolute technical uniformity. Its chief disadvantage is that this technique allows no variations in the way of individualized responses and fails to let the director capitalize on any interest that might be forthcoming if the chorus were permitted to reveal several differentiated personalities. Neither does it take into account the possibility that some of the choral speeches may express individual points of view. There is also the danger of vocal monotony, for if everyone speaks in unison and in the same key the effect produced may be likened to that made by a single section, say the first strings, of a symphony orchestra where the same sound with some very slight variations of timbre is simply multiplied by the number of instruments used. The harmonics and dynamic variations supplied by the other sections of the orchestra are lost in such an arrangement.

The alternative is to treat each member of the chorus as an individual and permit him to speak characteristic lines as an individual, and to move or gesticulate in accordance with the adopted personality.

The chorus itself can be broken into sections by separating the voice parts as in a singing choir. The tenors and basses or sopranos and altos may then be assigned appropriate passages befitting the contrasted vocal parts.

Variations may be obtained by alternating solo and choral passages, or by dividing the choral responses in other ways. For example, ominous and grave passages may be spoken by the alto and bass sections in whole or in part, while the lighter voices may speak those of lesser weight and import. Dark voices may be used antiphonally against the light. Or a solo voice may ask a question with the chorus delivering the response. Duets, quartets, sextets, and octets can be used as desired, and for strong punctuations the full chorus may come in to underline a single key word in a solo.

In this the director functions in the same way as the leader of a glee club or choir, and he should use musical terms to obtain his effects.

Timing vocal entrance cues presents a special problem. Without a leader to supply the beat, the attack on the opening syllable of a choral passage may be ragged. To avoid this, some other method of cueing must be found. A nod of the head by a single chorister who can be seen by the others may suffice, or the chorus may be drilled to time its cue from a previously spoken line. If the cue line is spoken in a clear-cut rhythm, the chorus can pick it up in the same rhythm after a single beat. Should this fail to work, the first few words or even the first sentence of a full-chorus passage may be spoken by a single voice and the choral cue taken from that.

Another more complicated system of cueing can be devised through movement. The chorus may begin to speak after having taken a specific number of steps in unison, or at the moment one of the characters or the chorus leader reaches a certain specified position or makes a particular gesture, the move or the end of the move constituting the cue.

Here is a demonstration of one way to orchestrate a choral passage. It is the opening of Eliot's *Murder in the Cathedral.*

FULL CHORUS

Here let us stand, (*beat*) close by the cathedral. (*beat*)

Here let us wait (*Two beats*)

SINGLE ALTO VOICE

Are we drawn by danger?

SINGLE SOPRANO VOICE

Is it the knowledge of safety, that draws our feet / Towards the cathedral?

FULL CHORUS

What danger can be / For us,

ALTOS ALONE

the poor,

FULL CHORUS

the poor women of Canterbury?

SINGLE SOPRANO VOICE

what tribulation

With which we are not already familiar?

FULL CHORUS

There is no danger

For us, (*beat, and continuing on one note, slowly*) and
there is no safety in the cathedral.

SINGLE ALTO VOICE

(*Strong, louder, steady tone. Ominously.*) Some
presage of an act,

SEMICHORUS, ALTOS

Which our eyes are compelled to witness,

FULL CHORUS

has forced our feet / Towards the cathedral.

SEMICHORUS, ALTOS

(*Deep, chanting*) We are forced to bear witness.

SINGLE SOPRANO VOICE

Since golden October

FOUR ALTO VOICES ADDED TO ABOVE

declined into sombre November

FULL CHORUS

And the apples were gathered and stored, (*gradual crescendo*)
and the land became brown sharp points of *death*
(*decrescendo*) *in a waste of water and mud,* (*beat*)
The New Year waits, (*pause*)

SINGLE VOICE

breathes,

SEMICHORUS, ALTOS

waits,

SEMICHORUS, SOPRANOS (*whispering*)

whispers in darkness.

FULL CHORUS (*resuming tempo, forte*)

While the laborer kicks off a muddy boot and stretches
his hand to the fire.

SINGLE VOICE, ALTO

The New Year waits,

FULL CHORUS

destiny waits for the coming.

FOUR ALTO VOICES

Who has stretched out his hand to the fire and remembered
the Saints at All Hallows,

FULL CHORUS

Remembered the marytrs and saints
who wait?

SINGLE VOICE, DEEP CONTRALTO

and who shall / Stretch out his hand to
the fire, and deny his master?

FULL CHORUS (*forte*)

who shall be warm / By the fire, and deny his master?
(*Pause*)

SINGLE SOPRANO

Seven years and the summer is over

CHORUS

Seven years since the Archbishop left us,

SINGLE SOPRANO

He who was always kind to his people.

SEMICHORUS, ALTOS (*low, cautious*)

But it would not be well if he should return.

CHORUS (*up*)

King rules or barons rule;

SINGLE ALTO

We have suffered various oppression,

SEMICHORUS, ALTOS

But mostly we are left to our own devices,

FULL CHORUS

And we are content if we are left alone.

SINGLE SOPRANO

We try to keep our households in order;

CHORUS (*quietly*)

The merchant, shy and cautious, tries to compile a
little fortune,

CHORUS

And the laborer

FOUR SOPRANOS

bends

CHORUS

to his piece of earth, earth color, his
own color, / Preferring to pass unobserved.
(*with gradual crescendo and faster tempo*)
Now I fear disturbance of the quiet seasons:
(*stronger*) Winter shall come bringing *death* from the sea,
(*Up*) Ruinous spring shall beat at our doors,
Root and shoot shall eat our eyes and our ears,
Disastrous summer burn up the beds of our streams.

SINGLE ALTO (*slowly, quietly*)

And the poor (*pause*)

FOUR ALTO VOICES

shall wait (*pause*)

SEMICHORUS, ALTOS

for another decaying October. (*pause*)

SINGLE SOPRANO

Why should the summer bring consolation
For autumn fires and winter fogs?

CHORUS

What shall we do in the heat of summer
But wait in barren orchards for another October?

SINGLE VOICE, ALTO (*terrified*)

Some malady is coming upon us.

SEMICHORUS, SOPRANOS

We wait.

SEMICHORUS, ALTOS

We wait,

CHORUS

And the saints and martyrs wait, for those who shall be
martyrs and saints.
Destiny waits in the hand of God,
shaping the still unshapen:

SOLO ALTO

I have seen these things in a
shaft of sunlight.

CHORUS

Destiny waits in the hand of God, not in the hands of
statesmen.
Who do, some well, (*pause*) some ill, planning and guessing,
(*lyrically*) Having their aims which turn in their hands
in the pattern of time.

SEMICHORUS, SOPRANOS

Come, happy December,

CHORUS

who shall observe you, who shall preserve you?
Shall the Son of Man be born again (*pause*)

SINGLE VOICE, ALTO

in the litter of scorn?

CHORUS

For us,

SEMICHORUS, ALTOS

the poor,

CHORUS

there is no action,
(*slowly*) But only to wait, (*pause*) and to witness.

Technical Rehearsals

Four or five days before the first dress rehearsal a costume parade should be scheduled, preferably before a run-through. The actors, in costume but without make-up, enter singly so that one costume may be examined at a time with the actor moving around, in character, and as required by the action. The object of the showing, it should be unnecessary to add, is to give the designer and costume crew a chance to see what further fittings and adjustments have to be made before the dress rehearsal, and to show the actors how to wear the clothes as well as to acquaint them with any special problems such as the handling of flowing skirts or capes.

If the director has any criticisms or suggestions to offer, they should be given to the designer after the showing. These should be minor for it is assumed that the director will have previously approved the sketches and seen the costumes in the process of manufacture.

Two sessions should be given over entirely to the technical aspects of the production, to be followed by a minimum of three dress rehearsals.

The first so-called technical rehearsal is held without the actors present. Its purpose is to give the technicians and running crews a chance to learn their assignments, to practice the shifts, to set the focus and levels of the lighting instruments, and run through the lighting cues. In a well-managed operation, the director will have reviewed the lighting requirements with the designer and the technical director before preparation of the light plot, and will have approved the completed scheme well in advance of the first technical rehearsal. It is advisable for the designer, the technical director, and the switchboard operators to be present at several early run-throughs in order to study the placement of actors, establish the location of emphatic acting areas, and to be apprised of any special lighting effects.

At this first technical rehearsal, the director should take pains to use stand-ins and have them walk through the moves and positions, otherwise the tendency is to light the setting instead of the actors. Particular attention should be paid to eliminating the hot spots that cause unwanted changes of light on faces. For some reason the downstage extremities of the stage never seem to be as bright as the center and this must be corrected if scenes are to be played at the edges.

This is usually a long and arduous session. No matter how carefully the light plot is followed or how long the operators have practiced the cueing, there are always corrections to be made and delays to be encountered. It takes time to refocus instruments, revise cue sheets, cut and install gelatins, and to practice transitions between one set of cues and the next. In complicated productions more than one such technical session without actors may be required.

Under ordinary circumstances the actors are called for the second technical rehearsal. The director should resist the temptation to use this occasion as a dress rehearsal and should try to attend only to technical matters, not exclusively to the lights and setting, but to problems involving the actors directly as in the handling of props, timing of exits and entrances, use of furniture and set accessories, coordination of speeches and light cues, adjustment of body positions for lights and other physical details.

It is not practical at this time to play straight through each act, although this, of course, is standard procedure for the dress rehearsals. Usually those passages are skipped in which there are no changes of scenery or lights. But long dimming cues must be timed to the actual length of the scene, in which case the actors should be made to play the whole scene in proper tempo. Except for these moments, the actors may not be required to read their lines as in performance, although it is usually best to have them walk through all their moves in sequence to insure their being properly lighted at all times. When side lighting is used, positions may have to be adjusted to prevent an actor in a shared scene from blocking the light from the face of his fellow performer.

The technical rehearsal must include practice in the opening and closing sequences of each act, or whenever the curtain is dropped or there is a blackout. At the start of each act the usual procedure is to bring the footlights or curtain-warmers on before the houselights start to dim so that the audience will not be left in the dark at any time before the actual rising of the curtain. If there is to be music, the cue is given before the dimming of houselights. These lights may be held at half for a short time to allow the audience to settle down. The houselights are then lowered to out, after which the curtain-warmers are dimmed to out and the cue given for the curtain to rise.

Dress Rehearsals

If the director has done his job well, if he has not postponed until the last moment the settlement of crucial details, if he has foreseen difficulties and taken steps to face them early in the preparatory period, there is little reason why the dress rehearsals should not go smoothly. There may be understandable tensions arising from the players' unfamiliarity with the physical aspects of the production that now confront them for the first time, but there is no reason why these should be serious. If major crises or seemingly insoluble problems do arise, they can usually be blamed on poor directorial planning. To avoid such impasses, the director should make it a point to put pressure on his cast in the two weeks preceding the dress, even doubling the number of rehearsals if need be to acquaint them with the handling of properties, the use of the furniture, and so on. This has the effect of lessening the pressure at the end.

The cast should be told that perfection in the first dress is not expected, and the director must not blow up when things do go awry despite careful forethought. He should proceed calmly to find the cause of any miscue and, having done so, make the necessary corrections. This is what rehearsals are for.

Nor should he be unduly startled upon viewing the results of the cast's first stabs at make-up. Fright wigs or the actor's misdirected attempts to alter his natural features, which often lead to grotesque distortions, are common problems to be taken in stride.

Photographs should be taken at the second dress, preferably between acts; and curtain calls rehearsed. Entrances, positions, and exits for the calls should be assigned before the rehearsal begins so that they may be tried at the end with the curtain cues. The director should plan the calls well in advance, or give detailed written instructions about them to the stage manager, who may be given the responsibility of staging them.

The final dress rehearsal should correspond in every respect to a regular performance just as though the audience were present. There should be no interruptions except those ordered by the director in cases of dire emergency. The custom of inviting a number of guests to this session, so that the actors may get used to responses from the house, is of little value and should be discouraged. A few scattered spectators are seldom responsive enough to provide any real measure of what the reactions of a full house are likely to be. And there is the other risk that well-wishers present may take it upon themselves to make suggestions or render criticisms at the last minute to their friends in the cast. Such gratuitous tips can wreak havoc with a performance and set the whole production off key. To prevent this, the director should caution players to make no changes whatever from the readings, business, or moves which have already been planned and rehearsed, except after consultation with him. If there are to be alterations, however slight, involving line readings, differences of vocal emphasis, new business, fresh aspects of characterization, or a try at new levels of intensity, these must be rehearsed so that everyone concerned is made aware of them.

On opening night it is unbecoming for the director to be seen in a conspicuous seat leading applause. His proper place is in the back of the house in a place convenient for taking notes. These are then duly given individually to the cast—not immediately after the performance, but just before the next.

On the subject of notes and note taking, a few final observations may be helpful.

It is demoralizing for a cast to be subjected to a series of run-throughs and a succession of dress rehearsals without eliciting some comment from the director. If he has not amassed a sheaf of critical or laudatory items to give his players after every run-through, it is a sign that he either believes the performance to be perfect and not susceptible to further improvement or that he has reached the end of his usefulness and can think of nothing more to tell the actors about improving the production. Prolonged silence is usually a confession of directorial inadequacy. When the director has nothing to say one must conclude that the preparation period has been unduly prolonged. Once the parts have been memorized and the actors are in control of their characters there must be continuous progress, otherwise the knowledge and fun of knowing that the whole is steadily improving are taken away, the repetitions become meaningless; the edge of enthusiasm is dulled, and general disaffection ensues.

In contrast, when the director's notes lead to sharpened effects, further clarification of meaning, elaboration of characterization, and increased subtleties in timing and movement, there is an awakened sense of accomplishment and advancement, and the notes are welcomed with gratitude.

Of what should the notes consist? Bernard Shaw has some advice to give on this point, and it is important enough to be memorized by every beginner:

> The notes taken by the director as he silently watches the players are a test of his competence. If, for example, he writes, "Show influence of Kierkegaard on Ibsen in this scene," or "The Oedipus complex must be very apparent here. Discuss with the Queen," the sooner he is packed out of the theatre and replaced the better. If they run "Ears too red," "Farther up to make room for X," "Pleecemin," "Reel and Ideel," "Mariar Ann," "He, not Ee," "Contrast," "Change speed: Andante," "Shoe sole arches not blacked," "Unladylike: keep knees together," "More dialogue to give them time to get off," "This comes too suddenly," "?Cut this???" and the like, the director knows his job and his place.[4]

The notes should deal with practical realities, faults in make-up, pronunciation, placement, tempo, costuming, and the like. Shaw doesn't mention it, but it costs little to try and balance criticism of the things the actor does wrong with praise for what he has done right. Negative remarks, nagging, and petty faultfinding are a source of discouragement to actors. But here again, if the compliments are to be of any real use, they should be on specific points of performance and not expressed in vague generalities.

If the director has not given his cast confidence in themselves by the night of the performance, along with a sense of exuberance in a job well done, he cannot mend matters with a pep talk just before the rise of the curtain. A volley of last-minute warnings and imprecations is disconcerting and futile. At most, he should wish them luck and give them his blessings, for his work is over now and the rest is up to them.

[4] *Theatre Arts*, Vol. XXXIII, August 1949. As quoted in Barnet, Berman, and Burto, *Aspects of the Drama*. Boston: Little, Brown and Company, 1962.

Appendix

Glossary

Index

APPENDIX

The Collegiate Theatre

Objectives

It is not the purpose of the theatre department in a liberal arts college to train students for the professional stage. A college is not a trade school with narrow vocational aims. Its broader responsibilities include the task of leading its students toward self-knowledge and to some understanding of the world and their fellow men, to cultivate in them the ability to think, to demonstrate how sets of given facts may be arranged into some order so that a reasonable conclusion may be drawn from them. The nerve center of the college is its Library, and the chief business of the students is scholarship and research. In its highest manifestations, a college education is a beckoning to young men and women to savor the joys of the life of the mind.

Where does the college theatre fit into such a picture?

In the first place, it should be emphasized that the college theatre is just that: a theatre in a college. It falls into the danger of losing its unique identification with a learning and learned community unless it operates as a true adjunct of the corporate enterprise. Its objectives should be closely aligned with the general objectives of the educational institution of which it is a part.

Yet the nature of the theatre itself sometimes stands in the way of such alignment. As a public art its purpose is something less than didactic, although in a college its end should be to elevate more often than to amuse its supporters. While it is true that the business of theatre is communication, it resembles a free-for-all forum more than it does a classroom. There is no continuity in the subjects it airs. Nor are its doors open only to students. They are open to the whole college community and sometimes to the general public outside that community. No theatre, in college or out, can exist as an effective medium of communication unless it has someone with whom to communicate. Its audience is an indispensable part of it, and the larger that audience is, the better, even in a college or university.

The presence of the audience, a necessary condition of theatre in any form, imposes another situation on the director and it is one which few of his colleagues on the faculty are called upon to face. He must offer the most gifted students opportunities to learn how to act and stage plays—a primary aim. Yet he has to face the fact that whatever he is able to teach them will be incomplete and unrealistic unless the end-product, that which they have learned, is submitted to the public judgment for approval or disapproval.

Needless to say, few if any professors of conventional subjects are required to present their students to the harsh glare of any such public examination. Nor are they compelled as he is to submit public evidence of their teaching ability, or lack of it, to the view of the community. Perhaps it would be better for American education if this were a universal requirement in all collegiate departments. Since it is not, the college director must accept it and face the challenge it represents as part of the game in any theatre.

It is a formidable challenge. It demands of him a standard of perfection in teaching rarely asked of his colleagues.

Consider the difference between him and the classroom teacher whose students pass the course with a grade of 70 or even 60. If such a grade means anything, it means that the student receiving it has understood little more than half the material. In contrast, the student actor who has memorized only 60 or 70 percent of his lines will not "pass" with the people who come to witness the performance. Unlike the academic judgment which grants degrees for considerably less than perfect work, the critical audience that has purchased the right of evaluating the accomplishments of every student participating in a production asks nothing less than 100 percent from each one of them. So must the director, who is thus called upon to be a perfectionist. The spur is in him. A failure in a course examination is a private matter between student, teacher, and dean, to be redressed at some later time by re-examination or by obtaining a higher average in subsequent tests. A failure on the stage is a public disgrace and cannot be rectified. Only in intercollegiate athletics are there similar pressing and absolute requirements that the student perform at his highest level of ability. For those interested in dramatics, work in the theatre may thus be the only activity in four years of college which demands totality of physical and mental commitment, and provides the only full-blown test of poise, confidence, and expertness under fire that the student will get before he enters the competitive world. This is one of the reasons why its theatre should be hailed and encouraged by the college as a most potent educational instrument.

It is also one of the reasons why pleasing the public becomes, or should become, a leading objective of both players and director, even though this may mean that students with indifferent talent may be deprived of the chance to appear in major productions. They stand in the way of the need to maintain this imposed standard of excellence.

There are those who will disagree with this contention. It has been argued that the educational benefits an individual student derives from playing a role before the public, however unsuited to it or lacking in talent he may be, justify using the unfitted. For those who support this opinion the audience is an unnecessary nuisance and can be disregarded since the main point is to provide an educational experience for all students regardless of talent, only provided they are interested in learning something from such an experience. The only thing necessary, they contend, is that the play itself be a masterpiece.

This view usually coincides with the attitude that the college theatre is primarily a place where the students can have fun, where they can teach themselves and play around with acting and directing in much the same way as children do finger painting. They equate the theatre with the classroom except that they deem what may be learned in it unworthy of college credit.

Let me repeat that the theatre is not a classroom. It remains, even in college, a place where a form of art is learned and practiced, an art moreover that requires considerable skill, intensive study, and devoted application if one hopes to become proficient in it. If it fails to communicate with its public or ignores that public by paying little or no attention to the quality of its acting talent or to the relation of that talent to the plays it selects for production, it can only operate in a cultish vacuum, and is really no theatre at all. Acting in it is like playing chamber music at home, a private family affair, pleasurable no doubt for the participants but for no one else.

Furthermore, the students in the audience have as much right as the players to demand their share of whatever educational benefits may be offered. It is doubtful that they would learn anything except disrespect for the medium on a steady diet of badly acted plays even if they represented the best in dramatic literature. It is a mistake to think that lasting satisfaction can be had merely by hearing the words of a text spoken. Unless the words are spoken well, and in a theatrical atmosphere that is at once imaginative and stimulating, and unless the roles are enacted with skill and power, student spectators would be better off if they stayed home and read the play.

Advocates of this "closed-end" type of amateur theatricals worry about the theatre's being too successful, that is, too successful at the box office. They seem to prefer that productions be unpopular and unattended, as if failure were proof of artistic integrity. Let it be admitted that the experience of failure can be chastening to the spirit. It may even eventually be an uplifting experience if the one who suffers it has a high moral character. But it is fatuous to adopt theatrical policies which court public failure on the grounds that it may ultimately be more rewarding and educative than success. Failure is uplifting only when it is overcome. To consider failure as evidence that the undertaking is not tainted with stains of the market place is nonsense. The half-empty house is seldom an indication of artistic worth. Somerset Maugham long ago pointed out the error of confusing commercial failure with artistic probity. And it is hardly complimentary to the cultivated and usually sophisticated taste of the audience in a college community to equate artistic success with the failure to please that audience.

College productions need not run a year to packed houses. But unless they sustain the interest of a solid section of their public, including a healthy representation from the student body, the theatre will make such a negligible impression on the community as to render it useless as a cultural force or anything else.

The College Director—Scholar or Showman?

Like his professional counterpart, the collegiate director must have imagination and skill to translate a script into vivid life on a stage. Both are charged with emphasizing and clarifying whatever it is that the playwright is saying and with seeing to it that this is stated in forceful and understandable ways.

The chief difference between them is that the director in a college is also a teacher, a member of an academic faculty. He must resolve whatever conflict of interest arises from the necessity of attracting a substantial audience. To do this, he has to minimize any differences between his obligation as a teacher to serve the presumed intellectual and artistic tastes of the students and his corollary responsibility as a theatre artist to provide rewarding theatrical experiences for a public. This latter responsibility is a substantial one if he is really dedicated to the art itself for its own sake and seriously concerned for its future.

The way out of such a difficulty, should it arise, is to refuse to acknowledge that the students' interests and those of the general public are really at variance. In choosing plays he must aim high, making no concessions whatever to those whose taste is unenlightened. The key to the solution of the problem is in his programs, and this subject is discussed in the section on play selection which follows.

The teacher-director has to bring these two sometimes contradictory personalities into some sort of reconciliation with each other. The nature of this duality may be illustrated by citing two extreme and intentionally exaggerated cases.

If he is *all teacher*, his main concern is with the individual student. He will be intent on developing that student's talents in, let us say, acting. In this he will be more coach than director, and he will spend just as much time teaching the untalented as the talented, since both, it is presumed, are paying the same amount of tuition.

Yet, as has been pointed out, he also has the responsibility of presenting plays to the public and he cannot be indifferent to the size of that public, although he is not under the same pressure as his professional counterpart to do everything possible, including truckling to it, to keep that audience large.

If he is *all director*, the audience can easily become his paramount concern. Fear of failure to please that audience, combined with the pressure of time, imposes upon him the obligation to get professional results in every production, regardless of the way these results are obtained. He may even be compelled to bring in professional actors, thus denying his students the chance to play anything but minor roles. What is worse, the development and training of his best students as individual artists may have to be pushed into the background or dropped altogether, along with the slow developers or the thinly talented who will get no chance at all to participate. Also neglected are those who would like to know something about the craft in general but who have no expectation of following it professionally. He is also in danger of thinking too much about his own reputation as an artist. To safeguard that, his every exertion must be aimed at creating productions that will be at once newsworthy, startling, and above all popular. If he happens to be a good actor, and I am one of those who believes the best directors are themselves good actors, he must put aside his obligation as a teacher to see to it that each role in a production is played in accordance with his own predigested plans. If the actors cannot fulfill his stringent requirements on their own, which is commonly the case with amateurs, the director will give them the readings, the gestures, the facial expressions, everything. For this is the fastest and in many ways the most efficient method he can use to convey to them exactly what it is he wants them to do.

In such a case, the actor learns how to play a particular part and sometimes how to play it well. But he does not necessarily learn anything about the art of acting, nor is he being trained to think like an actor. And this is something he must learn if he ever expects to come close to mastering the craft.

There is little difference in such a director's objectives and those of his counterpart in the professional theatre.

Somewhere between these two hypothetical opposites is the balanced individual who cares deeply about each student's personal development, and who does something about it without wholly ignoring the audience or abandoning his obligation to cultivate in them an interest in good drama and its enactment. He knows that he cannot provide pleasure for a cultivated public nor make his theatre count for something in the community unless the acting is of sufficiently high calibre to be enjoyed. For even the most indulgent public, in an environment which normally shows considerable enthusiasm for student activities, cannot be expected to respond favorably and over a long period to ineptitude in playing or to unimaginative staging.

Such a person walks a tightrope between coach and director. He makes an effort to suppress in himself any symptoms of that fatal Broadway syndrome which prompts its victims to dismiss summarily everything that does not contribute to surface shine and flashiness in performance. Curbing this urge can have the effect of letting the players use their own creative faculties, at least to some extent. The results may be less spectacular, and his productions may lack the high polish and precision found in the best professional work. But it may nonetheless be a true collective artistic enterprise of considerable worth.

Play Selection

The college director works for the most part with established scripts which have already been produced on Broadway or in the West End. Thus he is spared anguish and denied the joys which are the common lot of the professional whose job in the majority of cases is to hammer untried plays into some sort of workable shape. The cutting, rewriting, recasting and even redesigning that is now an accepted part of the pre-Broadway tryout process has all been done for him by the original director and producer. Dealing thus with pretested material, the college director can pretty well take the text for granted and address himself at once to the sole business of drawing effective performances from his young and usually inexperienced cast. Offsetting this advantage is his inability to command the services of the finest acting talent in the country, which is something the professional director can presumably do.

If a director is fortunate enough to have the first chance at a fine new manuscript by an established author, as we had at Yale in the case of Archibald MacLeish's *J.B.*, one of his chief objectives should be to show the author, in the test of performance, exactly what he has in his script. Some slight textual revisions may have to be made, but nothing like the drastic overhauling that is now standard procedure in New York. The stakes are not as high in the college theatre, and it may be assumed that the playwright will have ample time to effect needed revisions after he has digested the reactions of local audiences and local critics.

The test of how well a director resolves the dilemma of having to be a showman and a professor at one and the same time lies, as has been said, in the plays he chooses for production.

His problem is to find dramatic works worthy of his own and his students' time and effort. They should be on a level of artistic significance becoming to a scholarly community, and should offer the spectator something he seldom has a chance to see in the commercial playhouse. Programmatic appropriateness, the size and cost of physical production, the talent of the acting company and technical crews, all these are practical and important considerations bearing on the problem, and they must be faced. But in the end the choice of plays depends upon the man who makes the choice and follows from what sort of person he is. Needless to say the whole man is engaged in the process and this includes the sum of all his sensibilities, his taste, his subjective urges, his instinct and education, all interwoven with and colored by his concept of the functions of drama and the purpose of theatre.

A director who is essentially a tradesman by nature will be guided by his mercenary instincts; and the leading factor in his decisions will be his estimate of the play's box-office potential. The college theatre is not the most satisfactory area of operation for this type.

The timid soul will seldom venture beyond established hits, as much in fear of failure as in hopes for success.

Those who would be in the van of fashion will plump for the alien hybrids and the strangest experiments of the avant-garde while slighting conventional forms.

The unoriginal will favor those Broadway draws they have already seen and will do their best to duplicate the style and staging of the professional production.

The indecisive will form a committee and let its members do the choosing.

But the man with a mind of his own will do the plays he loves, the ones that affect him deeply and say something he believes should be said. And he will weigh every work in terms of the estimated satisfaction he and his company will get from doing it, to say nothing of the audience's satisfaction which he includes also.

His selections will be conditioned always by the fact that he is a creature who has learned to adapt himself to two environments, the world of learning and the world of the theatre. They may even represent attempts to reconcile the two.

To proceed on the basis that the purpose of a theatre, in college or not, is to give pleasure is perhaps an oversimplification. What sort of pleasure? Thoughtful men have found playgoing an enhancement to the spirit and a delight for the mind. In its long history the theatre has been many things, an agency of revelation, an instrument for correcting social ills, a means of self-expiation, self-analysis, or even self-defense. It has existed to evoke laughter, tears, or thrills, and in some modern works even revulsion and contempt.

If it is agreed that the best theatre enhances the spirit and delights the mind, the college director must then ask himself, "Whose spirit; whose mind?" What affords delight to a sophomore may be altogether different from that which pleases the Dean. The sophomore may find highest enjoyment in the guilt-ridden lucubrations of Genet or the obscurities of Beckett, while the Dean may be made captious and uncomfortable in the presence of anything but the most innocent and sentimental diversions.

The spectrum of taste is as wide in the collegiate audience as in any other, the only real difference being that in a college the same people, by and large, come to play after play. The undergraduates are the chief variable factor but even they come to be multiples of a generic type. What the director must realize is that he cannot hope to please all of that audience all the time. He must live in the hope of pleasing some of them all the time. If the pleased proportion happens to include the most intelligent and the most perceptive, so much the better.

It would seem safe to assume that the majority of the plays such a person would do would be significant examples of dramatic literature, plays which let those who work in them and those who come to see them make some headway in the search for knowledge, or for esthetic experience of the highest order. This would be in line with the thought that college theatre justifies its existence when the bulk of its offerings appeals strongly to the intellect and imagination of the community, but with this important proviso: whatever it offers must be within the range of the performers' technical abilities and therefore capable of being done well. A standard of performance must be maintained. It is the director's obligation toward the work itself to see that it is done as well as it can be done. There is nothing to be gained by destroying the effect of a masterpiece by poor playing.

I hasten to say that I do not mean by this that the audience should be subjected to a relentless and unchanging exposure to tragedy with the exclusion of all other types of drama. Farce can be an art form, too, with its own excellencies of arrangement and construction if not always of idea. The ardor of an over-zealous director who wants to do *Hamlet, Faust, J.B.* and *Brand* in a single season must be cooled by the firm hand of common sense. The theatre, like politics, is the art of the possible; and the old axiom, "Nothing to excess," applies equally to cultural drama at its highest level as well as to slapstick. An overplus of either deprives the theatre of one of its principal attractions, its variety.

All types should get attention, from tragedy through melodrama and from comedy to farce. There should be room in the year's program for works which tickle rather than edify. The one important condition is that each selection should be among the best representations of its particular type.

When Herman Hickman was football coach at Yale he said that one of his objectives was to keep the alumni "sullen but not mutinous." The director need not go that far to alienate his audience, but the chances are good that if he lays his bait for the sophomore with one type of play, and for the Dean with the next, he will keep both on the subscription list.

In either case he should avoid the stigma of being classed as a purveyor of idle amusement in competition with the local movie house for the public's patronage, just as much as he must shun the other extreme of being so culturally self-conscious that the public believes that a Phi Beta Kappa key is a prerequisite for admission. If he must err in either of these two directions, it is better that he should err in the direction of significance and go down with colors flying.

At an average rate of three plays a year, the college director can manage to stage at best about 120 productions.

All the more reason then that he should stay with the masterpieces, the great themes, as much as he can. If he is conscientious, nothing less will suffice.

He has the whole corpus of drama to choose from. If he is sensitive to the responsibility his environment places on him to acquaint his public with plays that have stirred or beguiled people throughout history, there is little danger that he will present for the majority of his offerings anything but the work of dramatists with the highest reputation and integrity, whether they be in the field of serious drama, farce, or even musical comedy. He stands the best chance of pleasing his audience with the masterpieces, although there is always the perverse critic who, after seeing *Hamlet,* will say he liked the production but hated the play.

Original plays written by the students themselves come under a special category. Whenever one of these with any merit comes along, it should be staged, even though it may be far from being a masterpiece, much less a finished work of art. The college theatre is the right place to nurture and develop potential writers for the stage. Audiences are usually willing to adjust their responses to student compositions and accept them as plays-in-being, rather than as classic examples of excellence in dramaturgy.

Although it is by no means universally true in current practice, the choice of plays should ultimately be in the hands of the director alone and no one else. Selection involves complex questions of theatre policy, continuity, quality judgments of the acting and production personnel, esthetic balance in the yearly schedule, casting, timing, production size, and other factors. No one is in a better position to weigh these matters and arrive at solid conclusions about them than the man whose whole life work is devoted to precisely these things. It is the director on whom the final responsibility for the success or failure of a production or a season rests. The reputation and the livelihood of the participating students or advisory committees are not at stake. His are.

He must be armed with persuasive reasons for his choices, of course, and must demonstrate in action that he has power and authority as an ideal spectator, knowing his audience, knowing plays, and knowing his business. He must prove in practice that he has the ability to make the decisions and to make them well.

He must work in full cooperation with his undergraduate dramatic group or the faculty advisory committee, if there be one. He should ask for their advice and listen carefully to their opinions, taking heed of the best. But just as he would not persist in bullheaded fashion to thrust plays upon his company which they as a group heartily rejected, so they in turn should not demand that he direct a play which in his opinion is offensive, or alien to his own tastes and interests, or too difficult to be staged well.

It is important that his taste be catholic, and not confined to particular types of plays or to those from a single historical period. His judgment should be broad enough to cause him to admire different plays for different reasons. One play may appeal to him because of its substance, another because of its timeliness. One may have an exciting story or unhackneyed characters, still another may attract him because it is written with style, point, and originality, or it may be tailor-made for his best actors. If he finds not one but a combination of these attributes in a single script, he should pick it.

After that it is merely a matter of staging it, not in any perfunctory fashion, but as though it were to be his very last production.

Purposeful Programming

A well-managed theatre with a subscription audience announces its program for the year as soon as possible after the beginning of the college term. Then the audience knows what it is buying. This procedure makes the director think in terms of his season as a whole and prompts him to consider the advantages of a purposeful design for the season as a season. It also relieves him automatically from the frantic searchings and last-minute improvisations that invariably ensue when the plays are chosen one at a time and without relation to each other.

There are many ideas on which to base an annual program. The plays may simply represent contrasting dramatic types: tragedy, comedy, melodrama, farce; or contrasting forms: satire, fantasy, a thesis-piece, a chronicle-history, a drama, or a sentimental play; or different samples of dramatic styles: realism, naturalism, or impressionism. These mixed bags have a variety that gives spice to a season.

Or, in contrast, a season may illustrate not variety but unity. The plays may all be comedies, differing in style or period yet linked by a common theme; or they may be satires with a common subject, or representative Expressionistic or Romantic plays drawn from various countries and periods.

Occasionally there may be opportunity to explore in depth the work of a single playwright. If such a cycle can be made to illustrate the various stages in the writer's development, the season can be singularly rewarding for an academic community.

Typical works from a single historical period or nation have appeal. The Civil War centennial provides occasion for a series of plays associated with that important milestone in our history. And there are always significant anniversaries in the lives of prominent historical or literary figures to be celebrated. Such programs always awaken interest on the part of other departments, the library, or the art gallery, and tend to enlarge the status of the offerings from isolated phenomena to important cultural events with widespread interest.

The director should be constantly on the alert for fresh material, and should not overlook many of the less-familiar works of established playwrights.[1] To do plays of quality that for one reason or another have failed in the commercial theatre is a challenge and a source of satisfaction for the daring producer. In spite of cool Broadway receptions many good works have been enthusiastically received in the educational theatre, including Anouilh's *Legend of Lovers,* Melville's *Billy Budd,* Sidney Howard's *Yellow Jack,* Denis Johnston's *The Moon in the Yellow River,* Williams' *Camino Real,* and Philip Barry's *Hotel Universe.*

In a three-play season, a sensible plan, although not necessarily a unified one, can be devised by differentiating the plays thus:

Play No. 1. A modern play by an established dramatist, preferably realistic but not an unrelieved tragedy.

Play No. 2. A period revival from the classical repertoire.

Play No. 3. A nonrealistic, experimental[2] script, representing the avant-garde, or an original play written by a student. Lacking the latter, one might choose an untried play from any other source.

The practical problem of having to enlist the interest and support of each incoming class can best be solved by opening each season with a play which has wide appeal. It should also be relatively easy to mount and dress, because at the start of the year the technical crews are likely to be green and somewhat disorganized. This play should not make heavy demands upon the actors. Every commencement leaves large gaps in the ranks of the company, and the opening bill may have to be chosen before the potentials of the new class are known. In fact, some colleges do not permit freshmen to take part in dramatics in any capacity until

[1] Such plays as James Bridie's *Jonah and the Whale,* Terence Rattigan's *Adventure Story,* Donagh MacDonagh's *Happy as Larry,* and Peter Ustinov's *House of Regrets.* There are plenty of others well worth reviving.

[2] An unsatisfactory term. Every play is an experiment, even a Shakespearean revival. Perhaps a better word, judging from recent samples, would be "outlandish."

they have successfully completed the work of the first semester (although they may play football), on the grounds that all their spare time is needed to become oriented to the real work of the college. The rule is preposterous, of course, but where it is in effect casting for the first and sometimes the second production is limited to the three upper classes. This is sufficient reason in itself for avoiding opening with a play that presents more than moderate difficulties.

The winter play has to be the "big" production even though intervening vacation periods may cause serious interruptions of rehearsals. It is a time when the pressure of mid-year examinations is over and the specter of finals far enough in the future to encourage widespread student participation. Hence the suggestion of a classical revival for the middle production.

Something fresh and new is most desirable for spring; it is the natural season for experiments. The audience will presumably have been so favorably impressed with what they have seen of the season already that they will now be ready to take anything, or almost anything. And a new, original script generates its own excitement, when it is given proper publicity.

It should be unnecessary to advise against programs made up exclusively of recent Broadway hits, but the number of college theatres in which this is done is large enough to warrant it.

The trouble with most warmed-over carbon copies of the hits is that they are not carbon copies. In spite of what enthusiastic relatives of the cast may say to the contrary, nonprofessional performances cannot stand comparison with the Broadway originals.

It is easy to fall back on the latest New York success to attract an audience, and equally easy for the director to save himself time and trouble by following the staging of the professional prompt book. But if he does this, in the long run he will have little to look back on in the way of uniqueness and originality in his production. If one must do Broadway's newest and latest, as may be the case when the theatre is at a distance from New York, it is to be hoped that the choices will fall on the plays that are artistic rather than popular successes.

A certain amount of audacity is required if programs are to rise above the commonplace. Chances have to be taken. The college theatre should revive good plays from the past but they need not always be the most familiar and well-worn masterpieces. A commendable courage and vigor is detected in those who dare to do *Cymbeline* or *The Winter's Tale* rather than *The Merchant of Venice* or *The Taming of the Shrew, Epicoene* instead of *Volpone, When We Dead Awaken* instead of *A Doll's House,* or *Thesmophoriazusae* instead of *The Frogs.*

Using the Talent

No director with experience will chose a season's program without first making careful reference to the quality and nature of the acting personnel, and particularly to his inventory of available talent for the leading roles. To decide on *Macbeth* just because "this is the year for Shakespeare" without making sure there are to be two people on hand with enough technical experience and some of the required physical attributes for the leads is to court disaster. In fact, before any consideration is given to specific playwrights or plays, the potentials of the acting group should be evaluated, and the plays should then be picked to fit the best talent.

Suppose one has a student who possesses vitality, charm, grace and humor and who also knows how to speak verse convincingly. Choose *Hamlet.*

If you happen to have one who combines all these qualities with a gift for character acting, if for instance this same student can play bumptious comic middle-aged men-of-the-world and has an added flair for acting lonely, disenchanted, embittered old men, then by all means put down *Peer Gynt* as a possibility. With luck, other actors with the right qualifications will appear for the supporting roles. But even if they don't, half the battle is won because you have someone who can be depended upon to play the star part.

One learns to wait for the right actors to appear. I directed two productions of *Hamlet* at Amherst College. The first was in 1938 after I had been directing there for more than ten years. The second production came ten years later. Both were considered to be successful. Twice in twenty years I found a student actor with natural endowments for the role. I consider this to be a good average.

The collegiate director must plan at long range to bring along his most promising charges in successively larger and more challenging parts from freshmen to senior year if he hopes to minimize the wide yearly fluctuations that are bound to occur in the quality of talent on hand. He can avoid periods of drought by remembering that the freshman spear-bearer may be his best choice for Brutus three years hence, or the little maid-in-waiting his future Juliet. By taking steps to plan their individual progress in successive parts he can oversee the development of promising novices so that they will be ready for leads when the time comes.

It should go without saying that when the director chooses the program in relation to his acting strength, he must play percentages, and be bold. If he waits for the perfect Hamlet to appear, someone who can step into the part and play it in a professional manner without any help from him, the odds are against his ever doing the play. Fortunately he has almost four full years in which to work with an actor, and it is remarkable what progress toward professional competence a gifted student can make in that time. The director must be able to identify a potential, or even a near-potential Blanche DuBois, Christine Mannon, Cyrano or Captain Boyle two or three years before scheduling their plays. When he can do this he has that knack which separates men from boys among college directors.

A word of caution should be said about assigning a series of successive leads to a single individual. No matter how gifted an actor, nor how much it would simplify the casting problem to let him star in one production after another, the practice is better avoided. Some colleges do not permit a student to act more than one leading role in a single year. The rule is severe, but audiences do tire of the same faces even in the short span of a college generation, and variety in casting is as vital to success as variety in play selection. Besides, nothing can be more demoralizing for the acting group as a whole than the realization that they have been permanently relegated to the background as mere supports for a fixed star.

Student Productions

No collegiate program is complete unless it contains, in addition to the major productions directed by the faculty, at least one or two presentations for which the students themselves are entirely responsible. Nothing is more rewarding and stimulating to a student with a genuine interest in the theatre than to be given a chance to show what he can do on his own. To satisfy this creative urge and capitalize on it is one of the obligations of the theatre department.

In many colleges the department includes production work on student presentations in its requirements for a major, and those participating receive course credits for it.

Generally these programs are made up of one-act plays, although it is not uncommon to include full-length plays in the student program.

If the directing and acting are done as part of an academic course in theatre, the director must perforce make comments and pass judgment on their respective worth. He must also be responsible for setting the dates since the danger of conflicts is ever-present in a crowded college schedule. Some control must also be exercised in the selection of programs and particular attention paid to the scale of the proposed productions since they can easily get out of hand. Otherwise the director should keep hands off and let the students work out their problems without interference from him.

Such productions should be open to the public without charge, with all expenses paid either from the departmental budget or with profits from the major productions.

Schedules

Six weeks of uninterrupted rehearsal time to technical and dress rehearsals are an absolute minimum for the preparation of a full-length play in the amateur theatre. There should be no less than five three-hour rehearsals each week, provided the play is simple and the production light. Elaborate and complex productions require a minimum of eight weeks to dress rehearsal. College authorities must be made to see that this much of the students' time must be given if the play is to be performed properly.

It should be remembered in this connection that professional performers are given four weeks of intensive rehearsing, seven hours a day being the limit permitted by Equity. In addition they have two to four weeks of playing out of town before the New York opening.

If professionals require no less than two hundred hours to perfect their performances it is only by the grace of providence that amateurs can be expected to bring theirs to a point where it may be shown to a critical public in any shorter time. Even with six weeks at his disposal, the college director still has less than half the number of rehearsal hours considered minimal by professionals.

Ideally, the first production should be shown just before Thanksgiving vacation. By then the football season is or should be over. An incidental advantage in scheduling the opening at this time is that it gives the director a vacation in which to block the second production! Auditions for the first play must be held, therefore, in the final week of September. This leaves four weeks in October and two in November before the final week of dress rehearsals and performances.

If the second production is scheduled for late March or before Easter vacation, there appears to be more than enough time on the calendar to ready it. But the director must reckon with the intervening Christmas vacation (two weeks) and the mid-year examination period (two weeks). If tryouts are held before Christmas and rehearsals begun in the second week of January, he will find that the months which seemed to stretch out ahead so reassuringly have dwindled to eight brief weeks. And even then these are not consecutive but broken by two lengthy interruptions, with resulting loss of momentum that costs him at least another week of rehearsals to remedy.

In the meantime he must prepare his third production and complete auditions for that before Easter vacation if he expects to have his minimum six weeks for the spring play. The third program, therefore, like the first, must be one of moderate difficulty. This means a fairly small cast, not more than one or possibly two sets, and an uncomplicated costume plot.

This schedule has been based on the optimum of three major productions per season. It is possible to produce four productions in a college year, but this is not recommended for small departments with a single director. If it is attempted, a maximum of six weeks' preparation time is all that can be allotted for each production, and then some overlapping will be necessary. The director must hold auditions for the oncoming play before he has reached performance with its predecessor, and the ensuing pressure on him can become intolerable.

Production dates for a four-play season can be scheduled roughly for the second week in November, the third week in January, the third week in March, and the third week in May. Such a schedule can only be maintained successfully if the acting group is large, and the technical crews fully manned and well organized.

To attempt more than four productions a year is folly, for the level of quality in performance is bound to be less than that of a routine stock-company. The cast can do little more than learn the lines, and the net result is routine or hackneyed playing, insufficient polishing, slap-dash and often frenzied last-minute adjustments, and in general a sketchy and often inadequate physical production.

Finances and Publicity

College productions should pay for themselves. It is not difficult to bring this about provided there is a modest public response. The college pays the salaries of the director and his staff. It also supplies the building and meets the cost of its maintenance. Some even supply the department with a modest subsidy for production expenses. If the administration can be persuaded to include the cost of a special student-rate season subscription in its "Activities Tax," normally imposed on the entire student body at the beginning of the college year, the theatre will then be in the happy position of finding itself in possession of a guaranteed sum on which to base its annual budget before it has sold a single subscription to the nonstudent public. The advantages of this system are not only monetary. It encourages undergraduates to attend performances, and many do just that because they have already paid for the privilege.

If there has ever been a college administrator who objected to the theatre paying its own expenses from box-office receipts, I have never heard of him. This is as it should be. To operate an academic theatre as a successful business is neither an indication that it lacks artistic ideals, nor a sign that it exists primarily to make money. It can come under such suspicion only if the plays it gives are of the obvious penny-catching type.

Most Americans expect to pay for value received. If the tickets are given away there is always the implication that the product is worthless. For this as well as for other reasons there should be a charge. It should be nominal, especially for students, for the objective is to provide as large an audience as possible with meaningful theatrical experiences, not to show a large profit.

Any theatre sustained by subsidy alone runs the risk of neglecting or disregarding its obligation to win public support by merit. On the other hand, if the academic theatre is put on a paying basis, the participants may be continually reminded of their responsibility to the paying public and made more fully aware that they are subject to the judgment of the community. The price of admission earns the public the right to enjoy itself as well as to pass judgment, and this alone should stimulate everyone concerned with the production to do his best. It also creates an environment and an atmosphere which, in this one respect at least, closely duplicates the conditions any profession-bound student will find in the commercial theatre. Such reminders that players are the servants of the public and that the activity in which they are engaged is not a private one for their own exclusive benefit are salutary.

There have been subsidized school-theatres in which members of the audience have been asked to submit critiques of the production in lieu of an admission fee. This is a policy of dubious value. Instead of attending the performance as a normal playgoer, the spectator is asked to come as a critic, to be psychologically prepared to perform a critical function, whether qualified for it or not. He attends not so much for the purpose of enjoying himself, but to dissect the play and the performances and to note down the points that will make his "review" effective. This tends to direct his attention to the weakness and faults of the production rather than to its strength. He has before him the models of so many professional reviewers, whose intent seems to be less concerned with honest appraisal than with demonstrating the critic's own superiority over the material, that he rarely can resist the temptation to imitate them. The results are seldom helpful.

A factor in this that is too easily forgotten is that most directors, playwrights, and casts with any competence at all are already only too painfully aware of what their production's shortcomings are. It is hardly to be expected that the lay public can supply them with important constructive suggestions which they themselves have not been able to think of in the two months of intensive work of preparation. If the play in question is a new one, it is doubtful if four or five hundred random critical reactions to it, each with perhaps a different suggestion, can be of any real value to the playwright. If he takes them all seriously he will be left in a state of dazed bewilderment, unable to decide what was really good or really bad about his work. He can learn just as much and probably more by making careful observation of the way the audience responds to his play from their seats, by their attention, their laughter, and their applause.

All legitimate means should be taken to publicize productions through newspaper articles, photographs, radio announcements, lectures and discussions, displays, posters, pamphlets and any other accepted channels of advertisement. The theatre is there to render a public service and the public must be made aware of it. In a college community there is little need for high-pressure salesmanship, indeed it will probably be resented. But publicity campaigns are necessary, and should be conducted with the restraint and taste becoming to a dignified artistic activity.

The director himself should initiate newspaper publicity. He may not have to write the articles himself although he must know how to do so if required. What is essential is that he supply the subject outlines for feature stories because no one else has as much knowledge and authority as he has to describe the salient features of the play and the style of the production.

A minimum of four feature articles is recommended. The first should contain an announcement of the play, a brief description of plot, and the names of the players. The second should supply details of the way in which the production will be staged, the names of the designer and technical staff, and other items bearing on any special production problems presented. The third should cover the play in depth and contain material on the playwright, with a description of all singular features in the play's viewpoint or theme. The fourth article should be a general recapitulation of the main points already covered and should stress the contributions of the leading actors.

Before the campaign to draw the audience begins, the director must publicize the tryouts. It is part of his job to track down acting material. In this he must be assiduous even though he may have to swallow his pride and personally invite certain key students to the audition. The best agency for drumming up interest in trials is the student dramatic organization. Whatever excitement and enthusiasm they may have for a project is instantly transmitted to the student body.

The Dramatic Society

Some mention should be made of the composition of this group. Ideally, it should represent every facet of the social, political, academic, and athletic configuration of the collegiate society. It is a mistake to restrict membership in the dramatic club to the esthetic segment of that society, or to the intellectuals alone. The theatre is a universal medium that addresses itself to people of every class and of every sort of esthetic and intellectual coloration. It is necessary therefore that all collegiate types be represented in it. It does no harm to the theatre's prestige to cast the captain of the football team in a minor part.

What should be the relationship between the director and the dramatic association?

Nowhere is the director's power so absolute as when he is onstage. How and when he exercises that power is often the measure of his success as an artist and as a man. But as a member of the faculty he is also the administrative head of an organization of students on whose cooperation he depends to get his productions before the public. In this position he should be very careful about the way he uses his authority. In fact the more sparingly and unobtrusively he exercises it the better off he will be. The director needs the student organization as much as they need him. Realizing this, the director will seek to function in relation to the society more as the chairman of a committee in which each member has an equal voice than as the president of a corporation or as a major general giving orders to his staff.

A clear definition of the two spheres of authority, the director's and the undergraduates', must be clearly established at the outset. In all matters pertaining to the staging of plays, the director's authority is supreme, of course. In casting he may and should seek the advice of senior members provided they are not themselves candidates for parts, but here again he must have the final word.

In the crucial area of play selection, the final decision as to what shall be done and not done must be the director's alone. Yet, he will be well advised to take the group as a whole or the members of its executive committee into his confidence before proceeding to a choice. He should call for their suggestions and recommendations at a preliminary meeting and at the same time ask them to read certain tentative choices he has previously made. He should outline to them frankly the problems which a particular season presents and what he wants to accomplish in it, stating the objectives in precise terms. Subsequently he will meet with them again and discuss their recommendations as well as his own. He will present to them a final list of possibilities, perhaps ten or a dozen plays from which three or four will be chosen. After ascertaining their reactions to this list and digesting the arguments, he will then, and only then, proceed to make his selection. When and if he rejects suggestions from the group he should explain in all candor why he did so.

The egotism of a director should not prevent him from realizing that the undergraduate body of a modern college contains an impressive and indeed an occasionally awesome amount of first-class talent for the stage. It is not impossible that one or two of his students may be more gifted than he is himself. All they may lack is his experience and maturity. A good teacher-director will be the first to recognize this possibility and use all the help he can get from such students to everybody's advantage. This would include their help in selecting the season's programs.

In colleges where it has been the custom for students to select the plays themselves, it may take some time for a new director to establish the group's confidence in his ability to choose the programs and to persuade them to yield this authority to him. But it must be done. Otherwise the director will find himself in the intolerable position of an employee of the undergraduates, hired to present works of their choosing which he may find of little interest or happen to dislike intensely. Serious conflicts and impasses will be avoided if both parties work together with the friendliness and mutual respect that mark most student-faculty relationships in an American college. Yet, inner disruptions do occur, sometimes with most unfortunate results. The best way to avoid them is to have incorporated in the constitution of the organization a full statement of policy which will include the aims of the theatre and a clear demarcation of areas of power between the director and the association.

The theatre's finances should be under the control of the director or the chairman of the theatre department. Fiscal responsibility is too critical a matter to permit it to be made subject to the fluctuations of managerial talent that occur four times in each college generation. The director represents the factor of continuity in this equation and the financial policy must be under his control as a matter of long-range planning, particularly if sensible budgets are to be drawn up and intelligent use made of annual profits. To give control of the purse strings to undergraduates is actually to give it to a comparatively minor member of the hierarchy, the business manager, who may not be in the least qualified to make decisions affecting the whole artistic future of the college theatre.

The students themselves should manage all matters pertaining to organization of the association, the conditions of eligibility for election to membership, the election of officers, honorary members, and so on.

Successful theatrical production depends on the contributions of many diverse talents, freely and enthusiastically given. One of the inescapable conditions is that the people engaged in it must work together on intimate terms. In a college there is little reason why the theatrical atmosphere should not be friendly. In the giving and the receiving of the theatre experience there should be joy and exuberance on both sides, for those who do the work and for those who see its fruits. A director honestly dedicated to the individual interests and the personal development of each of his students and not obviously in the business merely for purposes of self-aggrandizement will have little trouble in gaining the full cooperation of young men and women who are generally as dedicated and idealistic as he is, and often more so.

In the majority of cases all causes of friction will disappear once the students understand clearly that they and the director are together striving for the same thing—excellence in production.

Glossary

ABOVE Upstage, or away from the audience. An actor crossing above a table keeps it between himself and the footlights.

ACT CALL An order from the stage manager, usually "places, please" summoning actors to take their positions onstage or in the wings for beginning of an act.

ACT WARNING A half hour before curtain time the stage manager warns the cast in their dressing rooms that the curtain will rise in thirty minutes. He follows this with a "fifteen minute" call and then with a "five minute" call before calling places.

AD LIBBING (*ad libitum*, as one wishes) Improvising lines or business not contained in the text. An *ad-lib* is the term for such improvisation.

APRON That part of the stage which projects beyond the proscenium arch into the auditorium. The forestage.

ARC CROSS Movement in a curved line. Also *Curved Cross.*

ARENA STAGE A stage surrounded on all four sides by the audience. A "theatre-in-the-round."

ASBESTOS A fire-proof curtain hung just upstage of the proscenium.

ASIDE A line spoken directly to the audience, presumably unheard by others onstage.

A VISTA CHANGE (*cambiamento a vista*) A scene shift made with the curtain up and in view of the audience, except that the crew making the shift is not seen.

BACKDROP A large drapery or painted canvas supplying the rear or upstage masking of a set.

BACKING Any piece of scenery or material used to close the view of the audience through any stage opening.

BACK LIGHTING Light from the rear of the stage directed downward and forward to lend depth and plasticity to set and actors.

BACKSTAGE On the stage behind the front curtain, or the areas behind the setting including the dressing rooms.

BACK WALL Either the rear wall of the stage house or the rear wall of a setting.

BELOW The opposite of *above*. Toward the footlights. *Up, down, above,* and *below* derive from the raked stage that tilted upwards from the footlights to the back wall.

BLACKOUT To plunge the stage into total darkness by switching off the lights, or the condition this operation produces.

BODY POSITION The actor's physical stance in relation to an audience, whether facing full front, profile, or full back, or in any intermediate position in 360 degrees of arc.

BORDERLIGHTS Light strips hung upstage of a border.

BORDERS Strips of painted canvas or other material, usually three in number, stretched horizontally across the stage at set ceiling line to mask the flies.

BOX SETTING A standard interior set consisting of two side walls, a back wall, and a ceiling or a set of borders closing the top.

BREAKAWAY Scenery or properties constructed to break on cue.

BUILD To intensify gradually the impact of a speech or a scene by increasing pitch, volume, or movement, and deepening emotional tone.

BUSINESS Pantomimed action with or without properties.

CALL A posted notice or announcement of times of rehearsals, or performances, usually placed in or near the stage entrance.

CALL BOARD The backstage notice board where calls and messages for company and crews are posted.

CENTER LINE A line at the exact center of the stage drawn from the footlights to the back wall of the set. Used as a reference mark in blocking.

CLEAR STAGE An order, usually from the stage manager, given before the rise of the curtain or start of a scene to get unwanted personnel off the stage.

CLOSED TURN A turn away from the audience. The opposite of an *open turn* or *stage turn*.

COUNTER A small move in the opposite direction from a move made by another actor, made to adjust positions to avoid masking or to balance composition.

CROSS IN To move toward stage center.

CROSS, STRAIGHT A movement in a straight line.

CUE (*abbr. Q.*) Any prearranged signal, such as the last words in a speech, a piece of business, any action or lighting change that indicates to an actor, a stage manager, or any member of the crew that it is time to proceed to the next line, action or change. Usually led into by a warning.

CUE SHEET A list of numbered cues used by the stage manager, switchboard operator, and various other crew members.

CURTAIN LINE (1) The last line of a speech that provides the cue for the fall of the curtain. (2) An imaginary line where the front curtain touches the stage floor.

CURTAIN TIME The specific hour at which the performance is scheduled to begin (curtain usually goes up about ten minutes after stated time).

CYCLORAMA The sky drop, sometimes made of plaster, surrounding the back of the stage.

DIMMER An instrument used to change the intensity of stage lights.

DIM OUT To take out the lights on dimmer, the process usually being cued to a predetermined number of seconds or counts.

DIM UP To increase the light gradually to certain prearranged dimmer marks. To *dim down* is to decrease the amount of light without going to blackness.

DOWNSTAGE Toward the footlights.

DRESS (1) To step in the opposite direction of another's move. (*See also* Counter) (2) Abbr. for dress rehearsal.

DRESS PARADE A session in which actors wear their costumes to have them checked for fit, appropriateness, etc. Held long enough before the first dress rehearsal to allow for alterations, replacements, etc.

DRESS THE SET To add decoration, properties, hangings, etc., to the setting to enhance its reality or interest.

DRY UP To forget one's lines. Also to "fluff" or "blow."

EFFECT MACHINE A special lighting instrument for projecting painted slides on a screen, sometimes provided with a clockwork device to give effects of motion, as moving clouds, snowfall, etc.

FLAT A single piece of scenery, usually of standard size and made of canvas framed in wood, used with other similar units to create a set.

FLEXIBLE STAGE A theatre supplied with mechanisms that permit seats to be rearranged to form a playhouse in the proscenium, arena, or "three-quarter round" style, or some combination of these.

FLIES The loft above the stage where scenery and lights are hung.

FLOOR CLOTH The stage covering, often padded to absorb sound.

FLY GALLERY A narrow ledge projecting from the side of the stage and usually at some distance above the stage floor where the ropes controlling hung scenery and lights are operated and tied off.

FLYMAN A stagehand who operates the lines which lower or raise hung scenery or lights.

FOURTH WALL An imagined partition closing a three-sided set on the downstage side at the footlights. Sometimes thought of as at the back of the house.

FRESH ATTACK A direction to an actor to raise his energy level; to start a speech at a higher pitch, with increased volume, and a faster tempo to heighten interest or mark the transition from one idea to another.

FRONT PLAYING To play toward the audience.

GESTURE A movement, usually of the hands, arms, head, or shoulders to express thought or feeling, or to punctuate an idea, as distinguished from a cross which merely changes position.

GIVEN SCENE Wherein one actor is placed in a weak position in order to give prominence to another who is made dominant.

GREEN ROOM The actors' lounge and reception room backstage.

GRIDIRON (*abbr.* grid) A steel framework toward the top of the stage house supporting the blocks or sheaves through which lines are passed to raise and lower hung scenery and lights.

GRIP A stage crew member who handles scenery in the shifts.

GROUND ROW A low masking piece, sometimes cut to show the outline of a landscape, placed on the floor in front of cyclorama or backdrop.

HEIGHT The vertical relationship between the actor and the floor of the stage. Monotony in head heights is avoided by placing actors in various sitting and standing positions, by the use of platforms, etc.

HOLD Any pause or cessation in the play's action, sometimes unwanted as when an actor forgets his lines or his entrance.

HOUSE Auditorium, lobby, box office, and adjacent spaces in front of the curtain, as distinguished from backstage.

HOUSE SEATS Tickets reserved by the management for its own use, usually the best in the house.

IN ONE Designating a scene played below the first set of wings. In two: the same applied to the second set of wings; in three: the third, etc.

KILL To strike or eliminate. To kill a light means to turn it off.

LEVEL As used in this book, the term designates the actor's position with reference to his relative distance from the footlights to the back of the set.

MASKING (1) A piece of scenery or drapery used to conceal backstage areas and equipment from the audience's view. (2) The interference by one actor with the audience's unimpeded view of another.

OPEN TURN Any turn made toward the audience. A "stage turn."

OPEN UP To turn or face more toward the footlights.

O. P. SIDE Offstage area opposite the side where the prompter sits.

ORCHESTRA The first or main floor of the auditorium.

OUT FRONT In the auditorium or the theatre's public areas.

OVERLAP To respond to a cue before the end of another's speech; to telescope.

PACE The over-all speed of a scene, a speech, or a series of moves.

PARALLEL SCENE One in which the characters are not in apparent opposition or conflict.

PERMANENT SET A setting, the main features of which remain fixed throughout the action, changes in locale being effected by insertion of plugs or by minor rearrangements in placement of doors, windows, etc.

PICK UP CUES A direction to an actor to speak the moment he gets his cue, or even before.

PIT The area between the front row of seats and the stage, usually below floor level, in which musicians play.

PLACES An order warning the actors to take their positions onstage.

PLUG (1) To punch a line or otherwise increase its emphasis. (2) A piece of scenery inserted into the opening of a door flat or window flat to change its function.

POINTING Stressing or enlarging a speech or an action to make it more emphatic.

PRACTICAL Capable of actual use or operation, as a stage piano that must be played or a stage faucet that yields real water.

PRESET PANEL A series of dimmer banks used in conjunction with the switchboard enabling the operator to fix the dimmer settings for a number of scenes prior to use. Lights may then be changed from one cue to another merely by switching from one preset to another.

PROJECT A command to an actor to raise his voice or magnify an action so that it carries to the whole house.

PROMPTER'S BOX In opera houses and old theatres a small space beneath the front of the stage with an opening covered by a hood. Here the prompter sits with his head at stage level.

PROMPTER'S CHALK An 18th-century term for a line drawn or painted on the stage floor from the onstage edge of an entranceway or wing to show the actor where he had to stand offstage in order to stay out of sight line.

PROPERTIES Material objects, as letters, fans, cups, and the like which are used in stage action.

PROSCENIUM The permanent architectural wall separating stage house from auditorium. The audience looks through the proscenium opening or arch to view the stage.

RAKED STAGE A stage which slopes upward from the footlights toward the back of the set.

READ To register with the audience. A line "reads" when the spectators can hear it and understand it; an actor's make-up "reads" when its purpose carries across the footlights.

REPERTORY COMPANY A permanent acting company which repeats or rotates plays through a season or series of seasons, as distinguished from a stock company which presents a different play each week or so without subsequent revival.

RING DOWN To signal for the lowering of the curtain, or the actual process of lowering it. Opposite of *ring up*.

RUN THROUGH To rehearse a scene or an act without interruption.

SCRIM A gauze curtain.

SET (1) To establish a fixed routine, as a duel, a dance number, or any succession of movements or readings in a scene. (2) Scenery.

SHARED SCENE Any scene in which the participants are given equal emphasis in position, lighting, etc.

SHIFT To change the scenery, or as a noun the process itself.

SIDES Bound half-pages containing all of a single actor's lines and their brief accompanying four or five-word cues.

SIMULTANEOUS SET A scenic arrangement whereby several different locales or settings are shown at the same time, with the action passing from one to another. Derived from the "mansions" of the medieval stage.

SPIKE MARK A painted spot on the stage floor to indicate where a piece of furniture or scenery is to be placed.

SPILL Light leaks around the edges of a spotlight.

STAGE HOUSE The entire stage area behind the proscenium arch bounded by the rear wall of the stage, the permanent side walls, and the roof.

STAGE TURN (*See* OPEN TURN).

STAGE WAIT Any undesirable delay in the performance.

STOCK COMPANY (*See* REPERTORY COMPANY).

STRIKE To remove a setting, props, or furniture from positions onstage.

SWITCHBOARD An instrument panel controlling stage lights. Formerly placed offstage in one wing but now more often found at the rear of the balcony or in the orchestra pit. Advanced models are more elegantly termed *electronic consoles.*

TAKE FIVE Permission to stop the rehearsal for five minutes to give actors and others a chance to relax. Work is usually resumed after a lapse of ten minutes.

TAKE STAGE To draw audience attention. Sometimes used as a term of opprobrium as in the case of an actor who steals a scene by unwarranted moves or business, or a designer whose sets and costumes are ostentatious to the point of distraction.

TEASER A horizontal border at the top of the inner frame upstage of the proscenium opening, attached to the vertical framework on either side. These latter are known as the tormentors or "torms."

THROW AWAY To undercut or diminish the force of a line.

THUNDER SHEET A large rectangle of tin or galvanized iron hung backstage from a rope. When shaken it produces a sound like a thunder roll.

TOPPING Overcapping a preceding line by speaking louder or faster.

TORMENTOR LIGHTS Lighting instruments mounted on a pipe upstage of the tormentors.

TORMENTORS The vertical supports of the inner frame, upstage of the proscenium opening, connected at the top by a teaser.

TRANSLUCENCY A curtain of translucent material on which light may be thrown from the rear of the stage.

TRAP An opening in the stage floor through which an actor may enter from below the stage, or use as an exit.

TURN IN To face or step toward stage center.

TURN OUT To face or step away from stage center.

UPSTAGE Farther away from the footlights. To upstage another actor is to seize attention by moving farther toward the back of the stage than he is.

WINGS Left and right offstage areas. Also narrow standing pieces of scenery or legs forming the sides of a setting.

Index

Abbott, George, 13, 266
Academy, French, 33
Acting, art of, 6, 26, 166, 290, 312; and character portrayal, 275; craft of, 312; director's knowledge of, 13; educational benefits of, 309; exaggerated, 249; ham, 166; modern approach to, 290; movement in, 268; over-, 274; overintellectualization of, 290; problems, 231; profession of, 290; style, 99, 292, 293; teaching of, 290; unity of, 292
Acting areas, 115, 131, 161; appropriate, 136; described, 135; emotional "carry" of, 121; establishment, 142; expressive, 121; in French scenes, 134; in ground plan, 130; importance of, 121; large, 230; levels of, 150; and movement of characters, 150; overcrowding, 164; preselected, 150, 161, 196; selection of, 135, 225; sequence of, 121, 122; values of, 135, 136; variety, 194; weak, 121; whole stage as, 138, 148
Action, antecedent, 288; *concerted*, 122; dramatic, 53; flow of, 51; pause in, 214; propricty and aptness of, 272
Actor, attention of, 285, 292; audience response to, 231, 249; availability of, 255; awkward, 273; beginning, 274, 275; as collaborator with director, 124; creative sphere, 124; and director, 7, 119, 123, 127, 128, 166, 271, 278, 282; experienced, 275; feelings and instincts, 123, 290; freedom of interpretation, 124, 125; judgment, 119, 125; "no direction" method, 124; prerogatives, 119, 282; reading of parts, 256; role, 49, 124, 125, 126, 166, 259, 276, 290, 291; skill of, 290; star, 275; stock, 275; and verse plays, 90; voice, 126, 258
Actors, amateur, 6, 256, 259, 312; and blocking, 115, 122; concentration of, 231; conflict between, 120; "open call," 255; personality, 127, 271; and playwright, 245; potential directors, 125;

professional, 311; responsibility of, 125, 126; stage relationships, 268, 269; veteran and tryouts, 259
Actors Equity Association, 323
Acts, function of, 52, 53, 55, 59; titles for, 53, 54; working plan for, 141
Agamemnon, 249
Agitprop play, 29
All for Love, 36
Amherst College, 321
Anderson, Maxwell, 89, 93, 101, 151, 169, 195
Anouilh, Jean, 319
Anticlimax, 58
Antigone, 28
Antony and Cleopatra, 36
Aristotle, 28
Arsenic and Old Lace, 107
Atmosphere, 49–51
Audience, 46, 279, 281, 290, 301; alienation of, 162; attention, 51, 121, 164, 167, 246, 253, 285, 295; in college community, 310; as critics, 10, 326; and director, 248; emotions of, 108; importance, 268; intelligence, 248; and lighting, 50; paying, 246; relaxation, 249; response, 25, 26, 122, 162, 163, 167, 249, 292; and setting, 150; and tryouts, 248, 249
Auditions, in amateur theatre, 257; ensemble, 260–261; in professional theatre, 257; *see also* Casting
Augier, Emile, 39
Author, approach to subject, 99; and play content, 46; *see also* Playwright
Awake and Sing, 33

Beat, 286–287
Beckett, Samuel, 34, 57, 315
Behan, Brendan, 93
Billy Budd, 319
Blocking, 115, 122, 127–130, 141, 161, 163, 164, 169, 209, 225, 231, 293, 324; and actors, 115, 129, 272; corrections, 123, 153; and designer, 300; "free," 119, 120; by instinct, 162; key to, 206; master plan, 122; methods of, 116; New York directors and, 118; prerehearsal, 118, 119, 126, 127, 129, 199; principles, 161; process, 141; and prompt book, 161; and rehearsals, 268, 269; and relationships of characters, 162; results of, 127, 268; and role of actor, 118; of consecutive scenes, 194; self-, 122; in three-act play, 269; time of, 115
Body, balance, 273; use of as entity, 273
Bound East for Cardiff, 51
Brand, 316
Bridie, James, 14
Broadway and educational theatre, 313, 319, 320
Budgets, restricted, 255

"Call-backs," 261
Camelot, Toronto opening, 248
Camino Real, 34, 319
Carousel, 287
Cast, and director, 45, 271, 304; first meeting, 263; knowledge of plays, 29, 267; selection of, 22; self-confidence of, 128; and web of metaphor, 106

Casting, 245, 320; agencies, 255; amateurs in school theatres, 256; and budget, 255; card file system, 260; changes in, 264; and costumer, 261; and director, 254, 255; double, 264; "open call," 255; and playwright, 255; pre-, 259; procedures, 255; and producer, 255; in professional theatre, 257; and sight reading, 255; and stage manager, 255; and talent, 259
Cat on a Hot Tin Roof, 39, 40, 51
Ceremonial, ritualistic, 286
Cézanne, 33
Characters, analysis of, 46, 47, 48, 162; author's, 47; and director, 46, 49, 254, 255; dominant, 167; interpretations of, 47, 272, 289; placement of, 137, 141, 162, 163; range of, 47; reconstruction of, 289; relationships, 162, 163, 166, 174, 195; stereotypes of, 166, 276; subordinate, 167; textual evidence of, 48, 277
Chekhov, Anton, 11, 32, 33
Cherry Orchard, The, 10, 26, 263; as comedy, 11
Choral passage, orchestration of, 296
Choreographers, 22, 23
Choreography, 294; plan of, 123; synchronization with dialogue, 129
Chorus, directing of, 294, 295
Classicism, described, 35, 36
Climax, 55, 58, 59; in *Doctor's Dilemma*, 61; moment of, 55, 109
Close-up, use of, 163
Clues, 277
Coaching, 271; sessions, 272
Cocktail Party, The, 88, 89
Collegiate theatre, actors, 309, 310, 313, 319, 321, 322, 326, 329; audience, 308, 309, 311, 315, 316, 318, 320, 322, 325, 326, 327; budget, annual, 325; casting, 320–322, 324, 327, 328; college credit, 309; corporate enterprise, 307; development of writers and, 317; director, 308–318, 321–324, 327–330, as actor, 312, as showman, 313, as teacher, 308, 311, 329; as educational instrument, 309; faculty advisory committee, 317; financing, 325, 326, 329; novices, development of, 322; objectives, 307; performances, standard of, 315; plays, 311, 313–318, 319, 320, 321, 323, 326; one-act, 323, 'penny catching,' 325, students' original, 317, per year, 316; playwright and audience response, 313, 326, 327; production, 310, 320; expenses, 325; public, 309, 325, 326; publicity, 324, 327; program, season's, 51, 316, 318–322, 324, 329; programming, purposeful, 318; rehearsals, 323, 324; students and, 308, 310, 311, 317, 319, 322, 323, 325, 326, 329, committees, 317, faculty relationships, 329, original plays of, 319, requirements for, 308, subscription rate, 325; technical crews, 319; tryouts, publicized, 324, 327
Comédies humaines, 29
Comedy, 28, 29, 316; definition, 29; directors of, 23; Elizabethan, 101; and imagery, 100; Jonson-

ian, 47; of manners, 29; satirical, 61; and tragedy, minor types, 29
Conflict, 57
Constructivism, 34
Costume, crew, 300; importance of, 278; parade, 300
Country Wife, The, 108
Craft, actor's, 312; director's, 2, 43, 162, 167
Crossing, 129, 166, 168; and beginning actor, 274; body as unit in, 275; "geographical," 154
Crowd scenes, and designer, 294; directing of, 293; entrances and exits, 294
Cues, choral, 295, 296; curtain, 302; lighting, 50; speed in, 293; through movement, 296; vocal, 295
Curtain calls, rehearsals of, 302
Cutting, 245, 247, 248; and actor's role, 247; in amateur theatre, 247; and audience, 248, 249; and director, 13, 247, 252, 254; and performance, 249; prerehearsal, 247; problems of, 248, 249; reasons for, 246; in Shakespeare, 252; and subplots, 248; ways of, 252; working method for, 249

Dali, Salvador, 34
Dean, Alexander, 135
Death of a Salesman, 26, 42, 43, 51, 56, 95; climactic act, 45; emotional levels, 42; structure, 45; themes, 43
Denouement, 57, 59
De Quincey, Thomas, 3
Design, director's knowledge of, 14; balance in, 134; purposeful, 122
Designer, 300; and director, 7, 130, 131, 141, 150; problems of, 132; professional, 130; and script, 131
Devices, dramatic, and audience, 111; listed, 107; literary, 99; verbal, 96, 97
Dialects, 293
Dialogue, 51, 83, 84, 87, 89, 107, 132; and choreography, 129; and devices, 107; poetical, 89; and rhythm, 287; as song, 22; sound of, 87; and suspense, 109
Direction, 7, 24, 46; authority in, 125; drudgery of, 163; evaluation in, 129; good, 292; "no direction" method, 124; perspective in, 53; preparation for, 12; self-, 125; the tyro in, 10
Director, as actor, 312; and actors, 7, 45, 119, 123, 127, 166, 270, 271, 275, 278, 291; and audience, 249, 308; authority, 124, 328; and authors, 134, 153, 162; beginning, 10; and card file, 264; as chorus leader, 295; as coach, 270; collegiate, 256; in community theatre, 25; and conducting, 6; and core subjects, 13; craft of, 43, 162, 167; and criticism, 271; and designer, 130, 131, 141, 150; demands upon, 38; as drill-master, 269; experienced, 25, 129; as faculty member, 328; and final production, 8–9; and first reading, 262; flexibility of, 22; function, 3, 4, 5, 41, 46, 119, 162, 166; good, 12, 127, 167; as guide, 128; inadequacy, 303; infallible, 196; inventiveness, 13, 14; journeyman, 275; judgment,

291; knowledge of acting, 13; limitations of, 6; and lines, 282; as literary critic, 10, 12, 26; and manuscript, 245; masterplan, 6; notes on performance, at opening night, 303; personality, 7, 8, 23; and as play doctor, 12; and playwrights, 12, 41, 132, 214, 245, 246, 311; professional, 275, 310, 312, 313; qualifications, 11, 12, 20, 83; and script, 25, 26, 36, 131; and stagecraft, 275; and study of play, 27, 36, 37, 52, 111; and style of performance, 292; teacher-, 311; technical, 300; "to think like a," 135; in tryouts, 257
Directors, development of, 22, 24; psychological, 22, 23, 46
Discovery, dramatic, sudden or prolonged, 110
Doctor's Dilemma, The, 39, 40, 91; Act I, ground plan, 169; Act V, 248; scene analysis, 59; characters, 61, climaxes, 60; literary values of, 61
Doll's House, A, 30, 39, 40, 55, 66, 321; act titles, 53, 54; analysis of single scene, 67
Drama, beginnings of, 38, 39; classification of, 28, 107; conflict in, 57; cultural, 316; dance, 286; elements, 56; expressionistic, 34; functions of, 314; Greek, 107; subsurface, 107; symbolic, 4, 267; *see also* Verse Drama
Dramatic Association, business manager, 330; composition, 328; and director, 328; membership, 328; play selection, 328; policy, 329; and publicity, 328; student management, 330
Dramatist, 249; and clues, 277; and revelation, 50; *see also* Playwright
Dramatists, Irish, 92, 95
Dramatization, pictorial, 167
Drames, 29
Dream Play, The, 288
Dryden, John, 36

Eck, Philip, 159
Electra, 107, 109
Eliot, T. S., 88, 89, 294, 296; and Maxwell Anderson, 89
Emotion, expression of, 276, 291; feigned, 290; and hands, 273; and inflection, 267; parodies of, 276; and physical response, 268, 275
Emphasis, vocal, 166
Emperor Jones, The, 51
Enemy of the People, An, 30
Entrance of characters, 168, 199; flat, 198; mass, and rhythm, 288; strong, 132, 198
Epigram, 96
Evans, Maurice, 246, 254
Execution, area of, 6; precision in, 129
Exits, 168; mass, and rhythm, 288; strong, 132
Expressionism, 34

Failure, commercial, 310
Fantasy, 34
Farce, 29, 38, 110, 315, 316; movement in, 167
First reading, 262

Foreshadowing, objective and examples, 111
Formalism, 57
French scenes, 53, 58, 64, 65, 134, 136, 161; acting areas of, 139; composition, 64; definition, 64; diversity, 121; *en bloc*, 135; sequence, 162; subscenes in, 65; titles of, 134; unity, 139; *see also* Scenes
Fry, Christopher, and archaic vocabulary, 96, 97

Galsworthy, John, rule of three, 247
Genet, Jean, 315
Gesture, 166, 273, 284; hackneyed, 166; invisible, 285; mechanical, 273
Ghosts, 50, 111
Gielgud, John, 292
Glass Menagerie, The, 51
Gorki, Maxim, 32, 33, 34; norm of plays, 31; style of plays, 30
Ground plan, 130, 131, 135; in acting editions, 130; blocking, 130; exterior, 150, 151; mimeograph of, 294; revising, 22; scaled, 130, 141

Hamlet, 26, 30, 47, 96, 132, 276–282, 317, 321; full-length, 246; "G. I.," 254
Hands, onstage use of, 273
Homecoming, 249
Hostage, The, 93

Ibsen, Henrik, 30, 40, 50, 53, 54, 55, 66, 84, 85, 108; dramaturgic formula, 55; and foreshadowing, 111; norm of social plays, 29
"Illusion of the first time," 5
Imagery, in comedy, 99, 100, 102; and elements, 102; and metaphor, 99; in tragedy, 99, 102; in *Winterset*, 102
Images, emphasis and use of, 105
Importance of Being Ernest, The, 94, 96
Impressionism, 32, 33
Improvisation, and calculation, 291
Inflection, 281–284; and emotion, 267–268
Interpretation, director's procedure, 7–9; in revivals, 9–11; *see also* Characters
Irony, 107, 108; in dramatic reversal, 109

J. B., 27, 276, 279, 280, 281, 316; Yale production of, 280
John Gabriel Borkman, 84–87, 88
Julius Caesar, 294
Juno and the Paycock, 39, 92, 109

Kaufman, George S., 110
Kazan, Elia, 27, 42
Keats, John, 100
King Henry IV, 253
King Henry VI, 13
King Lear, 51

Lady's Not For Burning, The, 51, 96; anachronisms, 97; invective in, 97; language of, 96; metaphor and imagery in, 99, 100
Language, imaginative use of, 106; incongruities in, 97; metaphorical, 291
Lewis, Robert, 163
Libation Bearers, The, 110

Light, 49; changes of, 121, 300; in crowd scenes, 294; foot-, 301; house-, 301; hot spots, elimination of, 300; plot, 300, 301; symbolic, 50
Lighting, 49, 301; and audiences, 50; cues, 300; and director, 14, 50; importance of, 278; side-, 301; value of, 136
Liliom, 163
Lillo, George, 86
Lines, of approach, 206; in blocking rehearsals, 269; crossing, 275; exit, 168; and movement, 275; of motion, 165; misreading, 282; rhythmic, 286; stress in, 281; of separation, 206, 207; at technical rehearsals, 301; theatrical value of, 246
Logan, Joshua, 13
London Merchant, The, 86–87
Long Day's Journey into Night, 246
Lower Depths, The, 30, 31, 32

Macbeth, 40, 109, 252, 253, 321; dramatic reversal in, 110; symbolism of his nature, 49; textual evidence of character, 48
McClintic, Guthrie, 255
McCullers, Carson, 38
MacLeish, Archibald, 313
Maeterlinck, Maurice, 34
Make-up, 261, 302
Mamoulian, Rouben, 286
Manuscripts, *see* Scripts
Marriage of Olympe, 39
Maugham, W. Somerset, 310
Melodrama, 29, 38, 116, 316; "cliff-hanging" school of, 108
Member of the Wedding, The, 38, 39, 40
Memorization, 268, 269
Memory, associative, 291
Merton of the Movies, 110
Metaphor, 163, 291; and audience, 106; and cast, 106; in comedy, 99; cutting, 106; and designer, 131; and director, 105; repetitive, 106; in tragedy, 99; vocal emphasis, 106
Midsummer Night's Dream, A, 88, 89
Miller, Arthur, 43, 56, 95
Modes, dramatic, 35; Classical, 61; Romantic, 36, 61
Molnar, Ferenc, 163
Monet, Claude, 32, 33
Monodrama, 32, 123
Mood, 49; and dialogue, 84; and meaning, 50; and players, 51
Morley, Robert, 290
Motive, invented, 47
Mourning Becomes Electra, 246
Movement, stage, 231, 268; and audience attention, 167; and director, 166; and emotion, 165; excessive, 121; expressive, 165; imposed, 138; justification of, 162; motive for, 199; principles, 168; problems, 167; purpose, 16; reasons for, 164; and speech, 166; strong, 167; values of, 164
Moves, "carry" of, 165; consistency, 167; for emphasis, 164; esthetic, 166; practical, 164; reasons for, 164, 166; strong, 229
Murder in the Cathedral, 294, 296
Music, offstage, and rhythm, 288
My Heart's in the Highlands, 163

Naturalism, 30–33
Nō Drama, 34
Nonrealism, defined, 33; subdivisions, 34

O'Casey, Sean, 39, 93; and poetic prose, 92
Odets, Clifford, 32
Oedipus Rex, 28, 56, 110
Old Vic, 9, 14
O'Neill, Eugene, 246, 247, 249; and poetic prose, 91
Opening night, and director, 303
Ostrovski, Alexander, 51

Peer Gynt, 50, 252, 321
Performance, pitch of, 58; progress and improvement of, 303; rhythm of, 286; standard of, 4; test of, 249
Peter Pan, 34
Picturization, 167
Placement of characters, 141; purposeful, 195; reasons for, 150
Play, acts of, 53, 54; agitprop, 29; appeal of, 26, 106; build of, 268; climax, 58; contents, 37; copyrighted, 8; great, 26, 107; in-being, 317; literary values of, 13, 37, 99; meaning, 11, 37, 99; message of, 37; minor types of, 29; modern, 7; motives in, 47; "nature-imitating," 30; original student, 319; story, in, 37, 38; structure, 37, 45, 52, 55, 56, 58; style of, 5, 9, 27, 29–32, 34, 107, 109, 125, 267, 287; themes, 40, 42, 43, 46, 59; time, in, 46, 57; untried, 313; validity of, 11; verse or rhythmic, 88, 168, 169, 287; "well-made," 30
Playboy of the Western World, The, 93
Playing, ensemble, 269; "front-," 293
Playwright, 41, 47; and actors, 245; authority of, 246; and casting, 255; characters, 276; contract, 255; craft of, 46; and cutting, 246; and director, 12, 41, 132, 245; and first reading, 262; and ground plan, 151; legal rights, 11; and meaning of play, 11; medium of, 6; naturalist, 31; as owner of play, 245; problems of, 214; in Romanticism, 36; and settings, 130, 132–134, 150; skill of, 37; subjects, 39; technique of, 46; text, 7; and titles for acts, 53; at tryouts, 257; *see also* Dramatist
Playwriting, as art, 56; and director, 12
Plot, and act titles, 53; analysis of, 58, 59; characters of, 38; conclusion, 40; development, 56; framework, 37; function, 59; line, and movement, 168; linear, 55, 61; sequence of, 37; structure, 37, 54, algebraic, 55, differences in, 56, in *The Doctor's Dilemma*, 61; sub-, 36; synopsis of, 59; time continuum, 56; use of, 39, 40; value of, 38
Porgy and Bess, 286
Position, of defeat, 235; dominant, 208, 235; seated, 216
Postures, hackneyed, 166
Power of Darkness, The, 32
Producer, and director, 255

Production, successful, 5, 245, 330; master plan of, 6; stylized, 35
Programming, purposeful, 318
Prompt book, 115–128, 142, 162, 293; contents, 115; notations, 161; professional, 320; purpose, 115; and stage manager, 115; symbols in, 161
Properties, importance of, 20, 278
Prose, 89, 287; poetic, 91
Provincialisms, 293
Psychoanalysis, and director, 24
Psychology, and director, 24
Public, indifference of, 167; interest of, 311

Reading, aloud, 263; around the table, 267; in "call-back," 261; first, 245, 261, 264; and director, 258; interruptions in, 263; line, 269; mis-, 261, 282; and playwrights, 262; procedures for, 282; ways of handling, 262; *see also* Tryouts
Realism, 30
Reflections upon Theatrical Expression, 276
Rehearsals, 127; for amateurs, 323; around the table, 266, 267; blocking of, 269; coaching, 272; and director, 267; dress, 270, 300, 301, 302, 303; drill sessions, 272; ensemble, 292; and "gloves-off" discussion, 271; guests at, 303; number of, 302; period, 266; problems, 302; procedure for, 301; professional, 323; purpose, 302; of scenes, 270; schedule, 270; seminar approach, 267; on stage, 267, 268; technical, 300, 301; and textual sequence, 270
Rehearsing, methods, 270; purpose, 127
Repetition, a device, 96, 247
Response, 281; and emotion, 275, 285; empathic, 290; modification of, 278; problem, 281; searching for, 276; unwanted, public, 249
Revelation, 50; delayed, 43
Reversal, dramatic, 109, 175, 176, 177; and discovery, 109; effect of, 109; elements of, 109; examples of, 110; in farce, 110; and irony, 109; and suspense, 109
Reviewers, professional, 326
Revisions, textual, 313
Revivals, 8; and director, 9, 10; Shakespearian, 9
Rhythm, 285–287; and characters, 288; and cue line in chorus, 295; in dialogue, 287; in movement, 287; pattern, 286; in scenes of conflict, 288; speech-, 286, 287; in verse plays, 287; visual, 286
Richardson, Ralph, 292
Roles, character, 256; interpretation, 47; leading, in tryouts, 259; and life of actor, 166; reading of, 258; studying of, 52; tempo, 287
Romanticism, 35, 36
Romeo and Juliet, 9, 14, 29, 102, 104
Run-throughs, 270

Sandbox, The, 34
Sardou, Victorien, 33
Saroyan, William, 32, 58

Scenes, active, 209; architectonics of, 123; blocking, 135; climactic, 135, 293; crowd, 270; "emotional carry," 121; ensemble, 293; expository, 293; exterior, 132; form of, 199; key, 228; key point of, 229; progression of, 121, 122, 135; meaning, 135, 150; natures of, 293; of persuasion, 235; in rehearsal, 270; relationship, 293; rhythm, 199, 206; single, as entity, 121; sub-, 137; successive, *en bloc*, 194; two-character, 169; *see also* French scenes
Scripts, 26; reading new, 25, 27, 313; revision of, 8, 12, 313
Seale, Douglas, 13
Setting, and audience, 151; design, 150, 278; exterior, 150; formalized, 150; function in, 49; importance of, 49; lighting, 49; and plastic compositions, 132; small, and movement, 231; textural clues for, 150
Shakespeare, 28, 36, 40, 89, 102, 287, 321; cutting, 252; language, 96; and Renaissance, 96; uncut, 254
Shaw, George Bernard, 61, 62, 133, 134, 136, 174, 175, 176, 248, 290; on director's notes, 304; and discussion, 137; ground plan for *The Doctor's Dilemma*, 133; and poetic prose, 92; stage directions of, 132, 143, 144
Sightlines, and furniture, 131
Slapstick, 38, 316
Soliloquy, 123
Sophocles, 56, 107, 109
Sound effects, importance of, 50
Speech, climactic, 208; manner of, 293; metrical, 94; ranges of dramatic, 84; realistic, 94
Spurgeon, Caroline, 99, 102
Stage, arrangement, purpose, 119; business, 14, 20, 164; collegiate, 256; design, adaptation of, 131; direction, 6; manager, 115, 255, 261, 302; levels, 132; placement, problem of, 120; positions, importance and effectiveness of, 123, 268; properties and director, 14; static, 137; "take," 292; traffic problem, 231
Staging, plan of, 122; and dialogue, 132; improvisation in, 128; meaningful, 128
Stand-ins, 300
Stanislavsky, Constantin, 11, 84, 290; method, 23, 263, 291
Stock, actor, 275; theatres, 245
Storm, The, 51
Storms, playwright's use of, 51
Streetcar Named Desire, A, 39, 40, 93
Strindberg, August, 288
Styles, dramatic, 29; inconsistencies in, 292; literary, 83; naturalistic, 30; realistic, 32; *see also* Play, style
Subscenes, analysis of, 65
Supers, 294
Surrealism, 34
Suspense, 109; in melodrama, 108
Symbolism, 34, 35; in *Macbeth*, 49; in Maeterlinck, 34; in Yeats, 34
Synge, J. M., 91, 93

Talent, acting, today, 246; and casting, 255, 259
Teacher-director, 311

Teaching, modern, 290
Technique, actor's and director's, 270–291
Text, ambiguities, 282; and antecedent action, 288; and director, 7; and ground plan, 156; interpretation of, 6
Theatre of the Absurd, 32
Theatre, academic, 256, 307–330; amateur, 247, 256; American, 246; art of, 26, 163, 307; art of the possible, 316; business of, 307, 325; community, 25, 245; communication, means of, 50, 162, 307; studio, 163
Theatricalism, 33, 35
Time of Your Life, The, 33, 58
Tobias and the Angel, 14–21
Tolstoi, Leo, 32, 33
Tradition, in English drama, 93, 100
Tragedy, 28, 316; Aristotle's theories of, 28; of blood, 29; and comedy, 29; in Greece, 28; and imagery, 102; movement in, 167; in Renaissance England, 28; Sophoclean, 28
Troilus and Cressida, 10
Tryouts, 256, 257, 261; first, 258; onstage, 257; pre-Broadway, 248; and prechoice of actors, 259

Uncle Vanya, 51, 287
Understudy, 265
Uniformity, stylistic, 293; disadvantages, 295
Unity, 49, 292; Aristotelian, 36
Unmasking, 165

Values, dramatic, in text, 38; in timing, 56
Variety, law of, 216
Verse, blank, 287
Verse drama, 88–91
Visit to a Small Planet, A, 34
Vocabulary of characters, 83, 96, 97
Voice, modulations, 21; monotony, 295; and movement, 167; in rehearsal, 272; in tryouts, 258; volume, 293

Waiting for Godot, 34, 57
Wild Duck, The, 30, 108, 111
Williams, Tennessee, 40, 59, 319; and poetic prose, 91; use of meter, 93
Winterset, 10, 39, 41, 83, 89, 169, 195, 249, 288; French scenes, 226; ground plan, 151; images in, 102, 103, 104; language, 89, 102, 106; outdoor setting, 151; prerehearsal scheme, 195; Yale production of, 158–159, 195; synopsis of action, 235; and traffic problem, 231
Wycherley, William, 108

Yale, 13, 313; Drama School, 195, 249; productions, 53, 158–159, 196, 280
Yeats, W. B., 34
Young, Stark, 10

Zavadski, Yuri, 263
Zeffirelli, Franco, 9, 10, 14, 29